THE IRISH TIMES
BOOK
of the
YEAR
2002

EDITED BY
PETER MURTAGH

Gill & Macmillan

Gill & Macmillan Ltd
Hume Avenue
Park West
Dublin 12
with associated companies throughout the world
www.gillmacmillan.ie

© 2002 *The Irish Times*
0 7171 3443 1
Design by Identikit Design Consultants, Dublin
Index compiled by Helen Litton
Print origination by Carole Lynch
Printed by Butler & Tanner Ltd, Frome, Somerset

Contents

Introduction

Every western country has a publication that is seen as the 'newspaper of record', although the term 'newspaper of reference' is probably more appropriate in today's complex society. It denotes the newspaper which is regarded as the most comprehensive and reliable. It is the notice board of public life. It is the newspaper in which serious public issues are addressed. In Ireland, that newspaper is *The Irish Times*.

The relationship between such a newspaper and its readers is often very intimate. Readers develop something akin to a sense of ownership. They can become angry when they detect any departure from standards or when there are changes in content. They may often disagree with the editorial line – but they expect the newspaper to maintain its quality and its ethos.

Each publishing day, *The Irish Times* enters into a compact with its readers. The reader places his or her trust in the journalism of *The Irish Times*. In return for that trust, *The Irish Times* strives to provide a news service from Ireland and abroad which is comprehensive, accurate and up to date. It offers a range of opinion on public issues, domestic and international. It aims to inform and to stimulate. It tries to provoke and challenge. Sometimes, it even aims to entertain!

The putting together of a daily newspaper is necessarily an imperfect thing. Sometimes we get things wrong. When we do, we undertake to put them right for the record, as quickly as possible. We make no claim to impartiality. *The Irish Times* has views, positions and convictions. But we do strive to be fair. We give special consideration to minority viewpoints. And we always make room for the expression of views that may run counter to editorial policy.

The economics of publishing such a newspaper in a relatively small country are challenging. Similar newspapers in other, smaller European countries share that challenge. So do public service broadcasters, such as RTÉ. The origination, validation and publication of reliable information is an expensive process. Economies of scale which are attainable in larger countries are rarely possible. Quality newspapers seek to generate as much material as they can from their own resources. It is costly.

At *The Irish Times*, the economic model went somewhat wrong over recent years. Towards the middle of last year, as advertising revenues slumped across the world, it became clear that a gap was opening up between the newspaper's operating costs and its income. A programme of re-structuring was set in train. This has entailed the loss of 250 jobs across the organisation out of a workforce of more than 700. It has also entailed significant reductions in non-payroll costs.

The company's management and the unions which represent the staff worked extraordinarily well together to agree the plan for recovery. We have been well served by expert consultants. KPMG have been retained by the company itself. Farrell Grant Sparks and Paul Sweeney, Economic Consultants, were retained by the Dublin Print Group of Unions to examine the organisation and to make recommendations for the future. Those recommendations have been taken aboard in letter and in spirit.

Staff who departed have had the benefit of a good severance deal. Managers and editors have worked with staff in each section to identify efficiencies and savings. Many practices and procedures which were costly and wasteful have been identified and eliminated. It has not been an easy process but it has been pursued with commitment and professionalism. The company's recovery is under way and the future of *The Irish Times* is secure.

The new printing plant at Citywest, outside Dublin, is the most modern in the country and production of *The Irish Times* has been taking place there since early June. The press at Fleet Street is now silent, bringing to an end almost three centuries of newspaper printing in Dublin city centre.

What does it mean for the newspaper? What difference will it make for the readers of *The Irish Times*?

Some aspects of coverage are being reorganised to give more efficient service and better value for money. The newspaper's network of foreign correspondents will remain substantially in place. Staff bureaux will be maintained in the US, Brussels, London and Paris. The permanent bureau in Beijing has been closed but Asia Correspondent, Miriam Donohoe will continue to report from the region, travelling as necessary from Dublin. The newspaper's two offices in the US – at Washington and on Wall Street – have been reduced to one. Additional reporting from important locations around the globe will come from contracted correspondents such as Paddy Agnew in Rome, David Horowitz in Jeruslem, Declan Walsh in Africa, Rahul Bedi in India and Derek Scally in Berlin. Thus *The Irish Times* will remain the only Irish newspaper with its own international news service, bringing its readers a uniquely Irish perspective on world events.

Coverage of news from the regions of Ireland has been reorganised. Regional news remains a priority for the newspaper and the permanent Regional Desk will be maintained within the main Dublin News Desk. The newspaper's office in Belfast will remain operational with a number of senior journalists in place there. Different regions no longer have a dedicated day of the week for news presentation. Instead, a regional news section, at present published on Page 2 of the main newspaper, now draws news from all around the country.

There are changes in some of the supplements. This is facilitated by the coming on stream of the Citywest printing plant which will allow us to publish sections such as Business This Week and Property in one part, rather than in two parts as heretofore.Educational services have been re-organised. The weekly E&L supplement was replaced in the autumn by a section published within the main newspaper each Tuesday, dedicated to educational issues, parenting and career development. The successful Media Scope page continues. Day to day educational news and features will continue to be provided by the news team.

Other services such as Music in the Classroom and the annual Higher Options conference will continue. Meanwhile, growing numbers of students, parents and teachers are logging on to *Skoool.ie*, the interactive educational site operated by *The Irish Times* in collaboration with Allied

Irish Bank and Intel. In Septmber, the site was awarded the prestigious 'Golden Spider' prize – the on-line industry's equivalent of an Oscar.

The move to the new printing plant at Citywest now enables us to publish *The Irish Times* in one edition, rather than in two. This change was put into effect in July. Faster printing and better distribution will allow us to save significantly on costs while maintaining traditional news copy deadlines.

Within the editing process itself, the new Hermes publishing system allows us to streamline and simplify the flow of copy from the reporter through to the page. Copy for publication at *The Irish Times* has traditionally gone through an extensive series of supervisory checks. This process is simplified with on-screen makeup giving editors a quicker and more complete overview of material as it goes through the system.

Those who read *The Irish Times* on our website, Ireland.com, will be aware that full access to the newspaper and its archives is now available only on a paid-for basis. A reduced breaking news service will continue to be available free of charge. But in common with many newspapers around the world, *The Irish Times* has to face the reality than a quality service cannot be provided for nothing. It is anomalous – and unfair – that those who read the newspaper in print should pay €1.30 while those reading it on screen should have it free.

Since October, when the Citywest print plant became fully operational, *The Irish Times Magazine* has been printed there. This resulted in some design changes, both to the *Magazine* as well as the design and structure of the main section of the Saturday newspaper, including the Weekend supplement.

Beyond these changes which I have described above, *The Irish Times* will not be different from the newspaper which has been published heretofore. There will be no significant gaps in editorial coverage or in the range of editorial services. *The Irish Times* will continue to provide the news, analysis and comment which a well-informed readership is entitled to expect from a modern, quality newspaper.

By the time this *Irish Times Book of the Year 2002* is published, I will have stepped down as editor, after a tenure of sixteen years and there will be a new incumbent in the chair.

I believe I will have handed over a newspaper in fine shape. The readership data just to hand from the Joint National Readership survey, confirms the continuing growth of *The Irish Times* as Ireland's leading newspaper. Readership has grown by almost 70,000 in the past three years, contrasting with a drop of almost 100,000 in that period for the *Irish Independent*. Readership grew by 12.5 per cent in the year to end June 2002 alone – a remarkable achievement when set against the difficulties which we have gone through and a tribute to the standards and the professionalism of those who make the paper what it is. Moreover, *The Irish Times* continues to extend its dominance of the higher educated and influential ABC1 sectors of the population.

The re-organisation of the company and of the newspaper is now effectively complete. These have been very difficult months. But this is not the first time a great newspaper has had to hold steady and endure while the commercial structure within which it operates goes through difficulties. *The*

Irish Times is emerging as a more efficient, effective organisation and the newspaper will continue to go from strength to strength. New sections and services are at the planning stage. Improved news coverage from at home and abroad will be visible over the coming months. Above all else, the fundamental values and principles which have made *The Irish Times* what it is for almost a century and a half will endure.

Conor Brady
September 2002

Journalists and Photographers

Paddy Agnew is Rome Correspondent of *The Irish Times*.

Eileen Battersby is an *Irish Times* journalist specialising in literary and heritage matters.

Arthur Beesley is a business reporter with *The Irish Times*.

Alan Betson is a staff photographer with *The Irish Times*.

Rosita Boland is a feature writer with *The Irish Times*.

Mark Brennock is Political Correspondent of *The Irish Times*.

Harry Browne is a freelance journalist and *Irish Times* Radio Critic.

Vincent Browne writes a weekly column on the Opinion Page.

Cyril Byrne is a freelance photographer, based in Dublin.

Denis Coghlan was Chief Political Correspondent of *The Irish Times* until he left the paper this year.

James Connolly is a freelance photographer, based in Sligo.

Carol Coulter is *Irish Times* Legal Affairs Correspondent.

Kevin Courtney is a freelance journalist, specialising in rock music.

Paul Cullen is an *Irish Times* reporter and Development Correspondent, who has also specialised in the Flood Tribunal.

Kieran Doherty is a photographer who works for Reuters.

Eithne Donnellan is an *Irish Times* reporter.

Miriam Donohoe is *Irish Times* Asia Correspondent and was based in Beijing until this year. Back in Dublin, she also now writes about politics.

Keith Duggan is an *Irish Times* sports journalist who specialises in Gaelic Games and also writes a column in the sports supplement.

Jonathan Eyal is director of studies at the Royal United Services Institute in London, and a regular contributor to *The Irish Times*.

Brenda Fitzsimons is a staff photographer with *The Irish Times*.

Seán Flynn is *Irish Times* Education Editor.

Peter Hanan is a freelance illustrator and caricaturist. He illustrates the Saturday Profile.

Mary Hannigan is a sports writer. She compiles the Planet columns in the sports supplements, including the regular Planet Football.

Mary Holland is an *Irish Times* Opinion Page columnist.

Kathryn Holmquist is an *Irish Times* feature writer, specialising in parenting matters.

David Horovitz is *Irish Times* Jerusalem Correspondent. He also works for *Jerusalem Report*.

Joe Humphreys is an *Irish Times* reporter.

Tom Humphries is a sports journalist and also writes a weekly column, LockerRoom, in the Monday sports supplement.

Róisín Ingle is an *Irish Times* reporter and also writes a column in the Saturday Magazine.

Michael Jansen is a commentator on Arab affairs with *The Irish Times*, and is based in Nicosia.

Matt Kavanagh is a staff photographer with *The Irish Times*.

Colm Keena is a business reporter with *The Irish Times*, specialising in the Moriarty Tribunal.

Dan Keenan is Northern News Editor with *The Irish Times*.

John Kelly hosts 'The Mystery Train' on RTÉ Radio 1 and writes a weekly column, The Indefinite Article, in the Weekend section of Saturday's *Irish Times*.

Hugh Linehan is editor of The Ticket, *The Irish Times* weekly guide to what's on.

Eric Luke is a staff photographer with *The Irish Times*.

Diarmuid MacDermott is a freelance journalist, specialising in court reporting.

Dara MacDonaill is a staff photographer with *The Irish Times*.

Don MacMonagle is a freelance photographer, based in Killarney.

Trevor McBride is a freelance photographer, based in Cork.

Frank McDonald is Environment Editor with *The Irish Times*.

Patsy McGarry is Religious Affairs Correspondent with *The Irish Times*. He also edits the weekly Rite and Reason column on the Opinion Page.

John McManus is Deputy Business Editor with *The Irish Times*. He also writes a weekly Business Opinion column in Monday's business page.

Frank McNally is an *Irish Times* reporter. He also writes a weekly column, The Last Word, in Saturday's Weekend section.

Emmet Malone is Soccer Correspondent with *The Irish Times*.

Lara Marlowe is *Irish Times* Paris Correspondent. She also reports regularly from the Middle East.

Toby Melville is a photographer with the Press Association in London.

Frank Millar is London Editor of *The Irish Times*.

Frank Miller is a staff photographer with *The Irish Times*.

Mary Minihan is a freelance reporter.

Gerry Moriarty is Northern Editor of *The Irish Times*.

Kevin Myers writes An Irishman's Diary.

Moya Nolan is a freelance photographer, based in Dublin.

Breda O'Brien writes a column for *The Irish Times* Opinion Page.

Bryan O'Brien is a staff photographer with *The Irish Times*.

Tim O'Brien is Regional Development Correspondent with *The Irish Times*.

Conor O'Clery is North America Editor with *The Irish Times*, based in New York.

Alison O'Connor was a political reporter with *The Irish Times* until she left the paper this year.

Clare O'Dea was a business reporter with *The Irish Times* until she left the paper this year.

Caroline O'Doherty was a reporter with *The Irish Times* until she left the paper this year.

Niall O'Dowd is editor and founder of the *Irish Voice* newspaper of New York and an occasional contributor to *The Irish Times* Opinion Page.

Marie O'Halloran is an *Irish Times* reporter.

Joe O'Shaughnessy is a freelance photographer, based in Galway.

Fintan O'Toole is *Irish Times* theatre critic and also writes a column on the paper's Opinion Page.

Andrew Paton works for the Inpho sports picture agency in Dublin.

Derek Scally is Berlin Correspondent of *The Irish Times*.

Kathy Sheridan is a feature writer with *The Irish Times*.

David Sleator is a staff photographer with *The Irish Times*.

Patrick Smyth was Washington Correspondent of *The Irish Times* until this year. He is now based in Dublin from where he reports on foreign policy developments.

Jason South is an Australian photographer who spent a year with *The Irish Times*.

Joe St Leger was an *Irish Times* staff photographer until he left the paper this year.

Denis Staunton is Europe Correspondent with *The Irish Times*, based in Brussels.

Chris Stephen is an *Irish Times* foreign correspondent and freelance journalist, based in Moscow. He writes about Russian, Balkan and Near East affairs.

Cliff Taylor is Editor, News Centre, at *The Irish Times*.

Gerry Thornley is *Irish Times* Rugby Correspondent.

Martyn Turner is *The Irish Times* political cartoonist. His work appears on the Opinion Page.

Arminta Wallace is a sub editor and feature writer with *The Irish Times*.

John Waters is an *Irish Times* Opinion Page columnist.

Johnny Watterson is an *Irish Times* sports journalist, specialising in tennis.

Pádraig Yeates was *Irish Times* Industry and Employment Correspondent until he left the paper this year.

MONDAY, I OCTOBER 2001

'You Would Think They Would Wise Up'

Róisín Ingle

The blinds were pulled tight across the windows of the O'Hagan home on Tandragee Road in Lurgan yesterday. Visitors wearing suits came to pay their respects, some stopping briefly to look at a stark reminder of Friday night's tragedy.

You could still see the chalk marks on the pavement near the house, indicating where the bullets had fallen after investigative journalist Martin O'Hagan was shot dead by paramilitaries as he walked home from the pub with his wife, Marie.

The couple had moved there with their three children a year ago on Friday. This part of Tandragee Road separates the Catholic Collingwood area from the loyalist Mourneview Estate near where the killers, thought to be members of the LVF, abandoned the car they used in the attack. Bits of glass and debris littered the ground a few minutes away in Clonavon Lane, where it was later dumped.

People on their way to church strolled through the estate where the perpetrators are believed to have hidden on the night of the murder. 'Loyalists?' said one man of the killers. 'They make me ashamed to call myself a Protestant. Those people are a cancer in the Mourneview Estate, a cancer that we can't get rid of.'

Another well-dressed man, standing close to a mural which read 'Mid-Ulster Rat Pack: Defiant Until Victory' also expressed his disgust. 'There is shock and sadness across the Protestant and Catholic community,' he said. 'These things shouldn't happen.'

Books of condolences were opened at St Peter's Church on North Street, as well as in the local Church of Ireland. The messages were simple and personal. 'Martin was a fine upstanding hero

Martin O'Hagan, a reporter with the Dublin-based **Sunday World** *newspaper, had received a number of death threats over the years. He was shot dead as he walked home with his wife Marie from a local pub. Photograph: Pacemaker Belfast.*

who will never be forgotten; … he was always full of energy and enthusiasm, doing a job he loved.'

Those who queued up to sign after eleven o'clock Mass praised the bravery of the *Sunday World* journalist, whose commitment to exposing the criminal activities of paramilitaries on both sides eventually cost him his life. 'He was another Veronica Guerin', said one. Others repeated what most of the town seemed to be thinking over the weekend: 'I thought those days were behind us.'

A statement concerning the murder was read out at churches of all denominations around the town. The killing was, it said, the kind of event that 'we had hoped and prayed belonged to the past'.

At the Carnegie Inn, where Martin and his wife had spent most of Friday night, the atmosphere was subdued. He was a regular at this quiet pub, with its polished wood, green leather upholstery and mixed clientele. A few men sipped Guinness and watched the Rangers v. Celtic match. The owner, just returned from visiting the O'Hagan family, politely declined to comment and looked distraught as he stood behind the bar.

The couple had left the Carnegie, or Fa Joes, as it is known locally, at around 10.15 p.m. on Friday night, walking home together to the Tandragee Road. They were five doors from their house when a car drove slowly past. The reporter was shot twice in the back as he tried to protect his wife; the other shots hit some of the houses behind.

Journalists calling to the scene late on Friday night stood on the rain-splattered road behind police tape and blue flashing lights, as the RUC confirmed reports that the murdered man was a colleague. Locals peered over to where the journalist's body lay covered while forensic officers in white overalls searched for evidence.

Two young girls who had ventured down from their homes in the Mourneview Estate stood shivering in the rain. 'We heard the shots', said one. 'We were watching a video and we heard it. At first we thought it was fireworks, but then we realised. There were six or seven shots.'

The girl's mother arrived home shortly afterwards. 'I had to calm them down,' she said. 'They were crying and they just kept asking why? I told them it was because he was a Catholic. It is terrible. I am a Protestant, but we don't have any problems with anyone else. This doesn't make any sense. You would think after America they would wise up.'

Martin O'Hagan's body was taken away at about 1.30 a.m. on Saturday morning. There was a dry patch of ground in the rough shape of a man's body and a fresh pool of blood.

Before the removal of the body, some local Protestant youths began to challenge the RUC, shouting obscenities, while behind the blinds, Marie O'Hagan, who is from a Protestant background and has a close relative in the Mourneview Estate, sat consumed by shock and grief.

When someone objected quietly to their shouts, urging the youths to have respect for the O'Hagan family, they were ignored. 'You don't understand what life's like around here,' one teenager grinned.

TUESDAY, 2 OCTOBER 2001

A Grotesque Denial of Bloodshed

Fintan O'Toole

On Sunday week, unless there is a last-minute outbreak of sanity, we will be treated to an extraordinary spectacle. Coinciding with the Fianna Fáil Ard Fheis, the State will stage one of the most elaborate political ceremonies in its history.

After a religious service, the remains of ten IRA men, recently exhumed from their graves near the perimeter wall of Mountjoy Prison, will be draped in tricolours and loaded into ten hearses.

The cortège, accompanied by an Army motor-cycle escort, will then move at walking pace through the north side of the city towards the Pro-Cathedral, stopping on the way at the Garden of Remembrance and the GPO.

From the cathedral, the procession will eventually move back to Glasnevin Cemetery, where to the accompaniment of the setting sun and an oration by the Taoiseach, the remains will be buried. The whole event will be relayed live on television. The President and the entire Cabinet will officiate.

In the official version and in one part of the truth, all of this is a simple act of humanity. Nobody deserves to lie in a prison yard, and the families of the ten IRA men executed by the British in 1920 and 1921, among them the famous Kevin Barry, have every right to mourn their ancestors in

THE IRISH TIMES BOOK OF THE YEAR

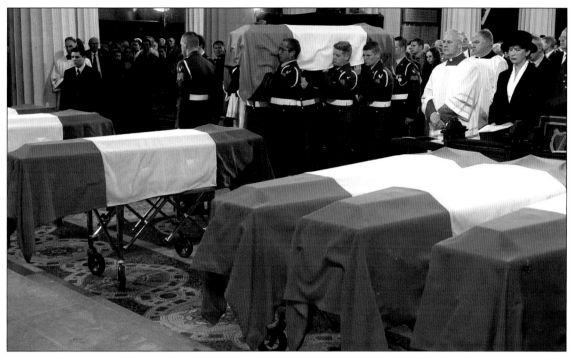

The remains of the volunteers of the War of Independence at requiem mass in the Pro-Cathedral. Photograph: Eric Luke.

hallowed ground. Nobody at all could object to the State helping the families to put these ghosts of history at rest.

Equally, however, nobody at all can deny the existence of a very specific Irish tradition of political funerals and martyrs. From the re-interment of Terence Bellew McManus onwards, militant Irish nationalists pioneered what might be called funerary propaganda.

As Patrick Pearse acknowledged in his oration at the graveside of O'Donovan Rossa, to hold the graves of martyrs is to claim your rights as the true inheritor of the past.

There are reasons why Fianna Fáil imagined that this would be a good time to claim the grave of Kevin Barry. When the last State funeral (that of Jack Lynch) was one in which the oration for a Fianna Fáil Taoiseach was given by a politician from another party (Des O'Malley), the need for an emotive event in which the party can claim to be the nation goes deep.

When the recent past that is being disinterred at the tribunals gives off a stench of corruption, the temptation to skip back into an apparently more idealistic time is obvious. When the party is so ideologically bankrupt, the temptation to wrap its nakedness in the green flag is strong. And when Sinn Féin is becoming a serious electoral threat, the desire to steal back the clothes it has borrowed is almost irresistible.

Yet even before the events of September 11th, an elaborate State funeral was a very bad idea. It was likely to achieve two things: sickening many citizens by its ghoulish cynicism and offering a great boost to those who want us to feel that the only difference between a terrorist and a patriot is the passage of time.

The official distinction that is being made between Kevin Barry and the contemporary IRA is that Kevin Barry was essentially a democrat fighting to uphold the mandate of the 1918 elections, which were won by Sinn Féin. It doesn't really stand up.

3

Donal O'Donovan, Barry's nephew and author of the excellent *Kevin Barry and His Time*, recalls a conversation between Barry and his sister, Kathy. Barry had just taken the oath of allegiance to the newly established Dáil. 'That's good', said Kathy, 'now you're a real army.' Barry's reply was, 'I don't know. Anyway, when this damned Dáil takes Dominion Home Rule, they needn't expect us to back them up.'

Nor was Barry's short military career very far from what we would now call terrorism. In July 1920, he took part in a raid on the home in Aughavannagh, Co Wicklow of the elected Nationalist MP, Willie Redmond. The following month, he was involved in an attack on a Church of Ireland rectory in Co Carlow. The clergyman fired a shotgun at his attackers from an upstairs

Elle Macpherson, supermodel and actress, at the launch of her new range of lingerie 'Elle Macpherson Intimates' at Brown Thomas, Dublin. Photograph: Dara MacDonaill.

window. The IRA men fired back but then left. 'We decided', as one of Barry's fellow raiders later recalled, 'not to go near the minister that night but to take him unawares' at some later time.

It should also be remembered that the September 1920 attack on British soldiers for which Kevin Barry was hanged was one in which civilians were recklessly endangered. The ambush was staged in a bakery off a busy city street. A bullet went through the window of the dairy next door, missing a baby in a pram by pure luck. Of the three soldiers who were killed, one, Matthew Whitehead, was, at seventeen, even younger than his killer, Kevin Barry.

None of this means that Kevin Barry was not a nice, bright, middle-class boy who, in normal times, would have ended up as a popular local GP and president of the rugby club. The State must acknowledge the circumstances of its own creation.

The elaborate act of piety that is being foisted on us is not, however, an act of acknowledgment. On the contrary, it is an act of denial, deliberately designed to sanitise the ambiguities of people like Kevin Barry whose idealistic certainty makes them reckless of other people's lives.

Before September 11th, it was a stupid mistake. After September 11th, it borders on the grotesque.

FRIDAY, 5 OCTOBER 2001

Lady Forced to Move as a Portrait

Clare O'Dea

The advent of the euro is forcing Lady Lavery from her Central Bank home. The original Lady Lavery portrait, which has graced Irish bank-notes since 1928, will be leaving its home in the Central Bank next year for the National Gallery.

The enigmatic Sir John Lavery's portrait of 'a beautiful Irish type' set against a Killarney background will be given on long-term loan to the gallery.

The bank has decided to release the portrait now because the image will disappear when the Irish Punt ceases to be legal tender on 9 February. The image is still visible as the watermark on the current series of notes, which was introduced between 1992 and 1996.

The familiar portrait has a colourful history. In 1927, the Currency Commission was set up to issue Irish bank notes and coins and decided to commission a portrait that would feature on the notes. After some debate, the Commission approached Sir John Lavery and asked him to paint 'a portrait of a beautiful female head treated in some emblematic fashion which might perhaps have some Irish association'.

The portrait, believed to be from an early portrait of Lady Lavery, an American-born society hostess, caused controversy when it was first reproduced on the new Irish Free State bank notes. The head and shoulders was not officially meant to be a portrait of a recognisable public figure but it was known that Sir John's model was his wife.

The painting has been seen by few people since it was presented to the Commission seventy-three years ago.

Although it will no longer be a witness to fiscal-policy dramas in the Central Bank board-room, the portrait will be well placed to capture public nostalgia for our old money in the National Gallery in years to come.

MONDAY, 8 OCTOBER 2001

Sometimes the Good Guys Don't Have to Finish Last

Tom Humphries

Niall Quinn sits down at the edge of the table at the top of the room with a big loopy grin dangling on his lips. The grin spreads across the top table and down through the rows of chairs where we hacks sit. He did it. The big guy did it. Irish goalscoring record. On his birthday. At home. Not a begrudger in the house.

'I'm thrilled really,' he says. 'I don't consider myself the greatest Irish goalscorer ever, that's for sure. I'm just pleased to have reached this kind of moment. I'm very proud. Even though I tried to play it down for the last sixteen months (pause) I really wanted it badly.'

And he laughs. We laugh. For the first time Mick McCarthy laughs at a press conference. The all-too-bearable lightness of Niall.

The way Niall tells it, it's been bread and roses all the way. From his debut goal at Anfield to his record-breaking goal here. The world has crowned him with laurels every evening. Get your forensic people, you wouldn't find a trace of bitterness in his bones.

Niall Quinn tots up all the blessings. You'd never know that this was a guy who did both his cruciates and came back the lonely way each time. He got just three games and no medal when Arsenal won their first league title under George Graham.

He got sold on a year before they won their second. He missed a World Cup because his club chairman wouldn't let him go. But he's always chosen to walk on the bright side of the road.

'I'm really pleased,' he says. 'It was sixteen months building up. It was great out there. After the goal (Ian Harte's), the next ball came in and I was away, but concentration slipped for a minute or two before that. All the promises I made. What I'd have to do if I scored. The pub in Clonmel are all having free drink, for a start.

'It felt wonderful coming off. Best I've ever felt being hooked. I've had a long old career, many great days, many hard days. It was up there with anything I've done for Ireland.'

And he's done lots. He made his debut fifteen years ago, coming into a team with names like Bonner, Moran, McCarthy, Hughton, Houghton,

McGrath, Stapleton and Aldridge. Scored his first Irish goal at Dalymount Park, of all places.

Scored some great ones after that: equalisers against Holland in the World Cup, England at Wembley in a Euro qualifier and Denmark at Lansdowne in a World Cup qualifier. He set up twice as many, and with Cascarino became the defining presence in our style of play.

'I only remember about two of them, England at Wembley. Holland World Cup goal — not the classiest of all time. And I suppose tonight. Half the crowd headed it in with me.'

From it all he picks the present as the best time.

'I would have to say, not just because Mick is here, the achievement here outshines what we did for other competitions. 1988 we stumbled over the finish line. In 1990 we were a little better. 1994 we almost threw it away. This time there has not been a fault.

'We have got ourselves in a situation where twenty-four points doesn't get us there. Which is unbelievable. We're proud. A great achievement up till now. We just have to go and do it.'

And stretching that record, Niall?

'Jaysus lads, give me a chance. I'd love to be involved, I'd love to go to the finals. If I'm going I'll have to come up with the odd one, naturally. I'll speak to Mick further on. I can't look as far ahead as some of the other lads.'

He can't look that far ahead, but what about the near future, the next few hours?

'Well', he says, 'I can't go as mad as I used to. I'll have a bit of a celebration.'

He frowns. 'I might as well tell you — I'll have a right good night.'

And he lopes off into the Lansdowne gloaming, one of those beloved heroes of Irish sport, one of the guys who keeps you believing.

Niall Quinn, Republic of Ireland, celebrates his goal against Cyprus at Lansdowne Road. Photograph: Dara MacDonaill.

TUESDAY, 9 OCTOBER 2001

Waiting on the West to Finish Their War

Lara Marlowe, in Faizabad, Northern Afghanistan

Everything in Afghanistan has its own mixed-up logic, so a few hours after the first night of British and American bombardments, the United Front, the armed opposition to the Taliban regime, finally made good their promise to fly me into the northeastern enclave they hold. Little matter that Front officials had announced they were suspending all flights for four days. I was about to arrive in the Front's main city, the capital of 'free Afghanistan'.

Forty of us piled into the back of the creaky Soviet Antonov 26 troop transporter, which was painted in green camouflage. All airspace over Afghanistan was supposed to be closed, so I could only hope the Front had notified the US air force in neighbouring Uzbekistan that we were not a Taliban suicide mission. We passed the meandering Amu Dariya river that marks the Tajik–Afghan frontier. From the window of the Antonov I could see only grey and sand colour.

Three years of drought have left Afghanistan dry as a bone, and many of its people on the verge of starvation — seven million, more than a third of the population, according to the UN.

Dominic McSorley and Phil Miller from the biggest Irish relief agency, Concern, shared my flight. Mr McSorley was unhappy about the bombardments. 'It's disastrous,' he said. 'We've been

Postmistress Laura Woods from Baldoyle, Dublin, with her dog, Lucy, and members of the Irish Postmasters Union protesting outside the Dáil against what they see as threats to the survival of sub-post offices throughout the country. Photograph: Frank Miller.

trying to operate under the threat of airstrikes which already crippled deliveries.' The World Food Programme was supposed to deliver 10,000 tonnes of food to Concern each week until the snow starts in November. But WFP withdrew its staff after the September 11th attacks on the US, and had delivered only 2,000 tonnes in the past month. Afghans at Concern's 'work for food programme' at Pulibeghem have seized tools and stopped a dozen local employees from leaving the site until they receive the 200 tonnes of food owed to them.

US officials predict the airstrikes will be 'long and sustained'. 'That means limited or no access for humanitarian relief,' Mr McSorley said. The US strategy of bomb and bread air drops made it likely that the most vulnerable would be left out — and that Taliban fighters will get plenty to eat.

'The humanitarian operation on the ground has been completely compromised,' Mr McSorley said. He showed me a Concern position paper issued the previous day. 'Air drops of humanitarian aid should not be used as a pretext or a cover for military action,' it says.

Below us, I could see only the same brown and grey, a few sand-coloured boxes that were houses, squatting in this inhospitable land. Not a sign of life. Had all Afghanistan gone to ground, like Osama bin Laden? Then the dunes started, immense, undulating forms, more dramatic than the Sahara desert. The riverbeds were dry and the desolation stretched to the horizon; valleys, canyons and mountains of sand. A dead star. The surface of Mars.

The Antonov crew asked us to crowd forward, to balance the weight of the aircraft. We were climbing to clear the outcroppings of the Hindu Kush, great tectonic plates that shifted thousands of years ago. The slightly orange-beige colour never varied, only the size and shapes of the mountains. The pilot veered before a high peak and we came upon a valley, faded and dusty but green. The passengers applauded when the wheels touched down in a whirlwind of dust.

Although we had paid for the flight, the co-pilot took up a collection for the pilot.

'State of Afghanistan is committed to Strugle Against Caltivating Producing and Trafficing of Narcotic,' said the hand-painted sign on the airport building, misspellings and all. The entire economy of the United Front enclave is based on opium poppies and relief aid. A photo portrait of Ahmed Shah Massoud, the Front's leader, hung below it, between broken windows filled with plywood. Massoud's assassination on 9 September is believed to have been a signal to the hijackers in the US to carry out their horrific mission.

Dozens of men and boys, barefoot or in sandals, wearing maroufi — baggy trousers with a long waistcoat over them — and cloth turbans or round kulla wool hats, stood on the dusty landing strip, staring, smiling, fingering their worry beads. In the capital of 'free Afghanistan', seat of Badakshan province, home to President Burhannudin Rabbani, with a population 100,000, donkeys outnumber vehicles. There is not a single paved road; all buildings are made of mud brick. There is electricity three nights a week, no running water.

Except for the Kalashnikovs slung casually over shoulders, the battered jeeps and two fancy guesthouses belonging to President Rabbani, Faizabad has changed little in 1,000 years. Ten years of Soviet occupation and the mujahideen attacks from surrounding mountains barely fazed it.

The only structural change in nine years of United Front rule is a massive compound for the presidential guard on the outskirts of town, surrounded by a mud brick wall with medieval turrets at each corner. We passed the bouz kashi playing ground, with mud brick bleachers, where the national sport is played for ten days every spring. Horsemen bat a headless goat around with sticks; outside the United Front enclave, the game has been banned by the Taliban.

We passed a school being built by US Concern. 'The teachers are given food for teaching, the students receive food for attending,' Phil Miller,

'Fox in the Snow' by Terence O'Connell catches the attention of Eoghan Clarke, 3, and Leah Deverell, 5, from Dún Laoghaire, and Ginnie, a young English pointer, at a preview of the Water Colour Society of Ireland annual exhibition in the County Hall, Dún Laoghaire. Photograph: Matt Kavanagh.

Concern's director in Faizabad explained: 'The girls get a special bonus.' We drove along the Kupcha River gorge to the old city, with its muddy paths and wood-shuttered stalls. It seemed odd that in a country at war, people could be so unconcerned and cheerful. 'People were very worried after Massoud died,' said Azam, an office manager. 'Now they are happy because the Americans are fighting terrorism. The Taliban will be finished. Our commanders will take Mazar, Takhar and Kunduz (provinces).' Only the mullahs had reservations about the US bombardment, because they are susceptible to bin Laden's discourse on Islam, Azam said. 'I talked to one of them today. He was afraid to say much, because he thought the people of Ahmed Shah Massoud might hear him and arrest him. In Afghanistan before, the mullahs were not

very influential. They learned this in Pakistan. It's the Taliban who gave the mullahs this power.'

The United Front style themselves as 'moderate' Muslims, but as Mr Miller of Concern learned, they are extremely strict. 'I had to obtain government permission to hire two women,' he says. 'We had to build a separate entrance for them, and employ an ugly old man to guard them. The government complained that I spoke to them three times in six months. I prefer the rural villages — they're more easy-going.' In one of the muddy streets of the terraced old town, I approached a fleeting form, shrouded in a white burqa. 'She doesn't want to talk to you,' my interpreter kept repeating. I insisted that he translate for me. 'I am not allowed to talk in the street,' the woman answered before hurrying away. 'She's afraid of the government people,' the interpreter explained, gesturing at 'No. 1 Guest House' — the seat of local government — on the incline above us.

Mohamed Nazir (26), President Rabbani's deputy, in charge of immigration, foreign relations and permits for the Panjshir Valley, sat in front of the guesthouse. He referred not to the United Front but to 'Islamic State troops'. 'Ninety per cent of the people are very happy about the bombardments,' he said.

Gen Pervez Musharaf, the President of Pakistan, said yesterday that the United Front must not benefit from the US bombardments. Mr Nazir laughed. 'The Pakistanis are pretending to go along with the Americans,' he said. 'But they've still got their devious plans for Afghanistan. Pakistan is a founder of terrorism. Pakistan founded the Taliban.'

But if the American onslaught continued, he predicted, 'It won't take long. They'll smoke out the Taliban.' But weren't the people of Faizabad afraid the Taliban might attack their idyllic valley in retaliation? Mr Nazir laughed again. 'People know the Taliban are over-powered. We want the Islamic State troops to occupy all of Afghanistan.' He looked across the old town, glowing in the late afternoon sun. The trees trembled in the breeze and the waters of the Kupcha roared beside us. Mr Nazir laughed softly. 'You know, it's always been hard for our people to get visas to visit the US,' he said, more to himself than to me. 'Faizabad is a very safe place. Maybe the safest in the world.'

Enjoying a hot October day in St Stephen's Green. Photograph: Brenda Fitzsimons.

FRIDAY, 12 OCTOBER 2001

Two Family Members Contracted AIDS

Eithne Donnellan

A woman who had three sons and three brothers with haemophilia told the Lindsay tribunal yesterday of the devastating effect on her life of AIDS, which two of them contracted from contaminated blood-clotting products.

She lost one of her sons to AIDS symptoms in the early 1990s when he was eleven, and one of her brothers died of AIDS-related symptoms a year later. Her two other brothers were now ill. Giving evidence using the pseudonym Eithne, the woman said the death of her son Simon (also a pseudonym) placed a strain on her relationship with her husband and changed her six surviving children completely.

'It was like moving from one family to another,' she said.

Of the effect on her parents and siblings of her brother's death, she said: 'It's destroyed everything we ever had.

She said her son was outgoing, loved football and lived for Michael Jackson. She recalled sitting in a doctor's office in the late 1980s when Dr Fred Jackson told her Simon was HIV positive and probably only had six years to live. She said the news was broken during a routine visit to hospital with her three sons for a check-up.

'I thought he was very cold,' she said, pointing out that Dr Jackson — now a consultant haematologist with the South Eastern Health Board and then working with the former director of the National Haemophilia Treatment Centre, Prof. Ian Temperley — didn't ask if she had anyone with her before delivering the bad news. Her son died in January 1993, twelve days after she took him home from Harcourt Street Hospital.

Another witness, Ms Anita Geoghegan, told the tribunal her father thought Prof. Temperley very 'cold-hearted' when, in 1994, he took her brother, John Scallan, who was HIV positive, to see him. After seeing them Prof. Temperley said to her father: 'This is the last time I'll be seeing you.' John, from Wexford, was a severe haemophiliac who was diagnosed HIV positive in 1987. He died of AIDS-related symptoms weeks after that visit to Prof. Temperley. He was thirty-four.

Ms Geoghegan said her brother was the life and soul of parties, had many girlfriends, bought himself a boat, and even bought a house from his hospital bed at one point. 'He was very much a young man going places in a hurry,' she said. One woman's magazine had voted him bachelor of the year.

He was a natural entrepreneur, worked in the family linen hire company and set up a paper business. The companies now employed 500, she said.

Of the effect the tragedy had on her family, she said her father subsequently developed bowel cancer and her mother and younger sister became ill. All their illnesses were stress-related, she claimed.

Ms Geoghegan read into the record a statement her brother had made to his solicitor before his death. In it he described being told of his diagnosis in September 1987 by Dr Jackson.

'He said, "I suppose you know you're HIV positive." As I informed him I had guessed but had never been told, he commented: "Well unfortunately you are." I had been tested approximately 1½ years before that.

'The effect of knowing I'm HIV positive is a constant subconscious niggle. I can't have children; my girlfriends will have to know.'

A third witness, using the pseudonym Veronica, said she contracted hepatitis C from a clotting agent she was given after she had a stillbirth. The diagnosis four years ago came 'like a bolt of thunder'. She and her husband 'cried like babies'.

Aged fifty, she said she did walks and mini-marathons for charity but now had no energy. She

Kofi Annan keeping the UN ship afloat.

often told her husband she wouldn't think twice about taking her own life.

She said she was afraid to tell friends and neighbours. 'I live a lie every day of my life.'

Now she was on sleeping tablets but they were of little use. She walked the floor at night suffering from excruciating joint pains.

'How it has affected me and my family and the

way I feel, I wouldn't wish it on my worst enemy,' she said.

Counsel for Dr Jackson and Prof. Temperley said it was always their intention to be as kind and gentle as possible when giving bad news.

WEDNESDAY, 17 OCTOBER 2001

Afghans the Victims of US Terrorism

Vincent Browne

All the news bulletins and news channels nowadays have 'anchormen' or 'experts' parading in front of huge maps of Afghanistan, explaining the detail of the military assault on the country.

We are told of the type of bomber used and from what base, the aircraft carriers from where the tomahawk missiles are fired. Sometimes we are told of the 'payload delivered'.

And not a hint of the devastation these 'payloads' deliver to the people of Afghanistan. The awful terror they bring, the devastation, the injury, the slaughter.

We have become morally desensitised to the abominations that are clinically conveyed to us night after night on our television screens.

Nobody at any of the news conferences challenges George Bush or Tony Blair or Donald Rumsfeld or Colin Powell about the outrages they are perpetrating. We are all part of the consensus that it is OK to bomb a country to a pulp with the vastness of the military might the world has ever known.

Nobody asks Tony Blair about the 'human rights of the suffering women of Afghanistan' that he talked about in that speech at the Labour Party conference two weeks ago.

How did the world get to believe that terror and slaughter delivered by a bomb in a car was an atrocity, while much more terror and much more slaughter delivered by airplane or missile is morally OK?

Remember all the talk some years ago about the godfathers of violence who sat in their comfortable, middle-class homes in Dundalk or Buncrana, while their cowardly minions delivered mayhem to the streets of Belfast or Derry or Claudy or Omagh?

What about the godfathers of violence sitting in their stately mansions in the White House or Downing Street or Chequers or Camp David, and their minions dropping far larger bombs from the security of thousands of feet beyond range of retaliation, causing far more mayhem in the homes and streets of Kabul, Kandahar, and Jalalabad?

And all for what?

Is it believable that the attack on America of September 11th could have been planned, directed and co-ordinated from caves in Afghanistan? Or that the organisation that was responsible for that attack originates in Afghanistan? A great deal of the emerging evidence suggests otherwise.

Last Wednesday *The New York Times* published a lengthy portrait of one of the organisers and perpetrators of the September 11th attack, Mohammed Atta. Atta came from a middle-class family in Cairo, where his father was a lawyer.

He went to Hamburg for several years to get a degree in urban planning and he later worked there. 'Officials' were quoted as saying there was 'strong evidence' Atta had trained in terrorist camps in Afghanistan in the late 1990s, but we are not told what that evidence is or what it is he could have been trained in that would have had any relevance to what happened on September 11th.

It is clear, however, that his radicalism emerged while he was in Hamburg, where he associated with people from the Turkish, Arab and African communities. He went to Florida in 2000 and trained as an airline pilot.

There is evidence that he received a large sum of money from someone in The United Arab Emirates, who 'may' have had an association with Osama bin Laden.

A report in Monday's *Los Angeles Times* quoted FBI sources as saying there were several people involved in plotting further attacks on the US and they were 'at large in the United States and across Europe and the Middle East'.

The *Los Angeles Times* also reported that several people suspected of involvement either in the September 11th attack or in planning further attacks were from Saudi Arabia and were resident either there or in the US.

CBS News on Monday evening quoted Prof. Vali Nasr of the University of San Diego as saying the Saudi government had 'appeased' Islamic extremists by funding and promoting a radical form of Islam that sees the US as the enemy.

Other reports from the US suggest that the real source of terrorism is Iran, where there are several persons wanted by the US, and, of course, Iraq remains a major suspect as a terrorist sponsor.

So what is the point of the assault on Afghanistan? Yes, Osama bin Laden and some of his associates are there, but if the vast bulk of those suspected of terrorism by the US are either in the US itself or in Hamburg or Iran or Saudi Arabia or Iraq, what good will it do if everyone in Afghanistan is obliterated?

How will it reduce the terrorist threat to the US if the vast majority of terrorists are in places other than Afghanistan?

If the anthrax attacks are the work of terrorists, does anyone believe that the packages containing it were sent from Afghanistan?

And just one other thing. If the point of the assault on Afghanistan is not to defeat terrorism but get Osama bin Laden and bring him to 'justice', why has the latest offer by the Taliban to send him to an agreed third country been dismissed?

What would it matter if he were taken to one of America's allies such as Egypt or even Pakistan or Turkey and 'brought to justice' there?

The reality is that Afghanistan is being devastated and hundreds are being slaughtered on the net issue of bringing bin Laden and his associates to

justice in the US rather than to some other third agreed country. That's what the slaughter is about. And that's putting it at its best.

WEDNESDAY, 24 OCTOBER 2001

'Day of Liberation' for Northern Ireland

Gerry Moriarty

So where were you when the IRA started disposing of its arsenals? Senator Edward Kennedy was in Washington. He described the news as 'a new day of liberation' for all the people of Northern Ireland.

It may have sounded a trifle exaggerated but on reflection it was an apposite phrase because for too long politics here have been imprisoned by dreary recrimination and perpetual crises — much of it revolving around the arms issue. It created a wearying atmosphere of political and public despondency.

This move could and should unlock that prison door after three decades of misery and suffering. And that effectively is how the IRA described their act of decommissioning. 'This unprecedented move is to save the peace process and to persuade others of our genuine intentions,' it said.

Up on the Shankill Road around the time of the IRA announcement people were commemorating the eighth anniversary of the IRA bombing that killed ten people, including the bomber Thomas Begley.

This positive IRA act was too late for the relatives of the dead, but generally they hoped this was the end of a conflict that through thirty years claimed the lives of over 3,600 people and mentally and physically damaged the lives of many thousands more.

Republican activist turned writer Danny Morrison was in a BBC studio remembering back twenty years to when he coined the phrase of the ballot box and the Armalite. 'It's now time for the ballot box,' he said.

A former IRA member was briefed in advance about the IRA statement but when he heard the formal announcement on the radio 'it left me half in a daze and half in a state of reflection'. But the republican movement was conditioned for the move and could live with it, he said.

'A historical watershed,' was how he portrayed the IRA statement. 'What it means is that for the first time the political wing of republicanism is taking precedence over the military wing.' Now that is historic.

Gen. John de Chastelain finally had a chance to earn his keep. He verified that the IRA had engaged in a meaningful act of decommissioning as the legislation demands but more importantly, as the Ulster Unionist leader Mr David Trimble required, to allow him to restore devolution.

Mr Trimble is expected to reinstate his three ministers in the Executive tomorrow, a move that will put pressure on the DUP to revoke their resignations. Mr Trimble has said all along that if this act of decommissioning meets the legislative requirement of arms being 'permanently unusable and permanently inaccessible' he would quickly move to restore devolution. And that was what he pledged after meeting Gen. de Chastelain last night.

Gen. de Chastelain has confirmed that the IRA met that requirement. The probability is that the DUP will follow the three UUP ministers back into government, to join the three SDLP and two Sinn Féin ministers.

The problem thereafter is how Mr Trimble can get himself re-elected as First Minister, assuming after all his trials and tribulations that he wouldn't prefer to leave that role to the previous acting First Minister Sir Reg Empey.

Members of the Caribbean theatre group Teyat Toutafe in Temple Bar Square. The performers from St. Lucia presented a Trinidadian play, **Mary Could Dance**, *at the Project. Photograph: Eric Luke.*

Mr Trimble has strongly indicated he wants to be back at the helm, and his closest aides have insisted he intends to seek re-election. That could only happen if he could command thirty unionist votes in the Assembly. At the moment he is at least one if not two votes short of that.

Ulster Unionist MLAs Ms Pauline Armitage and Mr Peter Weir have lost the UUP whip. Party sources believe they may be able to persuade Ms Armitage to return to the fold, but they have their doubts about Mr Weir. Self-interest is a wonderful motivator however and if the alternative is elections then Mr Trimble could yet find the necessary number of votes he needs.

Pro-agreement Ulster Unionist sources said last night there would be no unnecessary carping about the IRA statement or the subsequent statement from the Independent International Commission on Decommissioning (IICD) confirming that the IRA had followed the word with the deed.

Anti-agreement unionists, however, will attempt to seize on the lack of detail about what was decommissioned.

They may have their work cut out because Gen. de Chastelain confirmed that the material included 'arms, ammunition and explosives'.

Should some unionists say this could mean 'two guns, two bullets and two rotten sticks of gelignite', it will also be pointed out that the general described the act as 'significant' and that he is satisfied it meets the legislative demands under which he works. He has a reputation to maintain after all.

Moreover, Mr Trimble was happy to state last night that the arms disposed of were substantial.

The DUP and other No unionists may also try to exploit the fact that the IICD's mandate runs out in February.

This has raised concerns that some unionists, including some Ulster Unionists, will posit February as another deadline for complete IRA

Members of the Muslim community in the Islamic Cultural Centre of Ireland. Photograph: Moya Nolan.

decommissioning. Mr Jeffrey Donaldson, who is in Australia, already has said as much.

Rather oddly, both senior Sinn Féin and Yes Ulster Unionist sources say February won't prove a problem, again suggesting quite a degree of bilateral sequencing ahead of this IRA move. They appear comfortable with the prospect of the IICD's mandate being extended.

The next phase is to see some payoff for republicanism for its 'unprecedented move'.

Expect to see diggers and other dismantling equipment beginning work on some of the watchtowers in south Armagh very soon. Details of the demilitarisation plans are expected to be announced today.

Ultimately, the success of yesterday's republican and unionist risk-taking may depend on the general public instructing the politicians to get on with politics and to forget about petty fault-finding over the fine detail of the statements from the IRA and IICD.

It will take time to sink in, but yesterday truly was a momentous day.

There is much to analyse and much yet to happen to anchor the Belfast Agreement safely but it's worth taking time to reflect on the prospect that Northern Ireland could be on the verge of passing from conflict and sterile politics into a truly new dispensation.

IRA 'Thought Long and Hard About This'

Róisín Ingle

All eyes in Shorts pub in Crossmaglen swivelled towards the TV as the IRA statement was announced yesterday afternoon. It was raining outside and the tricolours which hang all over this IRA heartland drooped slightly under the weight of heavy showers. 'We will just have to wait and see,' said one man who seemed lost in thought as he sipped his glass of Guinness.

The pub is owned by well-known local republican Paddy Short. His daughter, Margaret, a teacher based in England, had come over for a few days to look after the pub.

'People around here probably feel that the IRA have thought long and hard about this. They have not come to this position lightly', she said. 'But there is the feeling that we don't want to go back to where we were. We will never be trampled on again.'

She talked about life in Crossmaglen, the constant whirr of helicopters, the soldiers on the streets, the intimidation by police officers. All over south Armagh, otherwise known as 'Bandit Country', observation towers protrude from misty mountains, wooden IRA signs are nailed to lampposts, soldiers stumble through fields and out from under hedges.

A masked IRA man with a machinegun peers down from a sign which reads 'Don't worry, be happy, welcome to Crossmaglen'. Another one declares 'Demilitarise. Brits Out'.

In the local bookies, two men sat with their arms folded behind the counter, checking dockets and taking money. They were tight-lipped at first.

'Cross' people do not say much, the older man explained. 'But I'm thinking what will be the next hurdle?' the younger man said suddenly as horses galloped around the racetrack on the TV screens. 'What will the unionists want next?'

Anyway, said the older man, giving up guns did not mean anything. 'Sure you can't decommission brains,' he said.

'And they won't be getting lorry loads of guns either. The guns haven't been used this past two years,' said the younger man, returning to his newspaper.

An elderly woman, hurrying home with her shopping, said she thought it was very good of the IRA to decommission.

'They are nice people. They have never caused any trouble around here. If they want to give up the guns, it is up to themselves,' she said.

A source in the local newspaper, the *Examiner*, said that what was needed now was 'clear skies over south Armagh and the uprooting of the observation posts'.

In Shorts bar, as the newscaster continued giving details of the latest decommissioning break-through, Margaret Short described the mood in Crossmaglen as cautious.

'We have never really seen any improvement here, despite the agreements and the peace process, so no one expects anything much,' she said.

'Secretly, though, everyone hopes that something will happen now, because if there is no hope, what else is there? But we need a gesture from the British government and we need one soon.'

Letters to the Editor October 2001

V a l i u m ,   N o t   I o d i n e

Sir, — The Naas dual-carriageway is in a mess because of the Luas and road works being carried out and it is very difficult to get to work. Hundreds of people have frayed nerves.

Perhaps it would be more in the interests of Irish health if Micheál Martin forgot about the iodine tablets for a while and dealt with a more immediate problem by dishing out Valium at the traffic lights between Naas and Dublin. — Yours, etc., Terry Healy, Hartwell Green, Kill, Co. Kildare. 9 October 2001.

L e g a c y   o f   t h e   H u n g e r S t r i k e s

Sir, — Robert Ballagh (Opinion, 5 October) appears to be trying to convince himself as well as others that the legacy of the 1981 hunter strike (the peace process) is something we should all be grateful for. He must be joking!

Mr Ballagh castigates what he terms 'establishment Ireland' for its marked lack of enthusiasm towards the hunger strike and its anniversary twenty years on. It doesn't seem to occur to him that it's not just establishment Ireland that stays away from his black-flag road-show but hundreds of thousands of ordinary people as well, because they have no wish to be associated in any way with an organisation that committed unspeakable acts of mass murder against innocent civilians in Britain and Ireland during a vicious sectarian campaign spanning thirty years, the real legacy of which we see almost nightly on our television screens.

Who does Mr Ballagh think is to blame when he sees working-class people from both communities in Northern Ireland stoning children going to school, burning each other's homes and churches, torching community halls and driving senior citizens from their abodes? Some legacy. — Yours, etc., Eddie Naughton, Weaver's Street, The Coombe, Dublin 8. 11 October 2001.

R e s p o n s e   t o   T e r r o r i s t A t t a c k s

Sir, — When I was a little boy in the 1960s I was already internalising a vague sense of inferiority due to something called 'Irish ancestry'. Eventually, as a young adult, I got the idea to travel here from my native New York, and I have been studying the place first hand since 1985.

Now, living in Dublin, I'm encountering the new incivility along with the wonderful affluence, and a less friendly atmosphere than I'm accustomed to in New York City. Lately, I've become so distressed by the responses I hear to the tragedy in the US that I want all Americans to know that we have fewer friends here than even I previously imagined.

After the memorial ceremony at the US embassy, which I attended, and the 'Late Late Show' interview with President McAleese (which was extraordinary) I've seldom heard any word of sympathy. I've received one call and one e-mail since September 11th, and a hundred of the same from the United States. Almost immediately, my associates in the art world and in the

An American passer-by who was in New York at the time of the twin towers attack remonstrates with members of the NGO Peace Alliance during their anti-war vigil outside the Department of Foreign Affairs in Dublin. Photograph: Matt Kavanagh.

world of letters here began to let their views be known. An alarming number of people I've talked to — a number still growing — believe the US deserved what it got (we are talking about more than 5,000 homicides, let alone that some of my interlocutors knew that I'd known some of the victims). I have been lectured repeatedly about 'world justice', and by some of the very people whose anti-Nice votes put the futures of millions of Eastern Europeans into question.

Few of these people knew that the US was already the largest food and supplies donor to Afghanistan. They want to blame the US for the factional fighting that took hold there after the Cold War. No doubt one day they will find a way to blame us for the faction fighting in Northern Ireland. I still haven't met anyone who understands the southern no-fly zone in Iraq, and our attempt to shield the Shi'ites, the Kuwaitis and the Saudis from

Saddam. Iraq, like North Korea, would starve or poison its people before giving up its weapons laboratories.

The Irish who have left me so appalled in the past three weeks are all fellow travellers in my estimate, and all are culpable in lowering the general standards of decency and sanity with their sham purity. They are pretending to represent some Cold-War era virtue. I see it another way. Whereas the Irish preserved Western civilisation during a former dark age, I see now an adolescent recklessness, even a romantic eagerness, to tear it all down. This is now a possibility.

Undoubtedly much good can come out of the attacks in the US, from greater civility at home to greater justice in the world and less want. It is a changed world. Yet, ever since President Bush, on the day after the attack, announced the word 'coalition', the animosity toward all things American has been palpable and growing in this town. The resentment about offering Shannon Airport to the US military campaign did not go unnoticed at home. Nor have I heard a single word of credit for how it has all been handled thus far. Instead, I hear countless cynical digs and the ubiquitous sanctimony I'd already come to know.

Unless there's a silent majority in this country quietly backing the admirable efforts of Mr Ahern, Mr Cowen, President McAleese et al., I will be leaving this place with a strong impression of Ireland's pompous ingratitude towards the US, let alone its foolishness on the world stage. I can think of nothing more serviceable to my country than to devote myself to drying up every dollar, every tourist, every last outmoded bit of the dream of Ireland.

I am once again embarrassed to have Irish blood in my veins, and I'm afraid this time I'm inconsolable. Ireland may be hopelessly insignificant in determining the shape of this world, but there's no excuse.

If there's another voice out there, for goodness' sake, speak out! — Yours, etc., Timothy O'Connor, Clontarf, Dublin 3. 17 October 2001.

Sir, — Timothy O'Connor's letter of 17 October really takes the biscuit for sheer arrogance and unwarranted bile — seemingly directed both at individual Irish citizens who dare to criticise US foreign policy and at the Irish nation's 'foolishness on the world stage' (an offensive accusation which he fails to support with any facts or with anything resembling a coherent argument).

He claims to have 'seldom heard any word of sympathy' for the suffering endured by America. Didn't he notice that Ireland had a national day of mourning on which all schools, businesses and State offices closed as a mark of respect? Hasn't he noticed the acres of sympathetic reportage in the Irish media? He then has the nerve to accuse us of 'lowering the general standards of decency'. More disturbingly, he berates our 'pompous ingratitude'. Perhaps he might tell us exactly what it is we are supposed to be grateful for, and why this gratitude should take the form of unqualified support for US military action.

It really is about time that Americans like Mr O'Connor came to grips with the simple fact that people around the world — not just in Ireland — are sick to the back teeth of American insensitivity towards the suffering of others.

Mr O'Connor sneers at those who 'lecture' him about 'world justice'. Are American lives the only lives to be valued? The slaughter of over 5,000 at the World Trade centre was an abominable act and I haven't heard anybody say the US 'deserved what it got'.

I do, though, hear people asking why Americans still don't understand that their shambolic and self-serving foreign policy has unleashed more than its fair share of Frankenstein's monsters — Osama bin Laden and the Taliban being two cases in point.

Mr O'Connor notes 'resentment' about Shannon Airport being offered for US military use as if this is to be automatically condemned. Well, yes, I do quite resent this — perhaps I've been under the misapprehension that Ireland is supposed to be neutral and that the Irish electorate should be consulted before our Government rushes to back a military campaign with unclear and ill-defined goals. It's called democracy, and our leaders have shown contempt for it.

Mr O'Connor's final bitter comments about thinking of 'nothing more serviceable to my country that to devote myself to drying up every dollar, every tourist, every last outmoded bit of the dream of Ireland' speak volumes. In other words, if we don't grovel at the table of American bounty, we will be punished.

If Mr O'Connor wants to know what 'pompous ingratitude' is, he should remove the plank from his own eye before daring to comment on the mote in another's. And if he wishes to promote 'decency' he could start by apologising for his vicious and inexcusable criticisms of the decent people of Ireland. — Yours, etc., Liam Carson, Jones Road, Drumcondra, Dublin 9. 19 October 2001.

A Bar Too Far

Sir, — 50p for a Mars Bar ... Do we just accept this? — Yours, etc., Mary Bowen, Nutley Road, Donnybrook, Dublin 4. 22 October 2001.

SATURDAY, 3 NOVEMBER 2001

From Shoeshine to Showtime

The Indefinite Article: John Kelly

Ibrahim Ferrer takes Lazarus with him wherever he goes. Showing me a short black stick with a carved head, he tells me that it has protected him for many years.

'An African woman gave it to my mother,' he says. 'It always goes with me.'

Back in Havana, he honours another Lazarus figure who stands like a Child of Prague in a domestic shrine. In one of the most memorable scenes in Wim Wenders's documentary, *The Buena Vista Social Club*, Ferrer is seen venerating his protector with gifts of candles, honey, perfume, flowers and rum.

'I like', he says, 'so I figure he does too.' The Lazarus stick is important to Ferrer because it links him directly to the mother he lost when he was only twelve years old. His father was already dead and, because he had no brothers and sisters, he was suddenly orphaned and alone. If asked to explain who he is, his answer is simple. He is 'the natural son' of Aurelia Ferrer and he comes from Santiago de Cuba. He'll neglect to tell you that he is also a septuagenarian superstar, but he most certainly is that too. As chief crooner of The Buena Vista Club, he is now almost as famous as Fidel — and a much better singer.

Dianne Kennedy and Neil Grundie, members of The Belfast Circus group, practising before their performance at Dublin City University as part of Arts Week 2001. The DCU Arts Week featured a wide range of performances including music, dance, comedy and poetry. Photograph: Bryan O'Brien.

'Well, I didn't have the opportunity to study music on a formal level,' he says. 'The first music I started to hear was tango, particularly Carlos Gardel. I know he came from Argentina, but I started singing it a lot. But after that I got interested in my own music — son and bolero, typical Cuban music. And the bolero was from Santiago. I was thirteen then; it was 1941.'

To suggest that he was born to sing is tempting. It sounds fanciful, but it seems that Ferrer was literally delivered during a social club dance. It is equally tempting to labour the influence of the biblical Lazarus, given the way his career has been transformed since the recording of *The Buena Vista Social Club* album back in 1996. The release was a huge success and it reminded everyone, not least the people whose shoes he had just been shining, that Ferrer was one of Cuba's great singers. For many years he had been a forgotten man — 'dumped', as he puts it — a victim of changing fashions. For him, and for other singers of the out-of-date bolero, it had been a time of shining shoes, selling lottery tickets and doing whatever it took to feed their families.

'For a time, after the triumph of the revolution, the bolero went out of fashion,' Ferrer says. 'It wasn't heard that much and the influence of the salsa started to emerge. It started to invade the music and the young people forgot about the bolero and got interested in outside influences.

'But now people who are involved in the bolero have become successful again, and one of the reasons is because they have managed to penetrate it and get to the heart if it. Yes, for a time I couldn't sing the bolero because it just wasn't popular. But now I just throw myself into it — for the love of the music.'

Many of the Buena Vista musicians first came together as part of The Afro-Cuban All-Stars, led by Juan de Marcos, a younger musician who wanted to pay tribute to the older pre-revolutionary music and get young and old to play together. The arrival of Ry Cooder brought his own talents and global attention to the subsequent Buena Vista project — and the Wenders film sealed it. Suddenly a non-mainstream recording became a massive hit and before long these 1940s and 1950s Cuban sounds were as ubiquitous as David Gray.

The downside, however, has been that audiences abroad now expect Cuban music to sound a certain way — the old way. Anything progressive poses aural difficulties simply because it doesn't sound like Rubén González or Ferrer, and this is a real worry for some of the younger musicians. After all, González is in his late eighties, Ferrer in his mid-seventies and so it is more important than ever that the preoccupations of the younger musicians are given a fair chance.

Not that Ferrer himself was necessarily stuck in pre-revolution mode. He was very interested in the Cuban music of the 1960s, most notably Los Zafiros, a doo-wop and rock 'n' roll influenced group who could count The Beatles among their fans.

On his *World Circuit* solo album, Ferrer recorded an old Los Zafiros hit, Herido de Sombras, and on this current tour he has been joined on stage by the twangy Los Zafiros guitar player, Manuel Galban.

'I was still a bit young,' laughs Ferrer. 'But yes, that music did interest me. We heard it a lot. I heard Elvis Presley a lot, but I preferred the music of tap. And I danced a lot. I don't know how good I was at it, but I liked to dance like Fred Astaire!'

When Rubén González played at Whelan's in Wexford Street back in 1997, Ferrer was there too. He stood at the side of the stage and broke hearts with his shy smile and his smooth voice singing songs like 'Perfidia' to a truly gobsmacked audience. There are those who still don't believe that that Whelan's show ever happened — most of the Buena Vista Social Club huddled on that tiny stage — but it did. A few weeks later, they were just about the hottest ticket on the planet and nobody would ever get quite so close to Ferrer again.

The story of his re-emergence is typical of the other 'rediscovered' musicians in *The Buena Vista*

Social Club. Ry Cooder was in town trying to track down as many of the old brigade as he could and Juan de Marcos went off in search of the singer. He called at Ferrer's house but he wasn't home; he was out shining shoes. When de Marcos finally found him, Ferrer at first declined the invitation to sing — but de Marcos insisted. Warily, the 'retired' singer wiped the polish off his hands and headed for the studios of Egrem, Cuba's only recording company.

When he arrived, a lot of his old friends were already there and, as he walked in, Rubén González began to play Ferrer's big hit, 'Candela'. Ferrer began singing, Cooder began recording and, over the next six days, *The Buena Vista Social Club* CD was made. Soon after that, Ferrer was back in studio to record *The Buena Vista Social Club Presents Ibrahim Ferrer*, a solo album featuring many of the same musicians.

Ferrer is a very happy man, singing all over the world. And for such a gentle, almost timid person, he is a remarkable showman, all singing and all dancing. He is genuinely enjoying the unexpected twist in his life and it shows.

As the talk turns to Frank Sinatra, Nat King Cole and Bing Crosby, I offer him a rum. He declines with a laugh. There's a show to do later and he's going for a nap.

SATURDAY, 10 NOVEMBER 2001

The Good Guy Who Outlived JR

Arminta Wallace

The silhouette is unmistakable, and so is the smile. It looks — if you don't look too closely — like J.R. Ewing is calmly drinking coffee downstairs in the Morrison Hotel, Dublin. J.R. Ewing: ultimate 1980s bad guy, star of the TV show 'Dallas', hell-raiser, womaniser, tormentor of trembly-lipped Sue Ellen and wimpy Bobby and petulant Cliff Barnes and all the rest — hell, is there anybody on the planet who doesn't know who J.R. is?

Of course, the man who rises to shake hands is not really J.R. It's the actor Larry Hagman, in Dublin to publicise a book whose climax is not the phenomenon that once was 'Dallas', but the recent liver transplant operation that saved his life. Perched at a table a discreet distance away is a blonde woman wrapped in a tangerine pashmina: Maj, Hagman's wife of almost half a century. Not very J.R. at all, despite the book's title, *Hello Darlin'*. But when you talk to Hagman, you have to keep pinching yourself because what comes out of his mouth is pure J.R., all quick-fire rhythms and outrageously overdone vowels.

'I'd been asked to do a book many times,' he's explaining. Minny tahmes. 'And I kept saying: "I'm too young. I'm not ready for that stuff yet." Well, I got to be seventy and I thought, there's not that many years left — I might as well do something, and get it right.'

He got it right. *Hello Darlin'* is a model of its kind, a great, gossipy read and — thanks to the input of the *US Weekly* journalist, Todd Gold — uncommonly well-written. However, I tell him, some of his stories are frankly unbelievable. He looks shocked.

'Really? Like what?' OK, what about the Great Dane? 'The Great Dane? Oh, no, that was true,' he protests. Desperate to do pretty much anything to get a foothold in the acting game, a young and impressionable Hagman was working for the impresario St John Terrell, driving a motley crew of chorus girls, choreographers, dancers and assorted dogs from New York to Florida. Forced to overnight in a motel with too many people and not enough rooms, he curled up on the floor while one of the women, and her dog, took the bed. He was woken by — well, consult page fifty-one for further details.

Hagman has assumed the look of wide-eyed innocence J.R. used to adopt when he was about

Larry Hagman. Photograph: Cyril Byrne.

to ruin some sweet-as-pie all-American family business. 'That was true,' he insists. 'Maj was with me.'

Maj, who is of Swedish origin and whose name is pronounced 'My', shakes her head. 'I wasn't with you,' she says. 'But I knew that whole group. It's for real.'

Hagman turns to me in triumph. 'What', he asks, 'would you think would not be real about it?' I mutter something about having lived a sheltered life. 'Oh. Oh, I see. Well, my dear', says Hagman, patting my arm, 'I'm sorry about that. No, actually, I'm glad. That sure is a lot better for you than the life I've lived.'

Reading *Hello Darlin'*, you'd have to disagree. Hagman's life has been peopled by a cast of characters weirder and more wonderful than anything the 'Dallas' scriptwriters — or those of his other TV smash hit, 'I Dream of Jeannie' — could have dreamed up. For example, his macho lawyer father,

who once gave him buzzard for dinner: 'Son, in Texas, we eat what we shoot'. Or his mother, the actress Mary Martin, a living legend in her own right. Hagman, who was raised by his grandparents, saw little of his mother during his teenage years, which come across in the book as a sort of showbiz hell.

'Not showbiz hell', he says now, 'so much as I just didn't have access to her. My stepfather kept me away, pretty much, and so there was no way of getting to know her. Then he died. I don't want to speak ill of the dead, but he's worth speaking ill of. He was a jerk.'

A jerk towards whom, according to the book, the twelve-year-old Hagman harboured murderous thoughts. 'Well, yeah', he says, taking a thoughtful sip of coffee. 'I had him in my crosshairs a couple times. But I didn't do it. Thank God.'

After his stepfather's death, Hagman and his

mother developed what he now calls 'a great relationship'. The day before she died, he sat holding her hand and they whistled Bach inventions together — a skill he hasn't lost in the meantime, as he happily demonstrates. 'I dunno why; mother didn't even like Bach very much.'

Like many of the stories in *Hello Darlin'*, it's cheesy but somehow cheering. Both on paper and in the flesh, Hagman comes across as one of life's good guys — easy-going, optimistic, family-orientated, for the environment, against Vietnam. Definitely not J.R. Where, I wonder idly, does he stand on George Bush? The answer is fired back like a bullet into a buzzard: 'George Bush is an asshole. He's no more qualified to be president of the United States than you are, or I am.'

For years, Hagman has battled the Californian bureaucracy, trying to have a National Weather Service radar tower removed from his neighbourhood, an idyllic town called Ojai, high above Los Angeles. 'Well, I hope I win that one — I'm fighting it, anyhow,' he says. 'They made a mistake, and they won't admit it. I went back east and talked to the second-in-command of that area of the government, black man, really nice guy. And he said: "Mr Hagman, you will never, ever, ever, ever, never, EVER get that tower moved." And I said: "Well, don't mince words — what do you really mean?" He said: "The bureaucracy up here hates you. You're a celebrity. You've made a lot of problems for them, cost them a lot of money."'

Warming to his theme, Hagman explains how the station is sited too high up in the mountains, how it emits microwave radiation which, every fifteen minutes or so, makes his TV sizzle for a minute at a time. Then he groans. 'Oh, now, see how I get wrapped up in this? The steam is starting to come out of my ears.'

Let's move to safer territory. 'Dallas' fans may be surprised to learn that the show's constant on-screen in-fighting wasn't even remotely matched in real life. J.R. and Bobby might have been deadly enemies, but Hagman and Patrick Duffy were

forever taking hunting and fishing trips together — still do, in fact. Kristin may have shot J.R., but Hagman gave Mary Crosby away at her wedding.

'I was very careful to keep everybody happy on that show,' says Hagman. 'There's no sense in working with dissension, you know? If anybody started to bitch, I'd just tell them to come into the dressing-room and say, "what's wrong, and is there anything I can do?"'

The approach seems to have paid off; he's even still friendly with J.R.'s ex-wife, Sue Ellen, aka the actress Linda Gray. 'I see a lot of Linda. In fact, I saw all of her in this show she's doing now in London, 'cos she has a nude scene. After twenty-five years, I finally get to see her nude, for God's sake.'

In 'Dallas', it was Sue Ellen who had the drink problem. In real life, Hagman — who had been, shall we say, fond of a drink since his late teens — had been averaging four bottles of champagne a day for fifteen years; eventually, it took its toll on his liver. At the age of sixty-four, he was told he needed a liver transplant. The book goes into plenty of gory detail about the operation and its aftermath, but the tone is light, almost jolly. Surely it wasn't as easy as he paints it? 'It was,' he says. 'I never had a minute of pain.'

And does he still have to take, what is it he says in the book, twenty-six pills five times a day? 'Oh, no. No, just twenty-six pills. For the day. Then I take vitamins and all that other stuff — about fifty pills, I guess. I dunno. I live well. I feel good.'

Last month, Hagman celebrated his seventieth birthday with an enormous party in the house in the Californian hills. In the same month, he and Maj hosted three charity fundraisers in the same house. How, in the rollercoaster romance business that is show-business, have they made it to nearly fifty years of marriage? Maj is adamant: separate bathrooms, she says. To the casual observer, though, the reason appears to be simply that the pair of them are great pals. They chat easily about their grandchildren, about her work as a designer, about Alaska and solar-powered houses and Tallulah Bankhead. In conversation they have the easy familiarity of a long-running comedy double act.

(Quick sample. A somewhat awed Maj is telling me about a recent function in Downing Street: 'And it was quietly said, you know, if you could donate five hundred thousand …' Hagman cuts in: 'I wonder if anybody did.' Maj: 'Everybody did.' Hagman: 'Oh, they did? I didn't.' Maj: 'You did.' Hagman: 'I did?' Maj: 'I did.' Hagman: 'You didn't? Oh God, I better go to work. Jeez.')

If he does go back to work, says Hagman, it certainly won't be on a TV series like 'Dallas'. Too much like hard work, he explains. Movies, now, they're a different story. 'I've done a few movies recently, and I wouldn't mind doing a few more. Where you come in, steal the movie, it's a big success, and that's that. Ten pages. Oh, yes.'

And downstairs in the Morrison hotel on a November evening in Dublin, J.R. grins his weasel grin.

WEDNESDAY, 7 NOVEMBER 2001

The Irish Times Seeks 250 Redundancies from Staff

Padraig Yeates

The *Irish Times* is seeking 250 redundancies from its 710 staff to address financial difficulties. The company told staff yesterday it was forecasting a group operating loss of £2 million this year, and that failure to cut costs would result in losses of £17 million next year.

The unions in the company are consulting members over the next few days and are due to meet on Monday to consider their response. The chairman of the union group, Mr John White, said it would 'not accept compulsory redundancy for any employee'.

Earlier, senior executives of the company, including the chairman of *The Irish Times* Ltd, Mr Don Reid, the commercial director, Ms Maeve Donovan, the director of human resources, Mr Michael Austen, and the editor, Mr Conor Brady, met union and staff representatives to explain the background to the job cuts.

Mr Brady said notwithstanding the cuts, the newspaper's 'character and ethos' would remain the same. It would 'remain independent of all external interests, primarily concerned with serious issues. It would continue to provide the most comprehensive news coverage and most informed opinion and analysis.'

Unions in the company are demanding full financial disclosure before deciding their stance.

A SIPTU spokesman said, 'We found it incredible that management was totally unprepared for this alleged crisis. We are completely opposed to compulsory redundancy and along with the group of unions are making arrangements for the earliest and widest investigation of the company's financial position.'

After a heated debate, the NUJ chapel passed a motion condemning 'the mismanagement responsible for the purported financial crisis'. The union said it would oppose compulsory redundancies.

The company has targeted 250 redundancies to achieve savings of £10 million annually and hopes to cut another £7½ million from non-wage operating costs. It hopes to begin its redundancy programme by the end of January.

SATURDAY, 10 NOVEMBER 2001

A Time of Challenge

Editorial

It has been a bad week for *The Irish Times*. The newspaper and its operating company must now face into a bleak period of hard choices and difficult operating decisions. A great gap has opened up between the newspaper's

Burka: Total cover up designed to keep one's "assets" hidden from public gaze...

Burke: see Burka...

TO ENBURKE: TO PULL THE WOOL OVER PEOPLES EYES.

earnings and its costs. On Tuesday, management told staff representatives that as part of a programme to return to profitable trading, 250 jobs have to go. Union representatives have said they will not accept forced redundancies. Both sides will get down to detailed discussions on Monday.

There can be little that is cheering in this situation. But the staff of the newspaper have been heartened by the volume of sympathy, the expressions of goodwill and the many messages of support from readers and advertisers alike. The message which *The Irish Times* wants to send back — very strongly — is that come what may, it will hold its place, without compromise, as Ireland's premier print medium, committed to its public role as a serious and unaligned newspaper.

Operating a quality newspaper — or a public service broadcasting station — is expensive, especially in a small country where economies of scale do not apply.

RTÉ, which announced further staff cuts during the week, finds itself in a comparable situation. The range and depth of this newspaper's editorial services are unique in Ireland and differentiate it from others which do not invest similarly. It has committed itself to giving readers an Irish view of world events by building up a modest but vigorous network of overseas bureaux. It has provided

consistently detailed coverage of Northern Ireland and the peace process. Its place as a noticeboard of public opinion is special. The things which go to give it this distinctive place and role in Irish society will not be abandoned. *The Irish Times* will remain *The Irish Times* in the fullest sense.

It is true that the organisation has been slow to get to grips with historical costs. Many of the jobs now under threat at *The Irish Times* have long disappeared in other newspapers.

A phased programme to manage down the problem had been put in place at the newspaper, based on the prevailing economic wisdom that the economy would slow to a soft landing after the peak of 2000. Unhappily, events overtook the process, braking the economy to a halt and drastically reducing advertising revenues.

We take pride in our place as a newspaper which is independent of all outside interests, unaligned with other business or financial elements. If the company and its staff are prepared to work together, the newspaper's present difficulties can and will be overcome.

The various stakeholders may have different approaches to the problems and there will be different interpretations of much of what has happened in the past. But they will be united in their determination to maintain the ethos, the principles and the standards which have made *The Irish Times* a great Irish institution and a newspaper which can hold its own with any in the world.

Of Course the Question Is, Is 2–0 Enough?

Mary Hannigan

Players' quotes: Err, where are the players? 'At a post-match reception,' we're told. Okay, so that explains why we've been waiting here like tulips in the VIP tunnel for forty minutes asking VIPs for their VIP thoughts on the game?

'Yep.'

Taoiseach? Is 2–0 enough?

'Hope so.'

Eddie Jordan? Pete St John? President? Ollie Byrne? Little boy waiting for autographs? The owner of Coventry City whose name no one can remember? Is 2–0 enough?

'Hope so,' they all smile, sympathetically.

Will we leave now? Mmm, maybe. Wait — here comes Roy Keane. Gird your loins. Roy? Is 2–0 enough?

'Well, I'm sure we'd have taken that before the match,' he reassures us. 'We obviously didn't want to concede an away goal so we're happy with that. We're all pretty calm about it in the dressing-room, we know there's a long way to go yet, a long journey on Monday and a tough match on Thursday.

'But we're capable of performing a lot better, we know that. We're talking about the World Cup finals here, so that's a great incentive for the players.'

An auld away goal would be nice, wouldn't it?

'Yeah but it's always dangerous to go looking for it — like tonight, you're stuck between a rock and a hard place: if you go too far forward looking for another goal you leave yourself open to breaks.

'Yeah it would be great to get the away goal, but the important thing is to keep it tight for the first half an hour in Iran, keep the fans quiet and build up a good solid base.'

Shay Given, Roy, our saviour?

'Shay's concentration levels are very good and he was very alive to that one-on-one. That's when they're dangerous, when they have good possession, they have decent players, but we knew that. Shay had to make another save soon after, but that's Shay's job.'

The knee, Roy, how's that blessed knee?

'Not too bad, but I'm well aware that sometimes it can take a while before it reacts. I said all along I'd play it by ear.'

So you're confident of playing in the second leg? we asked, the day before we learnt he wouldn't be playing in the second leg.

'I've said all along I'll just take it day by day. It doesn't feel too bad now but we'll see how it goes,' and with that he was off, carrying the blessed knee that had 'stiffened severely' by the time he woke next morning.

Next: Jason McAteer. Let's cut to the chase, Jace: is 2–0 enough?

'Mmm, it's the million dollar question, isn't it,' he says. 'If we get knocked out over there we'll be throwing it away, won't we,' he asks, rhetorically. Every head in the corridor nods, in an emphatic kind of way.

'If we do a professional job and defend like we can we should be alright.

'It was like a semi-final tonight, not like a qualifier — if you get beaten in a qualifier you can rectify it in the next game, but there was a lot of tension, a lot of nerves out there. We were firing the ball up to Niall and, for want of a better word, they were getting their arse and elbows on to the end of everything. We were just unfortunate with some chances, but then we got the penalty.'

Speaking of which?

'The ball ran free, I had a chance to cross, he lunged and caught me, simple: penalty.

'Maybe I should have scored in the second half — I might have done if Quinny had got his big

Roy Keane passes to Robbie Keane with attempted interception by Karim Bagheri (left), at the Republic of Ireland and Iran World Cup play-off in Lansdowne Road. Photograph: Eric Luke.

arse out of the way — that's a-r-s-e — but they defended well, they're no pushovers.

'A lot of people thought we'd turn them over easily but Iran are a good team. We knew that because we watched the videos. We knew they were capable of scoring an away goal but we kept a clean sheet.'

Niall Quinn?

'Can't stop lads, I'm in a mad rush,' he says before he stops and chats until we run out of questions. Any wonder the hacks love Quinny? Tie still alive, Niall?

'Ah, of course, but Jesus, we've a great chance. Yes, we'd have settled for 2–0, especially after the two great saves Shay made. If one of them had gone in it would have made it an awful lot more difficult.

'We're pleased, but we're not jumping up and down by any means — at the same time, though, we've given ourselves a great chance.'

The approach for the second leg?

'We'll have to think about it. There are two ways of approaching it, you either sit back and invite them on you or you go for the away goal, in which case, if you get it, the tie will probably be dead.'

Your preference? 'Not bothered. Whatever Mick says. He makes the decisions and he'll get the stick if it goes wrong.'

Big crowd in Tehran, scary? 'Nah, you're there to be counted in games like that. That's not a worry. Thanks lads.'

One more question? Is 2–0 enough? 'Hope so,' he smiles.

Funny, that's what the Taoiseach said.

Braving PR Fallout of Nuclear Plan Fiasco

Joe Humphreys

Whatever about the merits of Saturday's simulated nuclear accident as regards testing the national nuclear emergency plan, as a public relations exercise it came across as a genuine disaster.

Despite the fact Joe Jacob had been given advanced warning of the simulated incident, not to mention some six weeks to prepare his script following his infamous Marian Finucane interview, he remained as vague as ever regarding the advice to give the public in the case of a nuclear emergency.

Seven hours after the simulation began with an imaginary earthquake at the Wylfa nuclear power plant in Wales, the Minister of State for energy could offer no more advice than 'stay indoors'.

All other information would be decided upon in the context of the incident, he said.

Well, he was asked, what of this incident?

What advice would be given, for instance, on food consumption, or the ingestion of iodine? Ah, he replied, 'we are talking hypothetically at this point,' and he wasn't willing to speak about matters hypothetical.

Journalists called to this media 'briefing' were left scratching their heads at what Mr Jacob had described as 'an exercise in information management'.

It seemed advice couldn't be given on a hypothetical situation, even in the context of a hypothetical situation.

Members of the Irish Army on O'Connell Street, Dublin marking the UNIFIL Stand Down from the Lebanon. Photograph: Brenda Fitzsimons.

It didn't quite help to secure what was one of the Minister's stated aims of the day, namely restoring public confidence in the country's 'total state of readiness' for a nuclear emergency.

The second objective, he said, was to 'fine-tune' the National Emergency Plan for Nuclear Accidents, to give it its official title.

To meet both goals, the Department of Public Enterprise not only drafted in a team of consultants to evaluate the State's emergency response but also an external PR firm to manage the media's.

The exercise began at 5.15am with a phone call from consultants Environmental Resources Management (ERM) to a duty manager within the Radiological Protection Institute of Ireland (RPII).

This triggered a further series of calls, and the Emergency Response Co-Ordinating Committee — comprising representatives of Government Departments, the Garda Síochána and Met Éireann, among other bodies — was scrambled to the RPII's headquarters in Clonskeagh, Dublin.

ERM's director, Mr Sean O'Riordain, said relevant personnel were alerted to the day of the exercise, but not the time.

While he would not say how good the initial response was, he confirmed the different officials 'answered the phones'.

Adding to the crisis atmosphere was the fact that the press briefing, shortly after noon, was conducted in a cramped front lobby of the RPII building. The media was not allowed upstairs to see the committee at work.

Mr Jacob emphasised the exercise was 'not a reaction to anything'.

And just in case minds were turning to his RTÉ radio interview, he added hastily: 'it's not a reaction to the events of the 11th of September'.

He added he expected a report on the exercise to be available within days. Soon after, he said, the public would receive their long-awaited information leaflets on the emergency plan.

In the meantime, the public have at least learnt one fact: Wylfa and not Sellafield is the closest nuclear plant to the Republic. So it wasn't a completely wasted exercise then.

SATURDAY, 24 NOVEMBER 2001

Blowing the Whistle on What Makes Referees Tick

Keith Duggan

Admit it. You've snarled at him, cursed him, laughed hollowly at his pitiful stupidity. Maybe you have cocked a fist at him or undergone an out-of-body experience, astonished to find yourself not beside your kid in Row 38, Seat 16 but standing at a wire, foaming at the mouth and shouting passionately at a man whose name you don't even know and who can't hear you anyway. You have driven home obsessed by him, lain awake to fixate upon the neatness, the fussy notebook, that aggravating smile. Those polished boots.

You know that the sole reason God put him on this earth, gave him a life, was so that he could piss you off. And boy, does he excel at it. Sometimes, you have even tried to understand him, empathise with him, tell yourself that he is just doing his job.

But then your blood is boiling and he does something else, misses a detail or turns a blind eye or does that silly hand wave that makes you clench your jaw or something equally idiotic and all at once, you're seething again and you are convinced that it is a conspiracy and that this guy that you could seriously strangle is just a born bastard and he enjoys this, his pleasure is your anguish. And so you scream, past caring, beyond self-respect, to no one in particular, 'I CAN'T BELIEVE THIS F★★★★★★ REF'.

And then you immediately and suddenly feel better about life …

What do referees do when they are not reffing? They tell us they are real people, with mortgages and dodgy CD collections and a fondness for Kit Kats and everything but we players and fans are reluctant to believe them. It is more plausible that after a match at Lansdowne Road or the local park or gym, someone comes along and takes down the flags and the nets and then locks them up in a broom cupboard along with the referee. And there he sits, polishing his watch, whistle in his mouth, always ready.

It is best that we separate referees along those lines, see them as a breed apart. How else to explain, apart from masochism, why someone would voluntarily elect to stand in a field, often in front of sixty thousand people, and spend more than an hour making decisions that will, inevitably, displease people. Decisions that will make people mad. The best he can hope for is that nobody notices him, the worst is that the crowd will, in time-honoured fashion, sing insults to him.

'I love it,' says Tommy Sugrue, one of the GAA's most distinguished officials. 'Just the feeling when a game goes well that you contributed to it. Of all the games I did, the Derry–Dublin All-Ireland semi-final in 1993 stands out, there was such a beautiful flow to the game. A few early calls settled the players and after that, they just played. Also, the Derry-Down game in 1994, the so-called "game of the decade", stands out.'

The 'why' hit rugby referee Alain Rolland recently after he officiated at a Leicester–Saracens match, a classic, with the crowd close to the touchline and everybody — players, management, kids, just thrilled by the quality of the match that they were producing.

'And afterwards I was warming down and thinking, yeah, this is it, this is why. It is the sense that you are helping a game evolve into something special. And the thing is, the perfect compliment is when you are not noticed, when people forget you are there. It is the opposite of being a player when you strived for attention, for the headlines.'

Last weekend, Denise Rice, a Superleague referee and one of Ireland's FIBA ranked officials, found herself sitting on a train back from Cork after reffing a particularly poor basketball match.

'At times like that, you wonder why you bother,' she says. 'But when the games are good and the players are enjoying it and it's close, reffing is thoroughly enjoyable.'

Nobody refs for money. Nobody refs to try and improve their self-esteem. Nobody refs for the cool uniforms. Nobody refs for praise. Sport is full of stories about the hassle that whistle blowers endure. The problem is reaching crisis point in the English Premiership. Graham Poll received hate mail after a recent inflammatory match between Liverpool and Arsenal. David Elleray has a panic button in his house. In 1999, Hugh Dallas was cut open by a coin fired from the crowd. And that is at the highest level. A number of years back, Denis Cunningham was reffing a park game and found himself confronted by a player he had sent-off hurtling towards him. In a car. The most astonishing thing about that incident is that it wasn't without precedent.

The examples are myriad. Think of Alex Higgins or the now celebrated John McEnroe footage from the 1981 Wimbledon tournament. The public loved Superbrat because he made happen what is a fantasy for most sports fans: he forced the referee to sit and listen to his rant.

But there is a cultural tolerance of referee-abuse that filters through all sports at all levels. Sugrue remembers a match in Ruislip in 1992 between Tír Connail Gaels and Lavey being of such intensity that he was frightened for his safety leaving the ground. Rice was followed out to a car park after a game and verbally abused by a player using appalling language.

'The referee is an easy target,' says Sugrue. 'In my own sport, there is a attitude that the ref is basically there to be roared at, that he is a nuisance. You have to have a thick skin. People forget that without referees, there would not be games. But

A group of young people racing dumped sitting room chairs to their Hallowe'en bonfire site in Oakpark, Carlow.
Photograph: Jason South.

the abuse and intimidation is a problem and the only way to redress it is to teach kids from day one to respect the ref. Mistakes will be made undoubtedly but referees should not be hounded to the extent they are.'

There is no such thing as a born referee. It is a calling. Sugrue once likened it to the priesthood. Rolland, a former Irish senior international scrumhalf, started reffing because the appointed official failed to show. Obeying the old maxim that you should try everything once except Scottish folk dancing, he gave it a go. He was as amazed as anyone to find he had a gift for it and his ascent from Sunday morning cowpat games to internationals has been remarkable. He laughs now when he considers his former relationship with referees.

'I was a nightmare. The slag is I have been reffing for sixteen years but only had a whistle for three. But it helped because I know what annoyed me as a player.'

'So I always try and communicate with the players, let them know what they can and can't get away with, let them know the way I'm thinking. That diffuses a lot of the attention.'

Rugby is unique in that despite its aggressive nature, respect for the referee is paramount. It just doesn't pay to argue, let alone abuse. Rolland has no unpleasant experiences to report and is oblivious to crowd attitudes.

'If you are doing your job, you shouldn't even notice them. Anyway, people pay enough in; they are perfectly entitled to shout whatever they like as far as I'm concerned.'

Rice, despite her ranking, feels she has to work extra hard for credibility because of her gender. Incoming Americans, accustomed to male officials, often look at her in open amazement when she turns up to ref Superleague games, unsure whether to shake her hand or try and get her phone number. Last year, she became the first female referee to work an IBA Cup final and she also officiates at FIBA games in Europe. Abroad, there is no dissent but here it is a regular hazard of the job.

'I think a lot of it stems from just watching behaviour in other sports. Most of the time it is perfectly fine and you do understand that some-times players are just frustrated with themselves; they are letting off steam.'

Athletes, Sugrue points out, tend to forget what would happen if there was no referee. Games would be reduced to anarchy in shorts.

'You could call sixty fouls and be castigated in the papers the next day for ruining a game. But one of the first rules is that we protect the players. People want to see a flowing game, but if teams are belting one another, are you supposed to just let it go and have a fella end up in hospital?'

At heart, refs turn up for sports events for the precise reasons that fans and players do; for the love of the game. That they themselves will never be loved is not an issue. The perfect referee is invisible. All too often, though, he is in our sight-lines. The man in black.

Besides officiating, referees are useful psycho-logical props. Name the last losing manager to praise the brilliance of the referee?

Losing teams always have the consolation of telling one another that they would have won except they got screwed by the ref. And almost any sports fan can convince themselves that all the world's woes are down to one thing: the referee.

As the sports year winds down, the losers are licking their wounds and the glory-getters are getting shined up for the awards ceremonies. Nobody hates the referee in the off-season; he is just forgotten about.

Until of course, he next appears at your ground or gym, all prim and refereeish. And you know there is something about him, that he is destined to ruin your day. You feel your temple throbbing and so you take deep breaths and murmur: 'Refs are people too, refs are people too.'

Then the whistle blows.

SATURDAY, 24 NOVEMBER 2001

The Straight Talk

Kevin Courtney

'It's great to be gay!' announced Brendan Courtney at the launch of *GI* magazine last month. And he's right: there are a lot of advantages to being gay. You can wear colourful, figure-hugging designer clothes; you're on first-name terms with the girls at BT's cosmetic counter; you can even feel a lady's bosom and not get slapped in the face. And if you're Irish as well as gay, then the whole world loves you. Too bad I'm straight — I could be having the time of my life right now.

There's certainly never been a better time to be a gay Irishman. Dublin now has more homo-sexual men per capita than San Francisco and they're coming out of the closet faster than you can say, 'shut that door'. Despite the dire predic-tions of economic downturn, the Pink Pound is still the strongest currency around. Young, gay professionals have the highest disposable income, and they generally don't have families to support — gay couples being the ultimate DINKIES (double-income, no kids). *VIP*'s publisher, John Ryan, has created *GI* to cater to this burgeoning demographic. It's a mag whose time has, indeed, come out.

Our list of famous gay Irishmen is growing every day. In the last century, Oscar Wilde was our most celebrated literary queen, while Senator David Norris is probably our greatest living luvvie. They could soon be overshadowed by a new generation of media sweethearts, who are setting hearts a-flutter both at home and in the UK. There's Graham Norton, Channel 4's camp alternative to Pat Kenny. There's Brendan Courtney, presenter of 'Wanderlust', the travel-dating show on N2. Brendan graces the cover of issue one of *GI*, sharing a bicycle saddle with Brian Dowling, the winner of this year's 'Big Brother'.

Like Anna Nolan, last year's runner-up, Brian is gay, Irish and immensely popular with the viewers. Padraic Doorey didn't win on RTÉ's 'Treasure Island', but he was easily one of the most likeable of the castaways. Gay Irish guys have a mix of charm, wit and vulnerability that the public can't resist — everybody wants to mother them. (Notable exception: Shirley Temple Bar, who presents the dreadful 'Telly Bingo' — we just want to smother him with his own padded bra.) And then there's author Jamie O'Neill, whose novel, *At Swim, Two Boys*, tells the story of a gay affair between two young Irish fellas around the time of the 1916 Easter Rising. Now there's a Wilde premise indeed.

Yes, dahling, it's never been a better time to be gay, but where does that leave us heterosexuals, affectionately known to the gay community as 'breeders'? I hate to say it, guys, but we're sooo last season. There's probably never been a worse time to be middle-aged, Irish and uptightly hetero.

Straight Irishmen, no longer certain of their place in modern society, and less secure in their career, marriage and peer group, are undergoing a crisis of self-confidence, not the right frame of mind for having carefree fun down at The George every night. While gay Irishmen are finally coming out into their own, and enjoying what appears to be an endless love parade, us breeders aren't exactly feeling absolutely fabulous, sweetie. To be honest, we're feeling a little left out of the party. The bouncer has taken one look at our Gap gear and refused us entry.

Irish women, busy climbing the career and property ladder, have little time to stop for a relationship, so they increasingly prefer the company of gay men. You see, boyfriends are too much trouble to maintain: we require gallons of beer to keep us running, we're sluggish at the best of times and we demand constant care, attention and reassurance.

Having a gay friend to go out with is much less trouble — he's always up for a night out on the town, he'll compliment you on your fabulous outfit, he'll dance with you, listen attentively while you moan about being too busy to find a boyfriend and he won't expect a shag at the end of the night. You don't even have to call him up every day — he'll always be there for you. No wonder many women I know seem to have a gay man permanently attached to their arm.

Meanwhile, us ageing, balding breeders are cast adrift, with only John Waters to speak out on our behalf (God help us). Gay men seem to have a growing sense of community and belonging, while we heteros appear to possess an ever-shrinking support base.

There's no Bewildered Blokes Anonymous, no Society for Middle-Aged Men who've Missed the Boat, no Straight Outreach. Sure, we can meet in the local and talk football (yes, I know gay men can do that too), but there's still a big emotional gap right across our goal-line. We're trapped in our own straight little closets, hunched up and fearful, afraid to express ourselves in case people think we're nancy boys. OK, I know it's not always a picnic being gay, but when I see the likes of Brendan, Brian, Graham and Padraic having the time of their lives, I can't help feeling slightly envious.

But, since I'm not planning to change my sexual orientation in the near future, I'll just have to stumble on down the straight and lonely path. There are many obstacles to overcome, such as unimaginative dress sense, inability to dance, and a complete lack of interest in the music of Andrew Lloyd Webber. And there's another obstacle I sometimes have to skirt around — women whose 'gaydars' seem to have gone a bit wonky. In the past year, a small number of women — complete strangers — have introduced themselves with, 'I hope you don't mind me asking, but are you gay?' (Must be the way I hold my handbag.)

As a chat-up line, it probably ranks alongside, 'Hi, my name is Loreena Bobbit, like to come back to my place and see my carving knife collection?' As a greeting, it's rude — imagine walking up to a

The remains of the car that was carrying two locals is visible under the remains of a truck at a crash outside Drogheda on the N1. Photograph: Fran Caffrey.

woman and asking her if she's a lesbian. You'd be cut down like a chauvinist pig on a spit. My usual response is to splutter incoherently, blush, and then stammer out some awkward — and completely ineffectual — denial. Needless to say, this only reinforces my assailant's conviction that I'm a full-blown 'Friend of Dorothy'.

But I'm not going to get a complex about it (although I might just get rid of the handbag). I tell myself that these women are just fashion victims in search of a trendy gay accessory. Kim Basinger and Mickey Rourke in *9 1/2 Weeks* went out with the 1980s — this season's must-have relationship is Madonna and Rupert Everett in *The Next Best Thing*. Desperately seeking a gay-mate to take them out on the town and compliment them on their hairstyle, modern girls have got their gaydars on full power and bleeping loudly at the faintest effeminate signal. There's an ad for a certain drink, in which a

young man pretends to be gay, and finds himself surrounded by beautiful women. Hmmmm …

THURSDAY, 29 NOVEMBER 2001

Irish Times Trust to Confront Greatest Challenge

Fintan O'Toole

It is no secret that *The Irish Times* is in some trouble. In a very short time, the company has gone from unprecedented success to an almost unprecedented threat to its survival.

The scale of the crisis is in fact partly a result of the previous accomplishments.

In the past, when *The Irish Times* ran into difficulties, it was a small, intimate organisation that could change course with relative ease. Steady growth over the last fifteen years has made it a much larger, more complex operation. A big ship is much harder to turn around than a small one.

That the crisis has come after a long advertising boom and at a time when the paper's circulation is twice what it was in the 1970s, moreover, inevitably raises questions about the governance of the company.

Unlike the *Irish Press* which was in a long, slow decline before its eventual demise, *The Irish Times* is thriving in the media marketplace. If the paper is not the problem, what is?

The most obvious answer, and the one which tends to come from rival newspapers, is the fact that the paper is owned by a charitable trust, and therefore has no shareholders.

Private media barons find this principle rather offensive, and believe that only the pursuit of private profit can lead to commercial efficiency. The present crisis seems to provide support for this view.

It is, however, demonstrably wrong. The circulation of *The Irish Times* has more than doubled since it went out of private ownership in April 1974. Under the trust, the paper has massively increased both the number of jobs it provides for its staff and the coverage it offers its readers. It made a successful transition to new technology and led the way, not just for Irish newspapers, but for the global print media on the Internet.

Newspaper trusts also operate well in other countries, most notably in the UK where, as Hugo Young showed in this series on Monday, the Scott Trust's stewardship of the *Guardian* group has been marked by stability, commercial efficiency and well-judged expansion. One of the most successful niche publications in the Irish market, the *Farmers Journal*, is also owned by a trust.

Trusts may not be the only way to sustain a quality newspaper, as Elaine Lafferty's piece on *The New York Times* in this series has shown, but they are certainly not incompatible with viability and efficiency.

At the same time, the principle of ownership by a trust has immense advantages for both readers and journalists.

Private owners use their newspapers to make money, to exert political influence and to support their other business interests.

A trust like *The Irish Times* Trust makes money to survive, not the other way around. The newspaper's editorial line is independent, not just of political parties, but also of private advantage. Successive editors of *The Irish Times* since the establishment of the trust have testified to the absolute editorial independence which it has afforded them.

Given the immensely important role of the media in contemporary society, these are real blessings. *The Irish Times* may be, as its critics assert, prissy, arrogant, self-important and wrong-headed. But at least its mistakes and prejudices are honest ones. There is no hidden agenda.

The Irish Times Trust can take credit for the successes and for protecting the independence of a newspaper committed to social justice, non-violence and tolerance.

Conversely, however, it has to take at least some of the blame for the current crisis. Weaknesses that have been quietly inherent in the governing structures of *The Irish Times* for a quarter of a century have now become obvious. Arguably, *The Irish Times* Trust now faces its biggest challenge: the radical reform of its own structures.

It is worth noting that *The Irish Times* Trust differs in an important respect from the two other comparable media trusts on these islands in an important respect. In the case of both the Scott Trust and the Agricultural Trust which owns the *Farmers Journal*, the original owners did not benefit financially from their establishment.

In 1936, John Scott handed over the *Guardian* and assets worth the then enormous sum of £1 million to the Scott Trust. In 1963, John Mooney, who owned the *Farmers Journal*, turned down a lucrative offer from the Thompson Group and handed the paper over to a registered charity, the Agricultural Trust. Neither man was paid for his shares.

In 1974, however, the directors of *The Irish Times* sold their shares to the newly-established *The Irish Times* Trust for a total of just over £2 million, which the trust borrowed from the banks. This was probably somewhat less than the shares would have fetched on the stock market, but it was nonetheless a very large sum in 1974 prices.

As well as getting much more money for their shares than John Scott or John Mooney did, the leading *Irish Times* trustees also retained far more power. Both John Mooney and the Scott family kept a guaranteed place on the trusts they established. Neither, however, had a strong role in the day-to-day management of the companies.

As a relatively small and intimate operation, the *Farmers Journal* is run by its editor and chief executive, currently Matt Dempsey, with the unpaid trustees playing a broad watchdog role.

In the case of the Scott Trust, the trustees are quite separate from the commercial board of the company. Some executives are members of the trust, but it does not work the other way around: trustees do not join the company board.

The Irish Times Trust, by contrast, was constructed in such a way as to give the trustees as a whole a dominant role in the management of the company, and to give one trustee in particular, Major Thomas Bleakley McDowell, a very special position within both the trust and the company.

The Irish Times Limited, like any company, is run by its board of directors. The board can have anything between six and seventeen members, usually the latter. Two of these, the editor and the managing director, are automatic members. Other senior executives, as might be expected, are also on the board.

The trust, however, has the power to nominate from within its own ranks, a majority of the board — up to nine members. (There are currently eight trustees on the board.)

Even this appearance of relative equality between the executive directors and the so-called nominated directors (the trustees on the board) is deceptive, however.

Voting at board meetings is massively weighted in favour of the nominated directors. While each executive director has one vote, each nominated director has five.

In addition, the chairman has a casting vote if he or she is a nominated director, but doesn't if he or she is an executive director. The intention to give the trustees an almost complete hold of the governance of the company in the event of a vote could not be more clear.

If the trustees are more equal than the executives, moreover, one trustee is very clearly the first among equals. The articles of association of both the trust and the company make it very clear that Major McDowell is in the special position of being 'the A member'.

This in itself is explicitly guaranteed by a provision which states that any change in the right to remain as a governor for life of the A member will be put to a vote in which the A member is entitled to 'one vote plus such number of further votes as shall be equal to the total number of votes conferred on all other members of the company.'

The articles of association also underwrote Major McDowell's position as chairman of the trustees for as long as he wishes or until the other trustees ask him to step down.

As chairman of *The Irish Times* Ltd, he had the power to appoint and remove other directors and to remain as chief executive until he resigned. These latter powers ceased when he stepped down as chairman of *The Irish Times* Ltd. But his position as the A member will remain in place until his death when the A share will revert to the trust.

While the position of Major McDowell is certainly unusual, however, the key issue for the future of *The Irish Times* is the role of the trust as a whole in the actual management of the company.

The extremely personalised nature of the original trust and company structures make it clear that they were intended to suit the talents and accomplishments of one man, Major McDowell, and to cease when he ceased.

Whatever criticisms there might be of his extraordinary powers, no one doubted that Major McDowell was an extremely able manager with a track record of hands-on control within the newspaper industry in general and *The Irish Times* in particular.

His central role as the embodiment of the trust was thus not nearly as problematic as it might have been. Odd as the structures may have been, their oddness was a function of a single dominant personality, making them much more coherent in practice than they might have looked in theory. With the major's retirement, however, the inherent structural flaws are increasingly obvious.

Put simply, while the management of the company is vested in the executive directors, reporting to the board, ultimate authority is vested in the nominated directors whose members are not necessarily chosen for their commercial management skills.

Indeed, trust members are almost by definition people who are not involved in the newspaper business. Trustees cannot be current or former members of *The Irish Times* staff. They also, for obvious reasons, cannot have any connection with any other newspaper, magazine or broadcasting network.

Built into the structures of the paper's governance, therefore, is the stipulation that people with experience in journalism and media management can be massively outvoted on the board by people without it. That this is not a recipe for surviving and thriving in one of the most competitive media environments in the world should be obvious.

The proper function of the trustees, on the other hand, is that laid down elsewhere in the articles of association: to be broadly representative of the community throughout the whole of Ireland in ensuring that *The Irish Times* upholds the values of social justice, tolerance, fairness to minorities and serious journalism.

This clearly cannot be completely divorced from the actual business of producing the newspaper. Key decisions — the appointment of an editor and a managing director, new acquisitions, strategic investments — obviously affect the nature of the paper itself and need to have the approval of the trust.

But that overall monitoring role, like that of the Scott Trust, is very different from the ability to outvote the executive directors, if it comes to it, which *The Irish Times* Trust currently exerts.

If anything, the separation of executive management from the trust should lead to a strengthening, not a weakening of the trust itself. A much more open, broadly-based membership becomes possible when the immediate management role is removed.

A trust that actually does represent a cross-section of contemporary Irish life would not merely reflect successful practice elsewhere but would move beyond the notion of a clubbable, rather cosy feel that any self-perpetuating group tends to generate.

At a time when the possible demise of *The Irish Times* has reminded Irish society in general of the paper's values, a renewal of trust, in every sense of the word, is both an urgent necessity and an exciting possibility.

Letters to the Editor November 2001

Changing Times

Sir, — Irish Times, *Life Times and now Hard Times!* — *Yours, etc.,* David R. Noble, Blackrock, Co. Dublin. 12 November 2001.

Hard Times

Sir, — Can we now look forward to some 'glasnost' at The Irish Times? As one of the very many business people who have had their salaries and conditions reported in your paper, could I now look forward, finally, to reading all about yours?

You are a genuinely great newspaper. You will be even greater, and hopefully more understanding and less pompous, as the truth sinks in about yourself. — Yours, etc., Gerry Murphy, Brooklawn, Mount Merrion Avenue, Blackrock, Co. Dublin. 14 November 2001.

Killers of Garda Jerry McCabe

Sir, — I am proud to add my support to the many people, particularly Mrs Ann McCabe, who have expressed their opposition to the release of the killers of Jerry McCabe, before they have served their full sentence for his savage killing. We should be reminded that over twenty shots were fired into the body of this garda and six into his colleague as they sat in their patrol car while escorting a cash-carrying vehicle. The perpetrators of these barbaric acts surrounded the vehicle and opened fire on the detectives. If money was all that mattered to them they could have held the detectives at gunpoint without inflicting injury and death. That these criminals should have been convicted only of manslaughter, given their evil deeds, raises serious questions about the law and its application and adds insult to the bravery and sacrifice of Jerry McCabe and his colleague Ben O'Sullivan. To release these killers prematurely would be even more repugnant. By donating some of the proceeds of their crimes, criminals of this type can buy themselves into the protecting umbrella of the so-called republican movement. Republicanism in this country has suffered since the 1920s from this kind of convenient schizophrenia by allowing hardened criminals to be part of the republican family and the advantages that seem to go with it in the present climate. These criminals have not only hijacked the term 'republicanism' to suit their own

needs but have also been allowed to usurp our national flag for the same ends. Our flag, symbolising peace between orange and green, rightly adorned the coffin of the brave Irishman Garda Jerry McCabe. The irony that this flag, by its blatant misuse, could also be used on the coffin of his killers when they make their last journey, is an insult to our nation and to all honourable people who serve it. The Garda Síochána since its foundation has stood proudly and bravely against threats, intimidation and murder in its efforts to protect the lives and property of the people of this State. It is time that many of its critics came off the fence and supported it. We must stand unflinchingly in the support of this noble, brave and dignified lady, Ann McCabe, and ensure that her husband's sacrifice, not to mention that of his family and many more like them, has not been in vain and that these killers should serve every minute of their meagre sentences. — Yours, etc., Philip F. Callanan, Tullow, Co. Carlow. 21 November 2001.

Switching to the Euro

Sir, Has the 'free' EU/IRL calculator replaced the 'free' lunch? — Yours, etc., Con Sherin, Washington Park, Rathfarnham, Dublin 14. 27 November 2001.

SATURDAY, 1 DECEMBER 2001

When Your Face Just Doesn't Fit Any More

Gerry Thornley

In the wee hours of the night of Ireland's win away to Wales last month, at the Hilton Hotel where the squad was based, there was only a handful of IRFU officials celebrating in the same room as Warren Gatland. And they were all Connacht men.

Both that night and on the night of Ireland's victory over England, several IRFU officials could not bring themselves to congratulate the Irish

coach. After the earlier defeat in Murrayfield, and regardless of the win over England and the rattling of the All Blacks' cage a fortnight ago, there were still IRFU officials who had bullets with Gatland's name on them.

This week they flexed the muscles of their trigger fingers and fired. They like flexing their muscles every so often.

Many will wonder how the most successful year the Irish team have enjoyed since the Triple Crown and championship-winning season of 1985 culminated in this. Many will suspect there were other factors at work. That perhaps there was a row or, as some were immediately surmising, Gatland had asked for too much money.

In fact it never even came close to money. After Monday's round of interviews with Gatland, Eddie O'Sullivan and Brian O'Brien, the six-man IRFU sub-committee of Eddie Coleman, Noel Murphy, Syd Millar, John Lyons, Eddie Wigglesworth and Phillip Browne made their decision on Wednesday.

Coleman and Browne notified Gatland in the Berkeley that afternoon, and by tea-time Declan Kidney had been spotted arriving there.

The sub-committee made the final decision to remove Gatland but they have been granted the authority to take these decisions by the full committee. Not only was Thursday's monthly full committee meeting of the union not informed of the decision, but apparently none of the twenty or so present raised the matter.

But some of them did notice the unusual absence from the general meeting of Browne and Billy Glynn, a solicitor and long-time friend of Gatland's, and the union's lawyers had also been spotted in the Berkeley Court on Thursday.

Gatland was by then back home in Galway.

New Zealand artist Peter Robinson poses with his work at the first exhibition in the new gallery at the Guinness Storehouse. Photograph: Jason South.

By late yesterday morning the word was spreading through a stunned rugby community. One of the full committee said yesterday: 'There's going to be terrible aggro over this. People are going to be asking me why we made this decision and I'm not going to be able to answer it. I don't know why. People are already speculating that perhaps there was a commitment to Eddie, but one can only guess.'

Reports that O'Sullivan had been offered a lucrative contract to take over as USA Eagles coach the day before Monday's round of interviews with the management trio — reports which O'Sullivan yesterday verified — are unlikely to have forced the union's hand.

Many union officials had become rather smug about having got their much-lauded structures right, about the relative success of the provinces, and they now expect major success with the international team.

Some weren't happy Gatland was based in Galway, and didn't feel he spent enough time moving around the provinces. Gatland was never the cutest political animal, and he did not enjoy a particularly talkative relationship with them. They had criticised the coach loudly after the defeats to Argentina in the 1999 World Cup, and the subsequent mauling by England, and then, after an upturn in results, they took umbrage when Gatland began agitating for an extension to his contract (which was due to expire in April) to take in the 2003 World Cup, which was in line with the position of other Six Nations coaches.

After last September's defeat in Murrayfield, there was criticism in rugby circles of the Irish coach, which helped to fuel an orchestrated media campaign against Gatland. The head coach was blamed for selectorial mistakes and flawed preparation in Scotland, and the word was that he was doomed.

But then the record 36-6 win over Wales and the 20-14 win over England (so ending a run of seven defeats against them, and ending their run of eleven consecutive wins) made Murrayfield look more of a blip, and that feeling was re-inforced by the performance against the All Blacks two weeks ago.

Those behind the decision were, typically, tight-lipped yesterday.

'No, I'm not getting involved,' Murphy said. 'Philip Browne is handling the media. I'm not talking one bit about it.'

Coleman was not available for comment.

Browne, available for comment for the first time this week, shed little light as to the reasons behind this decision.

'What we're trying to do is move up another notch. I can't be specific in relation to the reasons why. I have to say that there was no one reason. There was a whole myriad of factors.'

Browne conceded that 'I'm sure quite a lot of people are astonished. We are trying to ensure we have the correct structures to move forward.

'We fully acknowledge the progress that has been made to date. Inevitably it was a very difficult decision and not taken lightly. It's disappointing for Warren and difficult for us.'

The new head coach, O'Sullivan, admitted: 'I'm delighted and honoured and pretty excited to be honest.'

He was officially informed at lunchtime on Thursday and says this is the culmination of fifteen years' involvement as a coach. 'I never managed to play for Ireland, which is something of a regret for me as I got close when I played for Munster, but this is pretty special.

'Obviously we've achieved a lot in the last two years and I want to consolidate that and then help to nudge the bar higher and higher. We've a pretty exciting bunch of players,' he said.

Though he admitted that he and Kidney had never formally coached together, they were of the same vintage and had both come through the Irish under-age structure.

Asked if Kidney was his choice as assistant, O'Sullivan said: 'Well, when I was asked my

immediate reaction was "no problem". We've already had a chat and we're very much on the same page.'

Kidney was not available for comment.

As for Gatland, one senses part of him will be relieved to be rid of all the sniping and the pressure, though he maintained last night that: 'I've enjoyed my time as Irish coach, and particularly in working with the players, and the support I've been afforded from the general public.'

A planned two-week trip back to New Zealand will now be extended to five weeks, but the Gatlands intend to stay in Galway. Along with his wife, Trudy, and children, Gabby (eight) and Bryn (six), he has been living here since 1996, and he and Trudy first set up home in Galway when he was Galwegians' coach from 1989 to 1993.

As to his coaching future?

'I'm not going to rush into any decision.'

MONDAY, 10 DECEMBER 2001

Opening up Lorry Load of Death and Misery

Caroline O'Doherty

The smart new office block in Wexford Business Park, two miles on the Rosslare side of Wexford town, has 'worker-friendly' written all over it. Instead of dreary brick and concrete, its architects have created walls of glass that extend right around the chunky centre and up to the top of the three-storey structure.

An American data processing firm, PFPC, is due to occupy the building in the New Year. A container load of office furniture arrived from Italy on Saturday morning — a bright, fresh, blue-skied day which made the discovery inside the container of eight bodies seem all the grimmer.

For at least four, and maybe eight, days they had lived in darkness. Squeezed into gaps among the

furniture, they must have had difficulty moving around to keep cramped limbs from turning numb.

When the ship ran into a storm sometime last Wednesday some of the furniture is likely to have shifted and the stowaways must have feared being crushed. They must have already been cold and terrified by the time the air supply began dwindling. Imprisoned in the container, they could not have known where they were, or how close they were to freedom.

Truck drivers are used to holding their breath and standing back when they pull open the doors of a newly delivered container.

The stale air and dust takes a moment to clear and there is always the possibility that something has worked its way loose and will coming bouncing to the ground.

But the driver of the Eagle Transport lorry with the jolly, yellow container on the back became even more cautious than usual when he approached it along with another man on Saturday morning and saw that the seal had been tampered with. In the past, tampered seals led to suspicions that the container had been robbed of some of its contents. Nowadays, however, the possibility of a secret human cargo tends to be the first thought of a trans-European lorry driver when he finds a broken seal.

When the two men looked inside, it was immediately obvious that the contents had been disturbed, and they noticed items of clothing. They closed the container and summoned Gardaí.

Eight corpses and five people seemingly close to death were scattered like rags among the boxes.

Within minutes, Gardaí, priests and doctors were arriving; politicians also came to inspect the scene. Local south-east TD Mr Brendan Howlin of Labour spoke for many when he said the discovery of the bodies was an appalling tragedy which had shocked the community, locally and nationally.

'The suffering endured by the dead and injured, including two small children, during the several days they spent in this sealed metal container is barely imaginable,' he said.

A Garda at work in the container in which eight refugees died in Drinagh, Wexford. Photograph: Bryan O'Brien.

'This tragedy demonstrates once again the desperate lengths to which people from deprived and often repressive backgrounds are prepared to go to try and improve circumstances for themselves and their children.'

All day on Saturday the container sat outside the office block as Garda forensic teams and the State Pathologist, Dr John Harbison, went back and forward, trying to glean what information they could from the dead before a series of hearses carried them away.

A few hundred yards away, walkers strolled by, enjoying the fresh air of the brisk morning while youngsters took full advantage of the construction workers' weekend off to hurtle their bikes around the smooth empty tarmac road. The doors of the container lay partially open, letting in the light so the officers could see to work.

WEDNESDAY, 12 DECEMBER 2001

Lord of the Rings

Hugh Linehan

'I can't believe it — you've seen it! You've actually seen it. What's it like?' I'm in an Oxford Street department store, shortly after leaving *The Fellowship of the Ring* screening in Soho, and the shop assistant has spotted the film's publicity brochure under my arm. There's an almost scary edge of hysteria to his voice as he calls over his colleagues, and I'm press-ganged into giving my first review. If I hadn't realised it before, here's evidence that it's pretty weird out there in Tolkien fanland at the moment.

There's been no shortage of advance publicity for *The Fellowship of the Ring*, the first in Peter Jackson's three-part adaptation of J.R.R. Tolkien's much-loved fantasy novel. Special supplements, in-depth profiles, location reports, star interviews — all the usual paraphernalia of the movie hype machine. But, up until this weekend, virtually nobody has been allowed see the actual film. Even

the press screening in London on Saturday morning, two days before the official world premiere, is held under unprecedented security conditions. Mobile phones and tape recorders are confiscated at the door, and we all submit to a metal detector, much to the disgruntlement of the assembled journalists, who settle grumpily into their seats for the three-hour epic, mumbling that they don't know what all the fuss is about. Do they seriously believe somebody would phone the soundtrack of the film down the line to some web pirate?

Well, yes they do, and they're probably right. On one level, *The Fellowship of the Ring* is just another big, blockbuster film. On another, though, it's the most eagerly-anticipated literary adaptation of all time — and that's not hype. Legions of Tolkien fanatics around the world are already having sleepless nights over the prospect of seeing their beloved book brought to life on the big screen. Will it fall short of their expectations? Will it be a travesty? Can it possibly match up to their own visualisations of the world of Middle Earth?

With all due respect to *Harry Potter* fans, the comparisons with Pottermania are some way wide of the mark. Potterites may be fervent in their particular faith, but the bespectacled schoolboy has only been with us for a few years, and *The Philosopher's Stone* is a no more than competent slice of commercial product by a journeyman director. *The Fellowship of the Ring*, by contrast, is a book which has enthralled several generations, which is being made by a self-confessed Tolkienophile with an interestingly quirky track record as a director, and which marks the first stage of one of the most ambitious film projects ever undertaken. The next instalment, *The Two Towers*, will be released next December, and *The Return of the King* in December 2003. Taken together, they amount to a ten-hour-long adaptation of Tolkien's novel.

There is, though, a difficulty with all this. As Jackson himself points out at a press conference later in the day, the world is divided into those who have read the book, and those who have

Lizanna Kirwan models a gold and silver sundial by Erika Marks and a two-piece waistcoat in Irish Salmon Leather by John Fitzgerald to publicise the National Crafts Fair of Ireland in the RDS. Photograph: Bryan O'Brien.

not, and the question remains as to whether it's possible to make a film which can please both constituencies.

'There's a lot said about the fans and how they're going to respond to the film,' he says. 'But I also felt a very strong responsibility towards audiences who'd never read the book. I don't know how it's going to break down, but my guess is that two-thirds of the people who see the movie will not have read the book. My primary responsibility was to create a film that could entertain everybody, so it was a kind of a tightrope to walk.'

First, then, an admission. This writer is definitively in the 'those who have' camp. It's with a slight shudder that I confess to having read the darned thing eleven times between the ages of twelve and fifteen (you'll notice I kept count), and

twice since then. I like to feel that I've recovered from the experience but, like lapsed Catholics and reformed Marxist-Leninists, the sacred text is imprinted indelibly on my consciousness. I can still tell you the names of most of the lesser Ents, can recite chunks of Elvish verse, and can draw an extremely detailed map of Middle Earth from memory. However, like the definition of a gentleman as a man who can play the accordion but doesn't, I have refrained from any of these activities for many years. But, somewhere within the blasé film critic who grabs his accustomed aisle seat on Saturday morning, there's a quivering, obsessional adolescent waiting to get out (nothing new there, then). And as the lights dim and the credits roll, that adolescent takes over completely. I am swept away. Three hours pass like a few minutes. At the end, I just wish I could see the next three hours immediately, now, straight away. Or, failing that, watch *The Fellowship* again.

Now, none of this is very healthy, I grant you, and it doesn't even necessarily tell you whether *The Fellowship of the Ring* is any good. But all pious intentions to view the film as an entity in its own right dissolve in the experience of seeing the story brought to life. As it happens, and after a day's reflection, I think it *is* pretty good: it's remarkably faithful to the structure and narrative arc of Tolkien's book; is very well cast and the visual rendering of Middle Earth through the New Zealand locations is quite wonderful.

There are elisions which hardcore fans may resent, but which make sense in terms of a filmic narrative. More seriously, perhaps, there's a kind of foreshortening effect, due to the compression of time; events which in the book take months or even years to unfold are rendered in a few days in the film. It's difficult to see how this could have been avoided, but it does rob the story of some of its epic grandeur. Certain sequences, such as those in the inn at Bree or the magical forest of Lothlórien, look as if they were truncated in the editing room.

'We got some wonderful footage that didn't make it into the film, and which will probably show up on the DVD some time next year,' says Jackson. 'But anyone who's read the book will know there was an enormous amount of detail, of subplot, in some cases characters that we had to leave out. In my view, in movie adaptations, there's only one thing that really happens, and that's simplification. To make a movie you have to decide on your central plot. In *The Fellowship of the Ring* the story is really Frodo and the Ring. It changes in the second and third films, but in the first film that was our focus, and any material that didn't relate directly to that had to be looked at.'

Tolkien's son and literary executor, Christopher, denied last week that he disapproved of the film, adding that his personal view was that the

books 'were particularly unsuitable for transformation into a visual dramatic form'. It's a reasonable point of view, and there are sequences where the film does become mired in exposition and explanation. But the sense of place is terrific, from the bucolic idyll of the Shire, the home of hobbits where the story begins, through the dangerous wilderness to the refuge of Rivendell (a sort of Elvish Berchtesgaden), on to the snowy peaks of the Misty Mountains and down into the ominous Mines of Moria. And the story is anchored by several strong central performances: Elijah Wood makes a remarkably good fist of what could have been a very wet role, as Frodo, the central hobbit hero; Ian McKellen is a satisfyingly grouchy Gandalf the Grey, the wizard who starts Frodo on his journey; Ian Holm makes a fine Bilbo Baggins; Christopher Lee is satisfyingly wicked as Gandalf's rival, Saruman; and Viggo Mortensen is impressively rugged as the warrior-king Aragorn.

Mortensen took over in his role from Irish actor Stuart Townsend after two weeks of shooting. 'We certainly take full responsibility for that,' says Jackson. 'I think Stuart is a fantastic actor. We tried to cast the film in a way that felt totally authentic to the book. Stuart himself actually auditioned for Frodo, not Aragorn. But we liked his screen quality and presence so much that we didn't think he was Frodo, but we thought he would make an interesting Aragorn. Then we just came to realise that it was a classic situation where we'd miscast the role. He was just too young. It's very difficult, very emotional and very upsetting to have to come to a parting of the ways like that. But he himself had said "You're crazy, I'm not Aragorn", and we said "You are. You'll be great". So we have a huge amount of responsibilty to take. But I believe in fate, and the day Viggo joined this film, fate played an incredibly kind hand to us.'

Received wisdom has it that it's only recent advances in digital animation and special effects which have made it possible to make the film now, but, as Viggo Mortensen rightly points out, it was never about the effects. 'People say it couldn't have been made before, but I think it could have been made in the Fifties or Sixties, with whatever effects were available, Ray Harryhausen stuff, whatever. All it needed was the will to do it.'

George Lucas has reportedly been sniffy about the technical standards of the New Zealand-based company, WETA Digital, which created the big effects set-pieces, such as the scene-setting prologue, with its thousands of orcs swarming across a bloody battlefield. But Lucas, not surprisingly, misses the point — yes, some sequences, such as those at the wizard Saruman's lair of Isengard, look a little cheesy, but if anything that works to the film's advantage. The obsessive attention to hi-tech detail which Lucas exemplifies is an aesthetic dead end, as his own recent, sterile efforts show. Here, effects are subordinated, as they should be, to story and character.

One of the impressive things about *The Fellowship of the Ring* is that it doesn't try to ingratiate itself with its audience by inserting anachronistic contemporary references (with the exception of one, rather good, dwarf-throwing gag). There are some attempts to redress what would nowadays be seen as the improper gender balance of the novel (*The Lord of the Rings* is not very PC at all) but no real violence has been done to the narrative.

'There's no doubt that Tolkien approached the story in a very English spirit, and we tried to honour that,' says Jackson. 'Basically, we're a bunch of Kiwi film-makers using American dollars to make an incredibly English story. That's the sole reason the world premiere is taking place here in London. It could easily have been in New Zealand or Los Angeles, but we wanted to respect the fact that this is where the story was born.'

It's this faithfulness which actually makes *The Fellowship of the Ring* most interesting as a film — the tyranny of the action movie formula, with its tediously predictable climaxes and pay-offs, is mercifully absent. It will be interesting to see how the two-thirds of the audience Jackson refers to will react to this, and to the fact that the film concludes on an open-ended, 'to be continued' note.

'The one thing I'm proud of when I sit down and see the film, is that it doesn't remind me of any other movie I've ever seen,' says Jackson. 'In this day and age there's an industry pumping out big-budget films, and to me this feels a bit like the biggest independent film ever made. It doesn't feel like a studio film. I'm proud of that, and I think that gives it a special spirit.' He's right. There's an oddness and a quirkiness to *The Fellowship of the Ring*, along with a peculiar sense of integrity, which is markedly absent from most films of this scale. And you don't have to have read the book for the umpteenth time to get it. Believe me — or I might just start chanting in Elvish again.

THURSDAY, 13 DECEMBER 2001

A Chance to Live His Fairytale of New York

Paul Cullen

Given that half the Dáil seems to have visited Ground Zero in New York over the past while, you could hardly blame Liam Lawlor for wanting to make the trip too.

So the Dublin West TD popped into a travel agent a few months ago and thoughtfully bought tickets for a Christmas trip to Manhattan for himself and his wife. Their son, Niall, lives just two blocks away from the World Trade Centre and his wife is expecting a child shortly.

But Liam's version of the Nativity had a cloud on the horizon. There was the nuisance of that prison sentence imposed by the High Court earlier in the year. He staved off Mountjoy only by an appeal to the Supreme Court, and its judgment was due, just like his daughter-in-law's baby, before Christmas.

You or I might worry about something like that. We might put our plans on hold. Or worry about having to forfeit the tickets. Even worry about whether we'd be given a visa.

Not Liam, though. No one, not the tribunal, the courts or the governor of Mountjoy jail, was going to play Scrooge to his family Christmas. It would be all right on the night.

And, in a way, it was. Yesterday's Supreme Court judgment did turn out more Groundhog Day than Ground Zero. For the third time in a row, the courts pasted him for his lack of co-operation with the Flood tribunal. A second one-week term in jail was confirmed.

By this stage, so many judges have thrown the book at him that he could set up a legal library. For once, the normally garrulous TD was not present in court, and could not be contacted afterwards.

Yet the five judges of the court did agree to defer his sentence to 2 January. Liam's Dáil work and his holiday would not be interfered with. The Lawlor family would, after all, have their fairytale Christmas in New York.

MONDAY, 17 DECEMBER 2001

Beijing Sees the Benefits of a Merry Christmas

Miriam Donohoe

I have never been in such good shape with eight days to go to Christmas. At this stage in the season I am usually all partied out, and Christmas Day can't come and go quick enough.

Liam Lumley on his property just north of the airport. A massive illegal dump borders his property. The neighbouring farm used to be the same height but tonnes of rubbish have turned the site into a toxic danger. Photograph: Jason South.

But I have a clear head. I haven't been over-eating. The shops are not crowded. The traffic flows like a dream, and taxis can be had with the same ease as every other month of the year. Oh, and I was able to get a seat on Friday night in our local, Frank's Place, beside the Workers' Stadium.

Despite the fact that we have perfect weather for Santa's sleighs, with a heavy snow-fall last week, you would never think it was Christmas in Beijing. Ask most Beijingers over fifty about Christmas and you will get a blank look or a shrug of the shoulders. 'Shengdan Jie', as it is known in Chinese, didn't feature at all in China up to ten years ago.

But where there's money to be made the Chinese are rarely behind the pack. And the commercial possibilities of Christmas are starting to be cashed in on. China's accession to the World Trade Organisation and Beijing's successful bid for the 2008 Olympics is helping to accelerate the country's westernisation. It is inevitable that more and more Chinese, especially the younger generation, will fall under the Christmas spell.

This is our first year away from home for the Christmas build up, and we miss it terribly. Okay, many restaurants and department stores are making an attempt, putting up trees, fairy lights and decorations.

But some of the efforts are not convincing. Not very realistic Santas stand outside shops handing out sweets, and waitresses wear Santa hats in restaurants. Shoppers in one of the biggest markets in Beijing, Hong Qiao, were this week greeted by a big sign 'Marry Christmas', instead of Merry Christmas. There will be no public holiday here for the Christmas period. It's all a bit bewildering for my two children, who have had no difficulty getting into the Christmas spirit in the past.

Yesterday, they were amazed to hear that Xiao Xiao, the sixteen-year-old daughter of a Chinese friend, would be going to school as normal on Christmas Day. Xiao Xiao, in turn, was fascinated to hear about the fuss made in Ireland, about Santa Claus, and the story of the Nativity. She said she knew some older teenagers who would be swapping small gifts on Christmas Day, but her family would not be marking the event.

The ever-growing foreign presence in China is having an impact, and the Beijing authorities are looking favourably on any event that encourages the Chinese population to spend money. China remains a nation of great savers and the government has already extended the number of public holidays in the year to encourage people to part with more of their money. Many Chinese working in multi-national firms find themselves getting caught up in the Christmas revelry of their western colleagues, and are also benefiting from the few days the company closes during Christmas week.

A tiny percentage of wealthy Chinese do celebrate, with artificial trees in their up-market apartments called 'trees of light' which are decorated with paper chains, paper flowers and paper lanterns. Their children hang up muslin stockings in the hope that Dun Che Lao Ren (China's Santa) will fill them with presents.

Although Christianity is not sanctioned in China, there are an estimated ten million baptised Christians, less than one per cent of the population, who celebrate the birth of Jesus at Christmas time. The popularity of midnight Mass has grown over the past few years among the Christian community with Catholic churches unable to hold the numbers who come out on Christmas Eve.

The 'underground' weekly Mass at the Canadian embassy has told worshippers they must register in advance to be sure of a place next week. But the majority of the population still remains immune to it all. Li Yan, a producer with CCTV, doesn't see why China should embrace Christmas: 'Why would we celebrate Christmas here when we have no religion? It wouldn't make any sense.'

We went shopping in Beijing's main shopping area this weekend. Wangfujing Street lacked the hustle and bustle of Patrick Street in Cork, or Grafton Street in Dublin, in the mad run-in to Christmas.

Only a small percentage of Beijing's eighty-strong Irish community is heading home for Christmas. One is a Montessori teacher, Gráinne Barry, from Griffith Avenue in Dublin, who has been living in Beijing since August. She boarded a plane for Dublin yesterday, never looking forward to a Christmas so much.

'It's just not the same here,' she said ruefully. I must admit we are pining too to be among the throngs in Dublin searching out that last-minute present, grabbing a coffee in Bewley's, visiting the live animal crib in Dawson Street, and having a pint with friends in the snug in Toner's of Baggot Street.

Roll on the end of the week when we will join the thousands from all over the world who will fly into Dublin Airport for the Christmas holiday. Mother, see you in Kilkenny on Christmas Eve. Will be home in good time for Midnight Mass. And, yes, cream on your mince pies please.

THURSDAY, 18 DECEMBER 2001

Judges Return Decisions to Politicians

Carol Coulter

Following the Sinnott judgment, it was probably not surprising that the Supreme Court would reassert the separation of powers and set limits on the capacity of the courts to order the Government to do things.

The implications of that route were spelled out by Mr Justice Hardiman when he warned: 'If citizens are taught to look to the courts for remedies for matters within the legislative or executive remit, they will progressively seek further remedies there, and progressively cease to look to the political arms of government.'

This is precisely what has been happening. In recent years certain categories of people have despaired of the capacity of the Government of the day — and the issues have survived many changes of government — to address their problems. The parents of children with special educational needs or disabilities spent years treading the weary path to politicians' clinic doors. Some of them even stood for election to highlight the absence of any facilities for their children. Eventually they went to the courts and found that their children did have constitutional rights, and the executive was obliged to uphold them. Then those concerned with the absence of any provision for highly troubled children, whose early lives had left them with behaviour very difficult for the existing institutions to cope with, helped them to seek the vindication of their rights in the courts.

Justice Peter Kelly photographed leaving the High Court. Photograph: Brenda Fitzsimons.

Following dozens and dozens of such cases, many of them heard by Mr Justice Kelly, the State put in place a plan of action, which included the establishment of a Special Residential Services Board. But there is still a shortage of places and children are still coming before the courts.

This was the context in which Mr Justice Kelly ordered the State to abide by its earlier commitments and build and bring into operation a number of special units for such children.

The State appealed eight of these orders and the Supreme Court yesterday upheld its appeal. It sent a clear signal that, when it comes to decisions on how the resources of the State are to be allocated, the executive has the right not only to decide, but to change its mind, without any interference from the judiciary. If people want a different allocation, they must address themselves to the political process.

Few people, either lawyers or members of the public, would argue with this principle. Judges are not elected to run the country. But people also know that politicians do not always, wittingly or unwittingly, uphold the Constitution. The issue is what to do if an individual's constitutional rights are not vindicated by the State.

The judgments of the Supreme Court majority have concentrated on Mr Justice Kelly's orders, introduced after years of foot-dragging by the State. They went too far, according to the court. However, it was pointed out that the court may make declarations that certain actions of the executive are unconstitutional, and the executive can, and usually does, undertake to remedy the omission in question. So recourse to the courts remains possible, even if the remedy is less definite.

But there may be another way. Mr Gerard Whyte, lecturer in constitutional law in Trinity College, pointed out that the political system has the mechanism of a constitutional referendum to reverse a decision of the Supreme Court that went too far in intruding on the executive's territory.

There have been such referendums, on issues as diverse as bail, abortion, and voting rights for non-citizens. But what government would propose a referendum saying the State had no obligation to look after disturbed children?

Stuck in Neutral: Ireland's Smug America-bashers

Niall O'Dowd

It is an issue that is particularly close to the bone for Irish Americans. Of the 3,000 who lost their lives at the World Trade Centre, an estimated twenty-five per cent have Irish backgrounds. In the case of the fire-fighters, at least 110 of the 343 killed were of Irish ancestry.

Anyone who has spent time with the families of such victims knows the fierce pride they continue to have in their Irish heritage and the cultural and social framework it provides for them. Thus, there is considerable shock and anger in the Irish-American community over Irish criticism of the United States and the war to defeat those who carried out September 11th.

The possibility of an Irish-American backlash over what has been perceived as rabid American bashing in Ireland should not be underestimated. Just one letter to the *Irish Voice*, from Patricia Farrell of Long Island, gives a flavour of how many Irish Americans feel.

She writes: 'What fools we Irish-Americans have been. Why did we keep the tradition alive here all these years? We must have been laughing stocks going to Ireland, sending money … My mother-in-law who scrubbed floors at night to support five kids always sent clothes and more home when she needed help herself … this has really put an end to anything I will ever have to do with Ireland.'

Her bitter comments are not unusual as the full impact of the war hits home and the extraordinary ordeal of those Americans who lost loved ones on September 11th becomes apparent.

At a time when the heroism and bravery of so many Irish-Americans is rightly being remembered in America and across the world, reports of anti-American sentiment have been flooding across the Atlantic from Ireland, ancestral home to the largest number of victims on September 11th.

Published criticisms in Ireland have received widespread distribution here. Comments such as comparing Bush and any Western leader who supports him to 'war criminals' are viewed with utter disbelief. It has been clear for some time that American actions, no matter how justified, are opposed by a certain mindset in Ireland which professes a bogus moral superiority when it comes to the use of force.

Many are the same people who justified every brutal crackdown by eastern European regimes under communism in order to protect the old order.

The reflexive anti-Americanism we have witnessed is unable to distinguish between military actions that are clearly correct and flow from a moral prerogative, and those that have no such clear-cut definition. There is a massive difference between the just wars in Afghanistan, and the US air campaign in Serbia to remove Milosevic, and other American actions which are correctly scrutinised and criticised such as in Vietnam and in Central America.

Nobody is arguing that American foreign policy in the past has been blameless in stirring many conflicts around the world. Yet it is barely stated in Ireland, for instance, that the biggest giver of humanitarian aid to Afghanistan, even under the Taliban, was the US.

This lack of nuance, and the outright condemnations of American foreign policy, sits strangely in a world where the question of whether you support armed actions to protect democracy or violence on behalf of religious fundamentalism has suddenly been placed front and centre.

Many Irish critics are using the Israeli-Palestinian conflict and American support for Israel as the convenient explanation for what happened on September 11th. Islamic fundamentalism, as vicious as any fascism that Hitler practised, is somehow excused in that context.

The fact that so many Arab countries have no democracy, no rights for women and malevolent dictatorships that harbour murderous Islamic fundamentalists is not as a result of American foreign policy but is of a much deeper historical origin. Yet the Irish critics are unable to acknowledge that because they are blinded by prejudice.

What is particularly insulting is the attempt by some to somehow shape a moral equivalence between the actions of President George Bush and Osama bin Laden, as if one was equal to the other.

To many Americans now, Ireland seems stuck in a time warp, as the questions and dithering about whether it should join an EU peacekeeping force for Afghanistan show.

Bin Laden and al-Qaeda are the Hitler and Wehrmacht of this generation, bent on mass destruction, and to pretend otherwise is ridiculous. As Martin Luther King Jnr has stated: 'It is not where you stand at times of comfort and convenience, but at times of challenge and controversy that is important.'

Right now Ireland is marooned in a no-man's-land. Perhaps that is why Irish attitudes are hard to fathom. A well-connected friend in Ireland seriously suggested last week that the US should have sent in ground troops only because that would have levelled the playing field and not so many Afghan civilians would have been killed.

War by the Marquis of Queensbury rules is a new phenomenon when we are facing the deadliest enemy since Hitler, who, with the speed of lightning would gladly obliterate London, Dublin and any other major city where the infidels live. As the *Observer* newspaper reported last weekend, bin Laden's lieutenants were ready to carry out a major bombing in London, plans for which had already

Yasser Arafat under fire.

been drawn up and which would have likely cost thousands of lives.

Are the Irish completely blind to such realities? In fairness, the national day of mourning and the steadfast support of the Irish government have shown the other side of the coin, and thousands of ordinary Irish believe that the US is doing the right thing.

Yet the recent survey by the Eurobarometer agency, which showed fifty-six per cent in Ireland opposing the use of Irish airports for American supply planes, reinforced American suspicions that the Irish want to remain the hurlers on the ditch of Europe, always ready to criticise, never to act.

What are the Irish waiting for? A nuclear explosion in London or Washington before they even think about acting?

As Dante has stated, the hottest place in hell will be reserved for those who remain neutral in a time of moral crisis. Ireland is in danger of entering that circle of the damned.

SATURDAY, 22 DECEMBER 2001

Trying to Beat Barbie's Many Winning Ways

Breda O'Brien

Ah, the dilemmas posed by motherhood. No, for once I am not referring to juggling paid work and the care of children, or even the lowered status of full-time motherhood. I am talking about the burning question animating many households this Christmas. Should girls be given Barbie dolls?

I hate Barbie. I was once caught by a sister-in-law punching my niece's Barbie doll in the face, which elicited a worried enquiry about my state of mental health. I always assumed any daughter of mine would share my contempt.

She doesn't.

From the age of three, which was the first time she saw the aforementioned niece's Barbie, it was

unconditional love. I tried a bit of propaganda, pointing out that Barbie was an anatomical monstrosity. Her body was half the length of her legs.

Had she ever seen a human being with legs like that? If she were life-size, given her measurements of 40, 18, 22, she would be so skinny that her bones would be sticking out, except for her bust which would be too heavy for her skinny body to support. In fact, the weight of it would probably make her fall over.

I only desisted when I saw my little girl's eyes fill with tears. 'But Mammy', she whispered, 'she's beautiful.'

Stumped, I stared at her. I never had nor wanted a Barbie or even a Cindy, but here was every fibre of my daughter's being yearning for my pet hate.

Perhaps the reason I hate Barbie so much is that if she were real her IQ measurement would be smaller than that of those mini-Alps she sports on her chest. Her coat of arms would have to include a cash register and 'Shop Till I Drop' would be her motto.

The story that Barbie was originally based on a character called Lilli, a woman of easy virtue who featured in a Hamburg newspaper cartoon, sounds like it was made up by a Barbie-basher like me but it is apparently true. The Lilli figure was sanitised and reinvented as Barbie.

Since her debut in the late 1950s, parents have been uneasy about her. Some saw Barbie's very provocative proportions as inappropriate for small girls. Others worried about the fact that she is the patron saint of materialist consumerism. Still others wondered whether she would spur vulnerable girls into anorexia.

Not even a professional Barbie-hater like me could lay that last responsibility entirely at Barbie's door since she is but one of thousands of cultural messages which pound our children emphasising that thin is beautiful.

It is in the area of the depiction of the female form that the feminist movement has been most resoundingly trounced. Despite feminism being more puritanical about women being viewed as sex objects than the most conservative Christian, popular culture is awash with sexual imagery which a younger generation seems to have embraced eagerly. What is Britney, hyper-sexual and virginal all at once, except a Barbie with a voice?

The new dolls on the market, Get Real Girls, sounded briefly interesting, but all they are really doing is replacing fluffy air-headed femininity with athleticism as an ideal. They exchange the tottering high heels for skis or soccer boots.

The Get Real Girls measure an allegedly more representative 33, 24, 33. Yet again, the image is bone thin, but just this time with bulging biceps and washboard abs. Their creator was too cute to make them completely androgynous, though. Each Get Real doll has real hair to brush and accessories to die for.

I am not so much a recovering feminist as to have ever given my son dolls, but there were some in the house which we moved into when he was a toddler. He took one look, tossed them over his shoulder and never looked at them again.

I did have a dilemma about giving him guns until his pacifist Dad pointed out that he had played with guns for thousands of hours when he was a boy and as yet was showing no symptoms of either being an axe murderer of a warmonger.

So my son got guns, to be followed by lasers, swords, knives and an axe with which he plays with great enthusiasm.

Those who say male and female roles are solely a social construction never reared children. Not that biology is destiny. My son loves babies and small children and is very good with them. Except for the fact that he despises Barbies and keeps pouring scorn on my daughter's love for them.

So there I was, hoist by my own petard. I had always emphasised the need to stand up for something you believe in even when others did not agree. My son never needed such tutorials. If I were to help my daughter learn that lesson, I would have to help her stand up for those loathed Barbies. I knew that our days as a Barbie-less house were numbered.

Then, at the Lios na nÓg Gaelscoil fundraising sale, there it was. A second-hand Barbie. It was money to a good cause and my daughter's dream fulfilled, all for 50p. My daughter was ecstatic. I did have a brief moment of worry that Barbie had had a previous incarnation as a voodoo doll until my daughter pointed out patiently that the holes in her hands and feet were to take accessories like shoes and hand bags.

My sister-in-law said archly: 'I suppose this Barbie will spend her time acting as an advocate for asylum-seekers? Or maybe drinking coffee where the producers receive a fair share of the profits?'

Worse was to come. Second-hand Barbie had hair as knotted as a whin bush. One night I could not stand it any longer and took a comb to it. Five minutes in, I was really beginning to enjoy the experience of combing hair without an accompanying chorus of howls and accusations of tearing someone's head off.

When Barbie was suitably groomed, I found myself saying: 'You know, she'd look a lot better without a fringe.' I looked up to see my daughter hugging herself with glee.

'You do know, Mammy, that you are playing with my Barbie?' No wonder the blasted doll has such a patronising smile.

Letters to the Editor December 2001

Sacking of Warren Gatland

Sir, — The IRFU's decision not to renew Warren Gatland's contract suggests that there's more truth to the classic Irishman jokes than we'd ever have thought.

As Irishmen ourselves, we are astonished at this breathtaking act of arrogance, parochialism and sheer stupidity. It's worthy of a Flann O'Brien novel, such is its bizarre and unfathomable illogicality.

As so often in the past, the IRFU have acted with cowardice, short-sightedness and a shameful lack of grace. In short, we are disgusted.

Of course that matters not in the world of the IRFU, where the remnants of amateurism, cronyism and backroom backscratching obviously still reign supreme. — *Yours, etc.,* Colm Black, Buccleuch Street, Edinburgh, Scotland. 4 December 2001.

Goodbye Elton John

Sir, — *With all the daily bad news of war and destruction in your newspaper, it was welcome to read some good news for a change (*The Irish Times, *3 December). Elton John will not be releasing any more songs.* — *Yours, etc.,* Paul Regan, Phoenix Park, Dublin 20. 8 December 2001.

Deaths of Stowaways

Sir, — *The folk memory of our island nation is filled with tales of the coffin ships wherein our forebears sailed. Yet even the worst of those vessels did not deny oxygen to the wretched human cargo.*

Surely, as a temporary emergency measure, we could cut a small vent near the floor level of steel containers, and another near ceiling level. This would evacuate the rising warm current from the heat of human bodies, priming a life-saving air intake via the lower vent. This remedy is quick and cheap, finished in five minutes with an angle-grinder.

It was all so sad. — *Yours, etc.,* Michael Reynolds, Ashford, Co. Wicklow. 11 December 2001.

Lorraine Eiffe, widow of Det. Sgt John Eiffe, turns to comfort their two-year-old daughter Rachel at the graveside in Ratboath. Det. Sgt Eiffe was accidentally shot during an operation to foil a bank robbery in Co. Laois. Photograph: Matt Kavanagh.

Sir, — Among the eight people found dead at Drinagh Business Park, Wexford, was a four-year-old child. His parents gave him into the care of relatives in the hope that he would have some chance of a better life in Britain.

It is hard to imagine the sheer desperation of that child's parents. They were prepared to be parted from him that he might have a future. The others who died were similarly attempting to grasp some opportunity of a life with dignity, a life devoid of misery, poverty and injustice.

Such is the plight, throughout the world, of countless millions of our brothers and sisters. And that is exactly what they are — our own flesh and blood, part of our human family. This immense tragedy on the threshold of Christmas challenges us, in a supposedly Christian country, to re-examine the core values of the Gospel.

On 25 December, we commemorate the coming among us of the One who says: 'I was a stranger and you made Me welcome'(Matthew 25:36). He identifies Himself with the hungry, the thirsty, the naked, the outcast, the sick and the imprisoned.

Britain, Ireland and the entire Western world urgently need to recover Christ's vision of humanity. On RTÉ's 'Questions and Answers', a few days after the Wexford tragedy, some callers rang in to express the opinion that 'we should look after our own first'. The truth is that those whose bodies were discovered in Wexford are 'our own'.

The only hope for this world is when we can begin to look at our fellow human beings and see the colour of their skin, or their ethnic background, as part of the unique beauty of their being human with us.

This vision must begin with ourselves. All racism and supremacism of any form is an insult to the God who has no favourites. It is a potent and deadly poison and it is rampant in our society. It is the task of Christians and all people of goodwill to counteract every expression of hostility towards those who come to us in such dire need. — Yours, etc., Father Patrick McCafferty, Sacred Heart Parish, Belfast 14. 18 December 2001.

Emergency Measures

Sir, — Apart from firing iodine tablets at the offending aircraft, how does the Government intend to enforce the no-fly zone? — Yours, etc., Brian Horgan, Rathfarnham, Dublin 14. 19 December 2001.

Criticising America

Sir, — For sheer audacity I have to hand it to Niall O'Dowd. Can this be the same man who has been publicly bleating over the years that we should show sensitivity to Sinn Féin/IRA, the man who has always been on hand to smooth the path for Sinn Féin representatives in the US, to explain and sympathise with their policies? — Yours, etc., David Herman, Meadow Grove, Dublin 16. 21 December 2001.

Sir, — At last The Irish Times publishes a thoughtful piece by Niall O'Dowd on Irish anti-Americanism. It then goes on to make his point in the letters page (19 December), where William Heap accuses America's 'democratically'(his quotation marks) elected leaders of wiping out en masse lives in other nations. He finishes his banal hyperbole by suggesting the 'American ethos' is reminiscent of the Nazis. Niall O'Dowd, you are wasting your time with these people, as in Ireland glib, politically correct ignorance is mistaken for profundity. — Yours, etc., Donal J. Leahy, Aughrim, Co. Wicklow. 21 December 2001.

TUESDAY AND WEDNESDAY, 1 AND 2 JANUARY 2002

Bubbly Greets Early Money-changers

Mary Minihan

Champagne does not usually flow at the Central Bank in Dublin at 10 a.m. but an exception was made yesterday for the introduction of the euro. Bank staff were surprised by the enthusiastic response to their offer to change pounds to euros on a frosty

Hugh O'Donnell of the Central Bank offers complimentary champagne to members of the public who queued to have their currency converted to euro at the Central Bank, Dublin. Photograph: Matt Kavanagh.

new year's morning and rewarded their chilly customers with champagne, whiskey and hot drinks.

'We don't normally have champagne in the Central Bank at this time of the morning, but I think we can say the euro is popular by the looks of it,' said a spokesman, Mr Neil Whoriskey.

More than 1,500 transactions were carried out at the bank yesterday, with the average involving £300 (€380.92). However, a significant number of customers wanted to exceed the bank's £500 exchange limit.

'We did have cases with some people with thousands of pounds, at least one customer with more than £3,000,' Mr Whoriskey said. 'We had to explain nicely to them that our limit was £500.'

About 100 people, mostly senior citizens, had gathered outside the bank by 10 a.m. In the afternoon, the queue stretched down the steps and round the corner to Dame Street. At 2.15 p.m., bank staff stopped additional people joining the queue and the last customer left the bank at 5 p.m.

Although shops were still accepting pounds and most city-centre cashpoints were dispensing euros, many preferred to exchange what was left of their 'old money' at the only bank in the State to open for business yesterday.

First in line was Mr Robert Wilson from Stoneybatter, who turned up at 7.45 a.m., but only because he thought the bank was opening at 9 a.m. Mr Wilson's long wait to change money for his mother and himself was rewarded with a bottle of champagne, presented to him by bank staff when the doors finally opened. He said the adoption of the euro would make it easier for him to follow his favourite football team, Arsenal, around Europe.

A Kildare man, Mr Edward Lynch, was waiting

to change £300 for the euro equivalent. 'What I'll get for that I don't know. I haven't a clue,' he said. However, once he got his hands on the euro notes, he was determined to 'try them out in the pub'.

Mr Tom Byrne from Walkinstown said he had no choice but to turn out early to get his hands on the new money. 'I have hungry grandchildren waiting to grab it,' he said. Did they understand the new currency? 'I hope so, because I certainly don't!'

New Year's Eve reveller Mr Andrew Mansfield from Upper Leeson Street in Dublin called at the bank after witnessing angry scenes in the early hours of yesterday morning. He said some of his fellow clubbers did not know cash points would close at 1.30 a.m. on New Year's Day and were left without enough money to get home.

'People were trying to get money out at College Green last night. There were a lot of very annoyed people with no money,' he said.

Mr James Tunney, from Finglas but living in Scotland, was collecting some euros to make his trip to France next week easier, while Ms Marion Winget from Tallaght said she simply wanted to see what the new money looked like.

TUESDAY AND WEDNESDAY, 1 AND 2 JANUARY 2002

Taoiseach Celebrates Euro Launch

Arthur Beesley

With the aplomb of a man on general election footing, Bertie Ahern chose a Drumcondra newsagent yesterday to carry out his first euro transaction. He bought sultana cake, milk and pears. He paid in punts, took the change in euro and smiled for the cameras. Easy.

Never one to underplay such occasions, he then sipped champagne with the shopkeepers,

Marion and Jim O'Neill. Like the bubbly, this was vintage Bertie.

According to Marion, the Taoiseach comes in for newspapers and fruit every day. She was up past 3.30 a.m. on New Year's Eve, but had the shop open by 10.30 a.m. in anticipation of the visit. Ms O'Neill's eighteen-year-old daughter, Sinéad, was up early, too. For her trouble, she received a Milky Bar from the Taoiseach.

As a gaggle of photographers jockeyed for position, a handful of Mr Ahern's supporters stood by the fruit shelf in the small shop. Yes, Mr Tom Cullen (seventy-two) felt slightly 'dicey' after New Year celebrations the night before.

But that was not to deter him. A long-standing Fianna Fáil supporter, he doesn't miss opportunities to see the great man. He had secured his position with a friend, Ms Phyllis MacArthur, long before the Taoiseach arrived at 1 p.m.

Yet the fuss seemed lost on Ms Ann O'Reilly, who wandered in to buy milk ahead of Mr Ahern. Asked about the euro she received in change, she said: 'I don't know, I'll have to get used to them.'

At five years old, Siobháin Murphy was among the youngest present. She was there with her father, James, brother, Tom, and sister, Emer, to witness what Bertie described as a significant symbolic purchase. 'Do you understand, Siobháin?' asked James. 'He's the leader of our country.'

Siobháin didn't. But others did. Thus the chairman of the Euro Changeover Board, Mr Philip Hamill, was present to advise that no hiccup had yet been reported in what has been described as an unprecedented logistical challenge.

Still, Mr Hamill had not had a late night. 'Our work was done. We were on call but we weren't called,' he said.

There, too, was the National Lottery chief executive, Mr Ray Bates, who observed the Taoiseach scratch a game card with a newly minted euro coin. Three stars were revealed, but the real prize will be fought for in the summer when an election is called.

Will Bertie still be in the job after the poll? 'We'll keep trying,' he said. All politics are local. So expect more walkabouts by the Taoiseach soon.

FRIDAY, 11 JANUARY 2002

Depressing Truth is that Intolerance Cannot be Legislated out of Existence

Dan Keenan

There have been bigger, deadlier and more protracted riots than that which flared in Ardoyne on Wednesday, reports of which got nowhere near the front pages and prompted no dramatic coverage on Sky News. But this riot was different.

How it started is not the point. Whether or not two people had an argument over a memorial to a murdered man which rapidly descended into anarchy is hardly news. Spats become riots in other places, too.

Why this outbreak of violence should be deemed so important is because it happened in north Belfast. It is this area of the city, and indeed the North, which has suffered most since 1969. Its cheek-by-jowl network of nationalist and unionist communities endures — perhaps facilitates — latent sectarian tension. The deprivation in parts is as endemic as it is predictable. It co-exists alongside the comfortable affluence of the Antrim and Somerton Roads, home to judges and bishops.

In short, north Belfast is a political, social and economic morass.

For the North's power-sharing executive, it symbolises the problem which must be addressed if 'normal' politics is to be seen to be worth it. If north Belfast cannot be changed, then the new political system will be held to be deficient.

It is no accident that as Wednesday's street argument became, thanks to nuclear-reaction rapidity, an all-out pitched battle, Stormont's recently appointed Executive Liaison Officer was meeting the Concerned Residents of Upper Ardoyne. For behind the grim scenes, the devolved government has been working collectively to sort out north Belfast. According to a senior Stormont official, there is now an idea in place which had been missing for twenty years, namely a realistic assessment of the area's needs and an integrated cross-departmental plan to meet them.

At the top of the pyramid are Messrs Trimble and Durkan. They have taken to heart the symbolism of their joint office and what newly acquired political gravitas they have. They are seeking to convince the neglected and aggrieved of north Belfast that the corner has been turned. They strive to make the point that political action is the vehicle to the progress which three decades of sectarian violence wrecked.

Prompted to act by the twelve-week confrontation between Ardoyne Catholics and Glenbryn Protestants on the road to Holy Cross girls' school, and that blast bomb last September which seemed to echo around the northern hemisphere, the First and Deputy First Ministers vowed to enable change.

To back up the fine words with action, work began at the second tier of government. Government departments have lined up to announce initiatives.

The DUP's Nigel Dodds, working hand in glove with the Housing Executive, has revealed expensive plans for housing improvement, new-build and industrial development.

Sinn Féin's Martin McGuinness has financed an education support programme which supplies schools with additional youth and community workers.

The Economic Development Minister, Sir Reg Empey, continues on the overseas marketing trail, trying to counter the revived rolling news network image of a city in seeming unending street conflict. Since November he's been to China, the

President Mary McAleese with Most Rev. Yaakov Pearlman (right) at his induction as Chief Rabbi of Ireland at the Synagogue, Terenure, Dublin, last night by Most Rev. Jonathan Sacks, Chief Rabbi of Great Britain and the Commonwealth (left). Photograph: Joe Leger.

US and Canada, and a further trip to New York is planned.

At street level, the North Belfast Community Action Project, chaired by a former Presbyterian moderator, the Rev. John Dunlop, was established. There is also a Community Forum. However, it is here, at the base of the pyramid, that things are most dicey.

What all those who are working for change in Ardoyne cannot alter is the inescapable reality that some people hate each other. From the community activist to David Trimble and at all points in between, the depressing truth is that intolerance cannot be legislated out of existence.

The blast-bomber can destroy more quickly than Sir Reg Empey can build, and no amount of tourist board PR genius or cash can erase the scenes of Wednesday's violence or the untold damage it does to both reputation and prospects.

However, while hatred proves enduring and resilient to those who wish it away, the causes of that hatred can be and are being addressed. It is here that hope lies.

Inspiration often comes from unexpected quarters, and the US State Department under a Republican administration falls into that category. The director of policy planning at the State Department, signalling Washington's intention to help foster greater understanding of unionists and their perceived plight, went out of his way on Wednesday to criticise despondency and pessimism.

In a speech aimed at Ireland but delivered in New York, Richard Haass stated a certain truth in saying: 'The reality is that there is no separating the future of one community from that of the other.'

He echoed a feeling shared in parts of Whitehall that there is no good reason for so many in the North to believe the glass of peaceful politics is half-empty since so much has been achieved since Good Friday 1998.

Yet for many unionists that is precisely how they see it. Unable to tear themselves away from the zero-sum-game notion of politics, they see a growing, confident and successful nationalist community which is gaining politically and numerically and in a swaggering manner.

They contrast this with the losses they feel, the 'concessions granted' and the inescapable fact that where once they dominated they now merely share. Unionist politics — once a monolith — has fragmented, and the loyalist paramilitaries feud among themselves.

Set against that background, striking out at parents and children going to school through 'our area' conforms to some form of base logic. People can do anything when cornered.

So, the task ahead is not so much to stop people hating as it is to stop them feeling threatened and defeated. The DUP MP Gregory Campbell said on Tuesday: 'The present system increases nationalist and republican confidence because it offers them progress … Unionists need convincing that an agreement is capable of addressing unionist concerns and grievances.'

He is in tune (though surely not deliberately) with the Secretary of State. Dr John Reid stated in his 'cold place for unionists' speech in November: 'Unionists worry about what the future holds, whether they will be able to feel at home for much longer in the land that they love.'

Whether this Secretary of State, this British government and this Northern Ireland Executive, working together with support and encouragement from the Bush administration, can address this key concern, remains to be seen.

As for north Belfast itself with its disparate band of Assembly members, duty falls on all of them — from Billy Hutchinson of the Progressive Unionist Party to Gerry Kelly of Sinn Féin — to find the answer.

A Fresh, Articulate Voice for Europe

Denis Staunton

When the 626 Members of the European Parliament elect a new president in Strasbourg on Tuesday, they will vote in secret for one of five candidates. The vote will be close, but few doubt that the outcome will see the Munster MEP, Pat Cox, emerging as the first Irishman to lead Europe's directly-elected parliament.

For the forty-nine-year-old watchmaker's son, Tuesday's election will be the crowning achievement of an extraordinary political career. As a member of a small political group in the parliament and a citizen of one of the EU's smallest states, Cox had few natural advantages.

What makes his feat more impressive is that he will have won office without the backing of a political party in his own country. What makes it unusual is that Cox is an unashamedly intellectual politician with a complex and somewhat inaccessible personality.

Although few European citizens could name the present president of the European Parliament, Ms Nicole Fontaine, the position is an increasingly important one. And many parliamentarians believe that Cox is the man who can help Europeans finally to feel a sense of ownership of their own parliament.

'We need to make the place what it is, more political, and we need to engage as a parliament in a very basic explanation of who are we and what we do and how we make a difference,' he says.

The European Parliament's powers have grown substantially over the past decade and, although it cannot initiate legislation, its approval is required for measures in most policy areas. Yet the parliament remains a Cinderella among EU institutions, derided as a tiresome inconvenience by many

Pat Cox, the first Irishman to lead Europe's directly-elected parliament.

Commission officials and representatives of national governments.

The parliament's president meets EU leaders for half an hour at the start of each summit and is included in the 'family photograph' when the summit ends. But Cox acknowledges that the leaders simply tolerate the president's presence, adding that the ritual reminds him of an old television advertisement for Guinness: 'This thirty minutes of darkness was brought to you by the European Parliament,' he says.

At a time when the EU's public face is the bumbling figure of the Commission President, Romano Prodi, Cox will represent a fresh, articulate voice at the centre of European politics. His ruthless dynamism will also stand in sharp contrast to the stately manner of Valery Giscard d'Estaing, the ancient French politician chosen to chair the

Convention on Europe's Future, which will start work in March.

Nobody questions Cox's political gifts or his intellectual grasp of policy. But he enjoys more respect than affection in the European Parliament and those close to him admit that he can be cold and insensitive to others.

In private, Cox can be witty and irreverent, a relaxed and engaging conversationalist with an endless fund of political anecdotes. In public, his eloquence can be impressive, but he is often long-winded, speaking in compound sentences which are riddled with sub-clauses and qualifications.

Pat Cox was born in Dublin in 1952 and moved to Limerick at the age of eight. His father, a watchmaker, worked at Shannon Airport after losing his job in West's jewellers on Grafton Street. Cox, who attended Christian Brothers schools in Limerick, describes his home as 'a happy if frugal household' with no strong political affiliations.

He was still at school when his father died and his mother went to work at Shannon Airport. He studied economics at Trinity College, Dublin, working during the holidays in the Shannon duty-free shop.

After graduation, Cox became an economist at the Institute for Public Administration and made his first trip to continental Europe. It was a visit to the European Parliament in Strasbourg. 'No member of my family had ever been to university and none, as far as I know, ever owned a passport. This was not unusual in Ireland at that time,' he said.

He returned to Limerick in the late 1970s to lecture in economics at NIHE, now the University of Limerick. In 1979, he unsuccessfully contested a local election on behalf of Fianna Fáil, a party which was dominated in Limerick by Desmond O'Malley, with whom Cox was later to have an irreparable breach.

Cox remained a member of Fianna Fáil for four years, but when he saw an RTÉ advertisement looking for current affairs presenters, he applied and was appointed.

Between 1982 and 1986, Cox became one of Ireland's best-known journalists, presenting the current affairs programme Today Tonight. He is remembered by former colleagues as a bright, courageous reporter who was equally comfortable investigating paramilitary links to crime in Northern Ireland or covering a US presidential election.

Following the formation of the Progressive Democrats in 1985, Mary Harney asked Cox to join, and he became the party's first general secretary. An energetic organiser, he was a welcome presence at branch meetings, not least on account of his high public profile as a television presenter.

He became an MEP for Munster in 1989 and played a key role in negotiating the party's programme for government with Fianna Fáil in the same year. He won a Dáil seat in Cork South-Central in 1992. Then, when O'Malley resigned the leadership the following year, Cox sought to succeed him.

After his defeat in the leadership contest, Cox increasingly believed that his future lay in Europe, and he wanted to defend his European seat, promising that he would give up his Dáil seat if elected. He left the PDs, fought the European election and defeated O'Malley by 3,000 votes. Although Cox has mended fences with most leading PDs since then, he and O'Malley remain on poor terms. When Cox resigned his seat in Cork South-Central, it was taken in a by-election by the late Hugh Coveney.

Back in Strasbourg, Cox was elected deputy leader of the Liberal group in the parliament and devoted himself wholeheartedly to European politics. He gained a reputation as a formidable speaker and an able deal-maker, encouraging the Liberals, who have only fifty-two seats, to form flexible alliances with other groups.

In 1998, he was the unanimous choice as leader of the group, becoming an important figure in the debate which led to the sacking of the European Commission the following year. Cox's speech on 11 January 1999, was a turning point in the debate over alleged corruption and croneyism by some Commissioners.

Although Commission officials maintain to this day that the accusations were overblown and that the Commission was treated unfairly, Cox captured the public mood by declaring: 'We have crossed the line from the politics of accounting to the wider politics of accountability.'

After the 1999 European elections, Cox made a deal with the conservative European People's Party (EPP) to support Nicole Fontaine for the post of president. In return, the EPP promised to back Cox in the next election.

Cox promises to lift the parliament's profile by forging links with the US Congress and the Duma in Moscow and introducing more political cut and thrust to the often sterile parliamentary debates. His most difficult task may be to negotiate a members' statute aimed at regularising MEPs' relationships with the thousands of lobbyists who surround the parliament and ending a stream of mini-scandals about expenses and petty corruption.

If Cox succeeds in raising the parliament's profile, he will leave office in 2004 as Ireland's most formidable politician on the European stage. Many former colleagues, including some who dislike him personally, hope that Cox will then return to domestic political life.

He will not rule out such a move. But, looking back on the meandering progress of his career so far, he says it is impossible to predict what will happen next.

'Who can ever say where all of those avenues go? I certainly wouldn't have thought when I voted in St Vincent's Primary School in Blarney Street in Cork in the 1999 European election that next Tuesday I'd find myself a credible possibility for the presidency of the House,' he says.

(Pat Cox was elected President of the Parliament on 15 January.)

FRIDAY, 18 JANUARY 2002

Political Kingmaker is Now a Fallen Idol as Enron Story Unravels

Conor O'Clery

At a Christmas buffet in Houston's exclusive River Oaks Country Club — membership fee $100,000 — someone standing in line loudly criticised Enron over its financial mismanagement, which had hit the pocketbooks of several members. There was, apparently, a sudden silence and heads turned. Queuing quietly within earshot was the embarrassed, balding figure of Enron chief executive, Kenneth Lay.

Until Enron collapsed, Ken and Linda Lay were probably the most respected and sought-after dinner guests in this socially conscious Texas city. They were at the very top of the tree — successful, wealthy and beneficent. They made their home among the elite in Houston's River Oaks district, which features grand mansions shrouded by huge oaks and magnolias.

Their address at 2121 Kirby Drive — until recently known only to friends — takes up all of the thirty-third floor at the top of 'Huntingdon', a walled and gated condominium with smoked picture windows. They don't flaunt their wealth, though they keep a house for their servants in a leafy street behind the condo. The Lays are 'new money' but they run around with 'old money', said Shelby Hodge, society writer for the Houston Chronicle. 'He's certainly not one of your Dallas ranch types; I don't think he ever wore a cowboy hat,' laughed a Houston publicist.

Among the 'old money' in Houston are Republican icons George and Barbara Bush, who belong to the more exclusive Bayou Club across town, where people like to play polo rather than golf. They were among the first Houston folk to be cultivated by Kenneth Lay, the son of a preacher with a doctorate in economics and a navy background, after he arrived in Houston in 1985.

He quickly made a name as an enthusiastic proponent of a new American business model, taking control of a modest gas pipeline company and making it into a financial powerhouse and the world's biggest trader in energy. In doing so, he helped make Houston one of the fastest growing and successful US cities.

The Lays maintained a certain reserve in their adopted city. They rarely appeared at the charity balls that dominate Houston social life but they often paid for $50,000 tables in support of worthy causes. They sponsored the arts, sometimes underwriting opera productions to the tune of $50,000.

They helped fund the Holocaust Museum, the ballet and the Anti-Defamation League, and endowed professorships at two city universities. Kenneth Lay sponsored Enron Field baseball stadium and gave generous endowments to the Texas Medical Centre. Enron employees contributed $3 million to United Way last year, which the company matched.

Raising money for charity is a full-time preoccupation of the Houston black-tie set. The Lays' neighbour in their condominium, Billye Halbouty, wife of a legendary wildcat oil driller, raised a staggering $2 million in two years for the Houston Grand Opera Ball.

The standing of George Senior and Barbara Bush is so high in Houston society that their name guarantees top dollar at any charity function. Here the Lays and the Bush family interacted socially. Ken Lay became honorary chair at Barbara Bush's Celebration of Reading at the Wortham Theatre Centre, where famous writers — Frank McCourt among them — hold readings every year to raise funds for literacy.

But Ken Lay had other, more significant interests in the Bush family. In tandem with his philanthropy, he lavished money on people in public service.

In Houston, money for charity brings social status but sponsoring politicians buys political clout. From the start he cultivated George Bush Senior. He became a major contributor of the then US president, and co-chaired a host committee for Mr Bush's 1990 economic summit in Houston, where he dined on hickory grilled veal with Margaret Thatcher and Francois Mitterand.

Ken Lay also chaired the host committee for the 1992 Republican National Convention in Houston, which selected George Bush for a second term. Enron benefited hugely when the first Bush administration secured passage of the 1992 Energy Act, which forced utility companies to carry Enron's electricity.

After George Senior retired, Ken and Linda adopted the young George Bush, personally giving him $47,500 in 1994 to help unseat Democratic governor Ann Richards, a former Enron beneficiary herself who had made Lay head of her Texas Business Council.

The Enron chief also donated money to Democrats during the Clinton era — $100,000 earned him a sleep-over in the White House — but he placed most of his bets on George W. They got so close, Bush called him 'Kenny Boy' — though he dispenses nicknames freely, said Houston political writer Alan Bernstein. (Bush calls him 'Benny'.) Enron and Lay gave a total of $550,000 to Bush's campaigns from 1993 to 2000. Enron paid $100,000 towards the 2001 Bush inauguration, and Ken Lay wrote a personal cheque for the same amount.

All of this was regarded as pretty unexceptional in a city with a history of corporate funding for those who run the political machinery. It was part of the culture. Houston's rise to prominence was due to similar figures over the years, like Jesse Jones, a crony of Franklin D Roosevelt, who brought the 1928 Democratic Convention to the oil town.

As Enron injected a vitality and prosperity into Houston, now home to 500 other energy companies and several major corporations such as Compaq and Continental Airlines, Lay's influence increased

Young actors John McEvoy as Walter Hartwright with Emer Brew as Laura Fairlie and Anne Catherick (she plays two parts), in **The Woman in White** *by Wilkie Collins and directed by Bernadette Meehan for Sligo Youth Theatre in The Factory Performance Space, Sligo. Photograph: David Sleator.*

accordingly. Almost every senior political figure in Texas, especially Republicans, received some Enron money, ranging from Texas Attorney-General John Cornyn to Supreme Court Judge Greg Abbot. This was widely tolerated, even when favours were done in return and apparent abuses surfaced.

There was little fuss in 1993, for example, when Wendy Gramm, wife of Senator Phil Gramm (who took $97,500 in Enron money over the years), was hired by Enron as a director five weeks after leaving the post of head of the US Commodity Futures Trading Commission, where she granted Enron a lucrative exemption from federal regulation on some commodities trading.

Wendy Gramm is now head of the Mercatus Centre (so anti-regulatory she has been named 'villain of the month' by the non-profit Clean Air Trust), to which Enron donated $50,000, further compromising her present role as a director of Enron charged with looking after shareholders' interests.

Another Enron director is John Mendelsohn, president of the prestigious MD Andersen Cancer Centre in Houston, which received $332,150 from the company.

There was an outcry when Republican Governor Rick Perry took a $25,000 contribution from Enron, the day after appointing a former Enron executive to head the Texas Public Utility Commission, as even Houston found it hard to swallow Perry's explanation that it was 'totally coincidental'.

As Governor from 1994 to 2000, the free-market ideals of Bush and Lay happily coincided and, like his father before him, he signed a de-regulatory law in 1999 clearing Enron's path into new markets. When George W. reached the White House last year, Lay was able to extend his influence, already considerable in Congress where most members had taken Enron money at some time or other, to the heart of the administration. He and Enron officials had several meetings with Vice-President Dick Cheney in the spring, helping to draft the President's energy plan. He played a role in shaping White House appointments that might affect his business.

In the most noted case, in May, Curtis Hebert, chairman of the Federal Energy Regulatory Commission, received what he termed an offensive phone call from the Enron chief executive, suggesting that he change his views on energy deregulation. Mr Hebert didn't and was quietly replaced in August by Lay's choice, former Texas utility regulator, Pat Wood. In another instance, a pro-deregulation officer in Pennsylvania, Nora Mead Brownwell, won a second term over officials' objections after Lay telephoned Karl Rove, the President's political adviser, on her behalf.

This autumn, even as Enron was sinking, Lay was discussing with White House budget director Mitch Daniels the repeal of the alternative minimum tax in a House stimulus package that would have delivered $254 million in tax rebates to Enron — though the package was killed in the Senate.

Kenneth Lay didn't get his way on everything. Despite his lobbying, President Bush abandoned a campaign pledge to impose mandatory limits on carbon-dioxide emissions that would have boosted Enron's natural gas interests. In the end, the former naval officer who liked to lecture people on the benefits of the free market was reduced to seeking government help as Enron collapsed, but this was beyond the capacity even of his friends in Washington.

Kenneth Lay is now a fallen idol in Houston. The city he helped so much is in a funk, its civic pride and prosperity hurting badly. A half-built $4 million mansion in River Oaks lies deserted, testimony to the sudden loss of fortunes for Enron shareholders.

There is deep anger in Houston at the way shareholders were left with nothing while Enron executives enriched themselves, and fury among the 4,500 workers laid off with investments and pensions made worthless by people they trusted. 'I bear Ken Lay's two-headed love child and he's not returning my calls,' declared a former employee on one of the internet sites in Houston that let off steam about Enron.

Some old friends are standing by him and the Lays are still listed as honorary chairs (including Celebration of Reading) by charities who hope their personal wealth will still be directed towards philanthropy.

But the really important invitations are no longer arriving at 2121 Kirby Drive. Ken Lay is not expected at the prestigious Davos World Economic Forum this year, where in 2001 he held forth as a 'real economy' player on the lessons of the dotcom bubble.

And shortly after the Lays received an invitation to a White House Christmas party for 600 on

12 December, with the scandal unfolding around them, they got the word verbally from Washington that it would be much appreciated if they didn't bother turning up.

They didn't.

SATURDAY, 19 JANUARY 2002

The WOW Factor

Frank McDonald

Bedevilled by planning problems and other delays, the National Gallery of Ireland's new Millennium Wing has been well worth waiting for. Because what it does is to transform a conventional art gallery into an exciting place for the public to view paintings or even just to enjoy a cup of coffee or a browse in the bookshop.

For the first time in its history, the gallery now has a real presence on the street. But few passers-by could imagine the truly breathtaking interior that lies behind its somewhat squashed Portland stone, glass and timber façade and the adjoining mid-eighteenth-century building, which the gallery's board was required to retain.

Though it is a double-height cube, the vestibule gives just a glimpse of what follows. Only when one passes beneath the steel canopy over its inner door is the vast volume of the wing's orientation court, rising right up to roof level, revealed with sensational effect. If there is anywhere in Dublin with a 'wow factor', this is it.

The unpainted plaster walls slashed with slits and other apertures, the steel-beamed bridge crossing it at a high level, the grand staircase at the opposite end and the wide openings to the glazed Winter Garden all combine to inspire awe and wonder. Ireland has never seen such a dramatic or dynamic space for art.

Compared with the small rooms and long corridors of IMMA, so wrong-headedly located in the Royal Hospital Kilmainham, the Millennium Wing's classically dispositioned galleries are tall and expansive; their unpainted plaster walls should be left as exactly they are, whatever the curators say about creating different 'moods'.

But the galleries take up only a proportion of the new wing. Space has been reserved on an upper mezzanine level for the nascent Centre for the Study of Irish Art and the Yeats Archive, and the gallery's other facilities include a large bookshop in black and blond wood, a small audio-visual room, a snack bar and a restaurant.

The restaurant occupies the glazed Winter Garden, overlooked by the bow-fronted windows of Number Five South Leinster Street. Unfortunately, its rear wall was in such 'rag order', according to Raymond Keaveney, the gallery's director, that it had to be consolidated and plastered over, instead of having the brickwork properly restored.

At the other end is one of the most curious sights in Dublin — a brick-fronted Regency ballroom, which is to become a private dining area. Though fitted out in white ash to look thoroughly modern, it is a bizarre, almost archaeological remnant, made even more so by the bridge that crosses diagonally over its slated roof.

The retention of Number Five and its ballroom, as required by An Bord Pleanála, means that the wing as completed is quite different to what London-based architects Benson and Forsyth originally planned. But whether or not their bold vision has been compromised — as its planning inspector, Pádraig Thornton, feared — is a moot point.

Certainly, the roof terrace is more ordinary and can't at present be opened to the public because of lack of disabled access, which is a shame because of the views it offers over the city; this will only be resolved when a 'finger building' is built on the staff car-park site off Clare Lane and plugged into the Millennium Wing.

One of Benson and Forsyth's great triumphs is the clarity of circulation within the building, which gives visitors numerous opportunities to 'look back at where they've been', as project architect Jim Hutcheson puts it, and to peer out through

The new extension to the National Gallery of Ireland. Photograph: Eric Luke.

openings of all shapes and sizes to confirm their mental maps of the city centre.

Its geometry also offers radically different perspectives. Thus, the orientation court appears to be much more truncated when viewed from the first-floor landing than it does from the entrance. One can also spot architectural references ranging from medieval cloisters to the wavy design motif associated with Alvar Aalto.

The architects floridly make the case that their building is firmly rooted in Dublin. What concerned them was not 'fashionable formal rhetoric [but] issues of formal integrity, of context and of achieving an appropriate expression of gravitas consistent with the cultural importance of the National Gallery of Ireland'.

Through its entry sequence from Clare Street — via the main orientation court and grand staircase to the existing atrium and the entrance hall of the original building — the new wing 'physically and visually articulates the relationship between the centre of Dublin, the playing fields of Trinty College, Merrion Square and Leinster Lawn'.

Continuing this geo-cultural theme, Benson and Forsyth describe the Clare Street façade as 'an inhabited wall' which 'mediates between the new building and the city' with well-located apertures offering framed views of Trinity College, Nassau Street and the north side of Merrion Square to 'anchor the visual memory of the visitor'.

The elevation 'mimics the height of the existing Georgian street façades', picking up the parapet line of Five South Leinster Street, and its proportions are also vertically articulated to two bays, reflecting the nature of the spaces behind as well as 'evoking the vertical modulation of its Georgian predecessors'.

Behind this wall, the new galleries and spaces are gathered around the orientation court and the glazed Winter Garden, which in turn echoes the Georgian garden that once occupied this site and spatially mediates between the façade of Number Five, the 'found object' of its retained Regency

ballroom and, of course, the new building.

'In this way, the Millennium Wing seeks to give expression to a dialogue between the art objects it contains and the city within which the building itself is contained.' And it does so. Benson & Forsyth maintain, by achieving 'the most sensitive relationship possible with the existing structures, which it both abuts and contains.'

Within the constraints laid down by An Bord Pleanála, the architects have certainly succeeded: that it now seems silly to have retained the ballroom is not their fault. Indeed, it is arguable that few, if any, Irish architects could have mastered the brief with such sophistication and vision; those invited to do so failed at the first fence.

Klaus Unger, one of the most senior architects in the Office of Public Works, which manages the project, believes that the new building will assume the same significance in Dublin as Mies van der Rohe's Neue Nationalgalerie in Berlin. 'It's a great uplift and shows the public that architecture really matters.' The result is a clear vindication of architectural competitions, even a 'huge act of faith' by the National Gallery, as Raymond Keaveney freely admits. Credit is due here to his former deputy, Dr Brian Kennedy, who provided the initial driving force for the project before departing for Australia some years ago.

The only scandalous aspect is that the Government put so little into it — a miserly €3.17 million, most of which it got back in VAT and PAYE receipts.

This forced the gallery to dig into its own reserves, to the tune of £4 (€5) million (which should have been spent on aquisitions) and to raise no less than £6 (€7.6) million from private donors.

That European taxpayers should have contributed three times as much as our own government, through a €9.52 million grant from the EU Regional Development Fund, is a shocking indictment of the Government and the value it assigns to a major public project. In France, it would have been paid out of the public purse.

Perhaps the gallery will have more success in securing Exchequer funds to re-roof and upgrade its older buildings so that they won't look so dowdy compared with the new wing, to refurbish Number Five South Leinster St as administrative offices and to build the so-called finger building — all of which will cost a lot more than €25.29 million.

In the meantime, one can only cast a cold eye on the very long and prominently displayed 'MM' foundation stone commemorating Sile de Valera, the Minister for Arts, the Gaeltacht and the Islands, who laid it. For she is a member of the same government that is not entitled to claim credit for this superb building.

SATURDAY, 19 JANUARY 2002

Dreaming About Lions and His Life on the Sea

Patsy McGarry

He was very old, but Ernest Hemingway once said of him, 'everything will be old but never the shine in Gregorio's eyes'. And it was true. Gregorio Fuentes was 100 when we met at his home near Havana in January 1998.

He lived in the tiny fishing village of Cojimar, east of the city. It was there Hemingway kept his fishing boat, *Pilar*, and Gregorio was its captain for over twenty years. In Cojimar they believe Gregorio was the inspiration for the elderly fisherman Santiago in Hemingway's Nobel Prize-winning novel *The Old Man and the Sea*.

'… Everything about him was old except his eyes and they were the same colour as the sea and were cheerful and undefeated.'

Arguably nobody spent more time with Hemingway than Gregorio. They would put to sea for days, just the two of them, fish for marlin, drink whiskey, talk, think, and occasionally Hemingway might write. On one such expedition in 1952 he

asked Gregorio what he should call the new novel he was writing.

'When *Pilar* Used Sail by the Sea,' suggested Gregorio.

'Say no more,' responded Hemingway, suddenly inspired, 'we'll call it The Old Man and the Sea.'

Hemingway grew up as a writer during his years with him, Gregorio believed. He knew all the stories, he said, all of which he believed had an autobiographical character. *Islands in the Stream* in particular was about *Pilar*, he said.

Gregorio, who died this week, and Hemingway first met during a storm at sea in the Gulf of Mexico in 1928. It was near Tortoise Island and Hemingway's boat had been badly damaged. Gregorio did all he could to help. He gave Hemingway provisions and waited with him until the US coast guard arrived to take the writer back to Key West in Florida.

He recalled that Hemingway spoke good Spanish and that they got on very well. Hemingway, who was just another guy as far as Gregorio was concerned, promised to contact him when he visited Havana again. And he did.

In fact Ernest Hemingway's first visit to Cuba was also in 1928. He was on the steamer *Orita*, which was sailing from La Rochelle in France to Key West in Florida. It docked for a few hours at Havana in the early morning of 2 April that year.

He went for a walk around the city and was seduced by it. He returned many times over the following years, before moving to live there in 1939.

During the 1930s he used stay at the recently restored and very beautiful Ambos Mundos hotel in Old Havana. There he would write and go for long walks through the city streets in the evening, calling regularly to La Bodeguita del Medio and the Floridita. Graffiti in La Bodeguita, written by him, reads: 'My mojito in La Bodeguita. My daiquiri in El Floridita.'

The mojito and daiquiri are potent cocktails. Towards the end of the 1930s he discovered Cojimar, its tiny harbour and its La Terraza restaurant. He also

Abdoulaye Math and Mary Lawlor (director of Front Line) at the Front Line Human Rights Defenders Conference in Dublin Castle. Photograph: Hugh McElveen.

renewed his acquaintance with Gregorio, who lived close to La Terraza. They began to fish together for marlin. 'Big, big ones,' Gregorio recalled.

Hemingway had a boat built and he called it *Pilar*. He asked Gregorio to be its captain. He agreed and was later described as the pillar of *Pilar*. 'La Mar' was how Hemingway addressed the sea.

'… The old man always thought of her as feminine and as something that gave or withheld great favours, and if she did wild or wicked things it was because she could not help them. The moon affects her as it does a woman, he thought.'

After their long fishing expeditions they would return to La Terraza and drink there with the local fishermen. 'They sat on the Terrace and many of the fishermen made fun of the old man and he was not angry.'

People from all over the world used to come to Cojimar to fish for marlin in those days, Gregorio remembered. They came from Spain, Italy, Russia, Africa. But that has all stopped now. Gregorio, who died this week, was fifty-five when *The Old Man and the Sea* was written. The description of Santiago in the novel fitted him perfectly. Photographs suggest he always looked old. The man was thin and gaunt with deep wrinkles in the back of his neck. The brown blotches of the benevolent skin cancer the sun brings from its reflection on the tropical sea were on his cheeks. The blotches ran well down the sides of his face and his hands and the deep-creased scars from handling heavy fish on the cords, but none of these scars was fresh. They were as old as erosions in a fishless desert.

He recalled Hemingway saying, when he won the Nobel Prize for Literature in 1954, 'We will have very much money now.' Hemingway dedicated the prize to the fishermen of Cojimar and went to the shrine of El Cobre at Santiago de Cuba, in the south-east of the island, where he left his Nobel medal at the feet of La Virgen de la Caridad Del Cobre, Cuba's patron saint.

Hemingway, Gregorio's grandson Rafael said, helped many people in Cojimar. Thanks to him also, they believe, the film of the novel, with Spencer Tracy as Santiago, was made at Cojimar in 1956. In gratitude for all his help, the fishermen collected propellers from their boats, melted them down and erected a bronze bust to Hemingway which still stands overlooking the little harbour.

An inscription on the plinth gives the writer's date of birth however as 1898. He was born in 1899.

A six kilometre stretch of sea off Havana has been named Hemingway's Mile. He gave it that name himself some time during the many hours of the many years he spend undulating on its waves, fishing. In 1950 he donated a cup as first prize in a fishing competition which is still held in May every year off Marina Hemingway in Havana.

In 1960 the prize was won by Fidel Castro, who had come to power in 1959. There is a photograph in La Terraza of Hemingway presenting Castro with the cup. By then Hemingway had been living in Havana for twenty years. In 1939 he bought Finca Vigia, an estate between the city and Cojimar. He lived there with his third wife Mary until he returned to the US in 1960. They say he used rise at dawn in that house each day and write for six hours while standing in over-sized moccasins before a typewriter.

The house is now known as Museo Hemingway and is as he left it in 1960. Visitors can look in but they cannot enter. Groups of middle-aged women guard it strictly.

It is beautiful, airy and bright, as befits Cuba's warm, wonderful climate. Magazines with jaded covers rest on the sitting-room table with bottles of Cinzano and Bacardi in a wine rack beside it, their labels browned by age.

The trophy room is a homage to machismo, with bullets and bullet casings neatly ordered on a table, and along its walls the heads of great animals killed on safari.

'… The old man had seen many great fish. He had seen many that weighed more than a thousand pounds and he had caught two of that size in his life, but never alone.

'Now alone and out of sight of land, he was fast to the biggest fish that he had ever seen and bigger than he had ever heard of.'

The writing room has a large mahogany table and shelves and shelves of books, too far inside the window to be identified. On the wall is a drawing of a bull etched in stone and presented to Hemingway by Picasso. *Pilar* is preserved in the garden of the house, as are the graves of four of his dogs.

He left *Pilar* to Gregorio when he returned to the US in 1960. Gregorio said he knew Hemingway had leukaemia and that he went to the US for treatment, intending to return. He never said goodbye, Gregorio recalled. Gregorio didn't talk about Hemingway's death. It still upset him.

In Cojimar they remember how tired Hemingway used to be in those last weeks with them and they believe he decided to take his own life because he did not want to endure a long, meaningless, debilitating, terminal disease.

'… He knew he was beaten now — finally and without remedy … He sailed lightly now and he had no thoughts nor any feelings of any kind. He was past everything now …'

In Gregorio's modest home on a slope there was a large picture of himself, Hemingway and *Pilar*. It was a reproduction of a 1990 painting by C. Salowski.

Gregorio liked to sit beneath this picture in his front room wearing a baseball cap with 'Capitan' written on it. It is how he received visitors who liked to talk to him about Hemingway.

He lived with one of his four daughters. He had seven grandchildren and seven great-grandchildren.

As part of his ninety-ninth birthday celebrations in 1996, his family brought him to see his birthplace on Lanzarote in the Canary Islands, off the north-west coast of Africa. But generally he lived quietly, remembering the past. Life's tempests had passed by.

'… The old man was sleeping again. He was still sleeping on his face and the boy was sitting by him watching him. The old man was dreaming about lions.'

(Quote extracts are from The Old Man and The Sea.*)*

WEDNESDAY, 23 JANUARY 2002

Murphy May Get Life Sentence for His Role in Omagh Bombing

Diarmaid MacDermott

Colm Murphy was yesterday convicted at the Special Criminal Court in Dublin of conspiring to cause the Omagh bomb which killed twenty-nine people, including a mother pregnant with twins, and injured over 300 in 1998.

Murphy faces a possible maximum sentence of life imprisonment. Following the conviction Murphy, a forty-nine-year-old father-of-four, who had been on bail, was remanded in custody for sentencing on Friday.

The building contractor and publican from Co. Armagh, with an address at Jordan's Corner, Ravensdale, Co. Louth, had pleaded not guilty to conspiring in Dundalk with another person not before the court to cause an explosion in the State or elsewhere between 13 and 16 August 1998.

The prosecution claimed Mr Murphy lent his mobile phone and another mobile phone he obtained from Mr Terence Morgan to the people who planted the Omagh bomb. Det. Garda James B. Hanley told the court that Murphy had admitted

he lent his phone to known republicans, knowing it would be used for moving bombs.

Mr Morgan gave evidence last November that he had lent his mobile phone to Murphy, but last Friday he retracted that evidence.

Det. Garda Hanley told the court that when asked if he knew his phone was going to be used in a criminal act, Murphy said: 'Yes, I knew it would be used for moving bombs. I knew these fellas were involved in moving bombs to Northern Ireland.' In another interview, Murphy was asked if he had been told by a named Real IRA man that his phone was to be used in planting the Omagh bomb and he replied: 'No, he didn't have to say it, he wouldn't talk about it. It was a disaster, nobody set out to kill anybody in Omagh, it was just a complete mess.'

Delivering the judgment, Mr Justice Robert Barr said the interview given by Murphy to Det. Garda Hanley and Det. Sgt Gerard Mc Grath at Monaghan Garda station on 23 February 1999 was 'crucial to the prosecution case'.

'It is relied upon as establishing that the accused procured Terence Morgan's phone on 14 August 1998 and passed it together with his own mobile phone to [a named dissident republican] in the knowledge that both were required by him in connection with the movement of a bomb for detonation at a location in Northern Ireland.'

The judge said the essence of the crime of conspiracy in the case was that the accused collaborated to provide two mobile phones in connection with conveying a bomb to Northern Ireland and that he knew the purpose for which the phones were required. He said the court had already ruled that the evidence of one of the teams of interrogators, Det. Garda Liam Donnelly and Det. Garda John Fahy, was inadmissible as interview notes had been rewritten.

But he said there was no evidence that other, more senior officers were aware of Garda Donnelly's wrongdoing and nothing to suggest the activities of other interrogators were tainted by it.

The judge said the defence had contended that there had been a 'dovetailing of evidence' by four

Etain O'Connor, Educational Co-ordinator of Achill and Currane IT Centre, photographed with her dog, Ollie. Photograph: Frank Miller.

prosecution witnesses — Detectives Garda Hanley and Mc Grath; Ms Lisa Purnell, an intelligence analyst working with the RUC and Det. Sgt Costello — about cell site analysis relating to the use of Murphy's mobile phone in Banbridge on 1 August 1998. But the court believed there was 'nothing to establish so-called "dovetailing" of evidence between the four prosecution witnesses concerned'.

Mr Justice Barr said the court rejected Mr Morgan's retraction of evidence 'and accepts the veracity of his original testimony beyond reasonable doubt'.

The judgment said the court was 'satisfied that the following facts which have been proved in evidence beyond reasonable doubt are collectively corroborative of the accused's confessions of guilt regarding his part in the conspiracy to plant and detonate the Omagh car-bomb':

1. The phone records which establish the movement of the accused's phone and the Morgan phone to and from Omagh at a time consistent with the bombing there on 15 August 1998.

2. Traffic between the two phones on that date.

3. Lies told by the accused to Terence Morgan by way of explanation for wishing to borrow his mobile phone on 14 August 1998.

4. Lies told by the accused to Detective Gardaí Reidy and King about not having loaned his mobile phone to anyone on the day of the Omagh bombing, which lies were retracted by him in later Garda interrogations.

5. The fact that the accused's admissions of guilt recorded in Garda interview notes are uncontradicted in evidence.

6. Telephone records relating to use of the accused's mobile phone at Banbridge on 1 August 1998 and the broad similarity between the traffic pattern there and the Omagh phone traffic in relation to the accused's and Morgan's phones.

7. The accused is a republican terrorist of long standing having been convicted of serious offences of that nature in this State and in the United States of America for each of which he served prison sentences. In the light of that background and his membership of a dissident terrorist group in Ireland which is not on cease-fire he is a person likely to be involved in terrorist activities of the sort charged against him.

8. Among others contacted by the accused's mobile phone shortly before the Banbridge bombing was [a named republican dissident] — to whom the accused is alleged to have stated he had supplied his own and Terence Morgan's phone on or about 15 August 1998 for use in connection with the Omagh bombing.

9. The accused is alleged to have conceded that [the named republican dissident] was then a member of the Real IRA. [The dissident] is recorded as having received three calls from the accused's mobile phone on 1 August 1998 at 13.05, 13.48 and 14.09.

The judgment added that it was 'highly likely' that Murphy would have feared that the mobile phone information 'would be used to connect him with actual participation in the transportation of the car-bomb to Omagh'. In order to 'distance himself from actual participation in the Omagh bombing per se, he had a strong incentive to tell the truth — that he had collaborated in the Omagh conspiracy in that he had provided two mobile phones for use in carrying out the intended objective but that that was the full extent of his part in the operation.'

(Two days later, on 25 January, Murphy was sentenced to fourteen years' imprisonment)

Options, Not Auctions

Editorial

We are now embarked upon the longest election campaign in history. There are about five months to go to polling day and four months to the formal start of the campaign.

Every party is offering to go into coalition with every other party — with the notable exception of Sinn Féin.

Big-name candidates are bartering for seats in State cars and, if lucky, State-owned aircraft. Manifestos are being polished. That old unseemly game of Dutch-auction politics, which served this State so badly for a period in the late 1970s and early 1980s, has opened. The bidding for votes with taxpayers' own money has begun.

The promises are being rolled out at the rate of four in the past week. The first Cabinet meeting of 2002 produced two. The Minister for Health, Mr Martin, announced that 709 acute hospital beds would be commissioned in public hospitals by the end of this year. That figure is 259 beds more than promised in the Government's Health Strategy late last year. The Minister for Public Enterprise, Ms O'Rourke, announced the beginning of the tendering process for the first line of the Dublin Metro which is to be built by 2007. She dressed up the eighteen-month-old decision in new election clothes. What stopped these ministers from providing these services over the last five years?

The promise to beat all was made by the Fine Gael leader, Mr Noonan, on Sunday when he said that tax credits would be offered to 400,000 taxpayers to recoup twenty per cent of their losses on Eircom shares. It is a daft notion. More than that, it is indefensible to ask the general body of taxpayers to pay for the gambling instincts of those who exercised their own free-will to splurge. It may appeal to the base instincts of aggrieved individuals but there are greater sectional injustices in society which could benefit from a €90 million give-away. The Taoiseach entered promise-land with his announcement that every school building should be surveyed over the next two years and a 'guaranteed standard' for each should be put in place. Where did sub-standard schools stand with the Celtic Tiger for almost five years?

The leader of the Labour Party, Mr Quinn, made a wise intervention in the electioneering frenzy yesterday when he called on all parties to put a halt to auction politics. He wanted the Irish people to have a sane and sensible debate on what the next coalition government should do. The voters were entitled to hear the manifestos of the political parties, properly costed, he said, so that they could make up their own minds on what kind of society they wanted for the next five years. Mr Quinn is right. There are almost five months to go to the election. The public should not have to put up with four promises a week from now to polling day. The drip-feed of goodies from government and opposition parties demeans politics and alienates voters. Have no lessons been learnt the hard way? The public needs option-politics, not auction-politics, before they cast their vote.

THURSDAY, 31 JANUARY 2002

Dublin Woman Hired Two People to Carry Out Assisted Suicide

Joe Humphreys

A Dublin woman suffering from depression is believed to have hired two people from the United States to assist her to commit suicide, *The Irish Times* has learned.

The woman, who was separated and in her forties, is understood to have employed the services

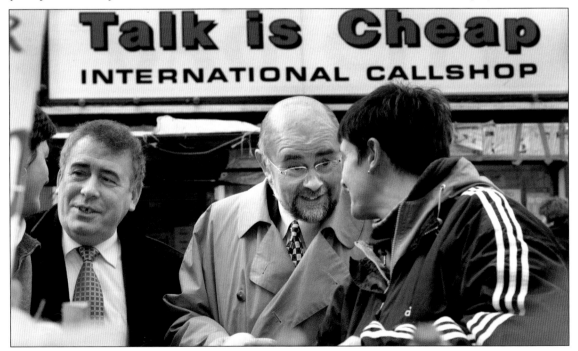

The Labour Party Leader Ruairí Quinn and the party's Dublin Central general election candidate Senator Joe Costello with traders in Moore Street. Photograph: Matt Kavanagh.

of an American organisation which offers help to perform suicide.

She is believed to have met the two at Dublin Airport last week and that subsequently they assisted her to kill herself at her apartment in Donnybrook.

Gardaí, who believe this is the first instance of assisted suicide in this jurisdiction, are investigating what happened. It is believed the woman paid the two individuals around €6,500. Gardaí also believe the two have already left the State.

A person close to the woman said she had not been suffering from any terminal physical illness but had 'extremely serious depression'. She was also said to have undergone numerous courses of treatment, without success, over several years. In addition, she was said to have indicated to others her intention to take her own life. 'She was quite rational about it. She felt it was the only rational choice,' said one source.

The woman had no children, and in recent months had been forced to give up her job because of her depression.

The Assistant State Pathologist, Dr Marie Cassidy, carried out a post-mortem on the woman's body at the weekend. Blood samples have been taken for examination and a toxicology report, which would identify the cause of death, is expected to be available within a number of weeks.

E-mail transmissions between the woman and a contact in the US in which details of the arrangement were discussed have been recovered. Gardaí are also said to be examining security tapes at Dublin Airport in the hope of finding film of the individuals meeting the woman.

The woman's apartment has already been examined by the Garda Technical Bureau. Detectives have been encouraged by the discovery of a number of fingerprints.

It is understood that Gardaí are seeking directions on the case from the Director of Public Prosecutions. They are also examining the possibility of seeking the extradition of the offenders from the US under a 1983 extradition treaty. They have

yet to confirm their identities. It is understood the woman made contact with the two through a confidential Internet 'chat-room'.

Numerous organisations in the US offer services to persons considering assisted suicide. However, none openly advertises the type of service performed in this case.

Assisted suicide is legal in just two EU states, Belgium and the Netherlands, and in only one state in the US, Oregon.

Under Irish law, anyone who 'aids, abets, counsels or procures the suicide of another' is liable upon conviction to be jailed for up to fourteen years.

Letters to the Editor
January 2002

Switching to the Euro

Sir, — So, the powers that be insist that we must at all times refer to the euro in the singular.

And there was I thinking that one of the main tenets underpinning the European ideal was the promotion and advancement of pluralism. — Yours, etc., Paul Delaney, Beacon Hill, Dalkey, Co. Dublin, 3 January 2002.

'Popstars'

A chara, — On Monday night's Questions & Answers on RTÉ, Eamon Gilmore TD said the sixteen-year-old who lied about her age on 'Popstars' showed great initiative. Will Mr Gilmore now confirm that he believes it is OK to lie about your age on application forms — and is his casual regard for the truth Labour Party policy?

Swear about your opponents, tell lies about your age — what else has Labour in store for us before polling day? — Is mise, Eimear McAuliffe, Cabinteely Avenue, Dublin 18. 16 January 2002.

Lying for a Cause

Sir, — Nadine Coyle, who lied about her age on 'Popstars', is in good company. Ireland's Antarctic hero,

Tom Crean, also lied about his age when he joined the British navy in 1893 in his personal bid for adventure. He was fifteen, a year younger than Nadine. — Yours, etc., Tim Magennis, Springhill Park, Killiney, Co. Dublin. 18 January 2002.

Switching to the Euro

Sir, — Please could we have an increase of one cent — or preferably three cent — in the price of The Irish Times? Each issue bought or sold involves trading with the one cent coin, which is very hard to handle. — Yours, etc., Rory Buckley, Woodpark, Ballinteer, Dublin 16. 18 January 2002.

Fine Gael's Election Offer

Sir, — Have I been hallucinating? Or did I hear correctly that the leader of Fine Gael proposes to

compensate Eircom shareholders if he is in a position to form a Government after the next election?

This cannot be true! It must be a joke. It is mind-boggling to think that a man would even contemplate such action after he opposed, tooth and nail, compensation for the sick, innocent victims of the contaminated blood scandal.

Presumably Eircom shareholders were all healthy individuals who purchased shares of their own free will. There was no coercion. They had a choice, and must have been aware of the old dictum, 'Never invest more than you can afford to lose'. Innocent victims of contaminated blood, on the other hand, were sick people who had no options open to them.

If this isn't political opportunism, what is? — Yours, etc., M.A. Farragher, Terenure, Dublin 6W. 24 January 2002.

All eyes on model Ruth Griffin, wearing a blue cotton granny print top, with denim eyelet mini skirt, at the showing of A-wear Spring/Summer Collections in Dublin. Photograph: Eric Luke.

MONDAY, 4 FEBRUARY 2002

Premiums for Flocks of Elusive Ewes Are the New DIRT

Business Opinion: John McManus

Let's talk about sheep. For those of you interested in such things there are 4,880,400 sheep living in the Republic. This figure comes from the December livestock survey published by the Central Statistics Office last week.

The survey is conducted every December and involves the CSO writing to 30,000 farmers and asking them in confidence how many sheep they own.

In order to encourage the farmers to tell the truth the CSO promises that it will not pass on the information to any third party, including the Department of Agriculture. As a result the survey is generally accepted as accurate and its figures used by Eurostat, the statistical service of the European Commission.

What the livestock survey does not measure is the level of fraud perpetrated by sheep farmers. To get this figure we have to carry out our own rather crude analysis. Our point of departure is the sheep cull carried out on the Cooley Peninsula last April after foot-and-mouth disease broke out. When all 276 flocks on the peninsula had been culled it emerged that more than 6,600 ewes on which headage premiums had been claimed were nowhere to be found.

It was also revealed that seventeen of the claimants had no sheep at all, fifty-one of them had seriously over-claimed and another 100 or so were unable to produce all the ewes for which they had claimed.

The number of ewes for which Cooley farmers had made false claims was eighteen per cent of the ewes for which claims were made. If we assume that farmers in the Cooley are no more or less corrupt than farmers anywhere else, we can extrapolate to get a bogus claim figure for the Republic as a whole.

According to the Department of Agriculture, €100 million (£78.8 million) was paid in ewe premiums in 2000, which suggests fraud along the lines of €18 million. Put another way, only €82 million of the premiums paid over in respect of 2000 was for ewes that actually existed. Funnily enough, if you multiply the number of eligible ewes that the CSO livestock survey says were in the Republic in December 2000 by the maximum premium payment of €24 you get … wait for it … €85.8 million.

Students of history will now start running for their copies of the Beef Tribunal report. They will remember that one of the things that got the ball rolling there was the 'discovery' that the Government was giving export credit insurance for beef exports that exceeded the annual beef exports of the Republic as calculated by the CSO.

Drawing such a comparison is entertaining but a little over-dramatic. The Department of Agriculture points out that the CSO Livestock Survey classifies one million sheep as 'others' rather than ewes. Some of these others could still qualify for the ewe premiums according to the Department.

Quite how many of them qualified the Department could not say, but you would have to add back pretty much the whole one million before you could reconcile the Livestock Survey with the 4.3 million ewes on which the Department paid out in 2000. According to the CSO the 'others' category is for ewes and rams that are to be culled and young sheep intended for the breeding flock.

On the other hand, the €24 per ewe premium is the maximum figure and only applies to farmers in disadvantaged areas. If you were to use a lower average figure in the calculations you would get an even bigger discrepancy between the Department's figure and the figure based on the Livestock Survey.

What cannot be disputed by the Department is that there is widespread, low-level fraud in the sheep industry.

The real question is not so much how much has been stolen, but to what extent the State turned a blind eye to it. History students will now start seeing parallels between what is going on in the sheep industry — and one has to suspect in the beef industry as well — and what went on in the banking industry with respect to Deposit Interest Retention Tax in the 1980s.

It is stretching credulity to think that the results of the Cooley cull came as a bolt out of the blue to the officials in the Department of Agriculture. One would have to suspect that — as was the case with DIRT fraud — the Department was aware of the problem but was not aware of any political will to face up to it.

Like DIRT evasion, premiums fraud is a victimless crime. The losers are — or at least were — the German tax payers whose contributions fund the Common Agriculture Policy.

The similarity does not stop there. The perpetrators of the fraud are, in the main, ordinary citizens and the amounts involved only run to a few thousand per fraudster.

It is only when you add all the individual amounts up and realise that it has been going on for years, if not decades, that you come up with the sort of headline-grabbing numbers that spurred the Public Accounts Committee into action over DIRT.

In the same way — and one suspects for the same reasons of political expediency — that successive ministers for finance dodged the issue of DIRT evasion until it became impossible to ignore, the various inhabitants of the ministerial suite at the Department of Agriculture have not afforded ewe premiums fraud any real priority until now.

The Department of Agriculture is answerable to the PAC and the subject is worthy if its attention. It could if it wished get stuck into it before the Dáil broke up for the coming election. A good starting point could be the investigation into 36,000 rural voters … sorry, sheep farmers … carried out by the

'Earth Angels'. **The Irish Times** *photographer Brenda Fitzsimons won the Photographer of the Year Award for this shot in February.*

Department on foot of the Cooley cull, which is supposed to be near completion.

FRIDAY, 8 FEBRUARY 2002

Rogue Trader 'a Bit Cocky' but just Seen as a 'Regular Guy' by His Colleagues

Conor O'Clery

As Allfirst executives in Baltimore work round the clock to complete their investigation into the loss of $750 million (€864 million), a fuller picture has emerged of the lone currency dealer at the centre of the scandal and how his rogue trades were uncovered.

John Rusnak was one of only two foreign currency traders at Allfirst. He made proprietary trades — i.e. he bought and sold currencies to make a profit for the bank — while his colleague conducted transactions for bank clients. It was a small treasury-debt operation, accounting for less than three per cent of AIB profits.

Working from a beige-coloured cubicle on the twelfth floor of Allfirst's city-centre tower, with a number of monitors constantly tuned to Bloomberg and Reuters financial news, Mr Rusnak would bet millions every day on the currency markets. Usually dressed in trader business-casual style of button-down shirt and khaki trousers, he would typically work in his cubicle from around 7 a.m. to late afternoon, doing up to 100 trades a day or more.

He had a reputation for being very quick and hard-working, and was 'a bit cocky', as one acquaintance put it, 'but a regular guy to go to a football game with or have a pint'. Once in 1997 he boasted that he made a $5,000 profit selling US dollars for German Deutschmarks in a transaction that took only seconds. 'If we could do that every time, we would be sitting back in our bathrobes smoking a pipe,' he said at the time.

Mr Rusnak, thirty-seven, is a native of Pennsylvania, where his father Emil was a steel worker and his mother Angelina registers death certificates for the state. He was employed first as a currency trader at Chemical Bank, a predecessor of JP Morgan Chase in New York, where he is remembered by a former colleague as 'a nice guy, good at what he did'.

He left New York, reportedly because he didn't like the pressure, and in 1993 joined the AIB-owned bank in Baltimore, then known as First

Allfirst employee John Rusnak, identified as the trader suspected of stealing $750 million from Allfirst bank, a subsidiary of Allied Irish Banks.

Maryland. Within a few months he and his wife Linda moved into a 119-year-old Victorian frame and clapboard house in the Baltimore neighbourhood of Mount Washington, which they bought for $217,500, taking out a $135,000 mortgage from Harbour Federal Savings.

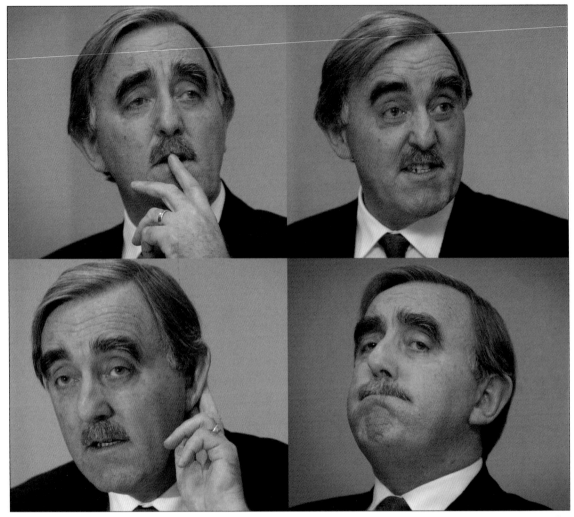

Michael Buckley, Group Chief Executive AIB, addressing the preliminary announcement of results. Photographs:
Bryan O'Brien.

They have since earned a reputation as modest people in the fashionable neighbourhood. 'They certainly aren't flashy — they didn't have any expensive or extravagant things, or live any kind of expensive lifestyle,' an acquaintance, Carol Brody, was reported as saying.

Mr Rusnak became an active parishioner at the Shrine of the Sacred Heart Catholic Church where his two children attended school, and he joined the board of Baltimore Clayworks, a non-profit ceramics and cultural centre. The family held a

lecture by an artist in their house not long ago.

'Upstanding' is a word used to describe Mr Rusnak by both a neighbour, Eva Glasgow, and by his boss, Allfirst president and chief executive Susan Keating. 'He was lovely, nice, fun, pleasant. I would never have thought he would be the kind of guy to do this,' Margery Pozefsky, also on the Clayworks board, told a *Baltimore Sun* reporter.

One thing that acquaintances noticed was that he was often preoccupied with his work, and recently seemed more and more stressed out, although at the bank he still gave an appearance of confidence and being in control. But two weeks ago he began requesting unusually large amounts of money for his trades and the first seeds of suspicion were sown in the mind of one member of the treasuries section responsible for verifying trades in currencies, equities and other bank business. This unit works from a different floor from the traders to maintain a separate oversight.

This bank official became concerned that Mr Rusnak was resisting oversight and complaining that with the limits imposed he could not trade effectively. On Friday he questioned Mr Rusnak about some of the contracts, many with expiry limits of 364 days taken out during 2001. He began trying to confirm the contracts actually existed.

It is now believed that last year and in recent weeks Mr Rusnak made many bets on the yen using complex financial instruments known as derivatives that are traded like stocks and bonds, almost certainly gambling that the Japanese currency would rise against the US dollar. He made bets on other currencies too. The greenback surged ahead throughout the year, defying predictions.

The losses for the bank should not have been serious. Traders buy options that enable them to exit losing positions at a price below the current market value. Without these offsetting options the bank would be left 'naked'. But everything seemed to be under control, with Mr Rusnak always working within the modest limits of the bank's risk-management plan.

'Most foreign exchange or currency markets are very loosely regulated at best,' said Alan Revercomb, options strategist at Ideaglobal. 'It's primarily internally controlled.'

The bank actually makes money from the illegal strategy if the original bet comes off, because no options were bought. But if the currency goes the other way, failure to purchase the option, as happened here, exposes the bank to huge unhedged losses. Each time he miscalculated, Mr Rusnak apparently lost on average an estimated $10 million

through not having a valid hedging option.

Mr Rusnak finished work as normal on Friday and went home. On Sunday afternoon, as the Asian markets were opening, the treasury official drove into the bank's office at Twenty-Seven South Charles Street and began to check out the options Mr Rusnak had declared. They had been taken out with the biggest and most respectable banks in the Asian-Pacific region, where the Bank of Tokyo and Hong Kong Shanghai Bank are the top currency traders.

It was then the awful truth began to become evident. One after another, the Asian banks told Allfirst that they knew nothing of the options contracts that Mr Rusnak had entered. The treasury official worked through the night tracking down more and more phoney transactions. Mr Rusnak was by then fully aware that the game was up. The official had called his house on Sunday afternoon to ask him more questions about the trades. On Monday morning he didn't turn up for work and refused to come to the telephone.

It took some time for the Asian banks to check out and verify that contracts simply didn't exist and for the Allfirst officials to 'back out' the fictitious trades and then rerun the value-at-risk models. At 5.30 p.m. on Monday the official notified Ms Keating and Frank Bramble, the AIB chief executive in the US, of an 'emergency situation'.

Other top executives out on business were summoned back to South Charles Street. Within thirty minutes, they had telephoned the news to group chief executive Michael Buckley in the Republic, where it was already getting late in the evening.

As the bank officials worked throughout Monday night revaluing all the last year's positions, the group treasurer, Pat Ryan, prepared to fly to Baltimore. By the time he arrived on Tuesday afternoon Allfirst, the star performer of AIB, was looking at a total loss of $750 million in up to 100 transactions dating from early 2001. It was the banking world's biggest scandal since Nick Leeson

Deputy Mr Dessie O'Malley on the plinth at Leinster House. Photograph: Alan Betson.

brought down Barings Bank with $1.4 billion in losses in 1995. The FBI had already been called in.

All the top officials expressed shock. 'We couldn't get our head around the fact that it was so big,' said one.

One theory being checked is that Mr Rusnak was able to rely on one or more treasury officials not to verify certain trades. An accomplice might have allowed him to post fictitious options trades and leave positions in the spot forex market un-hedged. Another is that there was external collusion. Pending the outcome of investigations, the vice-president/treasurer, the senior vice-presidents in charge of treasury funds and investment operations, and one staff member have been suspended.

'All are on full pay and are co-operating with the bank and other agencies,' said an Allfirst official. 'At this stage we don't think there is any money salted away.'

SATURDAY, 9 FEBRUARY 2002

Poor Drama and Bad Manners

Eileen Battersby

Not even the worst excesses of Tribunal Ireland could justify the vulgar travesty now on offer at the Abbey Theatre. To witness the sea-side comedy of *Hinterland*, a blatant exposé of the life, mainly the private life, of the disgraced former taoiseach, Charles Haughey, is as voyeuristically demeaning as the material it is based on. While I have no regard for Haughey or any member of the merry band he led through the most sordid period in Irish politics, the fact is that while the ridiculing of a society is fair comment, the ridiculing of one man's messy life is not. *Hinterland* is poor theatre. But far worse than that, it is bad manners.

Among the many problems of art and literary criticism is that it confers, indeed demands, a suspension of moral judgment. It is no use denouncing a novel under review because you don't approve of the characters, their behaviour or opinions.

Instead, the critic looks for a skilful handling of characterisation, dialogue, plot, narrative structure, language — and an overall cohesion. These are the elements by which a work is judged. The explicit nature of art often goes beyond that of polite society. In other words, one does not copulate in public — although simulations of such are acceptable on stage or on screen. Murder is another major theme in art, particularly in cinema and of course, fiction, and it is not necessarily confined to the thriller genre.

This suspension of moral judgment is problematic — consider the critical reaction to Bret Easton Ellis's novel *American Psycho* in 1991, when many critics initially responded with sermons rather than reviews. Loud was the outcry. I remember being castigated for reviewing it as a novel, not a moral outrage. Ultimately, however, it was judged as the novel it is.

Some critics and viewers looked askance at Lucian Freud's paintings because they depicted the ugliness of real-life bodies. Others praised the painterly genius of his brutal realism.

Hinterland cannot be treated in a similar way, such is the moronic obviousness of its satire. It has the savagery of a restoration comedy but none of the wit. Even a mildly informed ten-year-old will grasp most of the innuendo, never mind gags such as the one about the Georgian teapot — 'he gave its sister to Mrs Thatcher'.

The character Johnny Silvester is Haughey, so it seems cowardly to have changed the name. Brian Lenihan's liver transplant is here amended to a heart transplant — was that solely to facilitate the weak joke 'have a heart'?

As anyone who has been barely conscious during the past thirty years knows, Haughey is extremely easy to mimic. Many amateur mimics, myself included, can impersonate his voice, his gestures. Like Mary Robinson, he is an easy target.

Nor is it difficult to recreate the rhetoric. Remember 'Scrap Saturday'? Its scriptwriters replicated the Florentine grandiosity undercut by boot-boy argot with far more punch than this characterisation.

Patrick Malahide, the lead, mimics Haughey's voice and delivery, complete with an old man's shuffle. It's not acting. And in fairness, his impersonation lacks the darker aspects of the real-life character.

Instead of the complex, rather menacing persona of the former leader, we have Haughey as a greedy but benign idiot, claiming to love his son and his country, asking his wife: 'Have you no sense of humour?'

There is far more to the political story than spending public funds on private entertainment and cheating on a thinly written, still angry wife. Cornelius (Lenihan) is a quasi-comic Marley without the angst. The play has no interior life. The direction is unimaginative. There is no silence.

The only profundity is voiced by the disturbed son, an invented character, who tells his father: 'I am sorrowing.'

Hinterland is not Shakespeare because Haughey is not a tragic hero; he has no moral grandeur to lose. But his surviving the Arms Trial alone suggests that, beyond the big spending and grotesque self-delusions, there is something of near-sinister substance that demands scrutiny. A sloppy farce such as *Hinterland* is not the appropriate place for that political examination.

Nor should this play be condoned as the collective revenge of the Irish people on the man who betrayed the nation. It is to be hoped the revenge of the Irish people is somewhat more sophisticated than the knowing cackles that greeted the direct hits of each unsubtle reference on opening night.

Timing invariably highlights ironies. Coincidentally, the television drama 'No Tears',

Schoolchildren enjoying the first of **The Irish Times/RTÉ Music in the Classroom** *series, with the National Symphony Orchestra, at the National Concert hall. Photograph: Eric Luke.*

with its portrayal of a ruthless minister for health currently taking its toll on the reputation of the real-life health minister of that time, Michael Noonan, has concluded just as *Hinterland*, with its comic Johnny Silvester Haughey, begins its run. Both prove that art imitating life simplifies issues.

In both cases, 'art' has been overwhelmed by complexities. The blood scandal must be subjected to a meticulous documentary. Haughey's career warrants a serious investigation, not the naïve undergraduate revue treatment it has received from Sebastian Barry.

The surprise that Barry, a playwright with an international reputation based largely on the success of *The Steward of Christendom*, should have written this, adds to the surrealism of it all.

Of his seven plays thus far, the finest remains *Prayers of Sherkin*, which premièred in 1990. *Boss Grady's Boys* (1988) and *White Woman Street* (1992)

also share the two qualities that have dominated his work, grace and beauty — neither of which features in *Hinterland*. It is important to recognise that the *Steward*, having triumphed largely due to the performance of the late Donal McCann, remains to be fully tested, which won't happen until another actor tackles that role.

Had Hugh Leonard or Bernard Farrell, both fillers of theatres, written *Hinterland*, there would be righteous outpourings — but many critics regard Barry as above tastelessness. Not this time. The arrival of the high-stepping mistress in a Cruella de Vil-type coat and the exchanges that follow compound the text's multiple vulgarities.

Far from serving the nation in staging this silly trash, the national theatre has simply confirmed that the Irish love gossip. Most ironically of all, it has furnished the fallen squire with even more mythology and yet another escape route.

Mark Brew (14), Whitehall, Dublin, at the launch of the Irish Cancer Society's Daffodil Day 2002. Photograph: Joe St Leger.

SATURDAY, 16 FEBRUARY 2002

Will Someone Shout Stop!

Harry Browne

There's not a lot wrong with Marian Finucane. Really. She's got the voice, the manner, the warmth and the alert curiosity of a sound radio presenter. She's got one of the largest audiences in Irish radio,

notwithstanding the latest slippage in her listening figures. She's got the goodwill of the vast majority of people, who are prepared to overlook the occasional gaps in knowledge and flaps in syntax to which she is prone.

What she hasn't got is a programme that does her justice. 'Marian Finucane' (RTÉ Radio 1, Monday to Friday) has been, for most of its relatively short history, a pretty dire hour's listening, a show that raises more questions than it answers — chief among those questions being 'Why?' and 'Ya wha'?' Brenda Power was filling in for Marian this week, yet another case of the creeping colonisation of the airwaves by newspaper journalists (long may it last). She's fine — arguably even a slightly weak version of the kick in the arse the programme requires. Perhaps, as a feature writer, Power has an instinctive sense of how to walk through a potentially complex story, and her interviews have the shape that Marian's too often lack.

Finucane is terrific dealing with the focused, straightforward narratives and arguments that are the stuff of 'Liveline'. But get someone in the studio or on the phone with a bit of a life-story to tell, and odds are it will emerge awkward, roundabout, arse-backways even. Unfortunately, they make her do this sort of thing an awful lot.

Marian's autumn Joe Jacob interview was a gem thanks primarily to a simple conceit — the stopwatch running after a putative Sellafield plane crash — which the presenter stuck to, with just-audible wit and an unflappability to contrast with the poor panicking politician.

Many of her other interviews could do with a stopwatch too, but for a very different reason: someone needs to shout 'Stop!' after the first five aimless minutes.

We shouldn't be too harsh; the programme has an astonishing audience for such a short show. The fifty-five-minute length, however, is a big part of Marian Finucane's problem — listeners don't feel a particular show is going to recover from, say, a turgid first item (lots of them, aren't there?). It lacks the pace and variety to make us feel, yes, I'll stick with this, even though this item isn't my cuppa, because at least it'll be bright and breezy and the next one up will probably be better. We're more likely to think, jayzus, even Ian Dempsey would be preferable to this. And by the time we switch back, it's time for Pat Kenny.

And no, it's not all about Marian. Idiosyncratic would be a kind word for the programme's selection of stories — much of the time you can drop the 'syncra' from the middle of that word. A show that should be agenda-setting too often sounds like it picked up its agenda either from last week's Morning Ireland or from the crankiest of crank-calls.

Enough already. The best of us are prone to a slump and there's nothing wrong with Marian Finucane that the radio-heads don't know and can't do something about. As usual, we in the media are probably reading rather too much into relatively trivial declines in the show's JNLR figures.

Meanwhile, for years this column has been mocking Today FM for boasting about relatively trivial rises in its own figures.

This week it boasted yet another one, and frankly, it must be said, the station's series of trivial rises has consolidated into a definite trend. I would still maintain that Today FM's daytime programming is basically rubbish. I would insist that it makes a mockery of the words 'independent' and 'national' to apply them to a business that is in the process of being turned over in its entirety to a foreign media company. (What say we redesignate RTÉ as the 'independent national' broadcaster?) But I have to admit, Scottish Radio Holdings is getting what's shaping up as a sound little earner for its pounds sterling — whether or not it hangs on to Ireland's campest lad, Eamon Dunphy.

If it's big Q quality you're looking for, there's always the BBC. With Beeby indifference to the ecclesiastical calendar, it scheduled 'Pentecost' (BBC Radio 3) before we'd even got to Lent, but I doubt listeners were complaining. The timing was right in other ways; hot on the heels of two TV dramas that dealt with the very public events of Derry in 1972, this was Stewart Parker's exploration of a more private side of the 1974 Ulster Workers'

Actress Gretta Scacchi in the Irish Film Centre promoting her film **The Rage**. *Photograph: Brenda Fitzsimons.*

Council strike in Belfast.

Parker wrote the play's lead roles — mercilessly bickering Lenny and Marian — with Stephen Rea and Frances Tomelty in mind, but this BBC production, fourteen years after the playwright's death, marks the first time these two estimable actors have actually played the roles together. With Laura Hughes and Adrian Dunbar as the friends with whom they shelter on the peace line, and Valerie Lilley as the dead, old woman whose house they occupy, it's an impressive cast all round.

Impressive play, too, with characters who, inevitably, speechify all too freely, but who are tangible characters all the same. In a review, it's easier to quote some great speechifying than to transmit that tangibility: 'It's what I'm good at, isn't it, as you were at pains to point out — trading, buying and selling,' declaims antiques-dealer Marian to Lenny, very early on. 'I don't have to love it, just get on with it. Survival. It's one bloody useful knack, knowing the value of things to people, what they'll pay, what they'll think they're worth — the things that is. The people of course are not worth shit. I didn't have to love them either. You and I tend to diverge on that point, you having all that deep-seeded compassion for anything that snuffles into your shoulder … In my case the embattled bourgeoisie of Belfast was one long procession of avaricious gobshites, hell-bent on overloading their lounge cabinets with any bauble or knickknack, as long as it looked like it cost more than it did, as long as it was showy enough to advertise their grandeur, and their fashionable taste and stylishness, not to mention their absolutely bottomless vulgarity. It was bad enough before the shooting match started, it's grotesque at this point.'

Phew. Amazingly, we like this very un-RTÉ Marian. She's hard on Lenny, and tough on the old bourgeoisie too, but she tries to be terribly nice to the ghost of Lily Matthews. Lily is the Protestant widow who has recently died in her house, and she is none too pleased to see an 'idolator', and a separated one at that, taking her place. But Marian

hasn't moved so much as one of Lily's Coronation souvenirs: 'I've brought nothing with me, see — no Sacred Hearts, no holy water, not even a statue of yer woman.' 'Pentecost' is funny, complete with trombone breaks, but a comedy it ain't. There's all sorts of history and politics percolating around here — personal, sectarian, gender, the works. It's riveting, and while I understand the grief of radio-lovers who want to hear radio-plays, not stage-plays with the lights turned off, I'll definitely make an exception for this one: its dark, brooding Belfast nights, its prim ghost, its head games, are all perfect radio material, and Tomelty is completely and utterly amazing. Maybe Marian could learn something.

THURSDAY, 21 FEBRUARY 2002

Where Are the Protestant Churches on Abortion Poll?

Mary Holland

Where are the Protestant churches when Ireland needs them? Do they have anything to say about the abortion referendum? Or have they forgotten Yeats's proud statement that the community to which they claim to give spiritual leadership is 'no petty people' and that its views should form a part of the public debate.

There have been a few — a very few — contributions from individual Protestant churchmen. Dr John Neill, the Church of Ireland Bishop of Cashel and Ossory, has bravely raised his head above the parapet and criticised the 'serious hypocrisy' of the proposed constitutional amendment, which he described as 'cruel and naïve'.

Archdeacon Gordon Linney has argued, in this newspaper, that the decision to exclude the mental health of the woman as grounds for termination of pregnancy 'violates the fundamental view of the person as a unity of mind, body and spirit'. The

Adelaide Hospital has made clear its reservations on the issue. But from the main body of the Protestant churches, North and South, we have heard nothing. With less than two weeks to go till polling day, this is the dog that hasn't barked. The stance is in dramatic contrast to the Roman Catholic hierarchy's campaign for a Yes vote.

A million copies of the Catholic bishops' statement supporting the amendment, in both English and Irish, will be distributed in Catholic churches across the State. A website on the issue will be updated on a regular basis. On the Sunday before the vote a pastoral letter from each individual bishop will be read at all Masses in his diocese.

The silence of the Protestant churches is all the more curious because we know that representatives of the three major churches gave evidence to the all-party Oireachtas committee's hearings on abortion.

There were differences in emphasis between representatives of the Church of Ireland, the

Taoiseach Bertie Ahern at a press conference in Government Buildings where the Government launched its proposals for constitutional and legislative reform in relation to the twenty-fifth amendment of the constitution (Protection of Human Life in Pregnancy) Bill, 2001. Photograph: David Sleator.

Presbyterians and the Methodists. There were also divisions, as they all readily admitted, within their own congregations. But, taken overall, their arguments followed remarkably similar lines.

In the first place they were at pains to emphasise that they believed in the sanctity of human life and were wholly opposed to abortion in all but the most extreme circumstances. However, there was a consensus that situations could arise in which the termination of a woman's pregnancy would be 'the lesser of two evils'. They varied a little on what these extreme circumstances might be, but most of them appeared to accept that these should include rape, incest or severe foetal abnormality.

What they were agreed on is that abortion is too complex a problem to be dealt with through a constitutional amendment. They made it quite clear that what they wanted was legislation that would give precise legal definitions to the many moral, social and medical details involved. Thus the Rev. H.C. Miller, Church of Ireland Bishop of Down and Dromore, told the committee that his church's view was that 'the constitutional way is not the best method of dealing with this issue'.

Robert Cochran, representing the Methodists, argued that the Constitution was designed 'to lay out broad parameters of social policy'. It was never intended to deal with the detailed circumstances of individual cases, a fact which had been demonstrated by the X and C cases.

Dr Trevor Morrow, at that time Moderator of the Presbyterian Church, argued that it would 'be appropriate for a government representing not only majority but minority opinion' to proceed by way of legislation. Spokesmen for all three churches made the point that they were organised on an all-Ireland basis and that this made their task in giving evidence to the committee even more sensitive.

Their views have been ignored. This is a blatantly sectarian referendum and it is depressing that we have yet to hear a single political leader on this side of the Border oppose it on these grounds. We are much given to preening ourselves with the notion that successive governments have been sensitive to the views of the Protestant minority in this state, and generous in their treatment of them. Ergo, the argument goes, unionists have nothing to fear from the prospect of a united Ireland. Nobody seems able to make the connection that this is precisely what many Northern Protestants do not want to be part of: a state in which the moral teaching of the Roman Catholic Church is given precedence over their equally sincerely held beliefs.

The virtual invisibility of the Protestant churches in the present campaign is very different to their stance in 1983. At that time all of them expressed formal public opposition to the referendum on abortion. Not only that, members of the clergy were willing to speak on public platforms alongside disreputable people like myself.

One of my cherished memories of that time is a speech made by the Rev Victor Griffin, who was Dean of St Patrick's Cathedral in Dublin, which ended with an appeal along these lines:

'Remember Emmet, remember Tone! God save the Republic! Vote No!'

There is still time for the Protestant churches to make their voices heard in this debate. Many of us believe that they have a duty, not only to their own community but as citizens of this State, to do so. But they need to get their skates on. The referendum is less than two weeks away.

SATURDAY, 23 FEBRUARY 2002

One Lord A-Leaping and A-Dashing Downhill

The Saturday Profile: Johnny Watterson and Rachel Donnelly

Few who have plunged the equivalent of fifty floors down a mountain head first at eighty m.p.h. on an inverted tea tray have made such a sane impression. But in Lord Clifton

Clifton Wrottesley at the Salt Lake City Olympics.

Hugh Lancelot de Verdon Wrottesley's dash down the Salt Lake City track on Wednesday, which brought him closer to a Winter Olympic medal than any other Irish athlete since teams were entered in 1992, Ireland has woken up to the skeleton.

The skeleton is fringe material. It is to mainstream sport what haiku poetry is to pulp fiction. Wrottesley's fourth place in the event was astonishing.

The thirty-three-year-old baron was not expected to finish inside the top ten competitors. When in the practice run he claimed the seventh-fastest time, it was seen as an aberration, and when he found himself in the bronze medal position after the first of two runs, he was poised to become the biggest splash of these Winter Olympics.

Wrottesley emerged as a legitimate Irish athlete just before Christmas when he arrived in Dublin brandishing several bottles of the highly acclaimed wine, Chateau de Sours. He had convinced his uncle, Esme Johnstone, the Bordeaux vineyard owner, to sponsor the Irish team, a partnership that was so unusual it landed him on RTÉ's 'Marian Finucane' show.

Descent from James I, a French vineyard and a skeleton run in the Winter Olympics did not add up to a typical Irish package. But like Wrottesley himself, the idea had connections and charm, useful attributes in short supply.

Last July the dashing former Grenadier Guards captain, who served in Northern Ireland, married into one of the wealthiest families in Britain.

'I have been able to rationalise [the Irish tour] now,' he said. 'I served in Crossmaglen, but like many people in the Troubles I have moved on. I like to think Ireland has, too.'

His wife, Sascha Schwarzenbach, is the daughter of Swiss financier Urs Schwarzenbach, who founded Interexchange, Switzerland's largest foreign exchange company. Variously described as a multi-millionaire and a billionare, Schwarzenbach and his family, between sponsoring the top polo events (the Black Bears based at the Guards Polo Club at Windsor Park being the favourite team), can afford to spread themselves around the winter resorts of Europe; St Moritz, where Wrottesley married Sascha, being the favourite.

'I originally came to St Moritz to find out about my father, who died when I was two. He did the Cresta run and the bobsleigh. At one stage he had tried to put together an Irish team in the 1960s but nothing came of it.'

Although he was born in Dublin, Wrottesley spent only a short time in Ireland before moving on to be educated at Eton and Edinburgh University. He is a member of the 'gentleman's club' the Cavalry and Guards in London, but appears to be an infrequent visitor as there are no recent records of his attendance.

Wrottesley — pronounced 'Wroxley' — inherited his title from his grandfather in 1977 when he was nine years old. His father, Richard Francis Gerard Wrottesley, who established a pig farm in Co. Galway after he moved to Ireland from South Africa, was tragically killed in a car accident when Clifton's mother, Georgina, was pregnant.

'Dad died without a will, and I was made a ward of the Irish courts. There wasn't much left after that. He had lived in Galway four to five years before his death.

'We couldn't afford to go back to the UK so we went to Spain where it was more affordable. Then when my grandfather died his money paid for my education.'

The Wrottesley family fortunes in Staffordshire had earlier gone up in smoke after a stately home blaze in the 1950s. His father's funeral took place at St Anne's Church in Dawson Street, Dublin, and Georgina later married a Scots Guards officer.

One of Wrottesley's grandmothers is descended from the Wingfield family, which once owned the Powerscourt estate in Co. Wicklow.

Fittingly, as his celebrity curve rockets in Ireland, it was on the subject of the media that he made his maiden speech in the House of Lords on 18 December 1996.

Garda Tracy Corcoran from Nenagh with newly graduated colleagues at the Garda graduation ceremony in Templemore; 120 new Gardaí were presented with their certificates by the Minister for Defence, Michael Smith. From left: Shane Elliffe (Kildare), Brendan Leamy (Tramore), Nigel Bourke (Swinford) and Damien Broughall (Kildare). Photograph: Frank Miler.

Wrottesley, then only twenty-eight years old, admitted it was a subject he knew little about but thanked his fellow Lords for the opportunity to perform 'a somewhat daunting task'.

Of all the media, the press was 'the most anarchic, the most sensationalist, the most controversial,' but with youthful sensitivity he argued for self-regulation rather than strict new laws, adding: 'To deny to the poet or painter expression of what he or she feels is to impose a form of imprisonment.

'However, I concede that the articles written by many tabloid journalists can hardly be called prose, let alone poetry.'

With a touch of the historian, Wrottesley included the Magna Carta and observations on the media by a judge of the US Supreme Court in 1927 and quoted the French political thinker, Alexis de Tocqueville, all in a four-minute speech.

A Conservative, Wrottesley was not a particularly active member of the Lords, according to family friend and Conservative peer, Lord Glentoran, who won an Olympic gold medal for Britain in the bobsleds in 1964: 'He came in occasionally but he probably knew he wouldn't be there very long.'

Indeed, Wrottesley's time in the House of Lords was short-lived. The Vacher Dod Parliamentary Guide lists among the sixth Baron Wrottesley's special interests electoral and parliamentary reform, but in an ironic twist of fate just three years after he took his seat he lost it when all but ninety hereditary peers were removed under Labour's reform of the Upper House.

'He is quite shy and keeps himself to himself,' said Lord Glentoran. 'He has a serious commitment to everything and takes things extremely seriously. It [his Olympic performance] is a tremendous achievement, but I think he won't be terribly satisfied because of his previous ice experience and he will be working out whether he still has a chance for the next Olympics.'

'What's not known is that he was one of the fastest in the world on the Cresta Run and he only took up the skeleton two years ago, but he is an experienced ice-racer and like me has driven bobsleds.'

The Northern Ireland peer said luck on the day of competition plays a big part in winning medals. 'Luck was against him on the day, both for him and Alex Coomber [who won bronze for Britain in the skeleton bobsleds this week].

'They both went down late in the order, and Clifton's quite light, as she is, and it had been snowing heavily. In the end it becomes a bit of a lottery.'

Wrottesley left the Grenadier Guards in 1995 and is now a yacht-broker in London.

'What struck me about him was how he gave up his time talking to people and explaining everything to them in Salt Lake City.

'He is one of the best athletes I have seen in dealing with people. He's a good talker, very impressive,' said Olympic Council of Ireland president Pat Hickey.

'The Irish colours on his competitor's suit … all that was his own idea. He's a remarkable athlete. When I compare his attitude to some athletes in the summer games, it is unbelievable.'

Naturally his competition outfit came from a German fashion house, Escada, more famous for clothing female celebrities than little known athletes.

The Daily Telegraph recently pegged him as 'more Sloane than Tyrone', a description that after this week may fit less snugly.

His ancestors' names may be traced back to the Battle of Hastings in 1066 and appear in the Domesday Book, but in terms of his Irish qualification … if he could kick a football, Jack Charlton certainly would have selected the gentleman amateur.

Mummy, What's an Abortion?

Kathryn Holmquist

Many adults are feeling frustration, anger, sadness and — while it may seem churlish to admit it — boredom at being asked to address the issue of abortion yet again. But the subject is impossible to avoid, not just for adults, but children too.

With the age of knowledge about issues like sex, suicide and rape getting younger and younger, parents are finding themselves in the painful position of having to answer the kind of questions they wish their children didn't have to think about.

What do you say to your children when they pipe up from the back of the car and ask: 'What's an abortion, Daddy?' How do you respond when your child sees confusing posters that say, 'Vote Yes — Protect Women and Children' and 'Vote No — Babies Will Die'?

'These are issues that a child's mind cannot encompass,' says Ms Marie Murray, director of psychology at St Vincent's Hospital, Fairview.

This article, infused with the thoughtful advice of a psychologist experienced in family therapy, is meant to provide neutral guidance that all parents can use, no matter what their personal beliefs.

'What do you say when they ask what's abortion, what's rape and what's suicide?' Ms Murray asks. 'Such is the world in which we live and in which our children live, that we, as parents, must perform damage limitation exercises in relation to the levels of inappropriate material placed before the child. Once again children are being exposed to material that isn't in their best interests or which they cannot comprehend.'

Parents will of course speak to their own children according to their own value systems and beliefs. However, the manner in which they do so will have an impact on the children.

Begin with an understanding of your child's age and stage of intellectual and emotional development. What is your particular child's capacity to understand?

Some children may not have noticed the raging public debate and may not be curious, in which case don't invite trouble by asking your children questions. Other children may be extremely curious or upset and need your help. The first thing you need to do is to find out how much your children already know or think they know. They may have drawn conclusions from seeing posters or friends may have offered the schoolyard versions. You may be happy or unhappy with the information they have but the most important thing is to find out what they know.

You also need to find out if your children are upset or afraid as a result of this information or mis-information. Your children may even be feeling embarrassed to talk about it and ashamed that they know these secrets of the adult world in the same way that children are often embarrassed to talk to their parents about sex. Once you know where your children are at you need to let them know it is okay to ask questions. When they do, answer their questions in an honest, sincere and succinct way that provides just enough information to allay fears but no more than the young people are ready for.

However, if you are caught off guard, do not feel pressured to answer right away. Think about the language in which you will discuss it before you sit down with your children for a heart-to-heart. Ask yourself what is the likely impact on your children of the words that surround the debate; words like suicide, save, protect, rape and kill. Parents will want to discuss this in a manner that is sensitive, gentle, compassionate and age appropriate. So how do you do this?

Answer the young people's questions with calm and respect for their questions. Praise them for asking you because parents like to help children to understand important issues.

Remember that a simple answer is often all that

Referendum posters on Henry Street. Photograph: Alan Betson.

is required. There is always the danger of giving far more information than the children were seeking.

Before defining any word for children ask them what they think the word means. Take that as the basis of your reply.

For example, Ms Murray suggests that suicide can be described as 'a really sad and very unusual situation in which someone doesn't feel at all happy and even wants to die'. Rape can be described as 'when someone attacks and really hurts you'. Abortion may be described as, 'when people decide, for different reasons that a baby

Residents of Ringsend are rescued from their houses by foremen during the flooding of the Dodder River. Photograph: Alan Betson.

shouldn't be allowed to grow in its mummy's tummy and that is a very sad thing for anyone to have to think about, which is why everyone should be very kind to anyone with this worry'.

Your children may also want to know why adults are fighting about abortion. Explain to your children that everyone wants to do what they think is right for mothers and babies but they have different ideas about what that is.

At the end of the day as with any value and belief that you hold you will have to share it with your children in a way that is gentle, respectful, sensitive and for the child's higher good.

As a parent, one of your greatest fears may be that your children will hurt by knowing too young about words like abortion, rape and suicide. Don't worry — your children will not be hurt as long as you, the parent, are available to help them deal with the information.

SATURDAY, 23 FEBRUARY 2002

French Try to Make Sense of Irish Version of *The Scarlet Letter*

Lara Marlowe

The Irish couple had already left in the ambulance for Broussaille Hospital in Cannes when French gendarmes found the baby boy, wrapped in a hotel towel inside a plastic bag, hidden behind a curtain in the hotel corridor.

'I just saw a beautiful baby and that's it,' Mr Peter Van Santen, the director of the Miramar Beach Hotel in Théoule-sur-Mer, said.

In a dozen interviews about the tragedy, it was the only time I detected sadness. 'Unfortunately,' Mr Van Santen's words trailed off, 'without life.'

Since the gendarme's macabre discovery on the morning of 12 February, the lives of a twenty-one-year-old Irish woman and her thirty-five-year-old boyfriend have been altered forever.

In Ireland, politicians, the church hierarchy and the media have taken intense interest in the tragedy, which in other circumstances might have been treated as a routine criminal case on the French Riviera.

The young woman has been indicted on suspicion of murdering the infant, for which she risks life in prison.

Her boyfriend is in pre-trial detention in Grasse prison while he is investigated for 'failure to assist a person in danger' and 'failure to denounce a crime'.

If charged, tried and convicted, he could face a ten year prison sentence.

In some ill-defined way, the mysterious death of the baby boy on the Côte d'Azur seems trammelled up with the 6 March abortion referendum. (Ironically, the boyfriend's bail hearing will probably take place on the same day.)

To reduce it, as one source did, to 'an Irish obsession with anything involving Fallopian tubes', seems simplistic. The issues at stake make the story more resonant of Nathaniel Hawthorne's *The Scarlet Letter* or Theodore Dreiser's *American Tragedy* than a lurid tabloid tale.

For nine months, the young woman kept her unwanted pregnancy a secret from everyone, including — according to his family, friends and lawyer — from her boyfriend.

Not once did she consult a doctor, and she nearly died of a massive haemorrhage while giving birth.

She is still recovering in the penitentiary wing of Pasteur Hospital in Nice. Some time in the near future, probably next week, the young woman will be interviewed by the investigating magistrate, Judge Thierry Laurent.

In about a year from now, Judge Laurent will decide whether to send the Irish couple to the Alpes-Maritimes assize court for trial by nine jurors and three magistrates.

In the deposition that the young woman made to gendarmes on 13 February, she said her boyfriend did not know she was pregnant and that he was not the father of the infant. No one has broached the question of who the father might be. The paternity issue will be resolved by a DNA test in March.

Whether or not her boyfriend knew she was pregnant is crucial to his defence. Her sister, the airline staff who twice allowed her to board planes on 11 February, the hotel receptionist and the room service waiter did not realise she was pregnant.

She told friends and relatives who expressed concern at her weight that it was the result of an eating disorder, caused by homesickness and loneliness from her move to Luxembourg.

But could her boyfriend have failed to know she was expecting? Mr Gerard-Georges Girard, his lawyer, says the infant was conceived in May or June of last year, at a time when the couple were not together.

French police have begun an in-depth investigation into their personalities and relationship, which according to Mr Girard was founded on 'a certain sense of propriety'.

The boyfriend had been her teacher at convent school, where she may have become infatuated with him. They apparently started dating much later.

Her distraught parents have rented an apartment in Nice to be near their daughter. French law requires that they lodge a written request each time they want to see her. The judge has promised not to refuse requests from them, but this week they allegedly heard their daughter crying 'Mammy, Mammy,' and could not go to her.

Her boyfriend is described as an almost saintly person who was never a womaniser. Although his family is affluent, he had no interest in money and devoted his spare time to charity work in the east and north of Ireland and the former Soviet Union.

Those close to him were shocked by what they thought were psychologically cruel and tasteless methods of interrogation.

She clearly attempted to hide the birth from him. 'It was as if she didn't want the person accompanying her to know she had delivered the baby,' the hotel director told me the day after the infant's death.

Mr Girard says that when she went into labour on the night of 11 February, she told her boyfriend that her bloated stomach and pains were caused by digestive problems.

'She walked the halls of the hotel while he waited up,' the lawyer explained. 'Around 4 a.m., she came back to bed, and she seemed better. He fell asleep.

'He woke up between 10 and 10.30 a.m. By then it was over. She came back covered in blood,

Is Fianna Fáil doing enough to see him home safely?

The Fine Gael leader Michael Noonan at the launch in Dublin yesterday of a major billboard campaign by the party in the run up to the general election. Photograph: Frank Miller.

No referendum will change the reality of the nineteen women who travel to the UK every day for abortions. These women have health care needs that GPs (not psychiatrists) face every day. These patients and doctors need support, not regressive and dangerous legislation.

We need to defeat the referendum and then start to address these needs with a high-quality, accessible, GP-led service. — Yours, etc., Dr Mary Favier, General Practitioner, Dr Peadar O'Grady, Child Psychiatrist, Doctors for Choice, PO Box 6862, Dublin 2. 19 February 2002.

Sir, — On posters around Dublin for the referendum one can see: 'Pro Life Movement. To Protect Mothers and Children. Vote Yes.' And: 'Babies will die. Vote Pro-Life. Vote No.'

I am totally bewildered by all this propaganda. If I vote Yes I could be voting No. This type of confusion is just not on.

An Taoiseach Bertie Ahern, as leader of this country, should get on the television and explain what is going on and tell us simply what all this means. This is too serious a subject to be mucking about with innuendo. — Yours, etc., Ms Terry Healy, Hartwell Green, Kill, Co. Kildare. 20 February 2002.

Sir, — I never thought I would be in a position where the Government, legislature and Catholic Church of this country would violate my rights and dignity. There will have been many women in this position before, but today I must voice my anger and suffering at the inhuman treatment of women in this State.

Recently I was told that the sixteen-week-old foetus I was carrying had a severe chromosomal abnormality, incompatible with life, which would result in death soon after birth. This was a very much wanted baby, but the trauma of this news was vastly exacerbated by the thought of being forced to carry to full term a foetus which would never know extra-uterine life.

If charged, tried and convicted, he could face a ten year prison sentence.

In some ill-defined way, the mysterious death of the baby boy on the Côte d'Azur seems trammelled up with the 6 March abortion referendum. (Ironically, the boyfriend's bail hearing will probably take place on the same day.)

To reduce it, as one source did, to 'an Irish obsession with anything involving Fallopian tubes', seems simplistic. The issues at stake make the story more resonant of Nathaniel Hawthorne's *The Scarlet Letter* or Theodore Dreiser's *American Tragedy* than a lurid tabloid tale.

For nine months, the young woman kept her unwanted pregnancy a secret from everyone, including — according to his family, friends and lawyer — from her boyfriend.

Not once did she consult a doctor, and she nearly died of a massive haemorrhage while giving birth.

She is still recovering in the penitentiary wing of Pasteur Hospital in Nice. Some time in the near future, probably next week, the young woman will be interviewed by the investigating magistrate, Judge Thierry Laurent.

In about a year from now, Judge Laurent will decide whether to send the Irish couple to the Alpes-Maritimes assize court for trial by nine jurors and three magistrates.

In the deposition that the young woman made to gendarmes on 13 February, she said her boyfriend did not know she was pregnant and that he was not the father of the infant. No one has broached the question of who the father might be. The paternity issue will be resolved by a DNA test in March.

Whether or not her boyfriend knew she was pregnant is crucial to his defence. Her sister, the airline staff who twice allowed her to board planes on 11 February, the hotel receptionist and the room service waiter did not realise she was pregnant.

She told friends and relatives who expressed concern at her weight that it was the result of an eating disorder, caused by homesickness and loneliness from her move to Luxembourg.

But could her boyfriend have failed to know she was expecting? Mr Gerard-Georges Girard, his lawyer, says the infant was conceived in May or June of last year, at a time when the couple were not together.

French police have begun an in-depth investigation into their personalities and relationship, which according to Mr Girard was founded on 'a certain sense of propriety'.

The boyfriend had been her teacher at convent school, where she may have become infatuated with him. They apparently started dating much later.

Her distraught parents have rented an apartment in Nice to be near their daughter. French law requires that they lodge a written request each time they want to see her. The judge has promised not to refuse requests from them, but this week they allegedly heard their daughter crying 'Mammy, Mammy,' and could not go to her.

Her boyfriend is described as an almost saintly person who was never a womaniser. Although his family is affluent, he had no interest in money and devoted his spare time to charity work in the east and north of Ireland and the former Soviet Union.

Those close to him were shocked by what they thought were psychologically cruel and tasteless methods of interrogation.

She clearly attempted to hide the birth from him. 'It was as if she didn't want the person accompanying her to know she had delivered the baby,' the hotel director told me the day after the infant's death.

Mr Girard says that when she went into labour on the night of 11 February, she told her boyfriend that her bloated stomach and pains were caused by digestive problems.

'She walked the halls of the hotel while he waited up,' the lawyer explained. 'Around 4 a.m., she came back to bed, and she seemed better. He fell asleep.

'He woke up between 10 and 10.30 a.m. By then it was over. She came back covered in blood,

Robert Sweeney, the Mary's College prop, sings loudest with his team mates after they defeated Blackrock in the Leinster Senior Cup at Donnybrook. Photograph: Cyril Byrne.

and that's when he really got worried. The entire delivery happened out of his sight and knowledge.

'While he was asleep on the sixth floor, she gave birth alone, in the [public] toilet on the second floor.'

Mr Raymond Doumas, the public prosecutor whose recommendations Judge Laurent followed in initiating proceedings against the Irish couple, admits it is 'probable' that she tried to hide the delivery from her boyfriend.

'But he couldn't not see what was going on. You cannot give birth and hide it from the person you share a bed with.'

The prosecutor believes the infant died of suffocation when he was sealed inside the plastic bag.

The pathologist's report, expected next week, will prove it, he says. 'The alveoli in the lungs have a certain look — it can be verified in an absolutely scientific manner.' If she committed no crime, then the charge of 'failure to denounce a crime' will not hold up against him.

'We don't know if the results of the pathologist's report will be very affirmative, or nuanced,' says Mr Girard.

One question obsesses Mr Doumas. If, as she claimed in her deposition, the infant died of natural causes, how did it come to be hidden in a plastic bag on the sixth floor hotel corridor?

'It doesn't add up,' he says. 'If it was an unfortunate accident, they should have found the infant in the toilet where she had just given birth — not four floors up. I want to know who put it there.'

Rarely has a criminal investigation been fraught with so much potential for Franco-Irish misunderstanding.

The Irish couple's families may be quick to blame French authorities for what they see as bungling or unfair treatment — to which the French are likely to reply with memories of the botched Toscan du Plantier case.

And although the events at the Miramar Beach Hotel could have happened anywhere, the French have interpreted her denial of her pregnancy as a symptom of Irish inhibitions.

Ms Delphine Girard, the boyfriend's other lawyer, said she was stunned by telephone calls she received from the media in Ireland.

'They were so eager to condemn her,' she explains.

'No one tries to put themselves in her place. She's a young woman in distress, who's starting out in life with an enormous handicap.'

Ms Girard, who lived briefly with a family in Dublin as a teenager, believes that had the young woman been from any country other than Ireland, she might have sought help from a family planning clinic.

'She feels shame towards her parents, towards society and towards the church,' Ms Girard added.

'She's become a pariah. Even if she is not judged in court, she has already been judged morally by the society in which she lives, and which she grew up in.'

(The man was released on 20 April, and the woman on 24 April.)

Letters to the Editor
February 2002
Abortion Referendum

Sir, — As a feminist, I have never been more disgusted with an advertising campaign than with Labour's posters advocating a No vote in the abortion referendum.

'Let's trust women — protect women's right to life — vote no.' This is a disingenuous and cheap attempt to scare people into voting No and allowing widespread abortion in this county.

I am a Leaving Certificate student and believe, from listening to what all the leading medical and psychiatric experts in this country have to say, that deliberate abortion is never necessary to save women's lives. All the medical treatment needed to save a woman's life is allowed under the referendum. Ireland

has the best record in caring for pregnant women in the world without having the extensive abortion regime that Labour wishes dearly for.

Labour have conveniently disregarded all the evidence from both Britain and the US, where many women have died as a direct result of abortion procedures and many more suffer long-term consequences of abortion such as post-abortion syndrome and other physical problems.

It's time Labour started to really care for women and offered them choices other than abortion, which only damages and betrays women — Yours, etc., Mary Dillon, Ballymahon, Co. Longford.
18 February 2002.

Sir, — On behalf of Doctors for Choice, I wish to respond to the recent statement from Professors Clare and Casey in support of the proposed amendment to the Constitution. They state that abortion is not a psychiatric issue. As doctors we disagree.

Professors Clare and Casey are out of touch with the reality of medical practice in Ireland. Women who seek abortions are seen almost exclusively by general practitioners, not psychiatrists. GPs frequently see women who have significant psychological distress when faced with a crisis pregnancy. In rare cases this will include a risk of suicide (as in both the X and C cases) if there were to be an enforced continuation of pregnancy.

Women currently solve their difficulties by exercising their right to travel to the UK. This requires health and financial resources. By supporting this amendment Profs Clare and Casey agree with the prohibition of a termination of pregnancy for a woman who is suicidal and who is unable to travel for medical or financial reasons.

Secondly, this amendment, if passed, will for the first time allow the prosecution and imprisonment for twelve years of any woman who procures an abortion in this country, even if self-administered. Do Profs Clare and Casey support the imprisonment of vulnerable and distressed women? This is unprecedented in current medical practice and is itself a reason to vote No to the amendment.

The Fine Gael leader Michael Noonan at the launch in Dublin yesterday of a major billboard campaign by the party in the run up to the general election. Photograph: Frank Miller.

No referendum will change the reality of the nineteen women who travel to the UK every day for abortions. These women have health care needs that GPs (not psychiatrists) face every day. These patients and doctors need support, not regressive and dangerous legislation.

We need to defeat the referendum and then start to address these needs with a high-quality, accessible, GP-led service. — Yours, etc., Dr Mary Favier, General Practitioner, Dr Peadar O'Grady, Child Psychiatrist, Doctors for Choice, PO Box 6862, Dublin 2. 19 February 2002.

Sir, — On posters around Dublin for the referendum one can see: 'Pro Life Movement. To Protect Mothers and Children. Vote Yes.' And: 'Babies will die. Vote Pro-Life. Vote No.'

I am totally bewildered by all this propaganda. If I vote Yes I could be voting No. This type of confusion is just not on.

An Taoiseach Bertie Ahern, as leader of this country, should get on the television and explain what is going on and tell us simply what all this means. This is too serious a subject to be mucking about with innuendo. — Yours, etc., Ms Terry Healy, Hartwell Green, Kill, Co. Kildare. 20 February 2002.

Sir, — I never thought I would be in a position where the Government, legislature and Catholic Church of this country would violate my rights and dignity. There will have been many women in this position before, but today I must voice my anger and suffering at the inhuman treatment of women in this State.

Recently I was told that the sixteen-week-old foetus I was carrying had a severe chromosomal abnormality, incompatible with life, which would result in death soon after birth. This was a very much wanted baby, but the trauma of this news was vastly exacerbated by the thought of being forced to carry to full term a foetus which would never know extra-uterine life.

The current media focus on the forthcoming abortion referendum has thrown into sharp relief the very real lack of attention to the substantive issue of fatal abnormalities in the unborn, and the mental and physical detrimental impact on the mother.

The coincidence of the carers' dispute was a further reminder of the forgotten in this society, the people who cannot function outside an institution and the parents who cannot cope.

I am a self-employed professional, I have two sons aged twelve and ten, who would welcome a baby brother or sister, but who also need and deserve my full attention. They will never see that baby — but why should they also suffer the excessive trauma visited on their mother by Irish legislation?

All three of us are citizens of a State which is turning its back on the reality of the suffering and family distress caused to the living. I pay for private health care and insurance in this country, yet in order to bring about a dignified and healthy conclusion and safeguard my mental well-being my partner and I are forced to secretly seek contact numbers, book flights and accommodation, take trains and taxis to a strange hospital in a foreign city, to meet strange medical staff who see me as yet another statistic of the Irish problem, to be sent back to this country where there is no compassion — or else to carry on for a further five months, with all the attendant mental and physical strain, knowing that there will be a burial and not a baby to look forward to.

If there is a constitutional requirement to hold a referendum, I appeal, on behalf of the hundreds of women who undergo this untenable trauma every year, for recognition of severe foetal abnormalities as a case for humane intervention. It is a risible irony to allow the obstetric profession to carry out amniocentesis tests which identify these chromosomal abnormalities, and then demand that the harrowing results be ignored.

I do not advocate social abortion on demand. This, in my opinion, is a very separate issue.

I am angry that men I do not know and who don't know me, people like Des Hanafin and William Binchy and others who have been complicit with Fianna Fáil governments and the Catholic Church, have decided that my body is their demesne; that they have the right to decide how my family will cope with this very real tragedy; that, regardless of the emotional and physical distress for us, I must do what they want; that their bigoted will rules my body.

They are all instrumental in perpetuating a very real human misery, with which I have tragically come face to face.

I want to hear the response of the Taoiseach, the Tánaiste, the Attorney General, Cardinal Connell, to this specific aspect of the issue of the unborn. On behalf of other women and families who have suffered, I want to know this issue will be prioritised, addressed and resolved between the legislature and the medical profession outside of the current referendum marketing extravaganza.

The only people who will benefit from the obscene proliferation of posters and glossy leaflets are PR companies and printers. Neither a Yes nor a No vote will change the situation about which I write, but Yes will further criminalise anyone who tries to help. How backward can we be? — Yours, etc., Deirdre de Barra, Clonskeagh, Dublin 14. 25 February 2002.

MONDAY, 4 MARCH 2002

ASTI Leadership Continues to Go on War Footing

Seán Flynn

On the eve of a new rash of industrial action, you might think that the average teacher this weekend was looking forward to giving the Government a bit of a bloody nose. In fact, the reverse appears to be true. The comments of one experienced south Dublin teacher were typical.

'Most of us are totally fed up with all of this agitation. We don't want to worry parents or worry the kids in the run-in to the exams. We just want to get on with our jobs.'

In the past week, a small number of schools have been in contact with ASTI headquarters expressing alarm about the ban on supervision. Further complaints seem likely if there is serious disruption and schools are forced to close in the coming weeks.

The ASTI has recent experience of a grass-roots revolution. Last year, there was widespread anger when the executive refused to give members an opportunity to vote on the Labour Court document on pay. There was further anger months later when they were denied a vote on the Government's offer on supervision.

It was partly in response to this anger that the leadership conducted an extensive survey of members before Christmas. More than seventy per cent took part in the survey which provides the most accurate picture of opinion within the union. The results bear repetition.

Members were massively against further industrial action which would disrupt or close schools. Some seventy-four per cent defied the ASTI leadership by favouring co-operation with the benchmarking pay body. Teachers said they wanted to ban co-operation with new Department of Education programmes and other small-scale protests.

In summing up the mood of members in January, the ASTI's journal, *Aistir*, said members wanted 'non-disruptive action which targets Government'.

In this context, parents — and indeed many teachers — must wonder why the ASTI is again on a war footing this morning. The reason is because

Shelbourne players engulf Owen Heary on scoring the second goal for Shelbourne in the Eircom National League match with Shamrock Rovers at Tolka Park. Photograph: Eric Luke.

the results of this survey continue to be ignored by the leadership.

The ASTI is largely controlled by the 180-member Central Executive Committee (CEC) and the small, still more influential Standing Committee. The union maintains that these structures allow it to reflect feelings on the ground.

However, the union — like other trade unions and indeed political parties — is suffering because of the waves of apathy among members. Attendance at ASTI branch meetings is pitiful; less than ten per cent in some cases.

Inevitably, a small group can come to control the agenda but since others do not bother to get involved, they can scarcely complain. The ASTI, says one hardline member, is 'no more or no less democratic' than any big trade union.

Democracy in the ASTI is not helped by the fact that members are still obliged to vote at their branches rather than in schools. This makes it difficult for those who commute a long distance to school every day to participate in the union's democracy.

In recent months there has been solid evidence of the grass-roots drifting away from the union after the troubled pay campaign. Less than a quarter of members voted in a ballot on non co-operation with new Department programmes. Just over half bothered to vote when the supervision offer of €34 an hour was rejected by members last month.

The supervision offer was rightly condemned by many teachers because the payment was non-pensionable. It was also rejected by the Teachers' Union of Ireland (TUI) but, whereas the TUI saw the rejection as a bargaining chip in negotiation, the ASTI took a more hardline stance.

Its executive voted for a ban on supervision, but it also tabled four new demands including, in a bizarre twist, retrospective supervision payments for all retired teachers.

Commenting on this, one education source said the bar had been set 'impossibly high' by people who had 'no interest' in a negotiated settlement.

This weekend, the union's executive voted eighty-seven–sixty-nine to rule out any further talks on supervision until its thirty per cent pay claim is resolved.

The supervision issue now seems firmly deadlocked even though the Minister for Education, Dr Woods, has at last opened the way for pensionable payments. His response was welcomed by the TUI and the INTO, but the ASTI in characteristic fashion continues to fight on.

At this stage, it is not clear when ordinary members of the union will get another chance to have their say.

Not all members of the union's leadership are happy with the turn of events. The general secretary, Mr Charlie Lennon, and the union president, Ms Catherine Fitzpatrick, would prefer a more nuanced and less confrontational approach, but there is little tolerance of their views amongst the hardliners.

A leaflet which was harshly critical of both was sent anonymously to schools and the media last month. Others who have spoken out have also been targeted.

Mr Pierce Purcell, a former union president who has urged it to return to 'mainstream union activity', is facing possible expulsion and/or disciplinary action.

WEDNESDAY, 6 MARCH 2002

Contract for Aquatic Centre Awarded to Shelf Company

Arthur Beesley

The contract to operate the national aquatic centre at Abbotstown, Dublin, was awarded to a dormant London-registered shelf company with assets of £4 sterling (€6.54). The company, Waterworld UK, took only a 5.1 per cent shareholding in the

Irish entity which will run the centre, Dublin Waterworld.

The winner of the thirty-year contract could gain annual profits of about €1.9 million according to informed estimates which suggest the contract could be worth about €57 million. It is understood the Government was advised in June 2000 that the contract should be awarded to a management team or organisation with 'significant experience and a proven track record' of running centres of a similar scale internationally.

But Waterworld UK filed dormant accounts for the period to 31 May 2000. That month work on the eight-acre site began on foot of a letter of intent from Sports Campus Ireland, the Government agency established to develop a stadium at Abbotstown. The formal bidding process began in July 2000 and Waterworld UK was selected in December 2001. Its partners were the building firm Rohcon and S&P Architects.

Following a query from *The Irish Times* last night the Tánaiste, Ms Harney, said she had sought clarification from the Minister for Tourism, Sports and Recreation, Dr McDaid about the award of the contract. She said: 'I would be very concerned at any suggestion that a £4 dormant shelf company with no apparent track record or trading record could have won a competitive tender.'

Dr McDaid's spokeswoman — responding to the same query — said his department was 'not aware' that Waterworld UK was a dormant company. The Government approved the contract in January 2002, she said.

The broader Abbotstown initiative, dubbed the 'Bertie Bowl', is on hold after a High Point Rendel report estimated its cost at £704 million (€894 million), about twice the £350 million projected by Campus Stadium Ireland.

Waterworld UK is registered at Eight Grays Inn Square in London, the address of solicitors Cooke Matheson. Its registered number is 3367220. According to dormant accounts filed in the Companies Registration Office in London, it

had assets of £4 in 2000 and 1999. Shares were held by a firm registered in the British Virgin Islands, Ealing Trading Corp.

Filings in the Companies Registration Office in Dublin say that Waterworld UK subsequently took a £5 shareholding in Dublin Waterworld, whose total shareholding was worth £98. Mr John Moriarty is Dublin Waterworld's majority shareholder. Director of a Kerry-based firm, Moriarty Civil Engineering, he holds £59 worth of shares in Dublin Waterworld. Shares worth £19 are held by Mr Kieran Ruttledge, who is chief executive of Tralee Aquadome. Mr Liam Bohan, a former international swimmer, holds shares worth £15.

When Mr Moriarty was asked whether it was unusual that the expected beneficiary of the contract, Waterworld UK, took only a 5.1 per cent shareholding in the operating company, he said: 'It was stated in the bid that the directors of the operating company would include Kieran Ruttledge and Liam Bohan. These were the only two people named in relation to the operating company.'

Stating that the arrangements were confidential, he would not explain why Waterworld UK had apparently divested its rights to the benefits of the contract. A director of Waterworld UK, Mr Roger Currie, also declined to answer this question. Describing himself as an 'international consultant' to the waterpark industry, he said 'any question regarding operating detail' should be asked of Dublin Waterworld.

Mr Moriarty said: 'Waterworld UK was active through the work of its directors and this company was to be used as a vehicle for promoting the bid for the National Aquatic Centre. It was clearly stated in our bid that a new company would be set up to operate the centre. When the bid was under consideration we incorporated Dublin Waterworld Ltd.'

Campus Stadium Ireland said: 'The consortium bid made it clear that it was always intended to establish an Irish-based operations company. That company has now been established and is

Sonia O'Sullivan in Dublin for the World Cross Country with her daughters Ciara and Sophie. Photograph: Patrick Bolger/INPHO.

called Dublin Waterworld.' Rohcon declined to comment. S&P Architects said the arrangements between Waterworld UK and Dublin Waterworld 'are a matter for themselves'.

(*On 26 March the chairman of Campus Stadium Ireland, Mr Paddy Teahon, resigned following the controversy generated by Beesley's disclosure.*)

MONDAY, 11 MARCH 2002

Good Day for Politics, Bad One for Manners

Gerry Moriarty

How to figure David Trimble? Impossible. He may hold nothing but contempt for the South and by implication its people, but such a remarkable, provocative, complex character. Why does he despise us so? Let's try to supply an answer.

In terms of Ulster Unionist politics Saturday was a very good day for the First Minister, one of the best in recent years. But in terms of good neighbourliness and good manners — well, describing the Republic as a 'pathetic, sectarian, mono-ethnic, mono-cultural state' isn't going to impress too many southerners or, indeed, nationalists in the North.

It's a phrase Ian Paisley would have been proud of. But that's Mr Trimble's sincerely held view. Don't doubt it for a moment.

But why make such hostile, seemingly unnecessary, comments when for once he was on a roll. At the UUC gathering his opponents were a sorry bunch. There was some talk that former MP Mr William Ross or the Young Unionists might try to make life awkward for him. But not a bit of it, he had a free run. Why? Because his opponents knew they would take a hammering.

On Saturday, some dissidents muttered that decommissioning and the proposed amnesty for republican paramilitaries on the run could yet spell the end of Mr Trimble as UUP leader. It hardly made sense. They were blind to the fact that Mr Trimble had out-manoeuvred them.

And this is how. In the first instance, the amnesty is a matter for the British government. In an election period would the sceptics be so foolish as to try to depose Mr Trimble on something he has no control over, and which he will resolutely oppose in the House of Commons? Mr Trimble has pledged to act on decommissioning if the IRA does not deliver. It is possible it could move ahead of the general election in the South to boost Sinn Féin's chances. That would rebound to Mr Trimble's advantage.

But, even if it does not neutralise a few more bunkers, would any Ulster Unionist forgive say a Jeffrey Donaldson or a David Burnside if in August or November or January they called another divisive UUC meeting to force Mr Trimble's hand

against Sinn Féin — just months before Assembly elections when the party must present a unified face to withstand the DUP challenge?

Now, at last, Mr Trimble is taking control of his and his party's direction. Future strategy is his call, not his opponents'.

He could decide to again withdraw his ministers from the executive if the IRA fails to seal more of its dumps. It could even make electoral sense for him to pull such a stroke this time next year, six weeks short of Assembly polling. It might outflank the DUP and energise his supporters.

But it will be for Mr Trimble to decide, not Mr Donaldson nor Mr Burnside. Mr Trimble now has tactical mastery over IRA arms whereas before it had mastery of him. And considering the internecine battles, that is a remarkable achievement.

And there was more. On Saturday he devised the ruse of asking Northern Secretary John Reid to call a Border poll on the same day as the Assembly elections in May next year.

This would be five or six months after the census tells us if it is true that the number of Catholics in Northern Ireland is now in or around the forty-five per cent mark.

Odds are a May 2003 Border poll would again show a majority wish to retain the link with Britain. Mr Trimble says such a result would put the issue to bed for another generation, although that is unlikely because under the agreement seven years must elapse before another poll can be called.

But consider the beauty of a poll from Mr Trimble's tactical perspective. It would bring out middle-ground unionism, particularly the notoriously apathetic bloc which seldom bothers to vote. And if there were Assembly elections on the same day, the likelihood is they would vote for the UUP rather than the DUP.

And if John Reid says there are no grounds for a poll, then Mr Trimble can shrug his shoulders and say: 'It is obvious there is no majority public wish to break the union; let's get on with politics.' Win, win for the First Minister.

So, quite a successful weekend for Mr Trimble. The worm has turned. So why the apparently gratuitous lash at the Republic?

His spin doctors, if he had so instructed, could have explained it as a diversionary tactic to rally the atavistic, sectarian elements in the Ulster Unionist Council.

But no. At a subsequent press conference Mr Trimble was adamant his description of the South was 'the reality of the nature of the State'. Could we have some evidence to justify his portrayal of the Republic? a journalist asked him.

'Maybe you should go there and look at it,' he told the Mayo reporter. The truth of his view was 'self evident'.

Perhaps in the future he will be prevailed upon to elaborate upon his views. His comments are curious considering that in his address Mr Trimble warned against alienating the 'twenty to twenty-five per cent of Catholics who prefer the United Kingdom to a united Ireland'.

So if he despises the South, must he also despise Northern nationalists whose affinities and affection lie with the South? How will that persuade them to vote for the union? But Mr Trimble had no such concerns. 'A lot of Northern nationalists themselves realise that there are significant limitations in the society to the south of us,' he told us.

Here was Mr Trimble going out of his way to explain that his remarks were calculated and studied and intended to offend. Why? It just seems to be a visceral thing with the First Minister for all of the people of Northern Ireland.

WEDNESDAY, 13 MARCH 2002

Israeli Actions Fuel Hatred

David Horovitz

There could be no clearer proof of the depth of the hatred. The bloodied body of the Palestinian man was suspended, by the feet, from an electricity pylon in Ramallah's central square yesterday.

He had been killed as an alleged collaborator, suspected by gunmen from Yasser Arafat's Fatah faction of the PLO of having provided Israeli intelligence with information that, last week, enabled the Israeli army to kill three of its number.

The designer John Rocha launching the Anti-Racism emblem he designed as part of the National Anti-Racism Awareness Programme in Dublin. The Emblem, costing €2, can be worn as a pin, and went on sale nationwide to demonstrate support for a racist-free society. Photograph: Eric Luke.

The very centre of Ramallah was one of the few areas of the West Bank town to which Mr Arafat's loyalists had unfettered access yesterday.

Before dawn, the Israeli army sent a vast influx of troops into Ramallah — almost every Israeli combat fighter, and many reservists, were deployed there or in Gaza yesterday — taking control of most neighbourhoods, upping the military ante another few notches following the major raids on West Bank refugee camps in recent days.

In those earlier raids, hundreds of Palestinian males had obeyed army orders to assemble in main squares, where they were searched for explosives, disarmed of any weapons and, in many cases, blindfolded, handcuffed and questioned over any involvement in violence against Israel.

In Ramallah's al-Am'ari refugee camp yesterday, by contrast, Mr Arafat's Palestinian Authority ordered the local men 'to remain steadfast and to resist occupation'. So Israeli soldiers searched house-by-house and made dozens of arrests, again employing the handcuffs and blindfolds, witnesses said.

On Monday, Mr Arafat had accused Israel of 'Nazi' tactics — relating to instances where soldiers wrote numbers on detainees' arms.

The army's chief of staff, Gen. Shaul Mofaz, promised yesterday to stop the practice, in response to furious criticism by a member of parliament who is also a Holocaust survivor.

The intensified Israeli military action has clearly been timed ahead of tomorrow's scheduled arrival here of the American would-be peace broker, Gen. Anthony Zinni.

Presumably, Israel's Prime Minister, Mr Ariel Sharon, anticipates pressure from Mr Zinni to roll back the troops and work toward a ceasefire. Hence the desperate search now for the key militants who are building the bombs and training the bombers.

However, even Israeli military sources acknowledge that many of the most dangerous men have evaded them.

There can be no doubting the new hatreds fuelled not merely by the dozens of Palestinian deaths in the latest gun battles, but by the mass round-ups, blindfolding and handcuffing, and questioning of Palestinian males.

It may be no great surprise to hear a spokesman in Gaza for Hamas — a group which publicly calls for Israel's elimination — vowing yesterday 'to kill the occupier, to kill him everywhere, every village and every city'.

One of Mr Arafat's most senior advisers, Ahmed Abdel Rahman, could also be heard raging that 'talking peace with the Israelis was a historic mistake'.

Most Israelis feel exactly the same about talking peace with Mr Arafat, consider him to be bent on destroying Israel, and regard the army's activities as an overdue effort to try and thwart the suicide attacks and shootings.

All of which means that Mr Zinni faces a near-impossible task.

The intifada has destroyed the economy of both peoples. It has discredited the moderates. It has brought death and fear to every neighbourhood. Nowhere has been immune — not the café across the street from the Prime Minister's residence in Jerusalem (blown up by a Palestinian suicide bomber on Saturday night, with eleven Israelis killed); not the official offices of Mr Arafat on the Gaza beachfront (destroyed by Israeli missiles a few hours later).

Israel believes that Mr Arafat could still rein in the gunmen from his own Fatah faction and use his tens of thousands of policemen to smash the Islamic militants, if he wanted to, but says he instead chooses to encourage new attacks.

The Palestinians argue that Mr Sharon is bent on settling an old score with his Lebanon war enemy and on permanently reoccupying Palestinian areas.

And the blood-letting goes on.

FRIDAY, 15 MARCH 2002

An Irishman's Diary

Kevin Myers

Traffic is dead, and my life will never be quite the same again. Traffic was a soft-coated Irish wheaten terrier, and a more loyal animal never drew breath. He was steadfast and true, a dog who minded us with a vigilance which suggested that the patron saint of sentries had taken a special interest in shaping his genes.

He was not taught to be a sentinel. It was something he did. If we were on the beach he would find a high spot nearby, and sit there, keeping an eye on all movement, letting out a premonitory woof if there was something he didn't like. Otherwise his vigil was quiet, almost austere; but ceaseless withal.

He had been a typical wheaten puppy, waggy and inquisitive, fearless and friendly. The first other animal that he met after he left his litter was Tensing the cat. He bonded with Tensing in ways that I hesitate to write about in a family newspaper, but since I do not believe in the Himmler-wasn't-such-a-bad-chap school of obituaries, it is time to be fearless and frank.

Some time early in his life — the equivalent of our teens, I suppose — he took to licking Tensing's anus, while Tensing stood there, waving his tail languorously and purring little sighs of bliss. This might go on for an hour or more. You will note that both animals were males. Whether Traffic would have provided the same service to a female cat, I cannot say; and what precise pleasure he, Traffic, derived from this hobby is equally beyond my powers of exegesis.

Nothing that I know about cats suggests that the southern end of their alimentary canals is a proper playground for tongues, though Traffic could spend hour after hour there licking the little aperture, tight as a purse with draw-strings, while its owner hissed and groaned with pleasure. I have been trying to work out how many million pounds I would have to be paid to do what Traffic did with such lolloping enthusiasm, and have come to the conclusion that the number does not exist.

No matter. Until one day Tensing vanished, in the way cats do, and Traffic was beside himself with grief and disbelief. He would never see a cat again without giving chase — presumably in order to provide the same service. Of course, the cats wouldn't know that, and they would invariably turn on him, all gnashing snarl and flashing claw; and Traffic would simply howl with disappointment. If he had been able to speak cat, he would have said: 'All I want is to lick your scrummy …'

Liam Doran, General Secretary of the Irish Nurses' Organisation (INO), speaking at a press conference. Photograph: Dara MacDonaill.

Ben Good and his brothers Val and Alan training Irish Draughts Romell and Russell and Pride and Prejudice in the Phoenix Park in preparation for drawing the State Carriage with the Lord Mayor at the head of the Dublin St Patrick's Day Parade. Photograph: Alan Betson.

But of course he didn't speak cat; and his quest to be the champion lingual explorer of feline back passages came to naught.

And if you think from this tale that Traffic lacked something in the brains department, you would not be far wrong. A shoe — and not a particularly clever shoe — has more intelligence than poor Traffic had. In fact, he was the stupidest animal I've ever come across. A goldfish would learn things more quickly than Traffic would and, moreover, would remember them. Traffic could learn almost nothing.

He once collided with a car, and was sent bowling down the road like a skier tumbling downhill. It taught him nothing. He couldn't see an oncoming car without strolling in front of it and yawning as the wide-eyed driver entered a huge S-skid, his tyres burning a rubber signature on the road.

Aside from sentry and rear entry duty, what did Traffic like? Well, he loved sleeping for hour after hour, snuffling happily in his slumber, especially on the bed beside me. He loved his food. He loved to sit in the car behind the wheel, pretending to be the driver. He loved having huge, five-minutes pisses, a large sensuous smile on his face as he fire-hosed all over an astonished tree. His love of that pastime even survived the occasion when he cocked his leg against an electric fence, and then sleepily opened his bladder. His shrieks of agony rang across four counties.

And most of all, he loved us. His duty was to mind us, to guard us, to protect us; and sometimes to lick us, which was something — especially in the Tensing era — we were not always that keen about. When Tensing was gone, and other cats were repelling his advances, we felt more at ease about these lingual signs of affection.

The Michael Clark Dance Company performing Before and After the Fall *as part of International Dance Festival Ireland. Photograph: Brenda Fitzsimons.*

When he arrived nearly ten years ago, he was the only dog in the house. Over time, especially after we moved to the country, the dog population grew to eight; and he changed from being the playful puppy to becoming the elder statesman and leader of his canine tribe. He might sometimes growl at a dog to remind the other of his or her place in the hierarchy; but he was at the apex, and no one seriously doubted that.

Last week, we noticed lumps in his throat. The vet didn't like what he saw, though I refused to believe it was more than an infection. But it was. He had a malignant melanoma, which had occupied his body almost like an evil spirit possesses its victim. It was everywhere, racing through his system, diminishing and depleting him almost by the hour.

We had him put down on Tuesday. Death took him totally, as death does; but its utter totality is always astonishing. The body remains; but Traffic is gone, and just as conclusively, something precious and irreplaceable has vanished from my life, and for all time.

FRIDAY, 15 MARCH 2002

Perfect Day for Washing as Top AIB Figures Hung Out to Dry

Frank McNally

Conditions were perfect for washing yesterday, especially if you had a lot of dirty linen. Fortunately, the AIB press conference in Ballsbridge was almost as bright and breezy as the weather outside.

And when it got under way at 11 a.m., six executives from the bank's US subsidiary were already hanging out to dry.

Eugene Ludwig, the US banking expert whose report into the Allfirst fraud was being published, accepted that as the separate FBI inquiry proceeded, 'lurid details' might still come out in the wash. His preliminary cycle had uncovered a lot of the dirt, however, and AIB was clearly convinced by his account of how it lost €789 million. Short of giving the job to Lever Brothers, who will apparently give you your money back, they couldn't have done much better.

As the clean-out got under way it was also evident that those hard-to-shift group management people were still in place. In fairness to chairman Mr Lochlann Quinn and CEO Mr Michael Buckley, both had offered to resign, and both appeared suitably chastened yesterday. But their acceptance of criticism only went so far. The bottom line was that there was a difference between accountability, which they shared, and blame, which they didn't. It was a fine line, but it was the line on which the Allfirst executives were strung out.

Mr Ludwig recommended the bank improve its 'risk-control environment'. This may explain why television cameras were banned from the question-and-answer session.

At least the published document was a model of clarity. 'The Ludwig Report' sounded like a John Grisham thriller, and at a tightly-written fifty-seven pages, it was certainly entertaining.

Unusually for a banker, Mr Ludwig was not afraid of colourful language. His report warned of the dangers of trading by 'lone wolves,' and his implication was that Mr Rusnak had been howling at the moon for years.

Nevertheless, the report paints Rusnak as a complex character. A regular church-goer and a 'good family man', he could also be 'arrogant and abusive'.

On one issue, however, there were no contradictions, and the report sums it up in a section heading: 'Mr Rusnak was clever and devious.'

Mr Ludwig accepted that his inquiry was incomplete, since he had been unable to interview the main protagonist. But he had compiled enough evidence of what Mr Quinn called 'collusion by incompetence' in Allfirst's treasury and internal audit, and those responsible had paid the price.

Honourable Thing for the Bishop to Do is Apologise and then Resign

Alison O'Connor

Bishop Brendan Comiskey appeared on camera only very briefly during the BBC2 television documentary on the paedophile priest Seán Fortune shown this week.

Emerging from his car in a Wexford churchyard he was filmed singing his own version of Gloria Gaynor's 'I Will Survive'.

Given the circumstances, a burst of song seemed a little bizarre. However, the choice was curiously appropriate because of the bishop's incredible capacity for survival, despite the controversies which have surrounded his episcopal career.

One of those controversies — the case of Fr Seán Fortune — simply refuses to go away. The horrendous details of the abuse are all too familiar but what marks out the case is the fact that so many complaints were made to the Catholic Church at local, diocesan, and Vatican level about Fortune over many years.

However, from the Vatican down, the church refused to acknowledge its failure over Fortune, a serial abuser who wrecked many lives. The excellent BBC documentary 'Suing the Pope', by reporter Sarah McDonald, featured some of those people. Four men, Colm O'Gorman, Donncha McGloin, Pat Jackman and Damien McAlean, spoke on camera about their abuse. Monica Fitzpatrick from Fethard-on-Sea told how she believed the suicide of her son Peter was linked to Fortune.

Having spent almost seven years observing Dr Comiskey's handling of the fallout from this case, I can only marvel at his failure to deal with the issue. He heard his first complaint about

Fortune eighteen years ago when he was made Bishop in the Diocese of Ferns. After that he heard them regularly from parishioners who were getting increasingly desperate.

However, his statements on the matter, when he has been forced to give them, have sounded like those from a lawyer rather than a Bishop whose primary concern should be pastoral.

His victims have said a number of times they wanted to hear an explanation from the bishop, but their pleas have been in vain. This week his spokesman, Fr John Carroll, said that as a result of the four men publicly identifying themselves on the programme and their comments, Dr Comiskey felt he was permitted to write to them for the first time.

Up to this he had not felt free to do so lest it be 'misinterpreted as seeking to dissuade them from the legal route to justice, which is their natural right'.

However, this logic is nonsense given that two victims, Colm O'Gorman and Paul Molloy (who has since settled his civil action), spoke publicly, and were identified in *The Irish Times*, following Fortune's suicide in 1999.

In fact, Paul Molloy first identified himself to Dr Comiskey in 1988 when he wrote a letter telling the Bishop that Fortune had been abusing him as an altar boy. Paul said he received a letter in reply from the bishop.

Paul had revealed his abuse to the priest who replaced Fortune in Fethard-on-Sea. That priest brought Paul, who was then seventeen, to Dublin where he was questioned by another priest about the allegations.

Unfamiliar with Dublin, Paul believed he had been brought to Maynooth for this inquiry, but in fact, it was All Hallows. When details of the letter became public in 1995 Dr Comiskey, during an interview on RTÉ Radio 1, said: 'There was no such inquiry at Maynooth at any time.'

Dr Comiskey also said he had 'written no such letter apologising for the sexual misconduct of the priest'.

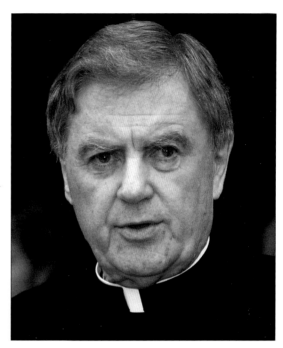

Bishop of Ferns Dr Brendan Comiskey speaking at a press conference outside his Wexford home where he announced that he had tendered his resignation to Rome. Photograph: David Sleator.

But Dr Comiskey was engaging in semantics. The inquiry had taken place in All Hallows and Paul is adamant he received a letter in reply from Dr Comiskey. He cannot remember the exact wording but said the bishop spoke of 'your time of trouble'.

'He could have been talking about my dog that died,' Paul remembers.

His mother Eileen also remembers the letter. 'I cannot believe or understand why he would say he didn't. I read it myself. It's not every day or just anybody who gets a letter from the bishop. Why would I say he sent a letter if he didn't? We have nothing to gain from it. I don't want to cause trouble for the bishop, but I cannot understand this. I told the truth to the Gardaí.'

Paul made his feelings clear in *The Irish Times* in 1999 after Fortune's suicide. 'I feel that the bishop put the welfare of the priest and the image of the

Catholic Church way ahead of his parishioners. I reported this in 1988 but they seemed to do nothing serious about it.' He also asked why the bishop had not made a statement to the Gardaí about the case, despite a request to do so.

At the same time, Colm O'Gorman also spoke publicly, saying the church and Dr Comiskey now had an opportunity to put things right. He is equally unimpressed and angry with the bishop for claiming he hadn't felt free to make contact with him until now because it may have been misinterpreted as trying to dissuade him from taking legal action.

'As far back as 1999 he was being asked to speak out and to act with some honesty and some compassion. Now he's saying one of the reasons he doesn't want to make public statements is that he would hurt the victims and may be seen to try and influence us. But I am a grown, intelligent, articulate person. I don't need him to take care of me. I need to hear his explanation.'

Those who look benignly on Dr Comiskey speak of his battle with alcoholism and the fact that he was in the throes of the disease when trying to deal with Fortune who was an arch manipulator. His victims, not just those who were sexually abused; but also those who were bullied; who had money taken from them; who had curses put on their children; who were forced to pay large sums of money so that sacraments would be administered

Fine Gael Leader Michael Noonan and Labour Leader Ruairí Quinn have tea poured for them by Tánaiste Mary Harney at Leinster House to promote the Alzheimer Society of Ireland's National Tea Day. Photograph: Bryan O'Brien.

or that they would be 'healed', take a less tolerant view.

At any rate the Bishop was treated for his addiction in 1995, and has apparently not taken a drink since. Therefore, he has had almost seven 'dry' years in which he could have made an effort to make some reparation for his lack of action to protect his flock. At this point, the only honourable option would be for him to apologise to them personally and resign.

(Bishop Comiskey resigned on 1 April 2002.)

MONDAY, 25 MARCH 2002

Is Bobby Molloy's Unit Powered Off? Or is He Just Out of Range?

Kathryn Holmquist

In Dún Laoghaire yesterday, I saw a Garda driving with a mobile phone in one hand and a steering wheel in the other. I was going to say something.

'Hi! (ahem) isn't what you're doing illegal?'

Then I noticed his shaven head and intimidating sunglasses and thought better of it. I didn't want to go there. He could be holding three mobile phones for all I care. It still wouldn't be worth it.

And anyway, maybe his defence would be that he was just 'idling'. But idling is driving in my book.

So I called the Garda Press Office. It is as confused as the rest of us at the chest-thumping, pre-general election edict from Bobby Molloy banning the use of mobile phones and — amazingly — radios used by Gardaí and emergency personnel.

Although it's still unclear to the Gardaí, apparently fixed hands-free sets are allowed.

Ahem, Minister, hello there?

Gardaí don't have fixed hands-free sets. Talking into handsets while chasing criminals in cars is what Gardaí do. If Bobby Molloy had ever seen 'Hill Street Blues' (not to mention Chief Wiggum in 'The Simpsons'), he would know that. So now Gardaí will have to pull into the side of the road before phoning ahead to set up road-blocks. Garda chases will become silent movies in the Keystone Cops mould.

The Garda Press Office was barely smothering its cynicism when it said it would 'take a couple more days poring over the legislation' before it had a clue what it meant. Strictly off the record, it was wondering how anybody could make sense of such a nonsensical load of rubbish.

Is the Government not capable of writing an unambiguous piece of legislation? Is it trying to drive us crazy, or merely disorient us in the run-up to the general election campaign? What does it want, a referendum on mobile phone usage?

The Road Traffic (Construction, Equipment and Use of Vehicles) (Amendment) (no 2) Regulations, 2002 reads: 'The driver of a mechanically propelled vehicle that is in a public place shall not hold or have on or about their person a mobile phone or similar apparatus while in the said vehicle, except when it is parked.'

Please define 'on or about their person'. Does that include the glove compartment, the baby seat, the briefcase, the cleavage?

In practice, drivers can't be searched. That solves that then. Obviously this means that the second you see a Garda or the Garda sees you, you both throw your mobile phones under the seat.

Mobile phones with 'hands-free' ear-pieces will not be allowed, but fixed hands-free sets will.

Could somebody please explain the difference between the two methods? Neither one involves hands, unless you're punching in a call, answering a call or checking your messages. In other words, THERE IS NO SUCH THING AS TOTALLY HANDS-FREE MOBILE PHONING.

A referendum's the only answer.

I can see it now: 'Article blah, blah, blah of the Constitution would read: to protect the safety of road-users, mobile phones may be present in the car but not on the person.

'A person may speak into a mobile phone microphone as long as they are not touching the phone as they do so or do not dial or answer a call in preparation for doing so.

'A driver may listen to a mobile phone held to the driver's ear by a passenger. However, the driver's own phone must be switched off, unless it is a hands-free set permanently attached to the dashboard.'

The Bar Library will have fun getting their heads around that one. A 'Prime Time Special' could feature psychiatrists debating the emotional trauma of having a ringing phone in the car which the driver is legally barred from answering, even

though the driver is sitting stationary in traffic (which is how most drivers spend their time).

Could there be mitigating circumstances? Say the driver is waiting for important news, for example, the price of AIB shares? Little Johnny or Imelda's Leaving Cert. results? A reasonable explanation of the shelf company behind Waterworld? The mobile phone is the life support to the beating heart of the economy.

Few drivers will stomach pulling the plug. So cars will be screeching to halts hither and thither on the roadsides.

But wait. The regulation states that 'Parked' means parked in such a location and manner that an offence under the Road Traffic Acts is not committed thereby.

Has Bobby Molloy tried to park lately? Legally, I mean.

Archbishop of Dublin and Primate of All Ireland, Cardinal Desmond Connell, encouraging a Yes vote on the Abortion Referendum when he spoke to the congregation attending mass in the Pro-Cathedral, Dublin. Photograph: Bryan O'Brien.

People will be driving around for twenty minutes at a time so they can find disc-parking spaces, making traffic jams worse than they already are.

People will inevitably risk it and pull in anywhere. The little brown men will have a field day.

Talk about stress. We might as well give up and sit on the side of the road lighting up joints.

Why not? The fine's less.

Letters to the Editor March 2002

Abortion Referendum Result

Sir, — I will definitely be voting No in the general election. — Yours, etc., Gerald Lee, St Agnes Park, Dublin 11. 11 March 2002.

Trimble on the Republic

Sir, — Your edition of last Saturday reported that the Orange Order sends 125 delegates to the Ulster Unionist Council. The order's internal rules make it an offence for members to be a Roman Catholic, to be married to one, to attend a Catholic church, to have Catholic parents or parents who are not married, to allow Catholics to play games or attend dances on a Sunday.

The Order mandates support for the British sovereign only on the basis that she/he is a Protestant and an Orange Order leader famously berated the British Prime Minister for betraying his religion by marrying a Roman Catholic.

It seems surprising, therefore, that the Unionist leader can accuse anyone else of being sectarian, mono-ethnic, mono-cultural or even 'pathetic'. — Yours, etc., Mick Finnegan, Bannow Road, Dublin 7. 12 March 2002.

Bush on Mugabe

Sir, — George 'Dubya' Bush becomes President of the US in a flawed election.

George 'Dubya' Bush says Robert Mugabe's election as President of Zimbabwe is 'flawed'.

Surreal, or wha' ? — Yours, etc., Dermot O'Shea, Meadow Grove, Churchtown, Dublin 16. 21 March 2002.

MONDAY, 1 APRIL 2002

Queen Mother Dies in Her Sleep at 101

Frank Millar and Jonathan Caine

Queen Elizabeth, the Queen Mother, who died on Saturday aged 101, was the most enduringly popular member of the British royal family during the past century. In part the result of her longevity, this derived too from her central role in the affairs of her country in the almost eighty years following her marriage to the future King George VI in 1923.

She claimed her place in the affections of the nation for her steely support of her husband in restoring the monarchy's fortunes after the abdication of King Edward VIII, for the love of divorcee Wallis Simpson, in 1936. But that special relationship which survived to her peaceful death on Saturday was cemented during the Second World War, when the bombing of Buckingham Palace and the royal couple's refusal to leave London enabled them to act as the symbols of national unity during Britain's gravest hour.

Thereafter the popularity of the reluctant king and queen was assured. And until her death, the Queen Mother remained Britain's favourite royal — with the exception of the period of Diana, Princess of Wales' ascendancy. Her unfailing sense of duty even in frail old age contributed to this — enabling her to rise above the failed marriages and

Irish artist Paul Regan with his exhibit 'Black Eyes, The Torch, The Dog' at the opening of his exhibition **Parade***, a series of new works by the artist that crosses sculpture with painting. The exhibition opened at the Guinness Storehouse in Dublin. Photograph: Matt Kavanagh.*

assorted troubles which would again beset the House of Windsor.

Her favourite grandchild, the Prince of Wales, captured popular sentiment in 1998 when he said she appeared 'indestructible'. Locked from public view and forced to use a wheelchair, that she was not well became tragically clear just six weeks ago when the Queen Mother was predeceased by Princess Margaret.

The Hon Elizabeth Angela Marguerite Bowes-Lyon was born on 4 August 1900, the ninth of ten children, fourth daughter of Lord and Lady Glamis, subsequently the Earl and Countess of Strathmore and Kinghorne. Although the birth took place in London, there is no record of exactly where. Staying at Glamis Castle, her father did not see his new daughter for six weeks, by which time the non-registered and non-christened Elizabeth had been taken to another family home, St Paul's Waldenbury in Hertforshire. Lord Glamis was fined 7s/6d for failing to report the birth on time.

Lady Elizabeth's childhood, typical of that enjoyed by the daughter of Edwardian aristocrats, came abruptly to an end with the outbreak of the First World War on 4 August 1914 — her fourteenth birthday. Glamis became a military hospital for the wounded, and Elizabeth was noted for her ability even then to cheer the patients. However, the war was not to be without personal tragedy. In 1915 one of Elizabeth's elder brothers, Fergus, was killed at the Battle of Loos.

Five years later, in May 1920, Elizabeth had her first adult encounter with her future husband, King George V's second son, Prince Albert. He reportedly told Lady Airlie, a close confidante of his mother Queen Mary, that he fell in love that evening.

Within the year the prince, created Duke of York, had secured Queen Mary's approval and proposed marriage. Lady Elizabeth turned him down.

His position aside, the duke had few obvious attractions. He suffered from a serious speech impediment and his health was far from robust. Elizabeth's view appears to have been shared at the time by his father who, on hearing of his son's intentions, reportedly remarked 'you'll be a lucky fellow if she accepts you'. Showing great foresight, Elizabeth's mother, writing to Lady Airlie, sympathised with the duke's plight and observed: 'He will be made or marred by his wife.'

The intervention of Queen Mary and Lady Airlie had the decisive impact on events. Resisting the duke was one thing, resisting the formidable queen was a different matter. In January 1923 the duke again proposed and was this time accepted.

By the early 1930s their lives and those of their daughters, the Princesses Elizabeth and Margaret Rose, seemed settled on the outer fringes of the monarchy. The Abdication Crisis would change all that, seeing the new Queen Elizabeth become the first British-born consort since Tudor times, and the last Empress of India.

Without doubt the deeply religious Duchess of York disapproved of Mrs Wallis Simpson. However, there appears no evidence that she plotted the downfall of the king for the advancement of her husband or herself. And certainly she never forgave Edward VIII for what she regarded as selfishness in forsaking his duty and thrusting the burden of the Crown on her unwilling husband.

'I never wanted this to happen. I'm quite unprepared for it,' George VI exclaimed at the time. But with the sense of duty that would characterise her life, his wife simply greeted the abdication with calm resignation: 'We must take what is coming and make the best of it.'

TUESDAY, 2 APRIL 2002

Answering the Call of the Wild

Rosita Boland

I found myself unexpectedly looking into a window of childhood recently. Wandering round Dublin Zoo on a weekday morning, when it was quiet and uncrowded, I came across one of the chimps' enclosures. Two female

Danielle Donnelly (left) in a 'Marie Claire' bikini and Natasha Byram in swimwear by 'Footprints' from the Clerys summer collection which was launched in Dublin city centre. Photograph: Bryan O'Brien.

chimps were inside, having a snooze in the straw. I read their little biography posted at the front of the enclosure. Both Judy and Betty had been brought to Ireland from Africa in the 1960s: they were, I realised in amazement, older than I am. I must have seen them several times before when I visited the zoo with my uncle as a child: I remember being particularly fascinated by the orang-utan, and the chimps. These same chimps.

Dublin Zoo these days is a surreal place that encompasses this museum-like time-travel experience and also contains one of the best modern developments in a European zoo — the African Plains. In these days when the word 'zoo' is used as a sort of vernacular shorthand for 'crazy place', it's fair to say that many people feel ambivalent about zoos.

Dublin Zoo has been around in some form since 1830, so it has a long-established name. However, sometimes reputations can be difficult to shift over time. If your last visit to Dublin Zoo was longer than a decade ago, you will have a different place in your head to that which exists today.

In my childhood, a visit to the zoo was an uneasy and furtive pleasure, usually because my uncle was so vocal about how unacceptable the conditions were for many of the animals. Due to him, even as a young child, I never felt the elephant, giraffe, rhino or alligator enclosures looked either big enough or exotic enough to be described as 'homely' for those animals.

There is no doubt that conditions in Dublin Zoo were less than ideal for many years of its long history — as, in fairness, they were less than ideal in several other zoos around the world. As late as the 1960s, zoos were offering elephant rides and chimpanzee tea parties, the public was encouraged to feed the animals, and the atmosphere and conditions were not far off a sideshow.

Dutch-born Leo Oosterweghel took up the job as director of Dublin Zoo last October; a zoo which he hadn't visited prior to arriving for the interview. He replaced Peter Wilson, who had

been seventeen years in the job. Dublin Zoo employs some fifty people between keepers, maintanance workers, and administrative support. In summer, those numbers go up. Visitor figures have been rising significantly in recent years: in 1996, they were 423,000; in 1998, 525,000; and in 2000, they hit 601,000.

For the fourteen years prior to his arrival in Ireland, Oosterweghel worked in Australian zoos, both in Perth and Melbourne, in addition to setting up a Wilderness Park in the Northern Territory. Melbourne Zoo is internationally famous for its bioclimatic zones and habitat-focused use of space for animals.

In layman's language, this means species from a certain area, such as Asia, are grouped together. They are kept in an environment which matches as closely as possible that to which they naturally belong.

The Great Flight Aviary, for instance, is an immense netted area of trees and flowers and shrubs, where birds fly freely, and which the public access through a raised, covered walkway, high off the ground. It couldn't be further from the traditional zoo method of birds displayed in separate cages, like curiosities in some cabinet of nature.

'Zoo design used to reflect displays in natural history museums,' says Oosterweghel. 'It was all about filing and exhibiting; all these cages lined up together, one by one.'

So what did he think of Dublin Zoo when he saw it first?

Oosterweghel chooses his words carefully. 'I thought the African Plains were great. I thought that there were opportunities to make other areas of the zoo better. There are strengths and weaknesses, but two attractive things for me were that Dublin Zoo gets Government funding, and that it does good business.'

Six months into the job, Oosterweghel has started making an extensive network of contacts, since he is effectively the public face of the zoo.

He has also been getting a feel for the history

of the zoo — which includes its problems — and getting to know the collection. The current ongoing project is the redevelopment of the old concrete pit enclosure used for the chimps, into a rocky bird island for the bald ibis.

'The priorities for years in the zoo have been with wildlife issues,' he says. 'Visitors and their needs were overlooked. But now we are focusing on their needs, and are improving visitor facilities.' There are plans to renovate the toilets and revamp the relentlessly burgers-and-chips-style restaurant. Both are badly-needed and long overdue.

The thirty-five-acre African Plains area, which opened in 1999, was the biggest single development at the zoo for decades, and has been deservedly popular. A huge lake commands a marvellously un-Irish-looking horizon, fringed by trailing grasses, and pampas. It manages to look both tranquil and alive with latent energy, like a Rousseau painting, where you sense that something dangerous is lurking unseen just out of the frame.

The long circular walk around the lake takes you past enclosures which incorporate the native mature trees and foliage.

There are no bars anywhere; instead, wooden barriers, which are periodically inset with full-length picture windows, giving the illusion of a much closer and more natural contact with the animals — among them, bongos (large antelopes), lions, red river hogs, giraffes, rhinos and hippos. It represents the habitat-based species-grouping approach, which Oosterweghel favours. It's true to say that many zoos worldwide are modifications of older incarnations on the same site. New zoos are seldom created. Is this in part due to the modern sceptical view of zoos as being unsuitable places to retain wild animals?

'It depends on what culture you're from,' Oosterweghel says. 'And how strong the anti-zoo

Leo Oosterweghel, who has been appointed director of Dublin Zoo, poses for photographs with ring-tailed lemurs. Photograph: Brenda Fitzsimons.

lobby is in that country.' He points out that while most north European countries would be supportive of zoos, Britain is not. Eastern Europe has many sub-standard zoos: 'The whole dancing bear thing still exists.' North America has pockets of anti-zoo feeling. He returns to the cultural point again. 'One Brazilian zoo feeds live pigeons to its big cats. That would be very difficult to do in Ireland, for instance.'

'Visitors to zoos want to be closer to the animals,' he says. 'But you have to balance visitor needs with animal needs.' The most popular creatures in the zoo, he says, are seals and penguins (because they're so active) and wild animals, such as the elephant, with the African Plains being the most popular area.

Oosterweghel sees himself staying in Dublin Zoo for the long haul. He appears well-prepared for the task of updating and improving the zoo.

Now fifty-two, he has been working with zoo animals since he was a teenager and became a volunteer at his local Dutch zoo. After that, 'animals became my career', he says. He has combined a lifetime of travel with his study of animals and insects (his speciality), curating and directing zoos in different countries.

'I want Dublin Zoo to be one of the best,' he says, six months into the job, now fully aware of the challenges he faces.

'I'm still on a steep learning curve.' He grins, clearly confident of manoeuvring that precipitous curve.

SATURDAY, 13 APRIL 2002

Yet Again, Irish Politics is Rocked by Repercussions of Sex Abuse Case

Fintan O'Toole

After he raped his daughter for the last time in June 1997, Patrick Naughton tried to rape her again in hospital.

There, in the bathroom, he told her that the story of his assaults on her was out, but he warned that after he spent some time in prison he would be back, and she was not to forget that.

In other words, Naughton was not merely a serial rapist who had begun to prey on his daughter when she was just nine years old, he was also a man who had issued specific threats about what would happen when he got out of prison.

Less than a week after Naughton was convicted, one of the country's most experienced and widely respected politicians, a man who — although technically a junior minister, had a seat at the cabinet table — wrote to the Minister for Justice.

Bobby Molloy's letter to John O'Donoghue of 6 November last showed considerable knowledge of the Naughton case. He was able, for example, to give the precise dates on which the trial had begun and ended, 22 and 31 October.

He knew that the rapist had not been sentenced and that the case was therefore at an extremely sensitive stage, when the judge, Mr Justice Philip O'Sullivan, was thinking through the precise demands of justice.

He chose to pass on a query from Naughton's sister as to whether the rapist who had threatened his daughter could walk the streets for a while longer. 'She is anxious to know if he must remain in prison until the appeal is heard or can he be released and continue to report to An Garda Síochána as previously required of him.'

This is the core of an affair in which, for the second time, after the resignation of Albert Reynolds over the fallout from the Brendan Smyth case, Irish politics has been rocked by the repercussions of child sexual abuse. That core itself is deeply rotten, eaten away by a rampant clientilism in which the political messenger-boy takes no moral responsibility for the message which he is delivering.

Around it, however, there is another layer of scandal. It is the revelation of a system in which this kind of thing is thought of as perfectly normal, a system that for all the sheaves of paper flying around this week, is still wrapped in obfuscation. For it is by no means clear that the full truth of what went on has yet been revealed.

We know that Mr Justice O'Sullivan got two phone calls on 19 March, while he was still considering the appropriate sentence for Naughton; one from the Department of Justice and another from an official in Bobby Molloy's office.

The immediate circumstances of the second call are not fundamentally in dispute. The official inquired of the judge whether he had received a letter from Anne Naughton. There are, however, contradictions and absurdities surrounding the official account of the first call. According to Mr Justice O'Sullivan, the Department of Justice official asked him if he would take a phone call at home from Bobby Molloy concerning the Naughton rape case.

The accounts of both Molloy and O'Donoghue come nowhere close to explaining how a call of this nature could have been made. In the first place, O'Donoghue claims that his officials did not know that the query from Molloy related to a court case at all. If this is so, how could the official have told the judge that Bobby Molloy wanted to speak to him about the Naughton rape case?

It is also difficult to understand how the Department of Justice official who spoke to the judge could have understood that the putative phone call from Molloy would refer to the Naughton rape case. This official, on John O'Donoghue's account, was prompted to call the judge by another civil servant in O'Donoghue's office, who had in turn been phoned by an official in Molloy's office.

This initial phone call specifically referred to Anne Naughton's letters, yet we are told the official who took it 'didn't know that the correspondence related to a case'. It seems extraordinary that someone being contacted in relation to Anne Naughton would not at least ask who she was.

Two other aspects of this call are deeply puzzling. One is so obvious that it has escaped comment. The official account says the Department of Justice official phoned the judge to find out the judge's phone number. This is like putting on your glasses to look for your glasses. In order to phone the judge, the Department official had to have his number already.

The only rational explanation is that the number being sought was in fact the judge's private home number. But here we run up against further inconsistencies.

According to John O'Donoghue, his official only asked for the judge's home number as an afterthought. The query was made only when the judge said he was leaving his office within the next minutes. We are left then with the bizarre claim that the initial purpose of calling the judge was to get the phone number of the office that was being called.

There is a further gaping hole in the official accounts. O'Donoghue's accounts in his written statement and media interviews are consistent: the call was made because Molloy wanted to speak to the judge. Molloy, however, interviewed yesterday on RTÉ's Morning Ireland, was absolutely clear: 'I didn't want to talk to the judge at all.'

If he didn't want to talk to the judge, why was a Department of Justice official trying to get the judge's private number for Bobby Molloy? And how did the official come to believe his job was to get the judge's number for Bobby Molloy?

O'Donoghue's statement says the original contact from Molloy's office on 19 March was to establish 'whether the judge had received correspondence from Ms Naughton'. This is not, however, what the Justice official actually asked the judge. He told Mr Justice O'Sullivan that Molloy or someone on his behalf wished to speak to him.

It is difficult to understand how a civil servant could take a request for information about whether a judge had received correspondence and turn it into a very specific attempt to arrange a call between the judge and the minister unless there was some other stage in this process which has not yet been revealed.

If Mr Justice O'Sullivan had not reconvened his court on Wednesday, the public would have known only that Bobby Molloy had made a query about correspondence from Anne Naughton which was inadvertently directed to the judge himself.

It would not have known that Molloy had been pushing the Department of Justice on the issue since March 2001 or that this pressure had eventually resulted in a call from the Department of Justice to Mr Justice O'Sullivan. In effect, a cover-up would have been achieved.

Even after the judge revealed the involvement of the Department of Justice, however, there were crucial omissions in the account given by John O'Donoghue.

Specifically stating that he was giving this information 'for the sake of completeness', O'Donoghue referred to three letters, two to him from Molloy on 13 March 2001, and 31 January 2002, and one from him to Molloy on 30 April 2001. This account, however, was radically incomplete. It did not mention twelve other letters.

The initial statement issued by O'Donoghue on Wednesday contained a long quote from his own reply to Molloy in April 2001. Yet, when the existence of further correspondence became known on Thursday, John O'Donoghue suggested that the full files had only become available. It seems a remarkable coincidence that the letter which exonerated the Minister was found on Wednesday, while the ones which put him in a less flattering light were not found until the following day.

Nor does O'Donoghue's explanation for the withholding of the other twelve letters — that he did not know of their existence at the time — seem to make much sense. Six of the letters were sent or received since the start of this year. All of them were personal correspondence from one minister to another, not routine pieces of administrative business.

There is, however, one credible explanation for why O'Donoghue would not have remembered these letters: that they were in some sense routine. If the letters were unusual, he would surely have remembered them. Conversely, if he forgot them, it may be because they were simply par for the course. What we may be looking at, in other words, is not a scandalous breach of the normal separation between the executive and the judiciary, but a far bigger scandal: that this kind of thing is common.

What has emerged, particularly in radio interviews this week, is that both O'Donoghue and Molloy felt there was nothing unusual about ministers contacting judges or about ministers from other departments trying to lean on the Department of Justice.

John O'Donoghue, on RTÉ's 'Five-Seven Live' on Wednesday, said: 'There are many, many legitimate reasons why a minister might in fact wish to speak to a judge, many, many legitimate reasons … I know that there are contacts from time to time.' He also said: 'It is true that people from time to time do send correspondence to the Minister for Justice. Various politicians around the country do that, individuals do that.'

Bobby Molloy, on 'Morning Ireland' yesterday, said of the letters: 'I see nothing wrong with any of these letters. I have sent letters like this before to ministers looking for information in response to requests from constituents and I think that other parties will have to admit that they have done the same. I see nothing wrong with it, seeking information.'

It is worth noting in this context that O'Donoghue's reply to Molloy's query about the possibility of Naughton being released was somewhat more nuanced than O'Donoghue has claimed. He actually told Molloy that Naughton could not be considered for temporary release because he had not been sentenced. The implication is that the request could at least be considered if the sentencing process were complete.

We know from the Philip Sheedy affair that John O'Donoghue has received requests for the temporary release of serving prisoners from senior colleagues. No less senior, indeed, than the Taoiseach who, in July 1998, asked him to consider Sheedy's temporary release.

This, after all, is why a woman like Anne Naughton would direct her inquiries about her brother's case through a senior politician rather than simply picking up the phone and asking her brother's solicitor. It is the expectation that expressions of interest from on high will be received with special attention that is at the heart of this scandal.

What we need to know is how often such expressions are in fact made and whether all the judges who receive them have Mr Justice O'Sullivan's courage to speak out.

MONDAY, 15 APRIL 2002

Value for Money in Public Finances High in Minds of Voters

Cliff Taylor

The boom is over, so where has the money gone? The Government's handling of the fruits of the Tiger economy will be a central issue in the forthcoming election campaign.

The Fianna Fáil/PD coalition trumpets the transformation of the economy under its stewardship, while the Opposition claims that billions have been frittered away and a huge opportunity missed.

One thing is for sure; whoever succeeds Charlie McCreevy as finance minister will have much tougher choices to make, as reality returns to the Exchequer arithmetic after a period when the normal rules appeared to be suspended and every budget brought lower taxes, higher spending … and the promise of more to come.

The Minister was not slow to use the opportunity, announcing a string of generous budgets. This strategy involved risks. By injecting so much money into the economy, the Government contributed further impetus to an economy threatened with overheating. Measures such as the big reduction in the top tax rate further pushed up already-soaring property prices.

The generous 2000 and 2001 budgets, in particular, risked adding fuel to an economy already firing on full cylinders. As it turned out, the boom ran out of steam in 2001, easing inflationary pressures.

A budget which looked over-generous when it was delivered in December 2000 did not carry the same risks by the middle of 2001 when the combination of foot-and-mouth disease and the technology downturn had taken the steam out of the economy.

Mr McCreevy's five budgets will be best remembered for their radical transformation of the tax system, significantly increasing the amount which employees take home.

Such has been the extent of the reform that the election campaign will be the first in many years where lavish 'tax packages' will not be used to lure voters. Ireland is no longer a highly taxed state and the public is now focusing much more on public services.

The transformation of the tax system has been fundamental and important. This is not to say Mr McCreevy finished the job. He might have done more for lower-income employees and high tax rates can still kick in at relatively low-income levels, particularly for single employees and single-income couples.

The Minister's individualisation agenda — of particular benefit to two-income families — was controversial. It did increase the incentive for couples to both stay in the workforce, but at the expense of attracting the ire of their single-income counterparts. It raised a fairness or equity issue which will feature in the campaign.

While Fianna Fáil and the PDs will not be slow to trumpet the tax reductions in their term in office, their record on spending will attract more Opposition fire. Investment spending has risen rapidly, although the ambitious targets in the National Development Plan are being missed. Shortage of money is not the main reason why the programme is behind schedule, rather factors such as planning delays and tardy assessment, decision-making and implementation have slowed progress.

The Government has provided the plan and started to put the money in place, but its management skills and those of the public service have fallen short in many cases and a strategic approach to setting and implementing investment priorities is missing. If the Republic's economic progress is to be sustained, this is a key issue.

The coalition spent too much time, it seems, arguing about high-profile projects such as the 'Bertie Bowl' and not enough setting in place a structure capable of delivering the development plan. However, it does deserve plaudits in one area — that of pension planning. The decision to pay money each year into a national pension fund to deal with an ageing population is a wise move and one which should not be reversed by any incoming administration.

The Government's key weakness in the area of public finances has been its control of current spending, which has been allowed to soar. Critically, the level of public services has not seemed to improve commensurately. In short, the Government has not ensured sufficient value for money from the extra cash it has spent.

This value-for-money question will be central to the forthcoming campaign. The public perception is that the billions poured into areas such as the health service are simply not reflected in a better quality of service. It is hard to argue with this conclusion.

Certainly, extra spending in some areas has been required merely to make up for gross under-funding from past cutbacks. However, as with investment spending, the Government has struggled to put in place coherent programmes which deliver planned improvements over a period of time; only in recent months, for example, has it published a medium-term health strategy, while its record on tackling social disadvantage is decidedly mixed.

Part of the Government's difficulties is raised expectations, particularly in public-sector pay, where health and education employees, among others, believe that in a modern economy they should be paid more. Part of the reason why higher spending does not always lead to better services is that it is going in extra pay to public servants (which is not to say that in many cases extra money is not deserved).

Rapidly rising current spending and the expectation of powerful public service groups that a process of benchmarking their pay will deliver substantial pay rises provides a dangerous backdrop to a deteriorating public finance position. Fortunately, the overall Exchequer position is still sound; however, the days when soaring tax revenues allowed the minister great latitude are over.

Normal transmission has now resumed and the next government will face the familiar need to decide how to allocate the limited resources at its disposal and, crucially, how to ensure that the money is well spent.

SATURDAY, 20 APRIL 2002

Stench of Death Fills Air in Jenin as Palestinians Recover Their Dead

Michael Jansen

We have no choice but to struggle up the rough slope within range of the Israeli soldiers posted on top of the hill opposite. Israeli tanks pulled back from Jenin yesterday after entering over two weeks ago.

A university student on his way home tells me he hasn't seen his family in eighteen days. 'They're OK. I was arrested on the first day and taken to an army camp with the other men. They held us for three days and then dumped us here.'

There are many like him. Young men with no baggage, walking. The death toll in the camp, estimated by Palestinians to be 500, will not be known until all the men in Israeli custody are counted in confinement or free to walk home.

I hitch a ride in a pick-up on the outskirts of the camp. The devastation begins at the very edge. Boys with a smattering of English step in as unpaid horror tour guides. We begin at a house blasted to its bare bones, picking our way over rubble. Here, at the beginning of the tour, the smell is of half-burnt rotting garbage.

We step out of the narrow confines of the alley into a wide plateau of rubble strewn with bright bits of torn clothing, chunks of plastic, rocks, clumps of cotton wool from quilts and mattresses. A huge bulldozer driven by a man proclaiming he comes from the Union of Palestinian Medical Relief Committees is waiting on the orders of a group of men plumbing the depths of the rubble for bodies.

The boys lead the way to a house where the smell of death is strong. 'You see there on the wall. Brains,' one of them remarks. A thick black splatter of something clings to the dusty outer wall. Inside the house there is more of the same — several people were killed standing against the wall. On the floor lies a brass vase containing a posey of pink silk roses.

The quarter is called Hawasheen for a family of Palestinians who settled here in 1948. The refugees first sheltered in tents, then tiny breeze-block huts which grew upwards into apartments housing extended families. The camp area holds some 14,000 people. At least 3,000 have been made homeless.

Men probing a small mound have found part of a torso and cover it with a cloth tugged from the rubble. Aya Oweiss takes my hand and leads me to her house. The entire front wall of their house has been blown away. 'They sent us to stay with our neighbour and moved into our house for ten days,' she says. 'When they left, they blew it up.'

The women sitting in their devastated salon watch men on the large mound search for a body, its presence indicated by the smell. A child's corpse is found and a canopy of pink cloth is erected over the grave site while they complete the exhumation. Elsewhere a multiple burial is uncovered, releasing a cloying, sweet stench.

Old people in dust-powdered clothing sit on piles of stone and shattered cement bloc, grim children reach out for a consoling handshake. They collect empty tank shells and scrap metal. People are wounded every day by unexploded ordnance and booby traps.

My companions and I catch a taxi for the return journey but as we alight from the car, we are greeted by a burst of machine-gun fire and several sharp explosions from an Israeli armoured personnel carrier on the hill above. We run uphill and join two dozen Palestinian civilians also running from the gunfire. To welcome us at the barrier are television teams in body armour and helmets.

The Minister for Justice, Equality and Law Reform John O'Donoghue photographed at the Garda graduation ceremony at Templemore Garda Training Centre. Photograph: Brenda Fitzsimons.

MONDAY, 22 APRIL 2002

France in Shock as Le Pen Squeezes Out Jospin

Lara Marlowe

A political earthquake shook France last night when the extreme right-wing leader Mr Jean-Marie Le Pen won a place on the ballot in the 5 May run-off for the French presidency.

Mr Le Pen's victory over fourteen other candidates, including the socialist Prime Minister, Mr Lionel Jospin, marks the first time in the history of the Fifth Republic that the extreme right will be represented in the second round. It is also the first time since 1969 that the left will not have a candidate in France's most important election.

The front-runner, President Jacques Chirac, received twenty per cent of the vote — the lowest score ever for an out-going president. Mr Le Pen obtained 17.2 per cent and Mr Jospin 16.3 per cent. The presidential election is now a contest between Mr Chirac's centre-right Gaullists and Mr Le Pen's extreme-right National Front.

Mr Le Pen wants to pull France out of the European Union and NATO and stop immigration. Although he has been extremely careful of his rhetoric during this campaign — the fourth time he has stood for the presidency — past statements earned him a reputation as racist, anti-Semitic and xenophobic, accusations repeated last night by the Socialist Party spokesman Mr Vincent Peillon.

Mr Le Pen's popularity rose steadily after the September 11th attacks, which seemed to vindicate his belief that Islam and immigration pose a danger for western civilisation. An incident last October, when Algerian football fans booed the Marseillaise at the Stade de France, further boosted his popularity.

'This blow to democracy is the responsibility of Mr Chirac, who centred the campaign on crime,' said the Communist Transport Minister, Mr Jean-Claude Gayssot.

Mr Nicolas Sarkozy, who is favoured to be prime minister if the Gaullists win the June legislative election, said Mr Le Pen's success was 'very worrying news for our country'. He blamed the Socialists for a 'lack of humility and arrogance' and claimed the fragmentation of the left — not Mr Chirac's campaign — destroyed Mr Jospin.

Mr Le Pen has for decades blamed France's large north African community for insecurity in France. Crime rose sixteen per cent during Mr Jospin's five-year term, a phenomenon which Mr Le Pen attributed to lax policies and a 'May 1968 mentality'.

The economic slowdown also helped Mr Le Pen, who has always performed better in times of high unemployment. He boasted last night that he received more workers' votes than any other candidate in the 1995 election.

Speaking from his campaign headquarters in St Cloud, west of Paris, minutes after news of his breakthrough, Mr Le Pen said he had beaten Mr Jospin 'because the French did not want their future to be reduced to a duel between Jospin and Chirac'. Asked how he would reassure voters who believe he is dangerous, he chided the television interviewer for distinguishing arbitrarily between left- and right-wing voters.

'The people are wrong less often than you in the establishment think,' he said.

In an interview with *The Irish Times* three days before the election, Mr Le Pen accused Messrs Chirac and Jospin of excluding three issues from the campaign: 'the dissolution of France in the euro-globalist magma, the close link between immigration and crime and les affaires' — the financial scandals surrounding Mr Chirac.

Mr Jospin's supporters wept in his party headquarters, and candidates from the left called on their voters to support Mr Chirac 'to block Le Pen's path'. Mr Jospin is expected to call on socialists to vote for Mr Chirac, his rival for five years. The

Extreme-right leader Jean-Marie Le Pen holds a press conference, watched by an unidentified bodyguard, at his party's headquarters in Saint Cloud outside Paris. Le Pen placed second in the first round of the presidential election and faced conservative President Jacques Chirac, who led results with about twenty per cent of votes. Socialist Prime Minister Lionel Jospin was disqualified after placing third and announced he would retire from politics. Photograph: Michel Euler/AP.

abstention rate of more than twenty-five per cent was the highest since the Fifth Republic was founded in 1958.

FRIDAY, APRIL 26 2002

Planning to Win the Grand National on a Donkey Once Again

Fintan O'Toole

It should be all over, even before it has started. If politics was a rational science, the Taoiseach's casual, almost contemptuous way of starting the race — announcing the dissolution of the Dáil to a near-empty chamber on Tuesday night — would have made sense. Why bother telling the Opposition in advance, when really they aren't even at the race?

Here, after all, is a Government that has solved two problems that once seemed insoluble: the Northern Ireland conflict and the historic inability of the Republic's economy to produce jobs. A lap of honour might seem more appropriate than a general election.

The only message that a grateful people might need to give to its triumphant leaders might be the traditional instruction which the *Guardian* newspaper trust gives to a newly-appointed editor: 'Carry on as heretofore.'

This, of course, is the message of the Fianna Fáil campaign launched yesterday: vote for us and you get more of the same, or, in colloquial terms, if it ain't broke why fix it? Passion, excitement and vision may be absent, but if the aim is simply to extend the shelf-life of what Bertie Ahern calls a golden age, such qualities are unnecessary.

For the Opposition parties to succeed, however, they need to convince the public that there is a lot to get worked up about, and that more of the same is either impossible or undesirable.

The first general election of the twenty-first century comes down to a simple question: what do we expect of ourselves? If we are pessimists inured to failure, if the old Irish fatalism is now part of our genetic code, then we must be enormously grateful for the last five years.

We must be in awe of the miracle that a squalid sectarian conflict is smouldering but not raging on this island. We must be amazed that mass unemployment and mass emigration have abated, at least for now. We must hug ourselves with delight that the wolves are not at the door, and give thanks and praise to the outgoing Government.

If, on the other hand, we see the Northern Ireland conflict as having been sustained in some measure by an appalling failure of imagination on the part of our own mainstream political culture, we will add the words 'about time, too' to our praise for the achievement of the Belfast Agreement.

If we see the economic calamities of the 1980s as a disgrace brought about largely by misgovernment, we will be less inclined to see the recent boom as anything more than an economy belatedly achieving the levels of wealth-creation it should have reached years before. If the old fatalism has died, we will not feel inclined to be grateful for the small mercies of not being driven into the external exile of emigration or the internal exile of poverty. We will at least listen to what the Opposition parties have to say.

Michael Noonan, leader of the Fine Gael party, surprises Pat and his dog on the campaign trail in Naas, Co Kildare. Photograph: Brenda Fitzsimons.

Director of Elections PJ Mara during a quiet moment at the launch of the Fianna Fáil manifesto in the Shelbourne Hotel, Dublin. Photograph: Bryan O'Brien.

All the signs are that the population is not especially grateful. One reason for this is a contradiction that is at the heart of mainstream politics in free-market economies.

On the one hand, a market philosophy tells the public that the State isn't all that important and that the private sector is where the action is, a message repeated yesterday in Bertie Ahern's economic manifesto. On the other, the politicians who espouse this philosophy also want the electorate to believe that their own roles as leaders of the State are so crucial that without them the country would have gone to the dogs.

The problem for Bertie Ahern and Mary Harney is that they have been too successful in getting across the first part of this message. The truth of the boom may well be that the role of the State — through infrastructure, incentives, educational investment, the brokering of social partnership and the subsidisation of private sector wages with tax cuts — has been crucial.

Ask most of its beneficiaries who they have to thank, however, and they will probably say themselves and the companies for which they work. As well as privatising public companies, the Government has also privatised gratitude.

At the same time, the prestige of government itself has been undermined by corruption on the one hand and the failure to deliver decent public services on the other. The public has watched the financial scandals, the attempts to interfere with the judicial process, the deeply worrying allegations of Garda misconduct in Donegal and elsewhere, and the unfolding revelations of dodgy dealings in the planning process.

It has sniffed the air of incompetence in public projects from the health service to the pool at Abbotstown. It has seen the State make enemies of the likes of Kathryn Sinnott and the Irish Haemophilia Association. And it has not been encouraged to feel such pride in the State that it ought to care passionately about who runs it.

It is all the more remarkable then that the main opposition parties have shown few signs that they intend to make the nature of the State itself an issue in this election campaign. Important as individual policies on the public finances or the allocation of spending unquestionably are, they all beg the question: can the State actually deliver on anybody's ideas?

One of the reasons the public seems sceptical and wary is, surely, that it suspects the answer is a flat No. This question runs across all the issues. The amount of money to be spent on health matters only if you believe that the money will be well used. A proposal to tackle crime by putting more Gardaí on the streets makes sense only if you are convinced that the Garda as a whole is in good shape.

Politicians talking about the fantastic things they will achieve in office are a little like jockeys planning a brilliant strategy for winning the Grand National on a donkey.

If, as seems likely from the opening skirmishes, the campaign is conducted as an argument about different ways of funding the same objectives, the electorate will probably decide that things aren't going to change much and it may as well stick with the crowd that's most comfortable running the system as it is now. To make a real contest of it, the Opposition needs to put flesh and blood on the sense of unease that is plainly present.

It needs to join up the dots between the various points of crisis over the last five years: the resignation of Ray Burke and the pursuit of Kathryn Sinnott, the attempted appointment of Hugh O'Flaherty and the jailing of Liam Lawlor, the conversion of large tracts of Wicklow into a toxic dump and the débâcle of the Bertie Bowl, the cynicism of the abortion referendum and the casual contempt for people with disabilities.

It needs to draw a clear picture of what we have and then another one of what a State that actually turns an economy into a society might look like. If they can't do this, Michael Noonan and Ruairí Quinn will be spending the next five years wondering how Bertie gets away with it.

SATURDAY, 27 APRIL 2002

Pressing Home the PDs' Promise of Prosperity

Róisín Ingle

When the Beatles organised a Magical Mystery Tour in 1967, it was slated by movie critics, but at least the destination was secret. Yesterday morning, when Mary's Magical Mystery Tour rolled out of Dublin, there was no mystery, just admiration for the brass neck of any party launching its political campaign in a village called Prosperous.

When the whisper came that we were off to the affluent-sounding Co. Kildare village (by people-carrier as opposed to psychedelic bus), it had us pondering what other places the PDs might have considered. A launch in Moneystown, Co. Wicklow (it's the economy, nitwit), could have worked, and surely there was some debate in party HQ about Ready-penny in Co. Kilkenny, another appropriate location to press home the PDs' election promise of continued economic success.

After a little investigation, we discovered another reason why the PDs may have felt some affinity with the town — founded in 1780, it wasn't long before Prosperous had fallen into decline and was being written off as 'little more than a heap of ruins'.

These days, though, it is more deserving of its name. Locals replied in the affirmative when asked whether Prosperous was prosperous. 'It is now,' said local Rita Wall. 'There have been a lot of changes. We have a tennis court and pitch and putt.'

The Prosperous Democrats were in fighting form when Mary Harney arrived at the Oak Partnership, a drama school run by her husband Brian Geoghegan's FÁS organisation, to be greeted by schoolchildren and the two Kildare PD candidates, John Dardis and Kate Walsh. Inside, Liz O'Donnell, Tom Parlon and Fiona O'Malley took their places on the small stage beside their leader, who told the assembled schoolchildren that they were there because 'Ireland is Prosperous and Prosperous is Ireland'.

Later, the crowd adjourned to Dowlings' pub across the road, a hostelry famous for being the place where Christy Moore came to prominence. It is also a venue fondly remembered by the Tánaiste, who used to shake her stuff on Dowlings' dancefloor in her youth.

Letters to the Editor April 2002

Ireland's Anti-Englishness

Sir, — As an Englishman living in Dublin for the last ten years I have made more friends here than in any other place on my travels. I can testify to the warmth, *generosity and hospitality of the Irish people towards people of different races and creeds. However, in recent years I have started to detect an alarming exception to the rule, namely the Irish attitude towards the English, particularly among the younger generation. Moreover, this attitude is not only supported by most of the media, but is actually encouraged.*

Some of my Irish friends who lived in England during the 1970s and 1980s when the Troubles were at their height have regaled me of stories of harsh treatment by my compatriots. However, these were usually isolated incidents involving ignorant people who confused the issue in the North with Irish nationality. What we are seeing now in Ireland is a kind of sanctioned racism that is far beyond the odd 'mickey-taking' and it is everywhere; many of my Irish friends have noticed it too.

Those who don't believe me might imagine sitting as an Englishman in an Irish bar when the English are playing another country — it doesn't matter which — at any sport. Any failure by the English is received with glee and celebrated with nothing short of venom by the majority. In an English bar, strangely, we always cheer for the Irish.

I am married to an Irish girl and would not live anywhere else, but my advice to any English people coming to live here is that the traditional Irish welcome is something reserved for everyone except us; and do not dream of expressing your Englishness in any outward manifestation as you will not enjoy the consequences. — Yours, etc., Martin Gascoine, Ballsbridge, Dublin 4. 2 April 2002.

Sir, — *Martin Gascoine (2 April) describes 'sanctioned racism' in Ireland against English people. His letter is given prominence on the Letters page and yet contains not one concrete example to support his point of view.*

Mr Gascoine says he has lived in Dublin for ten years, yet the best example he can suggest is to ask us to 'imagine' being an Englishman in an Irish bar watching the English soccer team in action. The Irish will always cheer the other team, he claims. He also states that the media back up this anti-English behaviour, while again offering no evidence.

I am also an Englishman who has lived in Ireland for the past fifteen years and I have often been irritated at the pro-British stance of some elements of the Irish media, especially when it comes to the conflict in the North. These elements bend over backwards so as not to offend British sensibilities. This fawning attitude is particularly obvious in relation to the British royal family — e.g. the continual promotion of an official visit to Ireland by Queen Elizabeth.

As for soccer matches, yes, I agree that most Irish people will cheer any team playing against England — a legacy of colonialism. During Italia '90 I watched Ireland play England in a packed Irish pub. There was no 'venom' directed at me, only good-humoured 'slagging'.

During my time living in Ireland I have heard much criticism of British government policy towards Ireland, but no personal abuse has ever been directed at me. I believe Mr Gascoine is inventing a problem where none exists. — Yours, etc., Mark Urwin, Court Farm, Mulhuddart, Dublin 15. 10 April 2002.

Sir, — *Mark Urwin's letter of 10 April was both accurate and quite courageous. He made a very valid point when referring to the Irish media who 'bend over backwards so as not to offend British sensibilities'.*

After the recent visit of Prince Charles to Ireland (and the media hype that accompanied 'the royal visit'), *I wrote a letter to your paper enquiring as to whether or not a full apology for the atrocity of Bloody Sunday would be appropriate from Prince Charles, in his position of Colonel in Chief of the Parachute Regiment.*

Surprise, surprise, my letter was not published, as I am sure neither will this one. — Yours, etc., Michael Farrelly, Blacrock. Co. Dublin. 12 April 2002.

Adams's Eulogy to the IRA

Sir, — *Following Gerry Adams's after-dinner speech at the 'Tírghrá' gathering eulogising 'one of the most effective guerilla armies in the world', I have four questions to put to him.*

1. Would it not be more fitting to say there would have been no war if it were not for the IRA, than claiming there would be no peace process without them?

2. Does the leader of Sinn Féin subscribe to the canon of violent republicanism as enunciated by Pádraig Pearse: 'Bloodshed is a cleansing and sanctifying thing and the nation which regards it as the final horror has lost its manhood'?

3. How can someone who claims to have moved into political peace-building celebrate, affirm or praise 'one of the most effective guerilla armies in the world'?

4. Since when did murder and mayhem become a noble cause?

Given the track record of Mr Adams and his colleagues, I am not expecting straight answers. — Yours, etc., Robert Dunlop, Brannockstown, Co. Kildare. 17 April 2002.

Complaining to Dublin Bus

Sir, — *Five months ago I sent a letter detailing a series of shortcomings in the 14A bus service to Dublin Bus head office.*

On no fewer than five occasions I telephoned to enquire when a response might be forthcoming, and on each occasion I was told that there was 'no customer service department' and 'did I want to speak with somebody in the garage?' I eventually agreed to be

The tricolour flying alongside flowers placed at the scene of the accident on the Stillorgan Road, in which two Gardaí lost their lives. Photograph: Eric Luke.

put through to someone in the garage, who asked me to read out my complaint so he could help me.

The offer was genuine and well intentioned. However, it is completely inappropriate for the bus service of a European capital city to operate in such an unprofessional manner.

This unprofessionalism must be compared with the sophisticated marketing and advertising system in place, where entire double-decker buses can be liveried from top to tail with full-colour corporate logos in a matter of days.

Dublin Bus has a shambles of customer service, with no commitment to its paying clients. I would like this fact on the public record. — Yours, etc., P. Corley, Fortfield Terrace, Dublin 6. 23 April 2002.

General Election 2002

A chara, — A lot of people done. More people to do. — Is mise, Jerry Twomey, Woodlawn Court, Dublin 9. 29 April 2002.

FRIDAY, 3 MAY 2002

Bertie Campaigns in Fast Lane at Speeds of Ninety-five M.P.H.

Tim O'Brien

The fast-moving Taoiseach might think he only breaks speed limits when on foot, but there was evidence to the contrary during his dash around the south-east yesterday. Mr Ahern's election cavalcade hit speeds of up to ninety-five m.p.h. yesterday as it dashed through the south-east five years after he launched the Republic's road safety strategy.

The speed of the campaign cavalcade has been criticised by the National Safety Council chairman Mr Eddie Shaw, who described such speeds as unacceptable. Mr Ahern, whose cavalcade reached speeds of eighty-five m.p.h. on Wednesday, arrived slightly behind schedule at 10.40 a.m. in New Ross, Co. Wexford, yesterday. After a quick visit to the auctioneering business of the son of local Fianna Fáil Junior Minister, Mr Hugh Byrne, and a quick huddle with reporters to discuss the overnight headlines, Mr Ahern's cavalcade was, unusually, behind schedule when it left for Wexford. Taking the N25 single carriageway road from New Ross to Wexford, the convoy of eight cars, some emblazoned with Fianna Fáil flags and posters, at times hit seventy-five m.p.h. in a forty m.p.h. zone, and passed a junction at eighty m.p.h., as well as reaching a top speed of ninety-five m.p.h.

The Taoiseach's convoy was ushered out of New Ross by gardaí at about 12.26 p.m. It speeded up to eighty m.p.h. by the time it was passing signs for Ballynaboola, about six miles from New Ross. The cavalcade arrived in Wexford at 12:43 p.m. and accomplished the twenty-two-mile journey in an almost incredible seventeen minutes. The road safety strategy, which largely focused on speed and drink driving, was never fully implemented. It was to have reduced deaths and serious injury on the roads by twenty per cent, over 1997 levels, by the end of this year.

Asked in Wexford town if he was concerned about the speed his cavalcade travels at, the Taoiseach smiled and said: 'Only walking. The only speed limit we break is when we are walking.'

When it was suggested that the journey from New Ross had broken the speed limit almost constantly the Taoiseach replied: 'Ah no. We were going slow today. When we are in the car we try to keep to the speed limit. When we are walking we break it.'

Having exhorted the party faithful to achieve a third Fianna Fáil seat in Wexford he insisted little funding was spent in the constituency when it was represented by the then ministers Mr Ivan Yeates and Mr Brendan Howlin.

An 'amended' Fianna Fáil election poster in Baggot Street. Photograph: Matt Kavanagh.

Mr Ahern's convoy sped off to Enniscorthy — at speeds which frequently touched seventy m.p.h. and reached eighty m.p.h. on a straight stretch of road alongside the Slaney, a few miles south of Enniscorthy.

Essential planks of the Irish strategy, such as random sample breath-testing and State-wide deployment of speed traps were never implemented as the Gardaí and other agencies were never given adequate funding.

The number of people killed on roads in Co. Wexford in the last four years was sixty-six.

Yesterday Mr Shaw, chairman of the National Safety Council, said: 'I don't think it acceptable to do those kind of speeds outside of the emergency services.

'I don't think it is right. It possibly shows the time constraints Mr Ahern is under in meeting so many appointments.

'If the reports of the speed of the Taoiseach's cavalcade are true then I don't think it is acceptable at all,' he concluded.

TUESDAY, 7 MAY 2002

Hoping to Avoid the Red Card as He Tries Again to Make His Mark

Kathy Sheridan

Just wondering, Michael, about this business of going bald-headed for Fianna Fáil — the Ceausescu gibe, the shimmying up lamp-posts to tell the nation they can't be let out on their own — when you've been so, um, cosy with the same people for years now?

Oops. Red rag to Rottweiler. He stops in his tracks. 'I'm in real competition with them. This is a very, very vigorous contest in which you have to shoulder people off the ball to score goals. This is not a fancy-dress competition.'

Crikey. Has no one else asked you about this? 'No. No one has been saying that kind of thing to me. Only Fianna Fáil at their briefings.' Selfish b ★★★★★ds.

The job now is to put clear blue water between the PDs and that lot. 'Honest politics, real results' is the slogan. McDowell — 'a passionate believer in clean capable political service,' it says on the pamphlet. You better believe it.

One woman with a set look on her face says she's undecided. 'Trust in politicians is an issue for me now.' His response is brief and business-like: 'Well, for myself, I've never betrayed the public trust.' No winsome smile, no attempt to cajole.

It's the same story with the woman who says she won't be voting for him because she 'didn't like the referendum — it showed no understanding of

Michael McDowell of the Progressive Democrats erecting a poster in Ranelagh, Dublin, against the possibility of a single-party government. Photograph: Frank Miller.

humanity'. Back on the street, he says there are people saying rosaries for him on account of the same referendum.

Michael McDowell is fighting for his political life and he still can't bring himself to turn on the smarm. Even the snippy dogs of fabulously affluent Orwell Road seem curiously muted as he bounds over the crunchy gravel, past the sporty Mercs and fragrant Labradors and on to the doorsteps on a bank holiday canvass.

He's canvassing in the middle of the FA Cup final; he doesn't even ask about the score when people finally drag themselves to the door.

A well-known arts figure with a particular interest in children says the PDs will not be getting his No 1 because he has a problem with taxation; he's not being asked to pay enough. Services have suffered, the PDs are over-reliant on market forces and tax reductions have created a culture of greed, he says.

'That may be a good middle-class position,' responds the old charmer, 'but if you had been living out in Neilstown where eighty per cent of households had no breadwinners and people who had jobs were worse off at work than on the dole — that's the kind of policy that reduced this country to its knees. I believe in cutting tax if it gets 400,000 people working and that's what it has done.'

Alas, poor arts man, your engagement got you nowhere. But you knew that anyway; that's the beauty of McDowell, there is no pretence. 'I see that culture of greed thing as vacuous,' snorts McDowell, as we canter down the street. 'What I see is an Ireland that's got up off its knees after twenty to thirty years of self-doubt, ideological cant and under-performance.'

It's his bugbear, that left-wing ideology. 'I despise it. They're far more concerned about how the cake is divided than whether there is any cake.' Anyway, the PDs have a way of extracting tax so you'd hardly notice.

'Capital gains tax produced £160 million in 1997. We cut the rate from forty per cent to twenty per cent and last year it produced £860 million. And the Labour Party wants to restore the rate from twenty to forty-two per cent. Now that's ideology.'

But back to that other lot. They are fighting this election on the basis that everything is 'hunky-dory,' and that doesn't suit the PDs at all. Health is a big issue, so is the economy — 'not that people are scrutinising the manifestos but there are concerns about jobs' — and they're also angry about Campus Ireland. Very angry.

Then out of the blue, two genteel elderly women answer the door and come very close to flinging their arms around him. 'One time we were

without water, you were the only one to take us seriously.'

His canvassing team turns up other tales about how he helped a woman to get a pram and had late-night advice about her tree for another. But hear this: Michael McDowell does not 'fix' things; he helps people to go about fixing things for themselves.

The real question though is how he can face into all this mullarkey again, five years after that devastating eleven-count twenty-seven-vote defeat to John Gormley. 'I believe in the political process,' he replies.

'Obviously there are huge temptations, family-wise, to be back in the Law Library. But the 400,000 people who are working in 2002 who were not working in 1997, they are the people I constantly have in mind.'

Anyway, his wife, Niamh Brennan, is no naïf. 'When Michael was elected in 1987, he took Joe Doyle's seat and I saw Joe and Peggy's upset that night. And I remember thinking that the only way out of this business is the red card. That's the reality.'

WEDNESDAY, 8 MAY 2002

'Politics is About Winning Votes — It's Not About How You Perform in Dáil Éireann'

Kathy Sheridan

Stay alert. No one is going to babysit you in this game.

You're perched against the range in a west Mayo kitchen, chatting with the voters, when you cop that the main man and his team have vanished. Yikes. They point you to the nearest exit. Out you run, fearing abandonment, only to be nearly crushed by the main man and team hurtling back in again.

What happened?

Fine Gael party leader Michael Noonan takes a break in Newcastlewest during canvassing in Co. Limerick. Photograph: Paul McErlane/Reuters.

'You never go out a different door to the one you came in,' says the poll-topping TD, in the way you might say the weather is nice. Eh? 'I'm a bit superstitious.'

No one blinks.

This is the electoral area of Erris-Achill, the strip of coastline that is the key to Michael Ring's supernatural, poll-topping, organisation-smashing feats. Everywhere — Ballina, Westport — is at least fifty miles away. Dublin is a conservative four hours on a quiet day.

You'll see a few Michael Ring posters on the long and winding road between Ballina and Belmullet. Not as many as for Tom Moffatt, or for Beverley Cooper-Flynn, who has the big fat No 1 graphic on her posters and not even a small-print mention of Fianna Fáil.

But everyone knows this is the Ring road, though he's fifty miles from home.

Down the coast, the people are the kind that city folk imagine disappeared into a black hole

around the time the Pope came to Ireland. Padre Pio pictures and Sacred Heart lamps, blazing turf fires, and at least three generations gathered together in welcoming, modest homes on a Sunday, a few rough fields away from the Atlantic shimmering in the evening sun.

'How're ya doin'? You know the aul job I'm on …'

That's one approach.

The second is more formal. 'I'd appreciate all the support you can give me. All I can say is I've done the best job possible. People can't say they haven't seen me since the last election.'

There's a third. That's when he doesn't get to open his mouth at all. Instead, he is yanked off the doorstep and landed in the kitchen without his feet touching the ground, to be plied with hugs and tea, open adoration and prayerful good wishes.

A few hours canvassing with Michael Ring, and being left at the door feels like rejection.

It means that his wiry little frame — already streaking ahead and clearing walls like a mountain goat — has to move all the faster. He is tired, very tired, and it's no wonder.

He works seventeen-hour days when there is no election. His sixteen-month-old Passat has 65,000 miles on the clock — 'and I drove every one of those miles myself.'

Even the Sinn Féin activist nods sympathetically when he calls. She stops short of inviting him in and hesitates when asked for a No 2 but looks pained about it. 'I don't like your leader … but I know how hard you work, Michael.'

Down the road, a quiet-spoken man tells the TD that they had to bring their seventeen-year-old mentally handicapped son all the way to Dublin, by train, to have his teeth seen to. Ring swallows hard; his compassion is no pose.

The only sour note is when someone adverts to his place near the top of the expenses claims. 'It's good to keep at the top anyway,' he replies brightly. But four bloody hours from Dublin, it grates …

Our driver is Henry Coyle, a young local boxer with bright, darting eyes, who shrugs that, sure, he has nothing better to do today. 'Ah, but Michael is sound. He comes to all the boxing matches.' (NB: 'sound' is as good as it gets in this age group.)

Henry's father is Cllr Gerry Coyle, who nearly triggers a mutiny in the packed car when he starts to sing (ah come on lads, the non-smoking, non-drinking Ring was out canvassing a disco at 2 a.m. last night) but, like his senior colleague, is deadly serious about an issue that is both national and intensely local. Planning.

The higgledy-piggledy arrangement of houses on this stunning coastline speaks for itself. But Gerry says Dublin people haven't a clue, don't know or don't care about the money sent home from Scotland by fourteen-year-old potato pickers to fund the new roof or the indoor toilet, and the sites left by grateful parents for when their children finally came home.

'In Dublin they think we're all lunatics … We have two Blue Flag beaches here because people were protecting the environment long before An Taisce was heard of.'

Michael Ring is standing in front of a disputed field leading down to the shoreline. Any objective person would want to protect that view, says *The Irish Times*. 'Well, go up and tell that to the son and daughter of the people in that house beside it who want to live where they belong,' he says.

He is fiercely, unashamedly, a man of the people. It's a mutual thing. Supporters like Ian McAndrew, a Bellmullet member of Údarás na Gaeltachta, are astonished when outsiders don't get it. 'If Fine Gael only had ten Michael Rings …' says Ian, hopelessly.

'Politics is about winning votes,' says Ring, who, by the way, has won ringing endorsements for his Dáil performances from Vincent Browne and several acerbic commentators. 'It's not about how you perform in Dáil Éireann. The votes are in Mayo.'

And the issues are no surprise: headage, social welfare, roads, orthodontics, medical cards …

But never, ever make the mistake of dismissing him as a parishpump politician or as merely 'colourful'. He knows he has risen way above that. 'If Fine Gael forms a government, the least I expect is a junior ministry. And if it's the Western Development job, I think I'd be the man for that senior ministry.' But as a man of the people, how would he find the time?

Simple. There would be a decree. Ministerial business Monday to Thursday. Constituency work Friday to Sunday.

Ring's biggest problem now, he says, is that 'every candidate is saying that I'm home and dry. It's the most dangerous thing in politics. I'm not happy with the way people are trying to take votes away from me on that basis. I've paid a price already in the organisation in conceding a lot of ground to the other candidates. And they're still saying I'm OK.' Who is saying that? 'All of them.'

Watch out, ye snakes of Mayo. There's only so far you can go with guys like Michael around.

SATURDAY, 11 MAY 2002

Sisterhood All Wrong About Women in Politics

Breda O'Brien

When the sisterhood urge us to vote for women, they really want us to vote for sisters. They want to elect women who believe that women are oppressed because of their gender, who are pro-choice and pro-divorce, who believe that domestic violence is almost exclusively a women's issue, who are convinced that young men are in dire need of re-education to make them more like young women.

They want women who believe that the mark of adult personhood is economic independence. So all women must have access to State subsidised childcare so that they can go out to work. Women who want to stay at home have to be given token support because of the exaltation of the value of choice, but that is the only reason.

Here's an example of what I mean. There is someone running for election who has always worked outside the home in a highly competitive environment despite being a mother. She has worked abroad, has been the primary wage-earner in her family for many years, and has extraordinary media and canvassing skills. She also has a very good chance of being elected. It would be fair to assume that the sisterhood would be enthusiastically supporting her. Except that her name is Dana Rosemary Scallon. Be careful what you wish for, sisters. You may get it.

There are two main reasons why there are so few women in politics, one politically correct but none the less true, the other heresy. Let's begin with the heresy. There are fewer women than men in politics because there are a heck of a lot of women who are bored senseless by politics.

In any workplace where men and women work together, other than in a media office or in a lobby group, the men will be the ones discussing politics. Women will be discussing the minutiae of life, such as how people are getting on with each other, or childminding problems or even washing powders.

This fact is seized upon by male chauvinists as proof that women are essentially trivial human beings without the ability to deal with weighty issues. To which one can only respond — bull manure. Men like politics for the same reason they like sport, because it's a game. They love the competition, the point-scoring, the jockeying for power and even the back-stabbing. Women dislike it for the same reasons.

Politics is a boys' game, and the women who are successful in it are the ones who are prepared to play by the boys' rules. There are a lot of heroic women in politics. They are called TDs' wives. They keep the show on the road in the family and in the constituency clinic. They make enormous sacrifices for which there are no public thanks whatever.

Since most women do not have wives or the equivalent, those who make a success of it are going to have to be exceptionally determined. Which brings us to the politically correct reason why so few women enter politics.

If you want to have a family life, and you live outside Dublin, do not become a TD. Even if you live in or close to Dublin you will be working extraordinary hours and expected to be available to constituents at any time they need you. Many women look at that life and quite rightly decide it is not for them.

Which leads us to an interesting paradox. Women who are willing to play by the boys' rules are much more likely to get elected and much more likely to please the sisters.

This is particularly true of women elected on a party ticket. But many people are cheesed off with the political parties, including many women, and as a result independents are likely to do well.

There are only three women likely to be elected as independents. They are Mildred Fox, Marian Harkin and Dana Rosemary Scallon, and while they have many differences, the one thing they have in common is that they are all anti-abortion, which is anathema to the sisters.

Not that I think any of them will be elected on a pro-life ticket alone. Dana certainly won't be. No, if she gets in, she will do so by being an astute politician running on an anti-politician ticket, and because she has charisma to burn. The photo of the campaign for me was the one of her wagging her finger at Bertie, while Margaret Cox's mouth twisted in cynical disbelief at her nemesis's cheek.

Dana and Bertie have a lot in common, both in their people skills and ability to surmount situations which would kill off anybody else.

Dana managed to let down and deeply wound a large part of her natural constituency, the anti-abortion activists, when she destroyed the referendum they had worked on for ten years. Yet she probably will still get elected. The way in which she has aligned herself with residents' groups in Galway is classic Dana, and very like the way in which she charmed the councillors into giving her an opportunity to run for President.

Mildred Fox is a hereditary politician who has grown into the role very nicely, both by assiduous work on behalf of her constituents and by having values for which she is willing to go out on a limb. Yet she would not be a favourite among the sisters, either. Marian Harkin would probably be the most acceptable to them, yet she will be elected not because she is a woman but because she is a dogged campaigner for the west.

A protestor is removed following clashes with Gardaí during the 'May Reclaim the Streets' rally in Dame Street, Dublin. Photograph: Matt Kavanagh.

Despite the sisters' exhortations, women and men will continue to vote for the person they feel best represents them. Voting for women because of their competence and their values makes sense. Voting for them because they are women is patronising nonsense.

WEDNESDAY, 15 MAY 2002

Feathers Fail to Fly as Fox Confronts Chicken

Frank McNally

In the protracted run-up to last night's debate, Fine Gael sought to portray the Taoiseach as a debate-fearing chicken, confident in the belief that Michael Noonan was an old fox, and that when the two finally met, feathers would fly.

The characterisation was only slightly off. This campaign has shown that if Mr Ahern resembles any member of the bird family, it's the old cartoon character, Road Runner: elusive, fast-moving (allegedly), and constantly dashing around the country going 'Beep Beep'.

And if Mr Noonan has resembled a crafty, four-legged creature, it has to be Road Runner's eternal but frustrated enemy, Wile E. Coyote.

So it was when the much-hyped debate came to pass. Wile E. appeared to have the bird cornered at last, pinned down in the areas of crime and health, on both of which the Taoiseach sounded defensive. Ethics came next on Prime Time's agenda, and here Mr Noonan had made a pre-emptive strike in the form of Fine Gael's anti-sleaze document, a cunningly designed election trap supplied by the Acme election trap company.

But inevitably, the coyote's plan misfired and the Road Runner was off again. Mr Ahern shaded the ethics debate, performed a quick lap of honour on Northern Ireland, and by the time he reached the safe ground of economics, you could almost hear him go 'Beep Beep' at the thought of a last whirlwind round of canvassing today.

Mr Noonan proved what everybody knew: that he is the better debater. Following the communications textbook, he told stories, where Mr Ahern recited facts. Cunningly, he also attributed certain story-telling skills to his opposite number, collected under the title of 'Alice in Bertieland'. But he needed a knock-out and this wasn't it.

In the event, the debate billed as 'the broadcasting event of the election campaign' was as dramatic as some of yesterday's weather reports. There were even uncanny similarities, blustery

Michael Noonan gets a custard pie in the face from Jessamine O'Connor minutes after arriving in Boyle, Co Roscommon. Photograph: James Connolly.

conditions, sunny intervals, the warm front exuded by Mr Ahern. But — ominously for Mr Noonan — the weather forecast and the latest polls both suggested rain in the south-west.

SATURDAY, 18 MAY 2002

Here We Go, Here We Go to Japan

Róisín Ingle

How many England supporters got to wish David Beckham good luck while standing so near him they could read the time from his watch?

Certainly not as many fans as got to mingle with the Irish World Cup squad at Dublin Airport yesterday. Supporters came out to greet the players as they set off to the Pacific island of Saipan — the team's base for a week before travelling on to Japan.

'Good luck, big lad,' some said casually to a beaming Niall Quinn as he strode from the team bus to the check-in counter surrounded by polite but determined autograph hunters.

With excitement at fever pitch, fans could barely believe the access they had to the parade of A-list footie folk ambling along beside them on their way to the World Cup in Japan. Keano, Stevo, Harty, Robbie, they yelled. At times the green jerseys of the players outnumbered the tasteful scarves on the uniforms of the smiling air hostesses.

Manager Mick McCarthy sat calmly on a chair amid the media frenzy in the Skyview Lounge, dressed in the squad's World Cup suit designed by Louis Copeland. His immediate plan was to sleep

Captain of Manchester United and the Republic of Ireland Roy Keane in his robes at UCC where he received an Honorary Doctorate of Law (LLD) from the National University of Ireland, in honour of his contribution to Irish life. Photograph: Alan Betson.

for eight hours on the plane. 'I am very relaxed. It will be nice to go out and concentrate on the football instead of all this,' he said.

Thursday's defeat to Nigeria was also on the minds of the players. 'We did let in a couple of bad goals,' said Keane as he rummaged through his kit bag. 'But better to let them in now than in a couple of weeks' time.'

Would his footballing prowess be even further increased by his recently-awarded honorary doctorate from Cork University? The sometimes grumpy midfielder grinned and said: 'Nah, it was a great honour, but it hasn't changed my life. Obviously I am getting a bit of stick over it.'

As the rain fell steadily outside, Keane wondered whether the heat in Japan might have an

effect on the team. 'We struggled a little in '94, in Florida,' he said. 'These days, though, the players are fitter and stronger and they look after themselves better. I am sure we will do well. I'm looking forward to it.'

Asked was he feeling fit enough for the challenge, the Ireland captain's answer was slightly worrying. 'Just about, yeh,' he said. 'As the years go by it gets harder.'

In between media interviews and obligatory photo ops with giant leprechauns the lads picked at bowls of fruit salad and munched on croissants until the physiotherapist Mick Byrne rounded them up for the flight. 'Here we go, lads,' he said in urgent tones. Here we go, indeed.

MONDAY, 20 MAY 2002

Ahern, Master of a Quiet Revolution that Produced Slick FF Machine

Fintan O'Toole

Liam Cosgrave, Fine Gael candidate, canvassing in Dalkey. Photograph: Alan Betson.

'It appeared to me that the Fianna Fáil ministers were behaving in a very disorganised manner. No one appeared to be in charge. At the meeting I attended, ministers came in and out at will, with some absent for periods.'

The speaker was the former Fianna Fáil attorney general, Eoghan Fitzsimons. The time was December 1994. The circumstances were those in which Bertie Ahern became leader of Fianna Fáil. Such was the state of disarray in the party that, far from disputing Fitzsimons's description, senior party figures reached for it as a lifeline. In the black farce of the last days of Albert Reynolds, it was better to plead guilty to hopeless disorganisation than to accept responsibility for anything.

Who would have thought then that, in 2002, Bertie Ahern would stroll to the easiest victory in the history of Irish politics? That in the early years of the twenty-first century, the Republic would be effectively a democratic version of a one-party state in which Fianna Fáil was the only credible candidate for power?

If there is a tiny glimmer of hope for the routed old-style opposition of Fine Gael and Labour, it lies in the example of Bertie Ahern himself. He took over a demoralised, fractious party in the throes of a historic decline and turned it into a machine so slick that it can leave its traditional enemies at the starting line without even getting into second gear.

Yet even that glimmer is a will o'the wisp, an elusive light that will lead those foolish enough to follow it even further into the mire. For the essential message of the election is that if Irish politics is framed as a contest to discover who is best at being Bertie, the winner will always be Bertie.

Being Bertie is a hard trick, and it is time that his opponents acknowledged the Taoiseach's achievements. He may instinctively be a cautious leader and a conservative politician, but there is a genuine radicalism in what he has done to his own party. By transforming Fianna Fáil's view of the Irish political universe, he has changed the nature of the political contest for good.

The change is obvious in the bottom line. In the old political world, Bertie Ahern's performance as party leader would have been quite poor. In 1997, Fianna Fáil got just thirty-nine per cent of the first preference, one of the worst totals in the party's history. On Friday, after the five most prosperous years the country has ever enjoyed, it got just over forty-one per cent. This is worse than, for example the party's 41.9 per cent in 1948, a figure that was seen at the time as abysmal.

By the old rules, Bertie is a failure. But he has changed the rules. In the old order, a general election was a contest between Fianna Fáil and the rest of the world. Fianna Fáil saw itself as a national movement rather than a political party.

Even a young, cosmopolitan figure like Micheál Martin was using this kind of rhetoric in the early 1990s. You were either part of the movement or you were a traitor, for, as Ray Burke once put it, 'Loyalty to Fianna Fáil is loyalty to the nation itself.' Or, as Brian Cowen said more recently, if in doubt leave them out. Those who were not with us were against not just us, but the nation.

To understand the quiet revolution that Bertie Ahern has overseen, all you have to do is look at a letter that his brother Noel sent to his Dublin middle-class constituents in the roads around Griffith Avenue on the eve of last week's election.

Sent from the Drumcondra address that is the ancestral home of the Ahern dynasty, Noel's letter had a heading that would have been utterly unimaginable in the pre-Bertie days: 'Message to Fine Gael voters'. The content was emollient: 'I presume as a committed Fine Gael voter that you will give your No 1 vote to the Fine Gael candidate.' Noel Ahern went on, however, to ask for a second preference for Fianna Fáil in order to keep out Sinn Féin candidate Dessie Ellis.

The letter is evidence of the attention to detail that puts the party's machine in a different class. But it was also an implicit declaration of something far more consequential. The Ahern dynasty was declaring the end of Civil War politics. Bertie has replaced 'if in doubt leave them out' with 'if in doubt, bring them in'. The Fianna Fáil world is no longer divided between Us and Them, but between Us and People Like Us. There are no strangers, only friends we haven't yet met.

During the election campaign, for example, Bertie was asked by Gerald Barry on RTÉ radio whether there was anything in the manifestos of either Labour or the Progressive Democrats that he fundamentally disagreed with. His answer was a straight 'No'. He is not in the disagreement business.

In narrow electoral terms, this means that Fianna Fáil can come close to an overall majority with forty-one per cent of the vote, because it gets transfers.

The inherited common culture — Catholic, rural, nationalist — is all but gone. The gap between rich and poor is so wide that there is a real sense in which they no longer inhabit the same place.

Bertie, the man who disagrees with nobody and understands all concerns, is the perfect balm for these anxieties. He embodies the notion of consensus, the illusion that we are all still on the one road, marching along, singing the soldier's song.

The great failure of Fine Gael and Labour — who together form what we might call the Loyal Opposition — is that they tried to fight fudge with fudge. They were telling the electorate what it knows already: that the health service is in dire straits, that casual violence stalks the streets, that we have a First World economy on top of a Third World level of public provision. They were trying to convince the voters that all of these problems would go away if the same system were run by different people.

They might have got somewhere if those people were genuinely new. But if a week can be a long time in politics, five years can be very short. Michael Noonan has never escaped the ghost of Brigid McCole. Ruairí Quinn is still remembered as a man who was so comfortable in government with Fianna Fáil that the join was seamless.

It is striking that in the massacre of the Loyal Opposition, it was high-profile figures, the ones who had wielded power as ministers or junior ministers in the 1980s and 1990s (Alan Dukes, Dick Spring, Niamh Breathnach), who lost out.

In the battle between Establishment and anti-Establishment, there was simply no room for the return of an old Establishment. If you were prepared to accept things as they are, the logic was to vote for Fianna Fáil. If you felt angry and excluded, the return of familiar fifty-something figures from the past was merely irrelevant.

Michael Noonan was promising to do the same things as Bertie Ahern, but more efficiently. Ruairí Quinn's vacuous slogan 'Ambitious For Ireland' was a classic Bertie-ism without Bertie's charm.

Thus the scale of Fianna Fáil's victory is far greater than the mere reversal of the trend that has seen outgoing governments punished at the polls. For what has happened, bizarrely, is that the electorate's anger at the Government's failures has fallen on the Loyal Opposition. A very large section of the electorate was ready to hear what James Larkin called 'the divine gospel of discontent'. It didn't like Bertie or feel that self-satisfaction was the appropriate response to the way we live now. There has been, indeed, exactly what Fine Gael and Labour prayed for: a popular revolt against the two-tier health system and the contempt for the weak which it symbolises.

The failure of the Loyal Opposition to capture that rage is far more devastating than the relative contentment of those who stuck with Fianna Fáil and the Progressive Democrats. The voters got the message but shot the messenger. They were willing to consider all sorts of alternatives — the outlaw romance of Sinn Féin, the anti-materialist message of the Greens, the individual valour of a Kathryn Sinnott.

But they simply didn't see Fine Gael and Labour as coming sufficiently within the meaning of the word 'alternative'. Their attitude to Ruairí Quinn and Michael Noonan was 'Get the hell out of my way, so I can have a good kick at Bertie.' When Ruairí and Michael didn't get out of the way, they kicked them in frustration instead.

The implications of this are far more profound than any short-term disaster that can be rectified by a new leader, hard work and a new marketing strategy. The electorate has decided, once and for all, that it knows what the mainstream of Irish politics is: Fianna Fáil and whatever Fianna Fáil needs to make up the numbers.

It has lost interest in the whole idea of merely replacing from time to time this natural Establishment with another one. It knows what consensus politics can and can't deliver, and that the new Ahern-model Fianna Fáil is just better at it than anyone else; one catch-all party is enough.

Fine Gael, in other words, is finished. For the foreseeable future, the party will not be what it has been for seventy years: the core around which any alternative government could be organised.

The gap between where it is now and where it would have to be for the electorate to take its leader seriously as a Taoiseach-in-waiting is too large to be bridged.

And no Labour leader can credibly convince his party that the way forward lies in working with Fine Gael rather than seeking to replace it as the second party. Labour, moreover, is now in a mortal struggle with Sinn Féin and the Socialist Party on one side of the class divide and the Greens on the other.

Anyone who thinks that that struggle can be fought with a love letter to a moribund Fine Gael in one hand and a glossy red rose from an imploding European social democratic movement in the other is sleepwalking towards the abyss.

And yet, in the early hours of Sunday morning, after Labour's hopes of taking a second seat in Dublin South Central were dashed by Sinn Féin, the party's extremely able TD Mary Upton was talking about the need for more consensual politics. You could almost hear Gerry Adams rubbing his hands gleefully in the background.

Labour, in any case, is in no shape to rescue Fine Gael from oblivion as it did in 1994, when Dick Spring put John Bruton into the Taoiseach's chair that Bertie Ahern thought was his. The two-and-a-half party system is gone.

This doesn't mean that the future has to be the infinite triumph of Bertie and his children. For one thing, the shape of the new government will probably confirm a drift to the right. With the hole in the public finances and the increased mandate for the PD policy of cutting taxes, the strong likelihood is that public services will be contracting, not expanding.

The arrogance which has been so obvious over the last five years will be enhanced by the electoral triumph. At the same time, the electorate has created a huge space on the left, indicating more strongly than ever before its willingness to listen to alternative strategies and welcome new faces.

A right-left divide is opening up. But the right is confident, capable and in complete control of political power. The left is incoherent, fragmented and incapable in the short term of matching the unity of purpose that Bertie Ahern has forged for his party.

In a neat reversal of stereotypes, the free-market right is a near-monopolistic cartel and the left is a free market in which competition is so intense as to be virtually anarchic.

If anyone can make a clear voice heard above the din of argument and recrimination, the electorate has indicated its willingness to listen.

MONDAY, 20 MAY 2002

A Cruel Trade Indeed for the Lonely Losers

Kathy Sheridan

The moment of menace was not when Nora Owen crumpled, sustained only by the humane embrace of Labour's Seán Ryan. Nor even when Mary O'Rourke kissed Donie Cassidy after he took her seat.

It was when Charlie McCreevy said to Mary: 'Well, you won't be going back to your knitting anyway.' He may even have repeated it. By then, this share of the audience had dived under the sofa.

Yes, you meant well, Charlie. The thing is, Mary never knitted, as she told you through bared teeth. She's been busy, being a senior government minister and stuff like that. And now she's nothing. And she was blaming you or someone very bloody like you for bulldozing her into one of those beastly arrangements with the lovely Donie Cassidy.

'Charlie,' she said mournfully, 'I never got a quota.' But nobody wanted to hear that. Selfish bastards.

Avril Doyle took a different tack. Asked what had gone wrong with the game plan, her reply was an acid: 'I didn't get enough votes.'

Austin Currie's defeat, he noted, came in his thirteenth election and thirteenth year in the Dáil — 'but I'm not superstitious'.

'Is it time to chuck it all in?' asked Brian Farrell, as if he'd just been pipped for the pitch and putt prize again.

After thirty-eight years in politics, said Currie, he had intended that this would be his last election

anyway. He quoted Enoch Powell (someone always does), who said that all political careers end in failure. 'I'm happy that I contributed to public life and will leave it at that.'

Dick Spring was one of several to quote Lord Birkenhead — 'Politics is a cruel trade' — though one of the few to credit the man. Then he twisted to look at Martin Ferris — fresh from wrapping the count centre in the Tricolour — and asked: 'Can I quote lords, Martin?' (I'd say so, Dick, having witnessed his colleague, Seán Crowe, wrestling with a large bottle of bubbly earlier on).

In a classic Spring combo of grace and grump, he drew on the memory of the late Tom McEllistrim's dignity in 1987 (when he lost to Spring by four votes) as his model in this hour.

He said that, if he had to, he would do the same all over again and warned about a raft of Springs ready to spring from the political traps. Then he wrecked it all by sniffing that the 'prospect of being a backbencher for the next five years' had not been a 'riveting' one anyway.

Well, Martin, Tom and Jim, do YOU feel stupid or what? And just in case they still hadn't got the message, he outlined the job requirements: 'I wish you luck in filling all those potholes because, by God, there's a lot of them out there in North Kerry.'

As Vincent Browne intoned that he was the 'outstanding politician of his generation', along with Alan Dukes, Dick left us with some final words to treasure. These came after a soothing Brian Farrell had heaped praise upon his graciousness and sent regards to Kristi and the children. 'I'll send you a postcard', drawled Dick.

Meanwhile, as Seán Haughey pulled streamers from his hair and Eamon Ó Cuiv wrestled with more bubbly, a procession of Fine Gael's best and brightest left their ghostly, pole-axed imprints on the screen: Frances Fitzgerald, Jim Mitchell, Alans Shatter and Dukes, Charlie Flanagan, Brian Hayes … They included a grandson of a founder of the State; a grandniece of Michael Collins; the party's

Nora Owen and Seán Ryan at the City West Hotel after results from the electronic voting count for Dublin North. Photograph: Dara MacDonaill.

John Dennihy, Fianna Fáil, turns to Kathryn Sinnott to console her at the moment of his election. Photograph: Ted McCarthy/Provision.

Tánaiste and Progressive Democrats leader Mary Harney TD in Paddy Power's betting shop on Baggot Street, Dublin, to collect her €260 win from her pre-election bet that the PDs would win eight seats or more. Photograph: Bryan O'Brien.

The Taoiseach Bertie Ahern applauds his running mate Dr Dermot Fitzpatrick after his election was confirmed (Richard McAuley, the party's communications director, is included left). Photograph: Matt Kavanagh.

Dick Spring of the Labour Party learning that he has lost his seat for North Kerry in the Election Count Centre, Tralee. Photograph: Bryan O'Brien.

Sinn Féin's Martin Ferris celebrates with Northern Ireland Education Minister and party colleague Martin McGuinness after being elected for North Kerry in the Election Count Centre, Tralee. Photograph: Bryan O'Brien.

deputy leader; a former leader. Having no Fine Gaeler in Dún Laoghaire was comparable to the Tories losing Kensington or Chelsea, said Ursula Halligan on TV3.

'It's like the St Valentine's Day massacre,' said Alan Dukes.

A bereft Richard Bruton said that the fallen would want those remaining to pick up the pieces and move on. Pat Rabbitte was cross: 'For half the population, sleaze didn't even feature … It's a new Ireland, an individualistic, materialistic Ireland.'

Sinn Féin's Pat Doherty wasn't buying that: 'Pat came close to blaming the people for the result that Labour got …' A cruel trade?

While the bodies were still warm and within minutes of Michael Noonan falling honourably on his sword, Brian Farrell was bludgeoning allcomers about whether John Bruton would be welcome back in the leadership slot. 'I have no ambitions at all in that regard,' said Bruton repeatedly, before taking Farrell to task. It's not easy to find your balance in a cauldron.

But yikes, who let the dog out? Yup, the Rottweiler was back, seeking whom he might devour. If Socialist Party man Joe Higgins got back on the 'It's the bins, stupid' platform, Michael McDowell was the 'Kick 'em in the shins and run' merchant.

Dick Spring took his hat off to him. Sort of. 'No constituency work, just turns up in a constituency and then heads the poll,' shrugged a thoroughly disillusioned Dick.

And the Rottweiler Party? 'Ran the most effective anti-Fianna Fáil campaign', said Fergus Finlay, 'the most cold-blooded and ruthless tactical decision I've ever seen.'

Upon which Mary Harney popped up to say that she was 'too nice' to force humble pie on those who had written them off.

And here was McDowell, almost puppyish in his effusive acknowledgement of his canvassing army. By yesterday, on Today FM's Sunday Supplement, he was back in ankle-biting form,

mercifully, insisting that the PDs shouldn't be taken for granted by anyone.

The double act is back: Rabbitte and McDowell. Let the games begin.

MONDAY, 20 MAY 2002

Who Gets What is Central Issue for Parties Now

Mark Brennock

For all the pious talk on both sides about how the negotiations to form the next government will be driven by policy, there are few issues of serious disagreement between the parties, and none of major conflict.

The new programme for government that will emerge from the talks starting on Monday will have a different emphasis than was set by the Government in its latter years. The invitation to 'get out and party' to celebrate the good times will be replaced by a more cautious tone, reflecting the deterioration in the Exchequer position.

The Taoiseach and Tánaiste will talk by phone today and are likely to have some discussion on the delicate issue of Cabinet positions. The PDs feel, quite reasonably, that the doubling of their number of seats in the election entitles them to a stronger role in government. Fianna Fáil feels, also quite reasonably, that their increased Dáil representation should not be followed by a reduced share of the spoils of office.

There are tensions within the coalition parties, too, over who gets what. In Fianna Fáil there are many who feel their talents should be recognised by elevation to Cabinet, including Seamus Brennan, Willie O'Dea, Eamon Ó Cuív, Martin Cullen, Noel Treacy and Eoin Ryan.

To make room for some of them would involve imposing pain on others. Members of the Cabinet seen as vulnerable to enforced retirement from the top table include Dr Michael Woods, Joe

Walsh, Michael Smith and Síle de Valera. The Taoiseach is notoriously slow to offend anyone, but as one senior source says, he faces the choice between offending those he demotes, or those he fails to promote.

The forced departure of Mary O'Rourke from Cabinet should create a vacancy for another woman, and Mary Hanafin appears to be in a strong position in this regard.

Others will have to wait to see just how adventurous Mr Ahern is going to be. Coalition with the PDs would probably involve ceding a second ministry to that party. Without significant involuntary retirements, Mr Ahern will have little room to manoeuvre.

The clamour for recognition is not confined to Cabinet aspirants. On the backbenches those who will feel their time has come for promotion to the junior ranks at least include Brian Lenihan, Dick Roche, Tony Killeen, Billy Kelleher and John McGuinness. Political geography would give hope to someone from Laois-Offaly (either Seán Fleming or John Moloney), Wexford (John Browne or Tony Dempsey), Mayo (and if it isn't to be Beverley Cooper-Flynn it must be newcomer John Carty), Limerick West (Michael Collins or John Cregan). Meanwhile, Pat The Cope Gallagher would feel deserving of some reward after agreeing to run for the Dáil again to win back a seat for the party in Donegal.

And then there are the Progressive Democrats. Before the election it appeared obvious that should they get two Cabinet posts, Liz O'Donnell would join Ms Harney as a full Minister. But that was before the return of Michael McDowell after his decisive role in the party's performance. The Attorney General is believed to have his mind set on a mainstream ministerial post. After his campaign contribution, it is difficult to see him being denied.

Tom Parlon would also fancy his chances of some advancement, and the party will press for two junior positions to accommodate him and Ms O'Donnell. Should they only get one, a committee

chairmanship or some other position would be sought.

Then of course there is policy. Both parties will begin negotiating on Monday on the basis of their manifestos. There is great convergence between them in most policy areas. The lack of difference is highlighted by the fact that the issue of whether and where to build a national stadium is seen as the most difficult between the parties.

But on the stadium, both parties have given themselves enough wriggle room to allow for a deal. Mr Ahern has said he will agree to a smaller stadium if necessary, and the Fianna Fáil manifesto said the rest of the ambitious sports campus was an aspiration, not a commitment. The PDs have said they are opposed to the '€1 billion project', leaving it open to them to accept a much smaller one. While they say they don't like the idea of building a stadium at Abbotstown, they have not ruled it out.

On tax cuts, the PDs are committed to reducing the top tax rate from forty-two per cent to forty per cent, while the Fianna Fáil idea is to have a vaguer commitment. Similarly with privatisation, Fianna Fáil will want a much vaguer commitment to selling off State companies than the PDs.

In the highly unlikely event of anything providing a stumbling block to the reformation of the FF/PD Coalition, Fianna Fáil has mapped out its alternative.

They believe they can secure the consistent support of four independents — or five, if Mildred Fox is elected. While the party hopes the availability of the independent option will temper PD demands, the opposite is also true. Fianna Fáil has already been in contact with several independents, and their demands appear very reasonable.

Jackie Healy-Rae appears keen to renew the existing arrangement and has a shorter list of constituency demands than last time. In 1997 he sought and got the re-opening of the Pretty Polly Factory in Killarney, and the beginning of work on the pier at Cromane, near Killorglin. Now, he said yesterday, his priorities include upgrading the Rathmore road to Killarney and the N86 to Dingle. 'But these must be addressed anyway,' he said.

Paddy McHugh, who was elected in Galway East as an independent, having failed to secure a Fianna Fáil nomination, has stated publicly his willingness 'in principle' to support a Fianna Fáil government. In return, he said yesterday, he wants commitments to the re-opening of Tuam Hospital and additional funding for national schools, water and sewage schemes and national secondary roads in the constituency.

James Breen in Clare has similar local issues he wants to pursue, while Niall Blaney in Donegal North East is also seen by Fianna Fáil as a likely supporter.

Fianna Fáil has attempted to spread its net beyond the 'Fianna Fáil family' independents, talking informally to Mayo independent Dr Jerry Cowley. Dr Cowley campaigned strongly on the issue of the upgrading of Castlebar hospital, and is also seeking improved supply of gas to Mayo towns and improved infrastructure for the county.

Even if a deal is done with the PDs, Fianna Fáil will be keen to keep some of the independents on side. For cautious Mr Ahern, it provides an insurance option against the possibility that the Coalition could break up over some unpredicted controversy. It would be his nature already to have the next general election date set in his head: June 2007.

Ireland manager Mick McCarthy watches team captain Roy Keane react to losing a point in a practice game while training in Saipan. Photograph: Kieran Doherty/Reuters.

THURSDAY, 23 MAY 2002

'People Were Not Happy but Life Goes On. Nobody Died.'

Interview: Tom Humphries with Roy Keane in Saipan

Q. So, after all the effort you put into getting the team here, what makes you announce that you are going home after a training ground row?

A. Well, it was the tip of the iceberg. I've basically had enough of certain things. I've come over here to do well and I want people around me to want to do well. If I feel we're not all wanting the same things, there's no point. It's been going on a while. It's the whole fact of being away. Like every other footballer. Maybe I should just be OK with it, but enough is enough. I'm banging my head against a brick wall regarding certain issues about this trip. This trip is the tip of the iceberg. From the training facilities to all sorts.

Q. Even here it's not right?

A. You've seen the training pitch and I'm not being a prima donna. Training pitch, travel arrangements, getting through the bloody airport when we were leaving, it's the combination of things. I would never say 'that's the reason or this is the reason', but enough is enough.

Q. Did you have reservations about the idea of flying seventeen hours here?

A. Yeah, exactly. Flying seventeen hours. It's different if we came here to a top training facility. The hotel is fine, but we've come here to work. You wonder why players get injured? Well, playing on a surface like that. I can't imagine any other country, countries in the world who are far worse off than us, playing on something like that. I don't think it's too much for us to ask, just for a pitch that's even watered. It's so dangerous. It's rock hard. One or two of the lads have picked up injuries. I'm amazed there hasn't been more but

give it time. But you know, we're the Irish team, it's a laugh and a joke. We shouldn't expect too much.

Q. Did you talk to people about it before you got here?

A. No, no, I was quite relaxed. Everything was fine. Starting from the airport though, and the farce of trying to get through the airport, and all the press and nothing organised and we get here and the skips (containing the team's training gear) are missing, blah blah blah! Here we go. This is not right. All I want is what's best for me and the team. I mean that. It's not right in anybody's eyes. It's a laugh and a joke, of course, some of it, always has been with us, but now I'm thinking enough is enough.

Q. It's fair to say though that you came on the trip unhappy with coverage of you missing Niall Quinn's testimonial.

A. Yeah. It was straightforward. I was injured, I wasn't fit. Then coming over on Wednesday on the plane I got a couple of complimentary papers and the word 'disrespectful' was mentioned. People said I should have been in the stand in a shirt and tie. Sure. I'm not that daft either. I was going away on Wednesday for five weeks, what was I supposed to do? Sit in the stand? Do you think I would have been left alone up there? Do you think Quinny would have been going 'ah, cheers Roy for coming.'

That wouldn't have been the case. It was a choice. I wasn't fit. To spend the last night with my wife and kids … as it happened I went to the pictures with my wife at about nine o clock after a day with the kids. It was that or be up in Sunderland sitting in the stand. I'd very little time with Theresa and the kids at the end of a long year.

I played Saturday, had treatment on Monday and Tuesday and left for here on Friday. Good luck to Quinny with what he's doing, but I don't need to be involved in the whole hullaballoo. My conscience is clear. Yeah, I wasn't happy, but I forgot about that.

Q. Was it something that could have been handled better by the FAI?

A. Again yeah. Without a doubt. They knew my situation. And Quinny did. They are the most important people, Quinny and Mick. They knew my situation. I've been seeing somebody in France who's been helping with my injuries. Then I picked up two dead legs against Arsenal. It had gone by Saturday (the one in my right leg) so I played against Charlton, but there was no way I could have travelled to France to have even done that work, because he does a lot of stretching on my legs and I wasn't fit. I wouldn't have made Quinny's game.

Either I went to France on Monday and after the stretching I'd have to rest for a day or two, or the dead leg would put me out. So I let them know. My priority was getting ready for the World Cup and, again, no disrespect to Quinny.

If people want to say that …

Q. Did you call Niall yourself?

A. I spoke to Mick Byrne who's the middle man for me, really. I spoke to Mick. If I thought for one minute it would offend, I would have gone up to save the hassle. But the choice of sitting in the stand or being at home with my family, there was only one winner.

Q. But you were asked to write a piece for the programme and declined?

A. Yeah, with Cathal Dervan. No way. Not with Cathal Dervan. The same man who three or four years ago insisted the fans boo for me. Michael Kennedy (Keane's agent) asked me, through Quinny. I said, if they wanted to do it through a different avenue … but it was just left. As soon as it happened, I knew the story would be that 'he refused to write a piece'.

Q. So Tuesday, you left for training, you seemed to be in good form. What happened?

A. It's a lot of things. There's a lot of things I don't understand when we come away like this — barbecue with the media, say. I don't understand the purpose of things. Or some of the gear going missing. The barbecue. Training pitch being wrong. No balls. Only two goals. There's differences of opinions about different things. Maybe I just don't get it,

Q. What bugged you about the barbecue? The media?

A. Yeah, I'm thinking, am I supposed to sit down with people, the likes of … I'm not going to mention any names because it gives them the satisfaction, but people who've slagged me and my family off. I know papers have to report. I accept criticism, constructive anyway, but not hypocrites. And I'm not talking just about the press there but people who were there with us being pally pally.

Things like that get under my skin. I've come away to train for the World Cup, not to have barbecues with the press but, if I don't go, I'm the only person who didn't turn up. It's all false.

Q. The team went out that night. Had you any problem with that?

A. I didn't fancy going out. We'll be away a long time. No problem at all. They needed to let off a bit of steam. I went to bed. I was tired. I'm getting old.

Q. As captain, do people come to you about these things?

A. The barbecue was mentioned. I questioned it, yeah. Believe it or not, at the time I didn't want to make a fuss. If the other players were comfortable …

Q. So what was the final straw then?

A. We'd no goalkeepers for the five-a-side.

Q. I saw you reacting badly to that. Why?

A. Ask any player, any footballer, anyone in the world, anybody — at the end of training you need a little game. Their attitude was that the keepers were tired. I completely disagreed with them. Tired? Well, is that not why we are all here? Explain that one to me. We've done about three hours work here, three hours work since Nigeria last Thursday. I know it's a relaxation but we could be in for a big shock next Saturday against Cameroon.

Q. But how does it go from there to you and Alan Kelly having a shouting match?

A. Obviously Alan disagreed. Packie said they'd worked hard. Alan said they worked hard. I said 'Do ye want a pat on the back for working hard — is that not why you are here?' I did mention that they wouldn't be too tired to play golf the next day and, fair play, they dragged themselves out! That was my stance and Kells took his stance. Few words, but I've had arguments like that hundreds of times. Unfortunately, there was press there and you could say it got heated between me and Alan, but Alan is a decent lad. I went to speak to Alan later.

You can laugh about it. These things happen. You get twenty-three lads away with each other. No big deal. It's over and gone. Done with.

Q. And when you came off the training ground and got on the bus on your own, had you decided then to come home?

A. Yeah. I'd had enough. I'm not asking too much — for everyone to want what's best. If it's a crime, fuck it, I'm guilty. Listen, people show it in different ways. Some people go to their rooms but it plays on me when something can be done about it. It's not being a prima donna. There's things you can't accept. That kind of pitch. No training kit. No balls. A seventeen-hour flight and there's no skips (containing the team's training gear). They said the skips were supposed to be here on Thursday. They should have been here two weeks ago, so there was no doubt! We're getting advised that we have to drink this stuff. It's not here yet, but when it does come you have to drink it. All the lads feel the same. I react differently. I know that's a downside. I am what I am, warts and all. Maybe you'll say I should have taken a step back. That's hindsight.

Q. So what happened?

A. It was a long night and a lot went through my head. I had to speak to people I respect. Obviously I had my family to think about but if it was up to me I wouldn't still be here. Couldn't

have got a flight until four o'clock Wednesday. I spoke to my wife. I spoke to Michael (Kennedy, his agent), I spoke to Alex Ferguson. He's a good man and he gave me good words of advice. You have to listen to these people. The manager (Ferguson) has the same temperament as me. He understood what I was going through. He told me to stick it out, but this is it.

Q. What were the arguments being put to you?

A. I knew I had my family to think about back in Ireland. My poor Dad, me Mam. My three brothers and sisters. It would be all very well for me going back to Manchester. I knew all that. I was seeing straight, you know, but I just couldn't justify myself being here. Not just this trip, there's the constant, negative criticism over the years chipping away. I'm thirty, I've had my few injuries. I travelled more than other players because of my commitments to United. That's not a complaint, it's just a fact and I just got to a stage where I said, I don't need this. So I spoke to the manager and I'll stick it out till after the World Cup and that will be it for me. Without a doubt.

Q. And how do you feel now that you are staying?

A. Today I'm thinking that the first game is next Saturday. I've got some of my family coming out before then to relax with. They're people I can switch off with and relax with. Obviously I room on my own and I'm in here (in his room) quite a bit, which is what I want anyway. If there was a flight yesterday, I'd have been gone.

Q. Being on your own on these trips, does it make you lower?

A. If I did want to room with somebody, maybe. On the whole, I prefer rooming on my own. We do it at United, pre-season we'd be away ten, twelve days. I know club level is different, the bonds are different but you can't have everything. I prefer to be on my own as regards using the telephone, getting up, reading, using the bath, whatever you might want. I could do something about it but I do accept I'm on my own. I've nobody to bounce things off or have a laugh with. That's the downside.

Q. So you spoke to Theresa (his wife), to Alex Ferguson and Michael Kennedy. Was there anyone from the team coming up to your room by this stage?

A. No. To be fair, I'd made my mind up. They were giving me breathing space. I didn't want to speak to anyone else. I spoke to Theresa and she said Michael was under pressure. It had been out on the news in Ireland. I don't know how that happened, only one or two people knew, but a ticket was booked for me, so maybe that way things got out. It's no good trying to blame any one person, it's a combination of things and myself. Enough was enough.

I spoke to Michael, he said the manager (Ferguson) had been on. He was on holidays but he'd seen the news. I had a good chat with him. He's someone I respect. In football, he's the only person I would listen to. We spoke about my family. I knew what he was saying but it helps when you get other people saying it. We'd discussed it before because of my injuries curtailing my international football. He said hang in there because of my family.

Q. What impact has it all had on the lads on the team?

A. Not sure, to be honest. I think when you are away things happen. To me it's gone now, what happened. I need to get my head down for two or three weeks. Get my head down for the country, enjoy it and leave with my head held high.

Q. How have you dealt with it in terms of your relationship with the team?

A. It's gone now. Me and Kells spoke, even. We had a laugh. We are grown men. I've had hundreds of thousands of those heated discussions. Every day in training at United. Really. I had lunch with Kells on the day it happened and — this is funny — we were saying how we were both the sort of people who fly off the handle easily and how we had to learn to control that. Then three hours later we had that row. Then today at lunch we were saying 'remember that discussion we had

yesterday!' It's forgotten about. We want what's best for each other. I'll get my head down for the next three weeks. I want to do well for the people of Ireland, for my family and for me personally.

Q. Do you think though that you exist as an island apart from the team? Take the Iran game, the players were baffled that you left the morning after the first leg without saying anything?

A. It was straightforward. Sunday morning, the manager (Ferguson) spoke to Mick McCarthy. I hadn't played for three weeks before that game. After the match I was feeling my knee, especially in the last twenty minutes. We were 2-0 up having not played that well. I felt the job was done. So, it was Sunday and the manager rang me. Mick Byrne and Mick McCarthy were there. It was agreed I'd go home. I just couldn't see us losing 3-0, but I probably would have taken the blame for it anyway if we did! The lads were having a warm-down, they were all in the rooms. It's not my scene. If I passed somebody in the corridor, I'd say goodbye. I didn't go round door to door. Even here, if I was leaving I wouldn't have gone door to door. That's not my scene.

Q. Do you know anyone else who gets as intense about football and getting it right?

A. Our manager, Alex Ferguson. Look, I just want what's best. Realistically, I didn't expect to come over here and find Highbury or Anfield waiting but I expected the pitch to be at least watered. We've had two injuries. Players are tired, fatigued after a long hard season and it would be softer out there on the hotel car park. If there is something wrong with wanting that, then what chance have we got? All the players feel the same. They react differently. Some people accept it easier. Maybe that's why some of our players are playing where they are. You have to want the best. You need to prepare. It's hard enough as it is, playing Cameroon next Saturday it's going to be so bloody hard. We could be in for a shock. Everybody could be in for a shock.

Q. Apart from facilities, is it too laid-back here for you?

A. To be fair, the hotel is nice, the sun is nice but it's a long way to come for that. That's my opinion. I think we've come to train hard, to get ready for the World Cup. Look at the facilities. We need to be taking it easy a little bit, I know. To be fair, I don't see anything wrong with the golf or the night out but, when we are working hard, can we not work for three hours solid on a good pitch? Instead, we've done three one-hour sessions.

Q. Why are the highs higher for you and the lows lower?

A. I try not to be like that, believe it or not. I'm trying to get level pegging. I don't want that, the highs and lows. I react. That's the way I am. That's what's made me what I am, good and bad, but I like me. I do like me. I don't think I'm a bad person. In my life, I'm trying to get things level. When I was younger I was up and down like a rollercoaster. I was up, out and in headlines, injured and winning trophies. High up, low down.

I'm trying to get things down, accepting things, but there's only so much you can accept.

Q. Do you get depressed?

A. No. I wouldn't say depressed. I can't go back to my room and switch off. It plays on my mind. I accept a lot of things, especially with the Irish team. People say I'm always moaning but, if I moaned about everything you'd have about 40 tapes there. I like my life simple, I really do. I didn't want the hassle I had yesterday, far from it. I didn't want the night I had last night. Do you think I slept like a baby? I slept okay in the end last night but that happens when you drain yourself taking things on board. I've decided I'm here for myself and the people of Ireland and my family. Sod everybody else. This will be my last trip. I can't go banging my head against a brick wall. I can't. Sometimes you have to make a stance. If there was a flight yesterday I'd be home now and I wouldn't have felt bad about it.

Republic of Ireland captain Roy Keane chats to manager Mick McCarthy during squad training at Adagym sports-grounds, Saipan. Photograph: David Maher/Sportsfile.

Q. When you went asleep, did you know you were staying?

A. At that stage, I was still going back. I woke at about 6.30 a.m. and I rang my wife. She said Michael Kennedy had been on, he was under pressure from the press. I rang him and he said to ring the manager (Ferguson). He'd been ringing me but couldn't get through to the hotel because of the phones here. I spoke to the gaffer, he said his piece. I decided. I think there was all sorts going on in the background. A lot of people were not happy but life goes on. Nobody died.

Q. What did you say to Mick McCarthy after training?

A. I told Mick I had enough. Basically that was it. We've had discussions already the other night about training facilities. You've got to prepare properly is my attitude.

Q. You hate the loveable Irish thing, don't you?

A. I suppose so. I accept it, I'm as Irish as anybody, but this has been going on for years. Training facilities, travel arrangements. It's easy to pass the buck. Everyone here does it. You got to prepare properly though, it's hard enough as it is. If I opened my mouth every time there's something wrong, I'd need my own newspaper.

Q. Had you any idea coming away that this was the end of your international career?

A. No. I was definitely going to the European Championships. Without a doubt. Maybe no friendly internationals but … It gets harder, no matter what you are doing. That's all. I had no intentions of quitting. I do love the ninety minutes, it's the rest of the crap. I'm sure the other players love their kids, but I can't worry about the other players. I have to worry about me. I travel a lot, I have four kids. I miss them. Everyone is different. All I can do is look after me and my family. The European Championships would have been my swansong. It's just come early.

Q. Any going back?

A. Unless there's drastic changes. No.

Q. Who are your friends in football?

A. There isn't anyone I wouldn't class as a friend. There's a lot of people I like. The Irish lads are all decent, good lads but I wouldn't be one to pick up the phone or send Christmas cards. A lot of people are like that. I have my family. I can go out with them and relax and switch off. It won't go beyond them. I've been that way for a long time. It's nothing to do with having a high profile. I've been a bit wary of people for a long time. It's a good thing.

Q. What's that song you've been heard to sing, 'Positively Fourth Street'?

A. My singing days are over. How does that one go again?

Q. You know. 'You've got a lot of nerve to say you are my friend, you just want to be on the side that's winning.'

A. Oh yeah, that one. In my defence, I was only joining in. Yeah, that would sum it up for me but there's people away from football I'd be comfortable with. You have to be like that, have to be a bit wary. People talk. I read things about myself. Players even. Niall Quinn did something, with Paul Kimmage I think, a few months ago. Jason did something too. Niall said, if Roy was buttering his toast it would have to be perfect. I'm thinking, what's Niall talking about? People think they know you. Daft things like that. I don't want to get on the PR machine though. I don't want it. I do like my life simple. People will laugh at that but people who know me … I was in UCC last week and it was a huge honour for me and my family, but a day like that, it takes its toll on me. I don't feel comfortable in places like that. I'm so grateful for it — that goes without saying — but give me my kids and walking my dog any day of the week. I do like my life simple and I have to laugh at myself because …

Q. Do you think you'll manage or would you prefer to walk away from football altogether?

A. It could go either way. I'd be very capable of walking away but I see the challenge of being a manager. I'd love to pull the strings of a big club, players, listen to people. I look at our manager and I think about it. I know it's stressful. People will say, if I'm going to walk away from this, what chance do I have of being a manager. I don't know. I think I'd enjoy that challenge. At the end of the day, I enjoy managing myself regarding looking after myself, stretching, weights. I'd enjoy stretching that. Good players and good people with me, people I could trust. I'd like that.

On the other hand, getting away from it, to a life where people leave you alone. I suppose the longer you're out of it … I'd love the idea of holidays at Christmas with my family, summers in Australia, doing courses or whatever. It's hard to imagine.

I have a four-year contract at United, though. That has its challenges. I'm hungry, I've probably never been as hungry as I am now for success. It still hurts me what happened at United this season. I need people around me to be hungry, too. It's the same with Ireland. I need people pulling the same way and wanting what's best.

Q. But isn't there more than one way to skin a cat?

A. Possibly. People do it different ways. Some people need an arm put around them. Yeah, I'm sure there are other ways. I watch people who I respect and if you know football it's about the different needs of different players.

People think because I go away with the Irish team I'm moaning, because it's not as good as Manchester United. That's nonsense. I want to have a good training pitch. At Manchester United they want the best of everything. That's the difference, they want it. Everybody. When we travel the treatment is fantastic because of that. People in the laundrette, the canteen, feel that way at United … A bad result and there's doom and gloom. Otherwise what are you playing the game for? I accept a lot of things. I know the FAI haven't got millions in the bank, but it's cost a lot of money to come out here and look … It's preparation. Fail to prepare. Prepare to fail.

Q. Why do you think Saipan was chosen as a venue for preparation?

A. Haven't a clue. Somebody came here once and it looked nice once. They thought they were making an effort because it's really far away. The important things weren't looked at. Travel, of course. A training pitch.

We had a lovely day yesterday, we went up to Suicide Cliff and learned the history. I enjoyed that, that's the nice side of it, but I keep saying to everybody we're here to prepare for the World Cup.

I was going to go back up there today to that cliff! Add an Irishman to the list (laughs).

It's gone now, this business. We'll just get on with it. Maybe it's the vibe I send out, the monster that's been built, some of it through my own doing but I don't expect anybody here to tiptoe around me. Alan Kelly took the piss out of the thing today. He came out at training with a balaclava on. I was glad. Alan would be a player I would talk to a lot. I don't want to be burning my bridges there! I'd be down to zero!

Q. How do you think you've come out of this whole thing?

A. I come off the worst, no matter what! Eventually the penny has to drop but you need to put the penny in. I'm learning but I'm only human. These things happen for a reason. You have to learn from these things, the bad things. Without a doubt. I think the best has still to come. I've made mistakes. I'm better for the mistakes. Introduce me to somebody who hasn't made mistakes and I'll shake his hand. Things happen for a reason. I'm sure the man upstairs is guiding me along the way, putting a few obstacles in the way but I feel very happy with life. I do. I just don't want us going home saying 'if only we'd prepared better'.

Q. And what have you learned?

A. Well, it's brought a decision that enough is enough. At this moment in time, I know this is my swansong. Not sure I'll be missed.

Q. It'll be duller!

A. It might be!

Q. You could be player-manager in the future?

A. Yeah. Nobody would play for me but we'd have great facilities!

Q. Well, you'd be the media choice.

A. Yeah? Right. That's that then!

FRIDAY, 24 MAY 2002

An Enmity of Long Standing

Tom Humphries

The long and fractious relationship between Roy Keane and Mick McCarthy came to an end yesterday in the unlikeliest of settings and the World Cup will unravel without one of its greatest stars. A deserted restaurant in a plush hotel on the pacific island of Saipan, with a string quartet jangling in the lobby, was the venue as ten minutes or so of vitriol was delivered by the player towards the Irish manager.

At the end there was nothing left to be said. Just goodbye.

The incident which occurred in the presence of the entire Irish squad and staff drew an emphatic line under a relationship which has been symbiotic but without respect from the start. Players who attended the meeting said they had never seen anything quite like what they witnessed.

'He questioned Mick as a manager and a person,' said one. 'I've never seen anyone abused in that way. He was white with rage.' When Keane finished he left the room.

'Is that it then?' asked Gary Kelly. 'Is it over?' It was. The team spoke among themselves for a while, but each contribution hinged on the shared knowledge that Roy Keane wouldn't be playing in this World Cup. The Irish squad moves on to Izumo on the Japanese mainland this morning and

they do so hoping that they are about to begin a fresh chapter in their World Cup preparations. One suspects, however, that the ghost of Roy Keane will follow them from now until the moment they arrive home.

As the player remained cosseted in his room last night, waiting for the second of just two flights off the island of Saipan today, the implications of one of the biggest stories ever to have broken across Irish sport were hitting home.

First, there was the almost poignant thought of Keane completely stripped of the armour of his team and being left abandoned to make his way home. When travelling with the Irish squad Keane is seldom seen in public without either team physio Mick Byrne or security man Tony Hickey, acting as wingman to protect him from intrusion.

Through the years his value to the squad has been such that allowances have been made for him, as they were for other great players of the past like Keane's close friend Paul McGrath. They have closed ranks around him, celebrated with him in his greatest moments, and suffered the lash of his tongue on the darker days. This morning they head off to the World Cup (a competition he dragged the team to by sheer force of will) without him, leaving him alone on a Pacific island which he despises, leaving him to face a gruelling journey home and a summer of tabloid inquisition. In the end, the team and manager decided that the price for accommodating Keane had become too high.

In a debate which will divide Irish sporting opinion for years, it is possible to have sympathy for both men. McCarthy's virtues are well advertised, and he has played his hand well and patiently this week, moving with a quiet serenity through a series of events which even a few months ago would have derailed him.

For his part, Roy Keane has considerable qualities which, in keeping with his intense desire for privacy, he keeps to himself. He admits that in terms of his public image, he has created something of a monster, yet he is capable of immense warmth and loyalty, flashes of high good humour and private generosity. He has an interest in the world around him which he somehow accommodates along with his lifestyle as a family man and a footballing obsessive.

There is a darker side to him, too, an aspect of him that can be almost frightening in its intensity, yet he burns off that black energy quickly and is willing to get on with things again. He is a loner and a passionate man and those qualities rarely find a good home in the raucous universe of football teams. He has been fortunate in that he met Alex Ferguson comparatively early in his career and found a kindred spirit who matched his obsession with excellence every step of the way.

This past week Keane has been unhappy certainly, but not consistently so. He has been quietly critical of McCarthy, but that in itself was no revelation; the pair appeared to have hammered out a working relationship in the past year or so.

Keane mixed sporadically with team-mates, especially senior players, and with his old friend Mick Byrne. The journey to Saipan was marked, however, by Keane's display of unhappiness with the communications structure within the FAI which he felt left him hanging over the issue of his non-attendance at Niall Quinn's testimonial game. He expressed his displeasure to several journalists on the way across, telling one that all media were scumbags.

Yet even in the height of the controversy which broke mid-week with the initial news that Keane had left the squad but had changed his mind and returned, he was approachable and talkative. He spent his days joining in what he considered to be the inadequate amount of training done by the team, and then either walking alone or resting in his room til early evening when the air cooled and he would go to the gym.

He had several discussions with McCarthy before yesterday's fatal derailment. On Monday evening he sat down with the manager to express his dissatisfaction with the non-arrival of the team's

training gear and other aspects of the preparations. On Tuesday, after his training-ground row with Alan Kelly, more talks followed.

McCarthy stressed to the player that if there were things wrong with the training set-up on the island, the week was to be regarded as rest and recreation anyway, and that serious work would begin when the team pitched camp at Izumo. The facilities there have been tailor-made for World Cup preparations. Keane, however, wanted McCarthy to accept more responsibility for what was wrong and said repeatedly that enough was enough and that he was going home.

Next morning, however, he took counsel from his friend and mentor Alex Ferguson and opted to stay. He subsequently fulfilled an agreement to this newspaper to provide an interview during which he publicly aired some of his grievances concerning the squad preparations and training. Publication gave rise to more questions and, seeking to end the

Republic of Ireland manager Mick McCarthy during the press conference at the Izumo Sports Park and Dome, Izumo, Japan. Photograph: Toby Melville/PA.

THE IRISH TIMES BOOK OF THE YEAR

cycle wherein team and media spoke of nothing else but Keane, McCarthy called yesterday's team meeting. It was a high-risk strategy, which brought an end to a relationship which had never quite flourished.

Older members of the Irish travelling party last night recalled the incident which marked the beginning of the enmity between the two men. It was 1992 and the US Cup, Roy Keane's first trip away with an Irish squad. The team's visit to the US wound up in Boston. On the final day, with an evening flight awaiting and with Jack Charlton off on one of his famous earners, several members of the squad decided to go playing golf. On their way they called into the south Boston bar of Frank Gillespie, an old friend of the team. There Keane and a couple of other players were already holding court. The golf was abandoned. The drinking embraced.

Time passed. In Charlton's absence, it was an unwritten rule that McCarthy took control of the squad. The big defender's natural sense of authority made that a logical choice. McCarthy, waiting impatiently at the team hotel, took matters into his own hands. He knew where to look for the missing players, so he asked Mick Byrne to pack the bags of all the players and load them on the bus. They'd pick up the drinkers on the way to the airport.

Duly the players were dragged from the pub in a state of high merriment. It had been a long season and had begun the summer holidays in convivial style. Keane, the shy emerging young star, was last on to the bus. He was wearing a Kiss-Me-Quick hat and a sloppy smile. McCarthy, irritated at how long the evacuations from the pub had taken, began to berate Keane.

'Look at you, look at the state of you,' he growled. 'You call yourself a footballer?'

Keane's rejoinder was quick and, to use the vernacular, came with studs up. 'And you call what you have a first touch?'

It was the sort of joke which might be made among footballing peers, but one which sat uneasily in the developing relationship between young tyro

and World Cup captain. Still it never seemed like anything more than a swift one-liner which got thrown in whenever Roy Keane anecdotes were swapped. By US '94, McCarthy had retired and Keane had become the star of the show. When McCarthy's barrack-square bark no longer drove Irish players on, it was Keane's incessant demands for more effort and better effort.

Players, right through to this week, have resented and appreciated his presence in about equal measure. In his autobiography, Jaap Stam, the former Manchester United defender, mused as to whether it was better to be picked to play with Keane or against Keane in the morning five-a-sides at United. Playing against him exposed you to the ferocious tackles; playing with him left your ears vulnerable to the blow-torch exhortations of a man who couldn't stand to see anything less than excellence.

And Keane's voice is generally unchallenged. He is tough and demanding, but what he extracts from himself has always made his presence, until yesterday, indispensable. It was that quality in Keane, that obsessive drive, which led McCarthy to appoint him team captain back in 1996 in an attempt to integrate him into the heart of the squad. The fracture at the heart of their relationship never healed, however. Keane got sent off in his first game under McCarthy and then, using the intermediary system which served as a substitute for communication between the two men, somehow failed to inform McCarthy that he would not be travelling to America for the US Cup in '96. McCarthy suffered the humiliation of taking a hoax call which he was convinced was Keane.

Both men appreciated that they would never have a relationship which involved in Keane's words 'going on holiday together, or even sending cards', but the hope was that the friction could be minimal. As results improved, the differences between the two men seemed to matter less.

This week, in close quarters in Saipan, has been different, though. Keane brought troubles with him and brooding in his room for long stretches of the day never freed himself of them.

For a man who is eternally hard on himself, the imperfections he saw in Saipan were hard to bear. He channelled his frustrations at McCarthy with whom he felt the buck should stop.

In the end McCarthy was left with little room for manoeuvre. Being abused in front of the entire squad was an unprecedented challenge to his authority. The nature and vehemence of the abuse seems to have been choice and novel, taking aback everyone who saw it.

When the storm abated, McCarthy had just three options. To quit. To play out the World Cup as a private laughing stock among his players, or thirdly to send home his greatest star.

In the end, the relationship between two of the country's most distinguished football men came down to a game of Call My Bluff. Would McCarthy surrender all authority in order to accommodate his best player, or would he risk being remembered as the man who sent home Roy Keane and who then struggled at the World Cup?

McCarthy did the brave thing, and yet for Keane and his troubles there can only be sympathy.

MONDAY, 27 MAY 2002

War of Words Across Great Divide

Mary Hannigan

On and on it rumbles and, judging by the tone of interviews with both protagonists in *Ireland on Sunday* yesterday, there's as much chance of a reconciliation between Roy Keane and Mick McCarthy this week as there is of Costa Rica winning the 2002 World Cup.

'There is absolutely no chance of that happening, never in a million years,' said Keane, when asked if there was any hope of him returning to the World Cup squad. 'I won't be going back, no matter who gets involved in the mediation, even if it's the Man upstairs … I couldn't play with certain players any more. I am finished. The only way I would go back now is if Mick left while certain other players retired.'

Keane insisted the reason he was speaking out, to journalist Peter Fitton, was because he wanted people to know his side of the story and the full facts of the ill-fated team meeting on Thursday. He claimed his attack on McCarthy was provoked by the manager accusing him, in front of the entire squad and backroom staff, of 'faking injury' and of 'letting down the country' and denied calling McCarthy an 'English c★★★' or ever doubting his 'Irishness'.

'I hope the people of Ireland understand my position,' he said. 'I'm giving this explanation for them. They deserve to know the truth. I am not asking for forgiveness, but I just want them to understand my side of the story. I know I have a temper, but I deal with life in real terms. I haven't got any halo. I only wished I had. But I do things for what I believe are the right reasons.'

Keane claimed that he 'exploded' at the meeting after McCarthy accused him of 'faking injury to miss squads and also of letting down the country'. 'It was a reference to my missing the final qualifier against Iran in Tehran,' he said. 'He knew what the truth of that was because he had spoken to Alex Ferguson about it. He agreed that my knee problem had to be considered and accepted that.

'Now, suddenly, the accusations were being repeated. And it was being done in front of all the players, not in private. In the privacy of a room with Mick I could have handled it, discussed it. But I exploded. It wasn't right to treat me that way.

'Mick was definitely putting a challenge down to me. Without a doubt it was all set up for me to react. I was being provoked and I swear on my children's life that it was being done deliberately.

'I did call Mick a wanker and, no, I don't feel I should apologise for that now. When your loyalty

Ireland's captain Roy Keane recovers from a sprint during a training session at the Adagym football pitch in Saipan after retracting his departure from the squad due to personal problems. Ireland, whose group contains Germany, Saudi Arabia and Cameroon, were on the small tropical island of Saipan to acclimatize for the humid conditions expected in Japan at the start of the World Cup 2002. Photograph: Kieran Doherty/Reuters.

to your country is questioned and faking injury is mentioned then I think you have a right to speak out. That's what happened with me. I had to defend my position.

'I said to Mick that I didn't respect him as a player, as a manager, or as a person. To be fair I used the expletive against him as well. I'm no angel, but these things hurt me to be accused in such a way. The language was strong, but that's always the case in football. It's not a debating society.

'Mick also showed the players a copy of *The Irish Times* and an interview I had done. He said I was turning against the players. It just wasn't true.

But he said that if I couldn't respect him then I shouldn't play for him and that's when I walked out.

'Sure, I called Mick a wanker. I'm not sorry about that, but I didn't refer to him being an Englishman, not an Irishman, in any way. I was just trying to defend myself from very serious and unfair allegations.

'There's no going back now. I don't feel an ounce of guilt about my part in what has happened. I will return to Ireland next week and walk down the main street in Cork with my head held high. I have nothing to be ashamed of. I don't think I should be apologising … I have huge pride in the Irish nation and that has not altered. But I will never be accused of faking injury and letting down my country, particularly when the accusations are made in front of the rest of the players. That's why I reacted like I did and I don't feel sorry about any aspect of it.'

While revealing that he received no support from anyone present at the team meeting Keane claimed that, privately, two players told him they backed everything he had said but would not speak out because they did not want to risk their chances of playing in the World Cup.

'When I left that room on Thursday night, no one except me knows how I felt. There are twenty players in there and ten staff and not one of them stood up and said: "Hey, come on". That's when you know your friends. Let's just say it did not feel good.'

But 'following the meeting several players came to see me — two of them said they had completely agreed with what I'd said but didn't want to place themselves in jeopardy, they wanted to play in the World Cup … I appreciated their honesty and I also appreciated their position.

'Some people are sheep and some are wolves. There are a lot of sheep over there and probably I am a wolf — that's my honest assessment,' he added.

While accepting that 'the manager … is the man who should be in charge', Keane insisted that 'as the captain I believe I am entitled to express my opinion. I do have a conscience and I try to do what's right. I'm not always shouting my mouth off, as some would have you believe. Look, I do lose my temper. And I did lose it in that meeting on Thursday night, but I feel I did the right thing. I had my honour to defend.'

Meanwhile, in the same newspaper, Mick McCarthy — who had vowed not to discuss Roy Keane again, but made an exception for the column he is paid to write — defended his position and gave his account of Thursday's team meeting.

'Roy was asked to explain why he felt we did not provide him with the best World Cup preparation possible.

'That is all I did … I asked him to tell me and the Irish squad what was causing him to run to the press like a scalded cat just hours after I had accepted his decision to renege on his international retirement.

'He treated me with honesty in his reply. Sadly, there was no dignity and precious little respect in his choice of language … I have never had to listen to such foul-mouthed abuse from any footballer in any dressing-room or any meeting room. I have never witnessed such an attack from any human being in any walk of life.

'I have had rows with Roy before but never at this level. It was vicious, it was unprecedented and it was unjust. I did not deserve it. I did not deserve to be treated like that by any human being. I was not going to take it.

'When Roy had finished his rant I threw him out of the squad … I was right, no matter what some people back in Dublin, people who were nowhere near that hotel room, have to say on the subject.

'Roy left me with no choice but to sack him. The honesty he displayed in that hotel dining-room was obnoxious, degrading to me and downright rude.

'I look at him after he waded in with one expletive after another, and I asked myself if this was my captain, if this was one of my players. Was this a man who could serve Ireland as a role model for our kids, for the youngsters who dream of following him on to the World Cup stage?

'The answer to all of that, judging by his behaviour in front of the other players and the backroom team in Saipan, is no.'

McCarthy made no reference in his article to Keane's allegation that he accused his captain of feigning injury to miss Republic of Ireland matches but insisted that the player, and nobody else, was responsible for his departure from the World Cup squad.

'Roy Keane is history now. He will never again get the chance to talk to me like that again. It was intolerable and it is over.

'We will move on, we will do Ireland proud in Japan these two weeks, without the best player we have. That was his doing and no one else's.

'Roy Keane drove us to the World Cup finals and drove himself out. You should all know that. And you should all ask yourself what sort of role model is he now.'

TUESDAY, 28 MAY 2002

An Emotional Rollercoaster Ride

Mary Hannigan

So, you're one of the folk out there who believes Roy Keane doesn't give a toss about playing for his country? Take it you missed his interview with RTÉ yesterday evening? If you read the transcript or heard it on radio it doesn't count. You needed to see his eyes, that muscle flexing in his jaw, to really, really understand just how he feels about it all.

Trust me. He wants to be at the World Cup even more than Mick McCarthy and his ghost-writer — the man who asked Ireland to boo Roy Keane at Lansdowne Road (sensitive choice of ghost-writer, Mick — must have been a good deal) — appear to revel in his absence from the very same tournament.

Perhaps you're one of the Law undergrads still toiling to get the degree you think will make you a cut above the rest and who resents a (spit) under-educated (sneer) footballer being crowned a doctorate of Law? Even if he's already achieved infinitely more and inspired and thrilled and given more sheer, unadulterated joy to those folk blessed with a pulse than you will screw in the course of your professional lifetime.

Oooops. Steady. Such emotion. Can't be having that. Forgive me. Have just watched Roy Keane's emotional interview on RTÉ and, damn it, your honour, I'm feeling emotional.

Hands up. I had the privilege and honour of watching him live and uninterrupted (apart from the missiles being thrown by the Juventus supporters in the tier above me) in Turin's Stadio delle Alpi in 1999 when he produced, quite simply, a sporting display of such majesty and selflessness that it damn well made me cry. Literally. Guilty, your honour. And proud of it. If you weren't there you'll never understand.

Before that night I classed myself as an agnostic. After that night I knew there was a God. Because He allowed me witness this magnificent creature's finest hour in the flesh. He could have delayed my flight from Gatwick. He chose not to. Despite the fog. God is good.

When I read the views of the miserable begrudgers, who could never tolerate Keane's success long before now, and heard the opinions of the fools who think Ireland is better off without his passion and drive, I thought, if only you were lucky enough to be in the Stadio delle Alpi that night. If only you saw what I saw.

Maybe then you'd reconsider your tired, trite, yawn-inducing declaration that this lad is only in it

Roy Keane's RTÉ interview with Tommie Gorman.

for the money. You know nothing. Absolutely nothing.

'I would be happier if the Irish nation stopped talking about Roy Keane,' Mick McCarthy told the *London Evening Standard* yesterday, before proceeding to speak at length about Roy Keane (as he had also done to yesterday's *Daily Mail*).

'I will not talk about him again for the duration of our World Cup bid,' he continued, before talking some more about … Roy Keane.

I will, I won't. I won't, I will. If the Irish defence is as indecisive against Cameroon next Saturday morning we can turn out the lights on our World Cup hopes.

The spinners have been at work since that infamous team meeting in Saipan last week — it's been Roy Keane versus Mick McCarthy, twenty-two players and roughly ten backroom staff. 'I didn't want to go through the media, I didn't want to be doing this interview today, I didn't want to be speaking to the *Mail* over the weekend, but when I got back in to London on Saturday morning my solicitor said: "Roy, you need to say something because there's an imbalance to the story" and I thought "he's right",' Keane told RTÉ last night.

'I might be a lot of things, but I'm not a liar,' he said, 'I try to live my life as honest as I can. I've made mistakes, probably more than anybody. I've done things I'm ashamed of over the years, but I'm sticking to my guns. I believe my gut feeling was right. What happened last week, to me, was wrong … I wouldn't wish it on anybody'.

McCarthy accused Keane of letting down his country. Good one Mick! Instead of getting down on your bended knees and thanking Roy Keane for getting YOU to the World Cup you smeared him, the player who dragged your team, screaming, to these finals.

McCarthy, Staunton, Quinn and Co. wouldn't be within an ass's roar of Japan this week if it wasn't for Roy Keane. And they know it. Last night, on RTÉ, Keane let his dignified mask slip. He let us know that he is hurt by this and that he cares about

it a lot more than he should. 'I'd love to play in the World Cup,' he said. And by jaysus, did he mean it. More fool he. He's rocked the boat and, as we know, there is no place for rebels with a cause in Irish football.

WEDNESDAY, 29 MAY 2002

Keane's Decision to Stay Away Ends a Long Saga

Emmet Malone in Izumo, Japan

Roy Keane announced last night that he would not, after all, be seeking to join up with Ireland's World Cup squad in Japan. In a statement issued on behalf of the 30-year-old midfielder, it was claimed that it would not be in 'the best interests of Irish football' for him to pursue the matter at this stage.

The news broke when Keane's solicitor, Mr Michael Kennedy, first phoned Niall Quinn and then the FAI's treasurer, Mr John Delaney, to tell them of his client's decision. Mr Delaney said Mr Kennedy told him: 'I've bad news — in the interests of Irish football Roy has decided to stay at home.'

The news was a blow to everybody who had worked behind the scenes to facilitate the player's return to Mick McCarthy's squad ahead of Saturday's first game of the World Cup finals against Cameroon, in Niigata. Mr Delaney, whom Mr Kennedy thanked for his efforts, said he had 'expressed my disappointment as I felt that earlier in the day and on Monday we were close to getting an agreement. But there must be closure now. This has been like someone in the family dying slowly, but this brings it to an end. It's been difficult, but we've got to move on now.'

The decision appears to end the speculation that has been rife since Keane travelled home from Saipan at the end of last week after a row with McCarthy.

Since Sunday, talks aimed at getting the pair to patch over their differences had been going on between the various parties involved and it had been hoped as late as last night at the Irish base in Izumo that the Irish captain might still travel in time to play this weekend.

A deal was actually brokered on Monday with Mr Kennedy reportedly telling FAI officials and senior players that Keane would offer an acceptable apology to McCarthy during his interview with RTÉ.

The player said very little in the interview that would have impressed McCarthy, however, and yesterday the Ireland manager made it clear that if the impasse was going to be resolved Keane would have to contact him directly and apologise.

It is a prospect that appears to have proven unpalatable to Ireland's best footballer and, having made it clear on Monday evening how much playing in the competition for a second time would mean to him, Keane now appears to find that missing out on a place on the game's greatest stage is preferable to making a potentially embarrassing phone call.

The news that Keane has ruled out the possibility of travelling to Japan may prompt mixed emotions in McCarthy who, on the one hand, looks virtually certain to be without his best player at these championships but who, on the other, may be relieved of some of the immense pressure he was under to find a way around the problem.

Yesterday McCarthy told the squad's other twenty-two players that he would resign if Keane was brought back without having to apologise. After a discussion amongst the various squad members, all agreed that they backed his stand on the issue.

Even after that, however, Quinn said he would be 'devastated' if Keane were absent from the finals. He said he would still vote for allowing the Corkman back into the squad if, as McCarthy said he would, the manager consulted all of the players and technical staff who were at the original Saipan

meeting after receiving any conciliatory messages from Keane.

Talks aimed at finding a solution appeared to have resumed almost as soon as the initial disappointment over Keane's remarks in Monday night's RTÉ interview had passed.

Mr Delaney was back in touch with Mr Kennedy while FAI general secretary Mr Brendan Menton travelled back from FIFA's congress in Seoul to liaise with senior squad members and McCarthy himself.

McCarthy expressed some distaste for the negotiations of recent days. He had, he said, tried to stop them on several occasions. 'I don't think that there should be negotiations going on to arrange an apology,' he said.

'If I feel the need to make one, I go and pick the phone up or I go and see the person I am apologising to.'

His insistence on forcing Keane into saying sorry personally now looks to have prompted Keane to abandon any hope of rejoining the squad, although the manager will take some heart from the words of Quinn yesterday who said that 'ultimately Roy is at fault — we can't escape that'.

Nevertheless, with supporters having organised small protests in Dublin and Cork even before the news broke last night, there may well be a backlash from fans who think not enough was done to facilitate a solution.

WEDNESDAY, 29 MAY 2002

Hamlet with FAI Buffoons but No Prince

Keith Duggan

The scarcely believable sequence of words and pictures that reached us from Japan yesterday suggested that the Irish camp has disintegrated to a level of dysfunction that is staggering. That Niall Quinn

Republic of Ireland striker Niall Quinn talks to the media about the Roy Keane affair at the Izumo Sports Park and Dome, Izumo, Japan. Quinn revealed how all twenty-two members of the Republic of Ireland's World Cup squad voted in favour of Roy Keane not being allowed to return to the Far East. Photograph: Toby Melville/PA.

has writ himself a large and celestial part in a sorry drama that really had nothing to do with him is the latest manifestation of a fatal and unforgivable lapse in management and administration.

When Mick McCarthy went on air to essentially contradict Quinn's verdict that the Roy Keane expulsion was beyond resolution it became clear that the natural orders that preserve the cohesion of any squad had ceased to exist.

The ultimate consequences of this shameful and petty episode are painfully set in stone at this stage. Mick McCarthy's position as Irish manager has become untenable and resignation will become the likelihood when Ireland's interests in this World Cup end — and arguably, they have already ceased.

It is uncertain anyway that McCarthy, a proud and honourable man, will wish to continue after the surreal collapse of his authority. The failure to right this fiasco renders it, sadly, the terrible and definitive legacy of an era through which McCarthy had painstakingly developed into a manager of considerable standing.

What ought to be his finest hour has freefallen into a nightmare of pride and pettiness that has somehow become a metaphor for what this country stands for.

Many people are understandably growing increasingly uneasy at the hysteria that this standoff between McCarthy and Roy Keane has provoked. The old maxim about football not being a matter of life or death has been invoked. And the thousands of calls and missives have been both fascinating and extreme. Why the madness?

What possessed a caller on RTÉ radio, an articulate and rational soccer fan who said that he has missed three Irish home soccer internationals

A wreath placed outside the FAI offices in Merrion Square, Dublin. The card reads 'Irish Football 1/6/1921–23/5/2002'. Photograph: Dara MacDonaill.

since 1973 — think of that — to declare he is going to cheer for Cameroon on Saturday? The reason is that many people believe that Roy Keane stands for a rare brilliance, the unflinching and unapologetic pursuit of excellence and that he has been obstructed and punished for that pursuit. Keane is no angel, as he has elaborated in his many media purges over the past few days. Last Tuesday in Saipan, he was hotheaded and hasty and foolish when he threatened to leave the island. But he reconsidered and he was probably privately embarrassed at the exposure the incident received.

Since then, he has never once lost focus of the reasons for his anger. His comments in this newspaper last Thursday were compelling and intelligent and justified.

In his reaction, Mick McCarthy demonstrated a succinct failure to manage. He allowed emotional slants to set in motion the swift chain of events that led to the sacking and dismissal of Roy Keane, the very soul of the Irish team. It was an act of terrible folly. The very fact that he had left himself open in recent days to a phone call from the Irish captain was an implicit acknowledgement of that ill-begotten haste.

Whatever Keane said to McCarthy was doubtless unpleasant but it ought to have been apparent that someone with his combustible temperament would react badly to being dressed down in front of his team-mates.

And the disgraceful hours of isolation that Keane endured following his dismissal were far more grievous and hurtful than any words, however foul and spiteful. To leave a player of ten years' standing to arrange his way home from a remote island is terrible.

That the FAI expected Roy Keane to apologise after that cold abandonment is a further example of their collective ineptitude. In private, Keane may well have met McCarthy half way but Niall Quinn's admission that the players were anxiously awaiting word of Keane's *mea culpa* live on television is funny and touching and tragic all at once.

Keane could not apologise because he believes there is nothing to apologise for. He raged against a cult of imperfection, of doing things wrong, of messing up, of plain carelessness that has long been the hallmark of the FAI. Mick McCarthy and his years of patient team-building have been betrayed by the FAI as much as Keane. But McCarthy has the misfortune of being manager. It was up to him to ensure that the mind-boggling cock-ups that so enervated Keane did not happen.

Roy Keane ought to have been flown back to Japan with no preconditions or daft demands. Team sports are primal and elastic; had McCarthy seen to welcome back Keane into the squad, then all reservations would have dissolved.

174

Players just want to play and on the strongest team possible. Chances are, the young stars of this side, Ireland's future, are devastated at the thought of not lining out alongside their childhood inspiration.

Now that Roy Keane will not wear the Irish shirt on Saturday morning, a shameful and mean hour in Irish sport and life has come to pass. Arguably the greatest Irish sportsman of all time has been denied the right to grace the high theatre of world sport in a summer that sees him at the peak of his fiery and singular genius.

And for what? The absence of a hollow apology? The appalling thing is that the worst is probably yet to come. If Niall Quinn's ravaged expression is an accurate reading, then the Republic's squad is mentally washed out. It can't even be said that this has affected preparation. It has as good as been utterly abandoned. Ironically, had Roy Keane made it to Japan, he would probably have been the most well rested and serene of all the Irish players. For him, there is no moral dilemma in this. Evidently, that was not the case in Japan.

On Saturday, Cameroon could inflict an on-field humiliation to match the behind-the-scenes embarrassments. The one hope is that Cameroon may grow scared of the notion of facing a side that might play with the desperation of the unhinged.

The sad thing is, of course, that many Irish people can't bring themselves to care anymore. Think back to the carnival night in Lansdowne Road a few weeks ago. It will be a long, long time before we arrive at such beautiful scenes again. Mick McCarthy did much to inspire them and somehow has let it all go up in flames. And the fall-out from this may well affect his reputation among clubs rumoured to be considering poaching him.

Everything is uncertain now. We may never witness Roy Keane's magnificence in Lansdowne again. We may not see McCarthy on the touch lines again. Irish soccer has taken a monumental blow and the buffoons who run the FAI have to stand up and accept the blame. Cathal Dervan may yet get to hear his miserable chorus of booing whenever Ireland next play at Lansdowne. But not, as he once wished, at Roy Keane.

If this is the end of Roy Keane's international career, then Ireland has become a smaller and meaner place.

Letters to the Editor
May 2002

General Election 2002

Sir, — I just love the the statement (29 April) by FG's Michael Noonan that he will deliver on healthcare.

Don't you know Michael Noonan that the women of Ireland know that you did not deliver for Bridget McCole.

She will not be forgotten. — Yours, etc., Ger Conway (Mrs), Scolarstown Road, Dublin 16. 1 May 2002.

Sir, — In the light of Minister for Sport Dr Jim McDaid's remarks about suicide, I strongly urge him not to resign.

If he were to resign there would be the possibility that he could return to general medical practice and I shudder to think of a patient suffering from depression and suicidal thoughts attending his surgery in search of sympathy, understanding and treatment.

Dr McDaid should stay in politics! It's really the only arena where his callous, uncaring and flippant attitudes are an asset rather than a liability. — Yours, etc., Darrin Morrissey, Dun Laoghaire, Co. Dublin. 3 May 2002.

Sir, — I find it very disappointing to read in today's The Irish Times *that the Taoiseach's cavalcade is showing incredible disregard for speed limits and for the safety of other road users. It seems ridiculous that speeds of eighty-five or ninety-five m.p.h. are fair game — to visit an auctioneering business. But the most distasteful*

Ruth Carroll, exhibition and gallery co-ordinator at the Royal Hibernian Academy, Gallagher Gallery, viewing exhibits in the 172nd RHA annual exhibition before the official opening in Ely Place, Dublin. Photograph: Matt Kavanagh.

aspect of this is that the Taoiseach could joke about speeding so soon after the deaths of two Gardaí in Stillorgan. All this from the party that promised 'Zero Tolerance'. — Yours, etc., Thomas Healy, Kildare. 4 May 2002.

Sir, — With the general election coming up I find I watch less TV, listen to little radio and read only the sports pages. My quality of life has improved already. Thank you, politicians! — Yours, etc., David R. Noble, Foster Avenue, Blackrock, Co. Dublin. 14 May 2002.

Sir, — When Michael Noonan became leader of Fine Gael he promised to 'give Fine Gael back to the people'. Obviously not too many people wanted it back! — Yours, etc., Cormac Duggan, Ballinode, Co. Monaghan. 21 May 2002.

Red Card for Roy Keane

Sir, — Does Roy Keane think he's better than the rest of us? The Irish people put up with sub-par services every day, from slow, unhygienic public transport, to hippy-bashing policemen, all the way up to 'brown-bag' politicians. Why would he have thought the FAI should be any different?

More importantly, why wouldn't he just do as the rest of us do and give his best shot regardless? Perhaps all those years working for a knight of the Queen has softened him somewhat. — Yours, etc., J. Best, Stoneybatter, Dublin 7. 25 May 2002.

Sir, — The Roy Keane episode highlights the contrast between two of the great sporting bodies in Ireland: the GAA, an amateur sport with professional administration, and the FAI, a professional sport with amateur administration. — Yours, etc., Rory O'Donnell, Boston, USA. 27 May 2002.

Sir, — And yet, somehow, life goes on. — Yours, etc., Seoirse Ó Dúnlaing, Scholarstown Road, Dublin 16. 27 May 2002.

MONDAY, 3 JUNE 2002

'Who Knows, Maybe He Invented Listowel'

Michael O'Regan, in Listowel

John B. Keane's funeral in Listowel on Saturday had all the ingredients of his powerful dramas. There were tears, laughter, a sombre farewell to a much-loved family man and friend, anecdotes capturing the essence of the man, and music, song and prayer. Commercial life came to a standstill in the north Kerry town, as large crowds marched behind the hearse to the Old Cemetery and lined the route for his last journey.

There was a poignant moment when the hearse, escorted by a guard-of-honour, paused outside John B. Keane's pub, where the playwright, novelist and poet had played host to locals and international visitors over the decades. He had done his writing in an upstairs room, sometimes late into the night, casting an occasional observant eye on the rhythm of life in William Street. It was in the pub that he had listened to the rich language of the people from the Stacks Mountains, who dropped in for a drink on their visits to the town on fair days and shopping expeditions in the 1950s and 60s. Part of his legacy is that their remarkable way of life has been chronicled in his considerable output over five decades.

Earlier, his son, Billy, had told the congregation at the Requiem Mass that the stop outside the pub was appropriate because his father never made a long journey without visiting a hostelry. The hearse then moved on to the John B. Keane Road, named after the famous local son and referred to by his children as 'Dad's road'. Danny Hannon, of the Lartigue Theatre, a friend since childhood, noted in his graveside oration that John B. Keane's last resting place was near places dear to his heart. Close by are the national school, St Michael's College, where he began his writing career, and the GAA pitch where, as he once told Danny

Mary Keane embraces the coffin of her late husband, Kerry playwright and author John B. Keane. Burial took place in Listowel Old Cemetery. Photograph: Matt Kavanagh.

Hannon, he had 'repelled football invaders from Ballylongford and Moyvane who had dared to challenge the football hierarchy of Listowel'. The funeral was an occasion for saluting a popular local man as much as an international literary celebrity. Danny Hannon noted how John B. Keane was rooted in his home town.

'He epitomised Listowel. Who knows, maybe he invented it. This is the town he cherished above all others. He loved its people, he treasured the streets and laneways where he walked. He was at his most joyful whenever the town was dressed in festive regalia.' John B. Keane's art, he said, was not one to be contemplated at a distance. 'It needs to be lived and loved at close quarters, because although much of what he wrote about was universal, its roots are deep in north Kerry. You

will not stray too far from this place today before you encounter those whimsical Keane specialities: the lovesick farmer, the successful TD, the country postman and the Irish parish priest. And if you do, you should be glad that there was an Irish writer who laid it all down on the page for posterity.' John B. Keane would have appreciated the irony of the pomp of church and State which surrounded the removal of his remains to the church on Friday and his burial on Saturday. The man who had railed against the State's policy of compulsory Irish in the schools of the 1960s, and had been sometimes critical of the hierarchical church, while remaining deeply spiritual, had the President, Mrs McAleese; two former taoisigh, Mr Liam Cosgrave and Dr Garret FitzGerald; the Minister for Health, Mr Martin; and the Minister for Arts, Culture

Michael McDonnell's Viking Ship on the River Shannon at Clonmacnois, Co. Offaly. Photograph: Frank Miller.

and the Gaeltacht, Ms de Valera, representing the Government, as well as the Bishop of Kerry, Dr Bill Murphy, and twenty-five priests, at his funeral. Fr Kieran O'Shea, parish priest of Knocknagoshel, and a lifelong friend, recalled how he had visited him a few days before he died. John B. Keane told him he had a short time to live and said simply: 'My next appointment is with the Man Above.' And, in an emotional farewell, Fr O'Shea remarked: 'Goodbye old pal, till we meet again.'

At the cemetery, Danny Hannon's final farewell to his old friend was by way of a poem written by the late Ray McAnally, whose powerful portrayal of the Bull McCabe in *The Field* won many plaudits, to mark John B. Keane's fiftieth birthday twenty-three years ago.

Some of the lines read:

Has he bugged the brains of Paradise?
Has he tapped the angel's phone?
Has God the Father special gifts
For John B. Keane alone?

TUESDAY, 4 JUNE 2002

Imagine There's No Leaving ... It's Easy if You Try

Róisín Ingle

I have to confess first off that I don't really remember much about my Leaving Cert. I know it happened in 1989. I know that I didn't study much. I know that at the time I was fully aware that the farce would have little bearing on The Rest Of My Life. And, what do you know, it didn't.

I do remember spending a few weeks before the exam learning history essays off by heart. Two hours after finishing the paper I wouldn't have been able to tell you a single thing about it. But then regurgitating information you won't recall afterwards is exactly what the Leaving Cert is all about.

I also remember consulting an Ouija board one night, asking John Lennon what themes we would be asked to explore in the Shakespeare play. Lennon was a fine songwriter but as it turns out he knows little or nothing about *King Lear*.

A friend took pity on me and dragged me down to Pembroke Library in Ballsbridge, Dublin, to study. My well-meaning friend eventually gave up. I spent most of the time watching the ants file through the cracks in the pavement outside thinking how uncomplicated their life must be.

I remember it was very sunny that year. Girls in short grey skirts sunned themselves between exams. They looked so cool perusing their colour coded notes. Some had been getting grinds at the Institute of Education. Some of them knew exactly what they wanted to be. I suppose I envied them, wished I had everything mapped out the way they seemed to. But the sane part of me knew there was something very weird about planning the rest of your life when you are only seventeen.

It didn't go unnoticed in the blazing heat that I was wearing black opaque tights. There was a good reason for this. A last minute panic attack meant I had written half the home-economics course in black pen on my thighs. Actually, the plan was to go to the bathroom and consult my legs

Republic of Ireland fan Joe O'Sullivan, from Glasnevin, watches Ireland's first World Cup game against Cameroon on a big screen at the Submarine Bar in Dublin. Photograph: Frank Miller.

in the middle of the exam. As I said, it was sunny. By the time I put my plan into action the writing had melted clean away.

English turned out okay. There was an essay on 'What it means to be Irish' or something. I wrote the kind of thing I thought the examiners wanted me to write. Ah, sure aren't we a great little nation all the same. Pity about the exam system.

I have to thank my sister for the fact that I passed maths, a subject that remains a complete mystery to me. I had done nothing. (And I don't mean nothing in the way all those swots used to say 'Ohmigawd, I have done nothing', when what they really meant was 'Yah, theorems rule'.)

The day before the exam my sister spent a few hours with me explaining the basics of the maths papers. I passed, which was all I really wanted. I was so glad I hadn't spent two years on it when it only took an afternoon.

I repeated the Leaving Cert a year later and remember even less about that. It was the summer of Italia '90 and I know I had at least one World Cup party so I can't have been taking it very seriously.

But I wish you good luck over the coming weeks. Just remember, while it might not feel like it now, there really are a lot more important things in life.

WEDNESDAY, 5 JUNE 2002

FF Remains Shy About Spending Control Plans

John McManus

Fianna Fáil assiduously avoided committing itself to economic targets during the election campaign and has reprised the tactic in the Programme for Government produced yesterday.

The absence of any target for government spending is the most surprising aspect of the Budgetary and Economic Policy section of the document. It had been expected that a tough target would be set as an indication of the new government's determination to deal with the holes that are appearing in the Exchequer finances; the most significant of which is the mismatch between revenue and expenditure.

Tax revenues are well below the levels predicted in the Budget, while spending is significantly ahead. An end-of-year deficit in excess of €1 billion is forecast if the trends that have emerged continue. Getting government spending back under control is the number one economic issue facing the new government, yet the programme is effectively silent on the issue.

There is no mention of any cutbacks — or even a review of — government spending. Measures that could boost revenues are also absent. The only commitments given on taxation are for further reductions in both the number of people paying tax and the amount they will pay. Business taxes will also be reduced. Similarly, there is no discussion of how the coalition plans to deal with the issue of public sector pay.

The report of the body charged with benchmarking public sector pay against the private sector is due at the end of the month. Pay increases of twenty per cent or more for some State sector workers are forecast. Implementing the twenty-five per cent of the awards that are due for payment immediately will put tremendous pressure on the public finances, yet the issue is ignored.

Progressive Democrat sources were keen to stress last night that the lack of any firm targets in the document should not be blown out of proportion. They acknowledged that the decision to avoid any parameters was driven by Fianna Fáil, but there is agreement on both sides as to what must be done, they stress.

Both parties worked on the assumption that the economy will grow by around five per cent a year over the next five years and that inflation will average three per cent a year.

Irish rock star Bono shares a joke with children with HIV/AIDS at the Missionaries of Charity AIDS hospice in Addis Ababa, Ethiopia. US Treasury Secretary Paul O'Neill (second from left) presents a check for US$400,000 to the hospice. Bono and O'Neill met with Ethiopian religious leaders on HIV/AIDS. O'Neill's visit to Ethiopia concludes a ten-day journey in Africa that has included visits to Ghana, South Africa and Uganda. Photograph: Sayyid Azim/AP Photo.

Much will hinge on the attitude of the next minister for finance. The key dynamic in the framing of budgetary policy is between the Taoiseach, Tánaiste and Minister for Finance. The identity of the first two is a given, but there are no guarantees that Mr Charlie McCreevy will be returned to the Department of Finance.

However, the vague nature of the economic parameters set out in the programme suggest that the Progressive Democrats must anticipate Mr McCreevy's return. Without Mr McCreevy in Finance, the junior partners would have much less reason to be confident that the hard economic issues will be tackled. In any event, failure to get the Exchequer finances under control will render most of the other commitments in the Budgetary and Economic Policy section redundant.

Taxation reform will remain at the heart of the coalition's economic policies, but a much less radical programme is proposed than the one implemented over the past five years.

The main commitments are to take all those on the minimum wage out of the tax net and ensure that eighty per cent of all earners pay tax only at the standard rate. Any 'improvements' in the income tax regime will come if economic resources permit.

There is a commitment to keep down taxes on work, which is seen as an indirect commitment not to raise employers' PRSI.

Addressing the 'infrastructural deficit' will be another priority, according to the document. The two parties had different views on how to raise the money to fund investment. The document is silent on the issue of a return to borrowing, but both parties made it clear during the election campaign that they will borrow, subject to the limits imposed by the EU growth and stability pact.

Fianna Fáil proposed topping up this debt with additional borrowing routed through a new government agency. The attraction of this was that up to half of the money borrowed by the agency would not count towards the EU limit. The Progressive Democrats favoured selling off State assets and raiding the reserves of the Central Bank and create a national development fund.

The compromise deal involves the establishment of the National Development Finance Agency that Fianna Fáil wants, but there will also be the PDs' National Development Fund. However, there is no commitment to actually activate the fund by selling any State companies.

It remains to be seen how the rather cumbersome structure that has been arrived at will work in practice.

WEDNESDAY, 5 JUNE 2002

Reminders that Summer Time is Here, Slightly Ahead of Schedule as Usual

Rome Letter: Paddy Agnew

Misty Lazio mornings, kinks in the hose-pipe, snakes that slither out from the water-pump house, flowers for Corpus Domini, end-of-year school exams, trips to the airport for family visitors, suntans and female midriffs — summer time is here, slightly ahead of schedule as usual.

This has been a long dry winter into spring, in these parts. Little rain has fallen and the landscape is already beginning to look thirsty. In such far from perfect circumstances, the baroness (herself) has decided to recreate Versailles, or more specifically the gardens thereof.

This has meant a lot of digging, earth-moving, pipe-laying, cursing and, last but not least, watering. As the heat gathers, too, our little reptile friends descend from the oak woods above us in search of a drop with which to soften a parched fang.

Thus it was that Alessandro, the plumber engaged on herself's post-Versailles *magnum opus*, enthusiastically reported a snake sighting in the water-pump house. A sighting is one thing, of course, but the important thing to establish is which type of snake was sighted.

Basically, we have two in these parts — the biscia (grass snake) and the vipera (viper). The former can look *Raiders of the Lost Ark* impressive but is in fact relatively harmless, while the latter looks like an insignificant, tiddly little thing but can kill you.

Whenever a snake is sighted, the immediate reaction (and this applied to Alessandro) is to claim that it was a vipera. On further investigation, it nearly always turns out to be a biscia. Your fearless correspondent (Harrison Ford is the role model) has occasionally had to slay a mighty biscia that opted to make his home in our garden, yet I have only once had a good close-up view of a vipera which, given his bad press, understandably tends to be wary of humankind. (On the occasion I did see one, the vipera in question was so concentrated on an imminent hit job on a hapless frog that he ignored the nearby human.)

The return of the 'biscia or vipera' question, however, like end-of-year school exams (next week) or the sudden and startling appearance of a hundred thousand, perfectly tanned shoulders and midriffs is a sure sign of this Italian time of year.

An equally sure indication, too, is the 'road closed' sign that blocks off our village on the first

Sunday in June as preparations are made for the Corpus Domini feast, celebrated with the laying of a carpet of flowers that form intricate patterns all the way round the village streets. Until a recent chat with Gilberto. I used to think that the laying of the flowers was basically the preserve of pious 'auld ones'. Not so.

At first glance, you would hardly imagine that Gilberto, who runs the lake's only taxi service, is big into flower patterns. He is a serious AC Milan supporter, chews a lot of gum, wears the odd chest medallion and drives according to the Schumacher school of Ferrari shunting.

Yet, during a recent early morning, madcap dash to the airport, Gilberto told me that he and his village cohorts (the Bracciano lot on the other side of the lake) were off to Siena for a flower *spettacolo*. In other words, Gilberto and cohorts have become so handy at the old flower patterns that they now occasionally travel the country to strut their stuff.

I am off on the 'airport run' this morning to greet the first of the summer visitors (sister of the baroness). As I adjust my peak cap for the long hot summer, I can at least report some good news.

In response to vigorous lobbying from your correspondent, the Italian government has wisely enacted emergency legislation that envisages immediate repatriation not only for those Irish tourists who order a cappuccino after their lunch or dinner but also for house guests who threaten to talk, whisper, cough, comment or otherwise make themselves heard during live broadcasts of World Cup games. Have a good one.

Damien Duff bows to the crowd after scoring Ireland's third goal against Saudi Arabia in Yokohama, Japan. Photograph: David Maher/Sportsfile.

THURSDAY, 6 JUNE 2002

Fine Gael Sends Mr Nice Guy to the Front as War Dust Settles

Denis Coghlan

In the crush outside Leinster House, the assembled journalists called 'Enda, Enda' as they sought his attention. It was the Bertie Ahern factor writ small.

But they were on first-name terms and familiarity of access was likely to translate into a honeymoon period for the new Fine Gael leader. The fifty-one-year-old Mr Kenny will certainly need it. After losing twenty-three Dáil seats, party members are still deeply traumatised. They will require careful handling if they are to be motivated and energised. The worst thing that could happen would be the re-emergence of old divisions.

The new Fine Gael leader won't go down that road. The first thing he promised was to create a strong Opposition in the 29th Dáil by using all the talents, assets and strengths of the party.

But while promising universal largesse, he already owed a few people. And Michael Ring was first and foremost. The ambitious, poll-topping TD, who outshone Mr Kenny in his home constituency of Mayo, had proposed him for the job and canvassed on his behalf.

After the victory, Mr Ring was quick to call for an end to 'moaning and groaning' within the party. And he was pleased Fine Gael would have 'a nice fresh face for its posters'.

It was a comment repeated by Kenny supporters, who spoke passionately of the need for the electorate to LIKE whoever led the party. The

Enda Kenny TD (centre) with deputies (from left) Gay Mitchell, Phil Hogan and Richard Bruton at Leinster House following his election as leader of the Fine Gael party. Photograph: Eric Luke.

message seemed to be that while previous incumbents, like John Bruton and Michael Noonan, had been smart and even streetwise, they had failed to connect with the electorate at a visceral level. In that regard, they felt Mr Kenny would get off to a flying start.

Ireland manager Mick McCarthy consoles Kevin Kilbane, who missed a penalty in the shoot-out following a 0-0 draw against Spain at Suwon, South Korea. Spain won the shoot-out 3-2 and progressed to the quarter finals. Photograph: Toby Melville/PA Photo.

The fact that he had secured the support of young Olwyn Enright as his seconder wouldn't hurt. And if he gives Richard Bruton a plum job next week, he could be expected to attract his mentors, Simon Coveney and Fergus O'Dowd.

Sixteen months ago Mr Kenny challenged Michael Noonan for the leadership and was blown away. On that occasion he offered to 'electrify the party' if he became leader, but was reluctant to identify his methods. A similar lack of specifics was evident yesterday during a brief meeting with the press. But that can be remedied. If there is one thing Fine Gael is not short of at the moment it is thinking time.

In terms of leadership, Mr Kenny lacks ministerial experience in a big-spending Department. His two-year stint at Cabinet, from 1995 to 1997, was spent at Trade and Tourism. Before that, he was a junior minister with responsibility for youth affairs from 1986 to 1987. But while popular within the party, he never hit the political big time.

Mr Kenny has to market himself as a competent, caring leader. And the soundbites are already beginning to flow. Another Mr Nice Guy has hit town. Smile, Enda, smile.

MONDAY, 17 JUNE 2002

Dream Dies on the Spot

Match report Emmet Malone

Republic of Ireland–1 Spain–1

And so the story ends with another game to be remembered for its heroics. This time, the memory of the heartbreak will also linger just a little while too. In years to come, though, it will be recalled that an Irish team determined beyond reason to live up to the boast of their 5,000 supporters that they could never be beaten took a star-studded Spain the distance and then some more.

After the ninety nerve-racking minutes of the game itself, Mick McCarthy's men dominated a

A dejected Robbie Keane holds his head in his hands after Ireland's defeat to Spain in the second round of the World Cup finals in Suwon, South Korea. Photograph: David Maher/Sportsfile.

Spanish side reduced to ten men by injury. And when the goal needed to win the game wouldn't come, it seemed we might see a rerun of those unforgettable scenes in Genoa twelve years ago. This time, though, penalties turned out to be the rock on which the dreams of this brave team finally foundered.

Robbie Keane, as he had done in the ninetieth minute of normal time, converted Ireland's first spot kick in the penalty shoot-out without fuss to give his side an early advantage. But a missed kick by Matt Holland and poor efforts by David Connolly and Kevin Kilbane that were saved by Real Madrid's remarkably composed twenty-one-year-old goalkeeper, Iker Casillas, left their team on the verge of defeat after Fernando Hierro and Baraja had both found the net for the Spaniards.

Juanfran and Juan Carlos Valeron went some way to handing the advantage straight back to the Irish by firing their penalties wide, but going into the last round of the required five kicks Steve Finnan needed to do better than Gaizka Mendieta if the process was going to be extended. After the right back pounded the ball into the roof of the goal there appeared to be just a glimmer of hope.

Cruelly, though, it was extinguished by the Lazio winger who badly scuffed his kick only to see it bounce over the leg of Shay Given and into the net.

From the dugout McCarthy and the players who hadn't been involved in the game when extra time had ended started to make their way towards the centre circle. Their World Cup adventure had ended with the same heartbreak Jack Charlton's men had imposed on the Romanians in Italy. Still, the Irish manager must have struggled to take it in that it is Jose Camacho's side rather than his own that will go on to play in next weekend's quarter-finals.

Maybe it just would have been easier had the Irish been well beaten and the game over as a contest before Ireland's supporters had been given the basis for believing it would be another of those magical evenings we were starting to grow accustomed to.

For a while that was indeed how it seemed likely to turn out. Ireland were behind within eight minutes of the start, when Fernando Morientes gave the Spanish the lead with a glancing header from so close in that Shay Given could barely have been expected to react never mind make a save. And during the spell that followed they dominated a game in which possession might have been shared rather evenly but only one side looked seriously capable of posing a threat to the other's goal. On nine separate occasions, in fact, either Raul or Morientes were hauled back after being caught fractionally off side. It was a dangerous game that the Irish defence was involved in, but they were certainly playing it well.

Crucial to the team's survival during that rocky spell was that Steve Staunton was consistently getting the better of his encounter with Raul, Real's twenty-three-year-old superstar. All around him, though, Irishmen were rising to the occasion. Steve Finnan, in particular, was outstanding, and Gary Breen, the goal aside, showed great composure as he and the rest of the defence repeatedly found themselves on the back foot.

During that first half the Spanish showed a team renowned for the tempo of its game that they knew a thing or two about playing their football at speed. Their work-rate and speed of movement provided the basis for their dominance, especially in midfield where Valeron, Baraja and Luis Enrique seemed endlessly capable of providing support to their front men when required but also of lending a hand to the team's determined effort to get bodies behind the ball while the Irish were in possession.

So while McCarthy's men saw a fair bit of the ball they achieved almost no penetration in attack. When the Spaniards dropped back into defence, they simply allowed the Irish to play in front of them, patiently waiting for the error that would allow them to break swiftly towards Given's goal.

Gradually, however, the Irish came to grips with the challenge, and as they improved the sparkle went out of the Spanish game. Key to the shift in the balance of the game was once again the switch by Damien Duff from central attack to his preferred role out on the flanks. This time it was on the right, but that appeared to matter little to the twenty-three-year-old who promptly started to tie some of the world's best defenders up in knots with a series of darting runs from deep positions.

With his adoption of the changed role having coincided with the arrival of Niall Quinn there was now some height to be aimed at in the Spanish box. The big Sunderland striker, on his last appearance for his country, can scarcely ever have thrown himself about to greater effect, and the thirty-five-year-old caused Hierro and Ivan Helguera a whole range of problems they had come ill-equipped to deal with.

As he did so, Quinn was well supported by Robbie Keane and later by Kevin Kilbane, whose influence grew dramatically after an opening hour in which he seemed incapable of troubling the Barcelona right back Puyol.

Even while he was struggling, though, Kilbane might have been the Irish hero had only his finishing been better, for twice the goal lay open before him and twice the Sunderland winger failed to grab the opportunity.

By far the more painful miss was his attempt to slot away the loose ball after a poorly directed Ian Harte penalty in the sixty-second minute had rebounded off Casillas and straight into his path. It looked as though the twenty-five-year-old should have attempted a diving header but he didn't and his shot was badly misdirected.

It was one of a growing number of close scrapes for the Spanish at the back, however, and by the time Hierro rather recklessly took two handfuls of Quinn's shirt and attempted to manhandle him into submission with the referee looking on, Camacho's men were working hard indeed to hang on.

Crucially, though, the game was virtually over at that point, and despite Duff's wizardry and the growing menace of Keane, the Irish had still not found a way of breaking their opponents down when they were gifted their second penalty. With Harte having again been substituted despite a generally improved performance, Keane this time stepped up to take the last-minute spot kick and coolly pushed the game into extra time.

When it started, though, none of the Irish players were aware until long afterwards that the Spanish substitute Albelda had been forced out of the game by the recurrence of a hamstring injury, and so his side was reduced to ten men.

The numerical advantage combined with the fact that Raul, also because of injury, and Morientes had both earlier been replaced, was obvious immediately with Mark Kinsella and Matt Holland now completing their takeover of the midfield.

The Irish assumed almost complete control, and though some of the play produced by both sides was understandably nervous the chances they

The President, Mary McAleese, with Taoiseach Bertie Ahern, who was in Áras an Uachtaráin receiving his seal of office. Photograph: Brenda Fitzsimons.

created reflected that they were now far more likely to go on and win it. Indeed Breen, Kilbane and Keane all went close again, but in the end time simply ran out.

Finally we were left to hope that history might repeat itself. But sadly it wasn't to be and Spain, for the first time in their long but mysteriously unrewarding association with this competition, won a game that had gone beyond ninety minutes. Perhaps it really is going to be their year.

The only thing certain for now is that, for all of this Irish team's vast reservoir of courage, they couldn't prevent it being Spain's night.

MONDAY, 17 JUNE 2002

The Seanad is Useless and Undemocratic

John Waters

One morning last week, I was on the NewsTalk 106 Breakfast Show with David McWilliams. I was debating equality with a moderately well-known feminist. Having spoken about her commitment to equality for nearly half an hour, it emerged that this individual was running as a candidate for one of the Trinity College seats in the Seanad election.

Having long commented on the brass neck of feminists, it shouldn't have surprised me that she saw no contradiction between pontificating about equality and running in an undemocratic election, but strangely it did. The CEO of the Equality Authority, Mr Niall Crowley, was on the same programme and he saw nothing wrong with the Seanad elections either, but the only thing that would surprise me about the Equality Authority would be news that it had done something to promote genuine equality.

Like roughly ninety-five per cent of the general electoral register, I do not have a vote in the

Seanad election. If I had been to Trinity College or one of the National University of Ireland colleges, I would have the right to vote. But because I left school at eighteen to work and pay taxes to subsidise the education of people attending university, I do not have any right to vote in the election for the Upper House of the Oireachtas.

You might imagine that the general tolerance for such a devaluation of the essential principles of democracy, in what aspires to being a modern state, would be a matter of public outrage and debate. It might at least, you would think, excite comment from those who claim in other contexts to be the watchdogs of civil and human rights, equality and democratic freedoms.

That it does not is due mainly to three factors: 1) virtually all the watchdogs of civil and human rights, equality and democratic freedoms have been to either Trinity or the NUI; 2) almost all opinion formers in this society can vote in Seanad elections also; 3) the Seanad is a completely irrelevant and useless talking shop which was created out of a post-colonial grandiosity seeking to replicate the House of Lords and nobody can think about it without falling asleep.

Given its anti-democratic nature, the sheer uselessness of the Seanad emerges as its only redeeming quality. Its main function is as a political life-support system for failed TDs. In all, there are sixty senators, eleven of whom are nominated by the Taoiseach, so as to ensure a government majority. A majority of senators (forty-three) are elected from panels of persons alleged to have 'knowledge and practical experience' under five vocational headings: 1) national language and culture, literature, art, education and so forth; 2) agriculture and fisheries; 3) labour; 4) industry and commerce; and 5) public administration and social services.

For these forty-three seats, only 900 local and national politicians may vote, and this arrangement ensures that the Seanad functions as a shadow of the Dáil, its composition reflecting the relative strengths of the major political parties. A provision in Article 19 of the Constitution whereby vocational groups, councils or associations might directly elect their representatives has not been activated by legislation.

The remaining six senators are elected by graduates of TCD and the NUI. There are 102,000 NUI and 39,000 TCD voters, each body electing three senators. NUI graduates do occasionally get hot under the collar about the undemocratic nature of this disproportion, but rarely extend their logic to the full picture.

A constitutional referendum in 1979 permitted the extension of voting rights to graduates of all third-level institutions, but no law has yet given effect to this. If it were not so useless, if it were more than a refuge for the casualties of bad vote-management strategies and the congenitally un-electable, if it had the slightest contribution to make to the democratic life of this nation, then, clearly, the fact that election for the Seanad is the locus of one of the most blatant instances of privilege in this society would matter a great deal. So yes, the Seanad's very irrelevance means the democratic deficit is not at first sight a major concern.

There is, however, the distinct likelihood that such an undemocratic construction is contributing to public cynicism by bringing the political system into disrepute. When these provisions were introduced by the 1937 Constitution, a degree was still a novelty and there was a perhaps understandable assumption that a university graduate was smarter than the average.

Today, some of the most spectacularly ignorant people in this society have emerged from the university system. Yet, despite the steady increase in the numbers of young people attending third level, there remains a considerable geographical/socio-economic complexion to the sector excluded from this privilege, and this overlaps significantly with the segment of the general electorate least likely to vote in any context.

On Friday last, I was back on NewsTalk to debate the undemocratic nature of the Seanad with

Senator David Norris, who has represented TCD in Seanad Éireann for many years. Mr Norris's position was simple: elitism is a good thing. It seems the election, albeit undemocratically, of special representatives of the most privileged caste in this society has something to do with 'excellence', which only the mediocre-minded could cavil with. The problem is that in politics, 'elitism' does not translate as 'excellence' but as oligarchy, monarchy or dictatorship.

WEDNESDAY, 19 JUNE 2002

Families Wait for the Bitter Confirmation of Loved Ones Who Are Lost

David Horovitz

Amit Maliah, a driver with Israel's Egged bus company, was slightly late for work yesterday morning, so his colleague, Rahamim Tsidkiyahu, went out on his 32A bus instead.

As Mr Maliah, now driving the next bus along the same route, neared the top of the hill that leads down from Jerusalem's southern Gilo neighbourhood toward the city centre, he and his passengers heard an almighty boom: Mr Tsidkiyahu's bus, at the bottom of the hill, had been blown up.

'All my passengers were panicking,' said Mr Maliah, who has worked for Egged for twelve years. 'Some of them were parents who feared for their children, whom they thought were on the bus ahead.'

'Rahamim's bus had been pretty full,' said Mr Maliah. Some children, hurrying to school, had apparently squeezed in while their parents waited for the next bus.

Mr Tsidkiyahu did not survive the horrific suicide-bombing. Along with eighteen of his passengers, he was killed by the bomber, who detonated his explosives — packed with screws and ball-bearings — near the entrance to the bus, at that stop by the bottom of the hill.

Rescue workers found the driver, still with his hands on the steering wheel, dead in his seat, as blood trickled down the steps by the door.

The white and red bus was reduced to a shell, its roof ripped away, every window smashed. And its passengers, every single one of them, according to police, was either killed or injured.

The dead were laid out under black plastic on stretchers, on the pavement just across from the mangled wreck of the vehicle in which they had perished. Almost all of them came from the Gilo neighbourhood.

Some of the casualties were, indeed, kids on their way to school. 'We're checking to see if all our pupils have arrived,' said Ruth Elmaliach, who teaches at the school adjacent to the bus stop. 'We fear that they have not.'

'There were bodies piled up near the door,' said Shalom Sabag, who was driving a car in front of the bus as it exploded and who dashed to help. 'I took off the bodies of two girls and a man. There was one girl I cannot forget. She had a long braid down her back and she lay on her stomach.'

Shlomi Calderon, who was driving a small lorry alongside the bus, having just dropped off his two children at kindergarten, said his vehicle was hit by parts of the bus, and that he saw at least two bodies blown out of the back windows. Hospitalised with minor injuries, he said the scene was 'indescribably horrible'.

At the city's Hadassah Hospital, the head nurse in the emergency room had a 'sixth sense' that the bombing was imminent, and began to lay out equipment, even before the sirens started wailing.

Her sixth sense was reinforced by an official alert: Police had taken the unusual step on Monday night of issuing a specific warning that a bomber had made his way to the city and was poised to strike.

So devastating was the force of the blast, so drastic the impact on the passengers, that as of late

Israeli policemen and medics work around the destroyed number 32A bus at Jerusalem's Pat junction near the neighbourhood of Gilo. A suspect Palestinian suicide bomber blew himself up, killing eighteen people and wounding many others. The blast was so powerful it ripped through the front of the bus and turned it into a mound of twisted wreckage. Photograph: Reuters.

yesterday afternoon, only a few of the bodies had been conclusively identified — fifty-one-year-old Mr Tsidkiyahu's among them.

But the families already knew that their loved ones were lost despite the lack of positive identification from the hospitals.

The bombed bus had been dragged away from the scene of the blast. Most of the blood had been hosed away. Small knots of demonstrators had gathered to chant 'Death to the Arabs'.

And they, the bereaved, were waiting at the national forensic centre for the bitter confirmation.

FRIDAY, 28 JUNE 2002

An Intelligent Start to Nice

Editorial

The Government has moved intelligently to address political concerns arising from the Treaty of Nice. Legislation published yesterday adds a new constitutional guarantee that Ireland could not join a common defence in the European Union without the approval of the people in a referendum.

A new Select Committee on European Affairs is to scrutinise EU legislation, promising more effective democratic accountability and will be in place before the second referendum on Nice is held in the autumn. The Government now hopes the debate can move on to discuss EU enlargement and maintaining Ireland's position in Europe.

Real progress has been made with these decisions. The two declarations on Ireland's military neutrality adopted at the European Council in Seville, which clarify the procedures to be followed for Irish involvement in EU military operations, are now to be supplemented by a constitutional entrenchment of the principle that a referendum would have to be held on any move to introduce a common defence.

This guarantee will help allay fears that Ireland could drift into a military alliance without a popular mandate. It should reduce the mistrust arising from Fianna Fáil's failure to hold a promised referendum on joining the Partnership for Peace. And yet it keeps open the Government's freedom to run a security and defence policy without being subject to the constant threats of constitutional challenge that would have arisen if military neutrality was to be written into the Constitution. Irish participation in operations conducted by the EU's Rapid Reaction Force remain subject to the 'triple lock' of United Nations mandate, Government decision and Oireachtas approval.

Equally important is the move towards more effective political scrutiny of EU business. Most

Nick Harris, author of a book on the vanishing of Dublin's Jewish Community, in the Irish Jewish Museum on Victoria Road, off South Circular Road, Dublin. Photograph: David Sleator

complaints about the democratic deficit in the EU concentrate on the secretive Council of Ministers and overlook the failure by national legislatures to make their own executives properly accountable on EU business. With the announcement that the new Select Committee on European Affairs is to begin its work next week and will have a legislative basis before the referendum is held, there is an opportunity for Ireland to adopt the best EU practice on parliamentary scrutiny. In the Convention on the Future of Europe and the subsequent treaty

A picture released by the Israeli Defence Forces shows what they say is a photo of a Palestinian baby dressed like a suicide bomber. The IDF said they found the photo during a search in a house of a wanted Palestinian man from Hebron, where Israeli army tanks and helicopters gunship pounded a Palestinian police building in an attempt to smoke out fifteen wanted Palestinian men Israel said had taken cover inside. Photograph: Reuters.

the question of democratic accountability is being addressed more comprehensively than ever before. It is essential that Ireland should participate fully and confidently in these negotiations, where the most important decisions will be made.

With these decisions behind it, the Government faces a gruelling campaign to convince voters that Ireland's vital interests are best preserved by ratifying the Nice Treaty. It needs to concentrate on getting that message across and demonstrate that it is prepared to listen and respond to counter-arguments rather than treating them dismissively. The Danish prime minister, Mr Anders Fogh Rasmussen's warning that a second No to Nice would be a 'political disaster' for the EU, illustrates how serious are the issues at stake.

Letters to the Editor June 2002
World Cup Coverage

Sir, — RTÉ should note well: the next time it produces the begging bowl, we, the licence-payers, will recall that we were paying to listen to Eamon Dunphy's treachery. — Yours, etc., Denis Mortell, Liberty Lane, Dublin 8. 5 June 2002.

Sir, — Grumpy Dunphy sat on a wall,/ Grumpy Dunphy had a great fall./ All Keane's horses and all Keane's men/ Will never put Dunphy together again. — Yours, etc., Donal Walsh, Newtownpark Avenue, Blackrock, Co Dublin. 5 June 2002.

Sir, — The result so far: Republic of Ireland, 2; Eamon Dunphy, 0. — Yours, etc., Dr Barry O'Sullivan, Castle Redmond, Midleton, Co Cork. 6 June 2002.

Sir, A recent letter-writer expressed the wish never to hear the name R** K**** again. May I add E**** D***** to the list? — Yours, etc., Terry Dolan, Dunboyne, Co Meath. 11 June 2002.

A clamped wheel appears to be all that remains of a car in North Great George's Street, Dublin. It appears the driver managed to remove the clamped wheel, replacing it with the spare, and drove off leaving the wheel in the parking space. Photograph: Eric Luke.

Alcohol and Young People

Sir, — Our son is sixteen years old, six feet tall, and well built; he can easily pass for eighteen or more. He has started to meet his friends in a pub in the evening and order beer as everyone else appears to be doing.

This may seem harmless, but it is illegal for him and the proprietor and may lead to occasional drunkenness and tomfoolery and damage to himself or others or property. He may get into trouble with the law and tarnish his future prospects. He may start down the slippery slope to a future drink or health problem.

So why is he there? He has a good home in a quiet neighbourhood, goes to a decent school, participates in active sports, has limited pocket money (tracked by his parents and a fraction of the 'norm'), but has earned

some income working one night a week during transition year at school, and has a summer job — both part of his education in the real world.

We as parents don't give bad example, drinking only shandies or glasses of wine on social occasions.

He goes to the pub because it is the only convivial venue open to him and his peers in the evenings, besides a few fast-food outlets where he would have to eat continuously or move out.

Teenagers need to get out of the home and meet their contemporaries, but in this country there is very little alternative to the pub. If they gather anywhere, they are perceived as a threat and if it is wet and cold why should they stay outdoors?

What can we do as concerned parents? Report the pub to the Gardaí or warn the publican? Experience shows such action results only in once-off action which blackens one's child unfairly in the eyes of the Gardaí, the publican and his friends, leading to other problems.

Facing the child and banning him from going to pubs will only lead to anger and deceit as there is no alternative venue for social contacts with friends who don't share the same sports; so we point out the dangers and encourage alternatives but stop short of forbidding.

In our opinion, without major investment evenly spread around the country in child and youth-friendly facilities, coupled with enforced compulsory identity cards, this problem cannot be properly tackled. — Yours, etc., Norman and Una Lee, Manor Avenue, Greystones, Co Wicklow. 17 June 2002.

The Nice Treaty

Sir, — The undertones of xenophobia and scaremongering in Anthony Coughlan's article (Opinion, June 24th) are an ugly addition to the debate on the Nice Treaty.

The following are some basic truths about the enlargement of Europe which Mr Coughlan omitted: Firstly, many of the applicant states are much more economically developed than Ireland was when we joined the Union. Indeed, as the Slovenian president confirmed last week in Dublin, his country will be a net contributor to the EU budget from the start — a level of prosperity Ireland took nearly thirty years to achieve.

Secondly, while enlargement will increase the EU population by twenty-eight per cent, that is only marginally greater than the twenty-two per cent increase brought about by the accession of Spain, Greece and Portugal in the 1980s — which, incidentally, did not lead to a mass exodus from the poorer to the wealthier regions of the EU.

Thirdly, while imports from the applicants to the EU increased by 300 per cent in the decade to 1999, exports from the EU to the applicants grew by 400 per cent.

Enlargement will offer even greater access to eastern European markets for Irish goods. This will ensure opportunities for stability and growth in the Irish economy.

Finally, while eastern European companies can at present undercut Irish prices due to weaker employee protection and product standards, upon joining the Union they will be forced to adopt the EU's progressive social legislation which will remove this unfair advantage — unfair to Irish businesses, and unfair to the workers of eastern Europe.

Last year's rejection of the Nice Treaty has caused concern and fear among the peoples of central and eastern Europe. Rejecting it twice will not only end the prospects for much-needed enlargement, but will irreparably damage Ireland's role in the Union and the prospects for consolidating and expanding our economic progress. There is no better way to ensure that Ireland loses 'power, money, influence' than by voting No.

Now that it is certain that we will have a chance to vote again on Nice, let's have an honest debate. — Yours, etc., Averil Power, Ballybrack, Co Dublin. 27 June 2002.

Sir, — It's about time the people of Ireland woke up and realised that we must finally accept that we cannot continue expecting the rest of our EU partners to sit idly by while we squabble and argue about the pros and cons of the Nice Treaty. Ireland has benefited hugely from membership of the European Union. Those of us who were forced to leave these shores in the 1980s can testify to that. Today we have a thriving economy built on many years of massive inward investment, generated in no small part by our membership of the Union. The development in our national infrastructure to date has been funded almost entirely by the EU.

The neutrality issue is a red herring; our neutrality was never in question.

The European Union, for better or worse, is an agreement between peoples with one common aim: that together they can greatly enhance their collective strengths and minimise the effect of their individual weaknesses. In the case of our little nation on the edge of one of the world's largest trading blocs, the benefits of this have been proven beyond any doubt.

Let us show a little confidence in ourselves and let us openly welcome the enlargement of the European Union and all that it brings. Is Ireland a team player within the EU or are we the spoiled child of Europe who, having got almost everything we asked for over the *past thirty years, now want to keep it all for ourselves when others want to come and share? — Yours, etc.,* A.P. O'Sullivan, Hole In The Wall Road, Dublin 13. 27 June 2002.

WEDNESDAY, 3 JULY 2002

Fire Rains from the Sky as Jets Collide over Germany

Derek Scally, in Uberlingen

The smell of pine cones and kerosene hangs in the air in the wooded hills of Germany overlooking Lake Constance. In a small clearing, pine trees are snapped in half like matches, others are scorched black, and yellow fibreglass insulation hangs from branches like snow. In a corner lies a twelve-metre red and white fragment of what was a Boeing cargo aircraft owned by the courier company DHL.

Shortly after midnight on Monday, its pilots tried in vain to avoid an oncoming Russian plane flying at the same altitude. Both planes collided in an explosion of fire and smoke, then plunged twelve kilometres into the dark woods.

Ms Maria Reichenbach, from the Black Forest, was visiting her cousin in a house 500 metres away. 'There was a bang like lightning and my nephew ran in from outdoors: "It's burning, it's burning".' From her cousin's balcony she saw 'an explosion of fire like a pyramid', a fire which burned into the morning. A neighbour saw 'a plane drop out of the sky like a stone'.

Sinn Féin's first Lord Mayor, Alex Maskey, stands for a moment after laying a wreath at Belfast's City Hall Cenotaph in memory of all the men who died at the Battle of the Somme. Mayor Maskey marked the anniversary of the Battle of the Somme ahead of the main ceremony, which he said he would not attend. Photograph: Paul McErlane/Reuters.

Miraculously, both planes came crashing to earth in deserted areas and there were no injuries among the 28,000 residents of Überlingen, a picturesque spa town near Friedrichshafen.

Sixty-five years after the explosion of the Hindenburg zeppelin, which killed thirty-six people, the sky over Lake Constance, on the Swiss-German border, was filled with exploding fire balls.

'I heard a crack and then I saw a bright light. I thought: "it's not a full moon". When I looked out the window, I saw the fire,' a resident told local radio.

The Russian plane, en route to Barcelona, crashed in a field north of Überlingen. Police kept the crash site sealed yesterday, but reports said a large part of the main cabin of the plane, a Tupelov 154, was intact on the ground, with many of the sixty-nine dead passengers still strapped into their seats. At least fifty of the dead are believed to be younger than eighteen and were on a UN-sponsored trip to Spain. Their relatives are expected in Germany today, when investigators will begin examining the plane's flight recorder.

The narrow streets of Überlingen were mainly deserted yesterday, with only small groups of locals on street corners discussing the tragedy in the skies over their town, one of the main air routes to Switzerland.

'We were used to a lot of air traffic but something like this will make sure it is a long time before we can calm down again,' said one woman.

The state premier, Mr Erwin Teufel, expressed his sympathy to the families of the victims. 'It is impossible to put yourself in the position of these families,' he said, whose loved ones were victims of a 'highly-improbable tragedy'. He also called for a revision of air traffic agreements, long a cause of friction between Germany and Switzerland. 'We are looking forward to discussing with Switzerland a way of reducing the over-burdened air corridor over Lake Constance.' He also called for the ratification of an already agreed air traffic policy between the countries.

Investigators have ruled out mechanical error as a cause of the collision, but now face a difficult task ahead determining what happened in the seconds before the impact.

The DHL Boeing crash killed its two pilots, Canadian Mr Brant Campiori and Mr Paul Phillips, a British father of three.

High in the hills overlooking the lake, two teams of investigators and firemen worked through the night and yesterday at the scene of the Boeing crash. Scattered on the ground over a fifty-metre radius were the surviving contents of the doomed cargo aircraft: a guidebook to Venice, chemistry papers and computer manuals lying among smouldering plastic DHL packaging.

The noxious fumes of melting plastic filled the air and small red and white fragments of the plane's exterior crunched under foot. The investigators have begun their meticulous search for clues.

MONDAY, 8 JULY 2002

A Subterranean Service, Always at Work

Colm Keena

The long-awaited Ansbacher report, despite its size, has failed to deliver the sort of bombshell revelation or revelations many may have expected.

It is the accumulated detail that is shocking. The dinner-party conversation which led to the opening of an Ansbacher account; the restaurant bills being settled by the customer putting the required amount into an offshore account belonging to the restaurateur; the widow being contacted to be told her late husband had a Cayman trust and subsequently gaining access to the money by way of travellers cheques and deposits to a London bank account.

A picture emerges of a busy subterranean banking service, always at work, helping people

Actor Edward Cosgrave dressed as Uncle Sam at America's 226th Birthday Party, the Fourth of July Independence Day celebrations hosted by the Ambassador of the United States of America at the Ambassador's Residence in the Phoenix Park. Photograph: Alan Betson.

hide money away where others won't be able to find it. While the fact that a particular person has been named as a customer of Ansbacher is not in itself proof of tax-evasion, the broad general picture which emerges is nevertheless of a whole class of people intent on evading tax.

In all cases the key person was the late Des Traynor. It seems that wherever he went he was able to find new customers for the bank he'd established in the Caribbean. He collected money before and after boardroom meetings, while waiting in the lobby for whoever he was lunching with that day in the Berkeley Court Hotel and when people dropped in to see him in his office.

The list of names includes some very significant figures from the Irish corporate world of the 1960s, 1970s, 1980s and 1990s.

They include members of the board of the Central Bank; members of the board of Cement Roadstone, one of the State's foremost companies; members of the boards of State companies.

The peculiar mix of people in the report is explained by its origins. Back in the late 1960s, Guinness & Mahon, according to the report, was run by three men from a 'similar Anglo-Irish Protestant privileged background'.

All three had gone to the same school. According to one of them, Mr William Forwood, they decided that what the bank needed was someone 'who was in touch with the outside world . . . They agreed there was only one man for the job, Desmond Traynor'.

Within a short time after his appointment, Mr Traynor had the run of the bank. He brought some of the clients he knew from his work with Haughey Boland into the offshore business he developed for the old merchant bank. As the offshore subsidiaries grew in size, their importance to the overall Guinness Mahon group business gave Mr Traynor increased power within the group.

The clients included old customers of Guinness & Mahon, many of them from a similar background to Mr Forwood and his colleagues' and representatives of the emerging Catholic capitalist class Mr Traynor knew from his Haughey Boland days.

Unfortunately the inspectors were not able to give a conclusive figure for the size of the offshore business built up.

In 1984 the Cayman bank had £203 million on deposit, with £25 million of this being redeposited in Dublin. In the years 1991 to 1997 Ansbacher and the related company, Hamilton Ross, passed £96 million through IIB bank in Dublin.

These figures give an indication of the scale, rather than a precise take. The Cayman bank had customers from Ireland, the UK, the US and Jamaica.

While significant figures from the world of Irish business were customers of Mr Traynor, very few are members of the super-rich league. Such people presumably had people other than Mr Traynor looking after their affairs.

The report is damning for Cement Roadstone Holdings (CRH), detailing as it does how Ansbacher held important meetings in the CRH headquarters in Dublin, how so many CRH directors had dealings with Ansbacher and how Ansbacher mail was delivered to the CRH head-quarters in Fitzwilliam Square and sorted by the caretaker there.

The inspectors write of Ms Joan Williams, secretary to Mr Traynor, openly counting cash at her desk and Mr Traynor's driver and the CRH caretaker personally delivering boxes of cash to Ansbacher clients' homes.

Mr Charles Haughey was, of course, Mr Traynor's most famous client. A busy, able and extremely discreet man, Mr Traynor was also engaged in collecting money from wealthy individuals for Mr Haughey.

A number of those on the Ansbacher list were close associates of Mr Haughey.

Some gave him, or his son's company Celtic Helicopters, financial assistance; some were financial supporters of Fianna Fáil and some were involved in the controversial Fianna Fáil fund-raising group, Taca. Mr Traynor's long friendship with Mr Haughey and work with Haughey Boland make this unsurprising.

This is, however, a key aspect of the overall Ansbacher story. It has no relevance at all for most of the customers other than they now find themselves associated with a scheme identified in the public mind with unease at aspects of public business during the Haughey era.

Also, of course, if Haughey had not been involved, this offshore-onshore unauthorised banking service would never have been the subject of such a detailed inquiry and comprehensive published report.

Some clients, it should be said, were supporters of Fine Gael and of course the late Hugh Coveney made use of Ansbacher in his business activities.

The report gives an insight into Irish business and finance during the period covered. Ansbacher took subterfuge to an extreme and, crucially, was not licensed to operate here. Its story forms part of a picture which includes bogus non-resident accounts in AIB, ACC and other banks and the sale of offshore bonds by NIB.

We also know of the dealings of Mr Michael Lowry and Mr Ben Dunne involving offshore accounts with AIB and Bank of Ireland and of the Irish Nationwide Isle of Man's refusal to send an official to give evidence to the Moriarty tribunal about an account belonging to Mr Lowry.

Perhaps, in time, new elements will be added to the scene.

No one may ever go to jail because of what has been revealed by the Ansbacher report. Nevertheless it is surely a ground-breaking event that it has been published at all. The public can now at least expect that the Revenue

Commissioners will collect all that is due. Openness, transparency and a limited amount of accountability.

MONDAY, 8 JULY 2002

Conspiracy to Defraud the State

Editorial

The Ansbacher report is not just a damning indictment of those wealthy and powerful individuals who evaded their due taxes, broke company law and engaged in criminal conspiracies from the 1970s to the 1990s, it reflects the failure of Irish regulatory authorities and professional bodies to uphold the standards required of them in the interest of the common good. There is a great deal to be ashamed of in the report and many lessons to be learned.

New and rigorous standards must be applied by the authorities.

It has taken nearly three years for this extensive report, conducted under the powers of the Companies Act, to be produced. The Tánaiste and Minister for Enterprise, Trade and Employment, Ms Harney, has paid a well-deserved tribute to the inspectors and officials involved for presenting a hard-hitting and clear document. It was her political determination and their hard work that ensured the preliminary information from the McCracken Tribunal, in 1997, was expanded into an in-depth investigation of the clients of Guinness Mahon Bank and Ansbacher Cayman.

Tax fraud involving hundreds of millions of

Ann Naughton in her clamped car at Bóthar Irwin, near Eyre Square in Galway city. Photograph: Joe O'Shaughnessy.

pounds was involved. Many of the most prominent Irish companies and individuals were found to be clients of the late Des Traynor, formerly of Haughey & Boland, who recruited new customers and operated their highly secretive, off-shore accounts. The most notable of those clients was former Taoiseach Mr Charles Haughey.

Nearly 200 prominent business people and companies have been named. Some of those were engaged in legitimate business dealings. But, while there is no accuser in the report and no individual is found guilty — on the important basis of a presumption of innocence — it is highly critical of certain companies and individuals. It finds the secretive financial transactions conducted by Ansbacher to be little more than a sham, a legal fiction, amounting to a criminal conspiracy where its clients sought to evade tax.

In a series of interviews at the weekend, the Minister for Justice, Mr McDowell, hoped for a change in Irish attitudes so that people who engaged in multi-million pound tax fraud were not regarded as heroes in their local yacht clubs while those who fiddled their social welfare payments were sent to jail. At the same time, however, Mr McDowell cautioned against public expectations that a rash of arrests and prosecutions would follow. Such a course would be difficult, he suggested, because of the lapse of time, the destruction of documents and the requirement to prove 'intent to defraud' in any criminal prosecution.

Nobody believes it will be easy to successfully prosecute some of the extremely wealthy individuals involved. But, if a determined attempt is not made, the consequences will do lasting damage to our democracy. The belief that there is one law for the rich and another for the poor will grow and flourish. The Ansbacher report lays bare criminal tax evasion by an elite within our society. It follows disclosures concerning illegal off-shore products sold by National Irish Bank and the evasion of DIRT tax by tens of thousands of wealthy citizens, aided and abetted by our major financial institutions.

There is no doubt that a tax-evasion culture has been deeply embedded in Irish society for generations. The real scandal is that it has been tacitly ignored or tolerated by successive governments and by those institutions of the State tasked with its elimination. Massive DIRT tax evasion was permitted in the 1980s and 1990s on the basis that any attempt to confront it would lead to a huge outflow of funds. Similarly, it has been suggested that attempts to properly regulate Guinness & Mahon could have led to its collapse. And attempts are now being made to minimise the importance of the Ansbacher report by suggesting that many other wealthy individuals operated similar tax-evasion schemes through banks in Jersey and the Isle of Man. Such diversionary tactics should not be tolerated. Sanctions should be applied immediately as breaches of the law and of regulations are identified.

A number of disciplinary options are available to the authorities in seeking to reassure the public. Companies and members of professions who conspired to break the law can be disqualified from further work. Criminal prosecutions can be taken, not least on the basis that individuals improperly availed of tax amnesties. And due taxes, along with harsh penalties, can be exacted by the Revenue Commissioners. Such a comprehensive response will require not just unambiguous Government support but the determination and co-operation of the Central Bank, the Revenue Commissioners, the Director of Public Prosecutions and the Director of Corporate Enforcement.

In recent years, we have borrowed a self-assessment system of taxation from the United States. But we have been reluctant to adopt the harsh penalties necessary to encourage widespread compliance. In New York, millionaires who believe that only 'little people' pay taxes are sent to prison. Here, belated co-operation with the Revenue Commissioners is a passport to freedom. Tax evasion by wealthy citizens twenty years ago was not without consequences. Their criminal behaviour ensured the quality of life of young people was impaired because of a lack of educational opportunity. Older people died prematurely because of inadequate health services. The public must be shown that such behaviour will not be tolerated. The most obvious — and public — penalty is a jail sentence for the guilty.

WEDNESDAY, 17 JULY 2002

IRA Statement of Apology Accorded a General Welcome

Dan Keenan

The IRA has apologised for the deaths and suffering of 'non-combatants' caused by its campaign of violence. The organisation issued its statement which contained an admission of 'past mistakes and of the hurt and pain we have caused to others' in Dublin yesterday, in advance of this weekend's thirtieth anniversary of Bloody Friday.

The IRA exploded more than twenty bombs in Belfast on 21 July 1972, killing nine and injuring hundreds. Television pictures of mutilated bodies being shovelled away by emergency services became one of the most enduring and harrowing images of the Troubles. The apology, the first of its kind by the IRA, was greeted in both London and Dublin, with Downing Street insisting it had no idea such an IRA statement was expected until shortly before it was released.

The Minister for Foreign Affairs, Mr Cowen, said: 'The challenge now is to redouble our efforts so that all parts of the community have confidence that Northern Ireland is now advancing to an irreversible peace and the pursuit of exclusively democratic politics.'

Other parties including the SDLP and Alliance welcomed it and hoped for further gestures. Unionists varied in their reaction. Some acknowledged it conditionally and expressed a preference for action over words. Others, mostly in the Rev Ian Paisley's DUP, dismissed it as cynical.

The Ulster Unionist leader struck a cautious note during a debate on Northern Ireland in the Commons last night.

Mr David Trimble said: 'It is quite significant that this statement says nothing at all about the recent violence that the IRA has been involved in, nothing about what their future conduct is going to be.'

He warned: 'If the government uses this statement as an excuse not to fulfil those undertakings, the government will create a very dangerous situation indeed.'

The Conservatives were more positive, saying the statement was 'significant and welcome'.

Relatives were divided. Some felt an apology could never undo the damage done, while others felt any remorse was better than none.

The IRA offered 'sincere apologies and condolences' and pointed out that loss of life had been inflicted on all sides. Reflecting on the past yet referring repeatedly to the future, the statement added that there should not be 'a hierarchy of victims in which some are deemed more or less worthy than others.

'The process of conflict resolution requires the equal acknowledgement of the grief and loss of others. On this anniversary, we are endeavouring to fulfil this responsibility to those we have hurt.'

Suspicions remain in unionist circles that the statement fits into a choreographed pattern of events designed to ease pressure on the Belfast Agreement and the concerns of unionists who have grown disillusioned with the 1998 peace deal and the parties who advocate it.

Republicans insist the statement is significant. Belfast's Sinn Féin Lord Mayor, Mr Alex Maskey, who broke with tradition this month and commemorated the victims of the Somme, called for the statement to be taken at face value.

The sense of crisis is deepening, with persistent questions over Mr David Trimble's leadership of the

Ulster Unionists and the advent of fresh Assembly elections next May in which, on current trends, anti-agreement unionists are destined to do well.

The process has been rocked by allegations linking the IRA with disturbances on Belfast streets for over a year and with the intelligence robbery at the Castlereagh police offices. The arrest of three Irishmen held on suspicion of links with FARC guerrillas in Colombia and the continuation of unclaimed sporadic murders have added to the pressure.

Many unionists claim the IRA ceasefire is bogus and should be declared as such by the Northern Secretary, Dr John Reid, who dismissed the loyalist UDA ceasefire as an empty gesture last year.

Dr Reid said last night that the statement could help foster confidence among sceptical unionists that the IRA will not return to violence. The British Prime Minister, under pressure to protect Mr Trimble and ease unionist nerves, is expected to sharpen a working definition of a ceasefire. A statement is due from Mr Blair next week before the House of Commons begins its summer recess.

SATURDAY, 20 JULY 2002

Bridge Due to Be Completed in October

Frank McDonald

Dundrum has acquired a modern landmark — and the long-delayed Luas light rail project a powerful symbol — with the construction of a spectacular bridge spanning one of Dublin's busiest junctions, at Taney Road.

Scheduled for completion in October at a cost of eleven million, the dramatic cable-stayed structure is already a source of awe for local residents and for the thousands of motorists who pass through the junction every day.

Its asymmetrical single pylon, standing fifty metres high, was consciously designed by consultant engineers Roughan O'Donovan as a landmark in an area that lacks vertical points of emphasis, apart from the tower of Taney Church.

But there was also a practical reason for the form of structure chosen by the engineers: it would permit the main span of the bridge, at 108.5 metres, to be erected without disrupting the flow of traffic, other than at weekends.

The deck is expected to be finished by the end of August. 'Thirty local residents were out the other night marvelling at the work continuing under arc lamps on this serious piece of infrastructure,' said Mr Éamonn Brady, the Luas information officer.

In terms of public perceptions, it has turned Luas Line B, from Sandyford to St Stephen's Green, into a concrete project much more dramatically than any of the road works or building demolitions along Line A from Tallaght to Middle Abbey Street.

Apart from the main span over Lower Churchtown Road, the Taney bridge — which is being built by Newry-based Graham Construction — has a 'back span' of 21.5 metres behind its inverted Y 'tuning-fork' pylon and two approach spans of eighteen and fourteen metres.

The deck is being erected using pre-cast concrete shells which are filled with concrete to form its soffit.

As it proceeds, the fifty-two galvanised steel cable stays are installed, eliminating the need for temporary supports that would have interfered with the road beneath.

Mr Cormac Allen, project architect for Luas Line B, said the bridge was designed in 1995 to take account of the existing road layout on the edge of Dundrum, as well as the radically altered layout following completion of the village's recently-opened bypass.

Having done his final-year thesis in the UCD School of Architecture a year earlier on the impact of Luas and the bypass on Dundrum, he joined his former tutor, Mr Alan Mee, in CIÉ's Light Rail Project Office to work on the architectural aspects of Line B.

Mr Allen says he was inspired by what had originally been built by the Victorian railway engineers, especially the village's granite-walled station on the old Harcourt Street line, with its 'beautifully scaled public forecourt' and its associated embankment.

'The closure of the Harcourt Street line in 1959, combined with the extension of Churchtown Road to Taney junction in the early 1970s, led to the complete destruction of the north end of the village . . . by a haphazard array of poorly-designed buildings.'

His main contribution to the project was to develop an urban design framework plan for the integration of Luas, and the Taney bridge in particular, into the essentially domestic scale of Dundrum. Seven years later, this strategy has yet to be implemented.

Its central feature was a civic space in front of the Luas station, to provide a new focal point for Dundrum, including an undercroft scheme infilling the village end of the bridge.

But the huge cost of the bypass, at €44.4 million, has probably jeopardised its realisation.

'It is crucial to the success of the project that these design proposals, which were incorporated in the Light Rail Order documentation, are executed.

'Otherwise, the bridge will remain architecturally incomplete in a sensitive urban setting,' Mr Allen said.

He left the Luas project in 1997 to work in the private sector having had enough of 'politicians talking about building a light rail system'.

In the intervening period, he has designed and built an art gallery, a theatre, an office block and a research building.

The bridge he played a part in designing is due for completion in October.

The Luas Bridge at Dundrum, under construction. Photograph: Alan Betson.

What Mr Mee finds amazing is that it's 'so uncannily like the first drawings that were done seven years ago' — proving, in effect, that dramatic bridges do not necessarily need a Calatrava.

The Luas project director, Mr Donal Mangan, said he was 'very proud of it. It's the product of young architects in the light rail office, CIÉ's engineering department and talented consultant engineers, in line with the highest tradition of Irish railway bridge-building.'

Somewhat surprisingly, neither local residents' associations nor An Taisce objected to the design. Any fears they had were put to rest by an assurance that the pylon would be no higher than the tower of Taney Church, a much-loved Dundrum landmark.

MONDAY, 22 JULY 2002

Licence to Browse at Spy Museum

Patrick Smyth

Eyes only — surveillance, corner F Street, Friday. Observed huge crowds for opening of Washington's new $40 million International Spy Museum which agent in place successfully penetrated and then exfiltrated, posing improbably as journalist.

Please advise Uncle that if station runs out of equipment, plenty of supplies here, ranging from invisible ink to coding machines and disguise kits. And plenty of ideas for Q — from old Soviet radio

Máirín Lynch, wife of the late Jack Lynch, unveiled a bronze statue of the former Taoiseach, Cork hurler and footballer in Blackpool Shopping Centre, Cork. The sculptor was James McCarthy. Photograph: Donna McBride/Provision.

in shoe to pipe, umbrella, lipstick, and cigarette guns. So many bugs, would need insecticide. Joke.

Tried out commissariat, disguised as shop. Tempted by hidden cameras in tie ($899). Was examining phone with secret built-in lie detector when approached by bagman posing as sales assistant.

'Are all these really legal?' asked him.

'Yes, of course,' replied. Then, 'Um. I don't know actually, I was only hired for the day . . .' Understand. Impeccable tradecraft. Strictly 'need to know'.

Washington's new museum, the first in the world devoted entirely to international espionage, will be a joy, a 'honey trap' to all small boys between the ages of seven and sixty, a veritable cornucopia of gadgets and interactive video games that test the powers of observation of budding spies.

Here, museum meets all singing and dancing high tech, and the world of intelligence make-belief blends seamlessly with showbiz.

Purists may balk that this is not exactly museum as centre of learning — the bookshop mixes serious history with Tom Clancy — and it makes no pretence to comprehensiveness. Its displays are largely a string of entertaining anecdotes — a natural history museum without the unsexy insects.

They range from Troy's wooden horse, to Jefferson's code machine, to the simulation of a submarine's sonar, to Mata Hari, to a lifesize mock-up of part of the tunnel dug by US agents from West to East Berlin, to the regular interweaving of the fictional (James Bond's Aston Martin with rotating number plates — I had a Corgi version of the original) with the real. This is pure entertainment.

But the museum has a deeply politically-safe quality to it. Some disquieting truths about American intelligence operations can be admitted, but only some, perhaps in keeping with these deeply patriotic times.

The museum can acknowledge that the great cryptographer, Alan Turing, key to cracking the Enigma machine at Bletchley, was disgracefully hounded from his job for his homosexuality and later committed suicide.

A corner dedicated to the McCarthy witchhunt era admits that the majority of those driven from work as communist sympathisers were entirely innocent.

And in the corridor devoted to the disastrous failure to anticipate Pearl Harbour the museum acknowledges that the US Army and Navy were so bitterly divided about who should be responsible for monitoring Japanese ship dispatches that the two had agreed to do it on alternate days.

Such damaging institutional bickering, reminiscent of the CIA-FBI dialogue of the deaf ahead of September 11th, was compounded by the refusal by the FBI's boss, J. Edgar Hoover, to believe the British master spy Dusko Popov's warnings.

But there is nothing about Hoover's notorious willingness to stray over the civil rights line domestically, or the CIA's deadly role in training and propping up some of the nastiest military dictatorships on the planet.

Indonesia? Chile? . . .

But enough party-pooping. Many of the anecdotes, told by audio tape or short video presentation by participants themselves, are riveting tales of derring do.

A personal favourite is the description given by two CIA agents, Sandy Grimes and Jean Vertefeuille, of the unmasking of one of the CIA's most damaging moles, Aldrich Ames, who had betrayed at least thirty of their agents.

Ames was interrogated along with a number of other agents by the two women in the process of whittling down potential sources of leaks. All were asked the same questions, including one hypothetical, devised by Vertefeuille, which would be his undoing.

When asked, 'If you were going to volunteer to the Soviets to become an agent of theirs, how would you go about doing it?' most responded with enthusiasm to the intellectual challenge.

But Ames, usually confident to the point of cockiness, was suddenly hesitant and almost incoherent.

'Usually he loved the what-if questions,' Grimes remembers.

Comparing notes later, the two women thought they had their man and slowly tightened the noose. Ames was bewildered when arrested. 'He thought we were two dumb broads,' Grimes recalls with a grin. One up for the sisterhood.

TUESDAY, 23 JULY 2002

Still Failing to Protect Our Children

Fintan O'Toole

Two young girls dead in the fields, one fifteen years old, the other fourteen. One the victim of a society which is afraid to challenge the official morality, the other of a society that is afraid of morality itself. One strangled by the rules, the other exposed to the dangers of a world that has no rules. One crushed between the narrow boundaries of what can be said and thought, the other made dizzy by the wide-open spaces where there are no boundaries from which to take your bearings. But both irredeemably dead.

Ann Lovett was found on a bitterly cold January day in 1984 by three boys who spotted her red schoolbag lying at the entrance to the grotto of the Blessed Virgin on a small hill outside Granard. At her side was the pair of scissors she had brought with her to cut the umbilical cord. The baby boy was lying on a moss-covered stone beneath the statue.

Ann was still just about alive, surrounded by her own blood, her arms bruised where she had gripped them against the pain. She died shortly afterwards in hospital from irreversible shock brought on by the combination of haemorrhaging and exposure.

Ann Lovett's death was reported by Emily O'Reilly in the *Sunday Tribune*. It struck most of us like the lash of a bull-hide whip. Many women wrote to the national father confessor, Gay Byrne, pouring out a torrent of secret shame, and Byrne read the letters in one of the most devastating radio programmes ever broadcast. Truths never told even to best friends and lovers — rapes, hidden pregnancies, babies buried in battered suitcases — seeped into the public mind. The version of Ireland that most of us carry in our heads changed for good. It is not that Ann Lovett's awful death stayed at the forefront of our collective consciousness, but it did take up residency in the back of our minds.

Say the words 'Ann Lovett' to most Irish people over thirty-five now and they know what you mean. Hers is the name we give to lies and hypocrisy, to the reality behind the official veneer of holy Ireland.

Ann Lovett's death did not, of itself, change Irish reality. But it helped to change Irish minds which, in some respects, amounts to the same thing. There is still pain and shame and concealment: only last week, another dead abandoned baby was found.

The prevailing culture has shifted profoundly, however. There is less hypocrisy about sex, less craw-thumping. The notion of justified cruelty against the young in the cause of upholding official morality is more or less gone.

Wind forward now to the death early last week, in a field in Ballindrait, Co Donegal, of Geraldine Chambers. She was even younger than Ann Lovett and her death is no less tragic. But the accoutrements of death are utterly different. Where Ann tried to dull the pain with the opium of religion, Geraldine sought oblivion with the morphine tablets that lay beside her, or with the bottle of vodka that was found nearby.

Where one died because she did not believe the world around her would say 'yes' to her need for sympathy, understanding and support, the other died because the world around her has forgotten how to say 'no'. A culture of extreme repression has been replaced by a culture of extreme tolerance. Haunted, perhaps, by the memory of Ann Lovett, adults are afraid to impose rules on teenagers. The awful loneliness of Ann Lovett has given way to a hedonistic conviviality, in which it is perfectly normal for fourteen-year-olds to go out for a night's drinking with the girls.

Repelled by its cruelty and hypocrisy, Irish society has dispensed with the church-based moral system from which it derived its rules. What it has not yet done is to develop the civic, social morality that is needed as a replacement. Adults, caught in this no man's land, are not sure what authority they have in setting rules for adolescents. Too many young people are left in a moral wilderness that is, in its way, almost as deathly as the airless room into which the old system locked them.

We need to be as shocked by the death of Geraldine Chambers as we were by the death of Ann Lovett. We need to ask what pain is being dulled by the drink and drugs and possibly the ultimate oblivion of suicide. We need to consider what message our children are getting from a public culture that celebrates conspicuous consumption and associates pleasure with expenditure. We need to look at an education system that condemns drop-outs like Geraldine to a sense of perpetual failure. We need to remember that the young deserve protection as well as freedom.

This is not about going back to the world in which Ann Lovett suffered and died. There is no lost paradise to be regained, and no way back to it even if there were. Even if we wanted to return to the priest with the blackthorn stick rooting the couples out of the ditches, there aren't enough priests to go around. At the back of the revolution in attitudes over the last twenty years was the belief that we could use freedom responsibly.

We've got the freedom. It's time for the responsibility.

Measuring Consumer Confidence by the Bin Load

On Wall Street: Conor O'Clery

Many analysts use anecdotal evidence to sustain their economic forecasts. Alan Greenspan likes to count the empty containers stacked at ports to judge import activity. Here's another one. I use an elevator to go up and down forty two storeys every day. Often my fellow button-pushers are employees of local restaurants, delivering carry-outs to residents. Eating-in is particularly popular in downtown Manhattan, where people are always rushing somewhere. I haven't seen so many delivery guys recently in the lifts.

Then I heard an interesting thing from my building manager. The city official in charge of garbage removal in lower Manhattan told him the other day he was spending an extra $1 million (€1.01 million) to buy three extra garbage trucks. The reason: more people are cooking for themselves rather than spending money on food deliveries, creating much more disposable rubbish.

Call it the ITT theory — the incremental trash theory. It is a sure sign that Americans, certainly my neighbours anyway, are cutting back on their optional spending.

According to polls, people across the United States are more worried about their financial future today than at any time since the 1970s. Especially hard hit by the market slide are the eighty million Americans who own stock.

People over the age of sixty are rolling back their spending or staying longer in work because their retirement assets are tied up in so-called 401(k)s, stock holdings where employees match employers' contributions, which have been shrinking fast — now disparagingly called 403(k)s or 402(k)s.

Enron employees lost $1 billion in employee retirement savings denominated in now-worthless stock.

WorldCom workers face similar wipe-outs.

These retirement savings plans have largely replaced old-fashioned cash pensions in the US, so the fall-out on Wall Street is more widespread that the crash of 1987. The percentage of the workforce that will receive a traditional pension has fallen from forty to twenty per cent in two decades.

Even the boringly safe mutual funds are shrinking, unable to resist the relentless pounding from the markets — the Dow Jones index fell on Monday to its first close below 8,000 for four years, after a month when the index had triple-digit falls on ten days.

Just as people in the 1990s saw the market going up, wanted in, and drove it up further, so today people see the market falling, want out, and drive stocks lower. Anyone who abandoned riskier stocks and put their savings into, say the supposedly rock-solid Vanguard 500 index mutual fund, would have seen their worth fall twenty five per cent this year.

The result is that many Americans are having to change their spending patterns.

Watch for falls in consumer confidence in the coming months. Newspapers in the US are full of interviews with families who have abandoned vacations or home repairs as their portfolios shrank, and retirees who spend their days behind a super-market register rather than on the golf course, as their savings produce less monthly income.

A quarter of American people in the sixty to seventy age group are working today, compared to one-fifth ten years ago, and confidence is falling in that cornerstone of the American dream — the belief that stocks are capable of generating wealth and providing for retirement for future generations.

Many Americans are raiding other assets to keep up with college tuition payments, home repairs or new car purchases. With the housing market booming (for how long?), home-owners are turning to a unique American way of turning property into disposable spending, applying for cheque books tied to their home equity value. Others are cutting down in practical ways, like dusting off old home cooking books and ordering fewer meals delivered to their homes.

In downturns there is always an upside. Some companies do well in recessions, like Wal-Mart, which offers cheaper household goods. The lesson from this story: Take your money out of Chinese takeaways and invest in grocery stores and companies that make garbage trucks.

THURSDAY, 25 JULY 2002

Population Rises by 8% to Slightly Less than 4m

Marie O'Halloran

Ireland's population increase over the past six years far outstrips any other EU country, according to preliminary Irish census figures which show a rise of eight per cent.

The population in the Republic is now at its highest level since 1871, at just under four million people.

Every major town with the exception of Cork city showed an increase in the number of residents, but the increases were greatest in the commuter-belt counties around Dublin.

The population of Dublin city and county increased by 6.1 per cent to 1.12 million, but this was lower than the eight per cent rise for the State overall.

The 'Census 2002 — Preliminary Report', published in Dublin yesterday by the Central Statistics Office, shows an increase of more than 290,000 since the last census six years ago.

Figures taken on 28 April this year by 4,000 enumerators in 100,000 streets and townlands, show a population of 3,917,336 compared to 3,626,087 in 1996.

Holiday makers at Salthill in Galway endure yet another shower of rain. **P**hotograph: Joe O'Shaughnessy.

The CSO highlights the remarkable growth in commuter counties around Dublin such as Kildare and Meath, and significant increases in other Leinster counties.

The figures confirm the projections for the National Spatial Strategy and according to a spokesman emphasise even more the need for a spatial strategy to balance growth between the greater Dublin area, where forty per cent of the population is based, and other regions, particularly the counties of the Border, midlands and western or BMW region.

Net immigration increased by just over 25,500 a year or 153,067 overall, made up of returning emigrants and non-nationals.

The figure is almost twice the national average recorded during the 1970s, one of only two other times when net immigration was recorded, since the foundation of the State. The second time was the last census period between 1991 and 1996.

Dr Aidan Punch, senior statistician at the Central Statistics Office, said Ireland stood out among EU countries for its sustained population growth.

Other EU countries had 'negative natural increases', and were not experiencing the 'increases, the growth rates we're getting. We are experiencing healthy population growth for the last five years.'

Ireland's annual population increase is 1.3 per cent, compared to 0.2 per cent in Belgium and Greece, or 0.4 per cent in Germany and just 0.5 per cent in France, where population growth is viewed as 'bullish'.

Commuter belt counties Kildare and Meath showed phenomenal population increases of more than twenty per cent, rising by 29,003 or 21.5 per cent in Kildare and 24,204 or 22.1 per cent in Meath. The number of residents in Lucan, Co Dublin, almost trebled in the same period, the highest increase of any area.

Overall, Leinster had the highest population increase of all the provinces, some 9.4 per cent or 180,747 with large increases in a number of counties including Carlow, Laois, Louth, Wicklow, Wexford and Westmeath of between 10.2 per cent and 13.8 per cent.

Co Leitrim, the smallest and least populous county in the State, also showed an increase for the first time since 1871. Its population rose by three per cent or 758 people from 25,057 to 25,815.

Cork city is the only major population area to show a population decrease of three per cent, or 3,849 people, but overall the county's population rose by 6.6 per cent, or 27,671.

Parts of Dublin showed significant decreases attributed in areas such as Ballymun and Sheriff Street to housing demolition and relocating of local communities, with a similar situation in the Glen in Cork city.

In other areas of Dublin, including Clontarf and Finglas, and in Bishopstown in Cork, ageing populations and 'empty nest syndrome' were cited as a reason for declining numbers.

The CSO was confident that it had 'very close to 100 per cent return' in the approximately

Ray Cosgrove of Dublin celebrates his goal during the Leinster Football Championship between Dublin and Kildare in Croke Park. Photograph: Frank Miller.

1.4 million forms that were sent out. Dr Punch said the enumerators were 'very tough' and 'left no stone unturned' to ensure all forms were returned.

Other information such as education, employment, ethnicity, age profile and computer ownership will be detailed in a more formal report, expected in 2003.

The statistics from the latest census show that there were 138,182 more births than deaths. Some 324,103 people were born in the State since 1996, while 185,921 people died. In 1841 the population of the twenty-six county area was 6.4 million, its highest ever since records began. The lowest population was in the late 1960s at just over 2.8 million.

Letters to the Editor July 2002

The Nice Treaty

Sir, — May I be permitted to protest most vehemently at the vulgar abuse to which our esteemed and respected President has recently been subjected by Mr John Gormley?

How dare he use the vernacular 'butt out' when giving unsolicited and unnecessary advice to (a) a married lady of unimpeachable character; and (b) the elected President of this country, who is entitled to the respect of each of its citizens?

Do we get the politicians we deserve? — Yours, etc., Colm O'Doherty, Finsbury Park, Dublin 14. 15 July 2002.

Sir, — I am surprised at the reaction of the anti-Europeans to the comments made by President McAleese and Seán Dorgan of the IDA. I am sure they would have held a party if President McAleese and Mr Dorgan had advocated a rejection of the Nice Treaty.

It appears to me that the anti-Europeans consider it completely acceptable, appropriate and democratic for an important individual to recommend a rejection of the treaty. But they consider it completely unacceptable, unappropriate and undemocratic for an important individual to come out and support it.

Perhaps they realise that when the people of Ireland hear the truth about Europe and the Nice Treaty the referendum will be passed by an overwhelming majority. — Yours, etc., Jason Fitzharris, Carlow. 15 July 2002.

IRA Apology for Bloody Friday

Sir, — Is it not strange that an organisation that recognises 'no hierarchy of victims' deems it suitable to regret the bloody slaughter of some innocents and not others? Is it not curious that it apologises for the foul murder of the victims while continuing to laud murderers as heroes and patriots?

If Sinn Féin/IRA thinks this statement negates decades of treachery against the Irish people, or excuses the ruthless terror campaign against our neighbours, it is mistaken. —Yours, etc., Martin Moran, Grange Road, Rathfarnham, Dublin 14. 19 July 2002.

Sir, — In the light of Sinn Féin/IRA's recent 'apology', I wonder where Det Garda Jerry McCabe might fit into their hierarchy of victims. — Yours, etc., Stuart Elliott, Swords, Co Dublin. 24 July 2002.

Israeli Air Strike in Gaza

Sir, — I would like to add my voice to that of the Israeli President Moshe Katsav in condemning utterly the horrific Israeli air force attack in Gaza.

Israel's government must take responsibility for this atrocity and do everything it can to prevent its air force doing this kind of thing in the future.

I am sick at heart at this, as I am at each and every attack on Israeli citizens. But a missile attack on an apartment building, after midnight when children and adults are asleep in their beds, is no more justifiable than a suicide bombing.

I am appalled and ashamed of the current Israeli government for sanctioning this and other similar operations. I am also appalled and ashamed of Prime Minister Ariel Sharon's cold-hearted response

to it, stating that it was 'one of our greatest successes'.
Has he any heart, any moral sense at all?

There is a huge divergence of opinion within both
the political establishment and civil society in Israel
about the policies of the current Israeli government. I
want to put it on record that such divergence of opinion
also extends to the 'local staff' of Israeli Embassies. —
Yours, etc., Dr Noreen O'Carroll, Press Officer,
Embassy of Israel, Dublin. 26 July 2002.

FRIDAY, 2 AUGUST 2002

Home to a Nation of Whingers

Miriam Donohoe

It is only when you come home after living abroad for a while that you realise what a nation of whingers we are. An alien paying a brief visit to this small but prosperous island would be forgiven for thinking that we were a country on the brink of social disaster and economic melt-down. We're in a mess, commentators tell us, and the party is over. Bertie Ahern got himself into trouble recently when he accused us of being whingers in the context of the Nice Treaty. Unfortunately, our whingeing is not confined to Nice.

I was only back in the country five minutes when I experienced some good-old fashioned Irish whingeing some weeks ago. We happened to land in Dublin airport a half an hour after the Irish soccer team arrived home after their successful World Cup campaign. Instead of celebrating our outstanding performance, we encountered a nation divided on whether the homecoming should be held in the city centre or the Phoenix Park. It has been one long whine every since.

The biggest whinge is about the price of everything. OK, prices have undoubtedly increased. (Though judging from the packed shops, travel agents, restaurants and pubs, this hasn't stopped people from spending.) When you consider that most people are earning more and paying less tax than a couple of years ago, this 'whinge' doesn't really stand up. Then there has been the traditional moan about 'the weather'. The tourist industry has been especially vocal this summer on the weather, complaining that times are very tough. On 'Morning Ireland' recently, we had an industry representative slamming Minister John O'Donoghue for giving only €3 million to the sectors to ease their current difficulties. Have they considered for one moment that the exorbitant prices they are charging visitors for bed and board may also have something to do with poor business? Maybe, Minister, you should have made it a condition when giving them money that they give it back to customers in some form when times get better and when the weather improves.

Reintegration back into Ireland would not have been complete without a good auld gripe from the farmers, who are currently arguing that CAP reforms will drive them off the land. Where have we heard that before from the agricultural sector? Sure that whinge goes right back to 1973, when we first joined the European Community. With increased prosperity, some higher class of whinge has crept in.

What about the woman who wrote into RTÉ Radio presenter Brenda Power recently and complained that she was finding it hard to say 'no' to friends wanting to stay in her holiday home in Spain? Or the friend who has to wait three months for delivery of his new car as the manufacturer can't keep up with demand? Is life tough or what?

The other disgraceful 'whinge' from people is that our country is being 'swamped' by immigrants and asylum-seekers. Turf out the foreign spongers is the well-worn cry.

In the last few weeks we have had some hysteria about the fact that a period of belt-tightening is on the way and public spending cuts are under way. Minister Charlie McCreevy even says tax increases might be introduced in his December budget. Shock horror. Perhaps this injection of reality would be no bad thing. Things have become too cushy. With the Celtic Tiger and prosperity has come higher expectations and an increased standard of living.

It is time to grab a hold of ourselves and stop for a moment to consider what we have. The vast majority of people in Ireland enjoy a good standard of living today. It's better than it has been for decades, it's a nice change from when times were really tough and when our young people were leaving in their thousands to find work abroad. One can't argue that there have been recent job losses, the latest being the announcement from Elan that 330 jobs will be shed before the end of the year, but let's not forget unemployment is still less than five per cent. In most developed countries this is regarded as full employment. The reality is if you want to work in Ireland you can, and in most

cases for fairly good rewards. The two-car, two-house, two-holidays-a-year family is not the rare thing it used to be.

Later this month, many teenagers will celebrate their Leaving Cert results not with a night on the town, but with a wild two-week holiday in Spain. Up to 10,000 of our citizens could afford to spend two weeks at the World Cup in Japan and South Korea, two of the most expensive countries in the world. I was amazed to be told by a shop assistant this week their most popular model of child's runner was sold out at just under €100 a pair. The vast majority of us have it good and it really isn't on to spend so many of our waking hours complaining.

We do have problems and it is a pity we don't hear more whingeing for things that really matter. For example, despite the Celtic Tiger and the fact we have come through a spectacular economic

Samantha Mumba performing at the O2 concert in the Phoenix Park. Photograph: Graham Hughes/Collins.

boom, there are still thousands of families in Ireland living on the bread line. We still have people begging on our streets. One of our most serious social problems is drug-addiction. So many young people abuse alcohol. What about our waste crisis? It is sad that real and serious problems like these are getting brushed aside in favour of more trivial ones. Or have I now joined the whingers?

SATURDAY, 3 AUGUST 2002

The Last Word in Deferential Interviewing

Radio Review: Harry Browne

Capitalism is in trouble! Who you gonna call? If you're Richard Curran, business editor at the *Irish Independent* and the latest substitute presenter on 'The Last Word' (Today FM, Monday to Friday), the man to ring is the boss himself, the one they call 'Tony'.

(On the radio, this friendly two-syllable name has definite advantages over 'Sir/Doctor AJF', though the first-name familiarity did sit oddly with the prevailing deference.) Such was the emergency, indeed, that normal programming and commercial imperatives were suspended for as long as it might take for Tony O'Reilly to ensure Richard and the rest of us that the global economy is safe in the hands of Wall Street. And how long was that? This rare interview with Ireland's mega-mogul kicked off at about 5.29 p.m. on Tuesday, at a time when the show's presenter would normally be reading a few listeners' comments before the 5.30 p.m. headlines, and it continued utterly uninterrupted, without so much as an ad for the Indo, until just after 6 p.m. Hey, when Tony is on the line, the order of business is suspended.

So was it thirty-two minutes that changed the world? Only if the world had been labouring under some considerable doubt that Tony is a bright boy

who can string together a sentence or two. To be sure, he's all that and more, and he knows it. But by golly this was an exercise desperately in search of a point, as even Curran seemed to realise toward the end when he struggled to find a polite way of asking 'Tony, what makes you tick?' — and Tony manfully insisted on talking about the importance of mineral exploration to Ireland's economy, before finally squeezing out some patriotic guff for the masses.

O'Reilly spoke with the stentorian confidence of a man who has become too accustomed to having his every banality received as though it were an Olympian pronouncement. Of course there were banalities aplenty here — in this respect Tony simply joins a long list of business pundits who have been intoning 'the system works' ad nauseum in recent months — and only occasionally did he bother dressing them up with a memorable word or phrase. One did come near to 6 p.m., after Curran asked O'Reilly another softball of a leading question about the Nice referendum and the economy; 'I take a more cosmic view . . .' Tony began, and it was just as well Richard didn't laugh, coz Tony wasn't joking.

Tony's view on the hoary old Boston v. Berlin debate was that 'Berlin looks better from Ireland when you're in Boston', which was pretty cosmic until he explained that this just means US companies like investing here because of access to the German market. O'Reilly's other startling truths were based on his experience as a chief executive in the US. He contrasted the old economy, of which he sounded inordinately fond, with the rather dodgier new economy, garnishing his comments with helpful examples about the predictability of, eg, ketchup sales. Amid Tony's fifty-seven varieties of cliché about business morality and the free market, however, some ironies lurked, unnoted by Curran but interesting all the same. The working and workable 'system' that O'Reilly described had very little to do with untrammelled enterprise; in fact, again and again he returned to the importance of the trammels, as it were, the complex set of laws and regulations that ensure corporate good behaviour. Since the discussion focused on the US, he referred specifically to anti-trust legislation such as the Sherman Act that seemingly means bosses can't even talk business on the yacht or the golf course, and the close scrutiny from the Securities and Exchange Commission of any potential board-room manipulations.

As for the market, this seemed to have an entirely more detrimental effect: shareholders, especially those pesky pension-fund managers, put extraordinary pressure on CEOs to maximise reported earnings, Tony told us. He didn't quite link this pressure directly to the recently publicised fraudsters, and Curran didn't encourage him, but the implication was there.

Is this anything approaching an adequate description of corporate reality? Surprisingly, Curran didn't challenge his own boss's 'pity the poor bosses' overtones, though he might have noted that regulation has clearly proven to be inadequate, at best, in several cases; that ordinary shareholders are the very ones who have been kicked in the teeth by the likes of Enron and WorldCom; that pension funds have suffered while chief executives have benefited obscenely from share speculation, etc. Okay, you can't expect too much from such a strange and misguided interview; what was interesting, all the same, is that the

Adrian Sweeney of Donegal under pressure from Dublin's Coman Goggins during the All Ireland Football Championships quarter final between Dublin and Donegal in Croke Park. Photograph: Bryan O'Brien.

leading light of Irish business appears to believe that corporations require a strong state sector to save them from the pressures imposed by the stock market. It makes you wonder if perhaps they should be paying a lot more tax.

WEDNESDAY, 7 AUGUST 2002

An Irishman's Diary

Kevin Myers

Inter-denominational schools: ah, how the heart sinks at those very words, and at the virtuous intent they convey. All those determinedly secular middle-class mothers, veterans of various Nicaragua, Guatemala and anti-apartheid support groups in their youth, who used to roll their own cigarettes in Bewleys on Saturday mornings, where they mastered the right-on, knowing, put-down look, or the head-bobbing sign of agreement. Far out, man.

Dabbled on the outskirts of lesbianism, vegetarianism and not shaving their legs under their long Indian print dresses, all of which proved conclusively that they were pretty hip. But one day they settled down with their boyfriend, a law graduate who ran a free legal aid centre, and bought their first car, a Morris Traveller or a Deux-Cheveaux, and moved to Ranelagh, and while he sort of imperceptibly drifts into the family law firm — specialising in conveyancing — she starts producing 2.4 babies called Conor and Simon and Alexandra and Emma.

Then it's schools: where do you send them? Well, of course the inter-denominational school, naturally, where they can learn to respect all religions equally, and where no religion is seen to have a monopoly on right, for we all have so much to learn from one another, from our different philosophies, and our different world experiences. And there'd be pictures of Mahatma Gandhi and Nelson Mandela and Martin Luther King on the walls, and the children would be raised in a world where there was no difference between religions or races.

Sorry, Ranelagh-woman. Wrong. For the history of religion is the history of emphasising difference, not celebrating it. Yet in the Ranelagh world of benign unbelief, it's easy to pass off affable agnosticism as ecumenism. And if unbelief means that people don't kill people out of religious conviction, well and good: in fact splendid, and I'm all in favour of it. But the fashionable tepidities of the Dublin 6 bien-pensant are mere coffee-morning tittle-tattle compared with the dark passions which go into the making and the maintenance of religious beliefs.

There is a single, central difference between the Catholic Church and the main reformed religion here, the Church of Ireland, and that difference has remained unbridged and unbridgeable despite forty years of the ecumenical movement. No amount of inter-denominational pussy-footing in Ranelagh is going to change the towering importance to the Catholic Church of the doctrine of transubstantiation.

The Roman Catholic dogma is that during the consecration, the host actually becomes the body of Jesus Christ, the Son of God, and Redeemer of All Mankind; not symbolically, not in a complex piece of imagery, but in full reality. This piece of human flesh, of tongue and breast and bowel, is then consumed by the worshipful.

Well naturally Ranelagh-woman doesn't want to go into the gory details of all that. She's Catholic all right, but not that kind of yucky Catholic. Her form of Catholicism is inclusive and warm and forgiving, and it's all about the Third World and AIDS and soon, she hopes, women priests.

Once again, Ranelagh woman. Wrong. That's not Catholicism. That's being nice. Which is not the same thing. Eating a person's body is not being nice. It's being weird. But Catholicism is weird. All religion is weird. And the doctrine of transubstantiation is certainly weird. But without it, the Catholic Church is an organisation with lots

Model Lorenzo Barbera wearing an Etro three-quarter length suede jacket, with Etro woolcheck trousers, and model Martha Christie with the Tackle booklet, at the launch of the Brown Thomas Autumn/Winter menswear collection, with the Irish Cancer Society launch of Tackle, a men's awareness campaign, in Dublin yesterday. Photograph: Eric Luke.

of buildings and money, rather like AIB.

Of course, an entire generation or more have been brought up on happy-clappy Catholicism, with not too much talk about the differences between the Churches. But the fellows at the top, they know the irreducible chasm between the Churches is the Eucharist; and that's why they insist the communion wafer can't be distributed to all comers, just as you wouldn't invite any old stranger off the street to mind your children. Go on. Pop some real God into your mouth.

No, it's not easy to accept. It's not meant to be. It's doctrine, not a simple mathematical equation. So that's why religion isn't a minor lifestyle choice, along with Habitat or Next, AIB or Bank of Ireland. Religion is something which commits you to life-governing beliefs. The key is in the word: its root is *ligare*, Latin for bind, as in ligament.

That's why the lesson of Dunboyne isn't about sectarianism, but about the intellectual religious integrity of its head teacher, Tomás Ó Dúlaing. He at least understands that 'inter-denominationalism' ceases at the consecration; and that consecration is the central pillar of the Catholic Church. Far from it being a pillar for the Church of Ireland, it is a barrier between it and Rome, and he equally understands that Protestant children cannot be expected to be taught as doctrine something that is anathema to their church.

But, of course, the Catholic Church over recent decades neglected to teach its faithful how profoundly it differs from the Protestant faiths. Its priests were far too busy building ugly concrete wigwams in which to conduct folk-masses, with altar-girls performing Riverdance and strewing rose-petals over the congregation, to remember what lies at its heart.

The reality is there is no such thing as inter-denominationalism, and that at best, there is multi-denominationalism. Of course, the failure of the Catholic Church to define and defend that central truth has confused the Catholics of Dunboyne, not to speak of An Foras Patrúnachta, never mind our right-on Ranelagh woman. It is an object lesson that, even intellectually, sound walls make good neighbours, and that rapprochement based on well-meaning ignorance invariably ends in tears.

SATURDAY, 10 AUGUST 2002

A Case of Broken Hearts

Róisín Ingle

I'm still not finished moving. It has been months now and there are boxes in the bedroom still unpacked. These are marked in black felt tip with enlightening phrases that I felt would be helpful when the time came to identify their contents. Miscellaneous Stuff sits beside Things I Need and the one I really dread opening, Bits and Pieces. It's like I wanted to write Can't Be Bothered Sorting Through This Crap but there wasn't room on the cardboard crisp box. So they sit there in anonymous piles, growing scarier by the day.

Then there is a battered suitcase that has followed me everywhere. From Dublin, to Birmingham, to London, to Dublin, to Belfast and back to Dublin again. It doesn't need announcing because its contents spill out the sides.

But if I did mark it, I would call it simply Letters and probably never go near it again. At least until I'm advancing in years and want to remember

that I had a life once. I wonder how impressed I'll be as an old timer when reminded I used to hang out at the roller disco an ever-so-slightly excessive three times a week.

This suitcase is filled with pages and pages scrawled from friends, missives about everything and about nothing, all stuck in pink envelopes and posted in the days before e-mail and text messages. I rarely send or receive letters anymore. When I do get them, they tend to be the nasty kind written in green ink that I'm more inclined to file in my dustbin than in the suitcase.

Along with the letters, the case is filled with out-of-focus photographs, ticket stubs for events I can't

Susan McCarthy, Bandon, Co. Cork, with Fast Silver, an Irish Draft Stallion, on the opening day of the Kerrygold Horse Show, at the RDS, Ballsbridge. Photograph: Eric Luke.

remember attending and birthday cards from people I wouldn't recognise. But at the bottom, wrapped in black tissue paper and pink ribbon, is a little bundle of memories I'll probably always carry around.

Every time I move house, that perfect package leers at me. As I moved from Belfast to Dublin I really thought I would do it … I thought I might open the ribbon and face the contents. But I didn't.

These are letters twenty-one-year-old me sent to seventeen-year-old Sam who broke my heart into a thousand pieces despite not having an ounce of cruelty in his bones. We met at a gig in Birmingham where he was pressing buttons on the sound desk. I'm having a party, I said. Would you like to come? Alright then, he said. He was beautiful. Inside, outside, every way.

There followed three weeks of exquisite kisses because when things are this pure, anything else would just spoil it. Wouldn't it? Three weeks of feeding ducks and exchanging meaningful glances. Reading about the Kray twins in the rain. Eating space dust that exploded in your mouth.

Then one day he didn't call. And the letters began. Long and winding missives full of anguish and recriminations and vaguely psychotic ramblings. In hindsight, I can see I was coming on a little too strong. The letters were wrapped up in black tissue paper (the misery! the drama!) and never sent.

But being me, I made the fatal mistake of showing him one of these rants, probably more for a critical analysis of my Emily Dickinson-style poetry than anything else, and the next day he met me in a coffee shop with a letter of his own. The gist of it was 'I'm sorry. I think you need a husband, not a boyfriend. I don't want to stand in your way.' He walked me to the bus stop and I used up a whole packet of paper hankies on the way.

Two years later, I got married. Five years later, I was crying again. And I wanted to find Sam. He was in Gran Canaria working as the Spanish equivalent of a red coat, which made me feel a little better because I thought he might be an under-ground film director or something equally cool. We spoke briefly and blandly. I have to admit I fantasised about me turning up at his hotel on a package holiday and us living happily ever after. But the thought of him in that uniform made me cringe.

And then I fell in love. Properly this time. With a gorgeous man who likes that I come on far too strong and is learning to love any vaguely psychotic tendencies.

For the first time in ten years, I realise that this particular bundle of memories doesn't matter anymore. In a box marked Revelations, I pack the painfully corny but truthful notion that romantic wounds, no matter how deep, eventually fade. Just like the ink on an unsent letter.

And these ancient infatuations, no matter how well they are packaged, just can't compete with the real thing. I think about this but don't quite have the courage to pull gently at the pink ribbon, peel back the black tissue paper and take a match to the contents. It wouldn't be fair. I think old timer me might like to remember how it felt.

SATURDAY, 10 AUGUST 2002

Donaldson and Empey New 'Dream Ticket'?

Frank Millar

Jeffery Donaldson and Reg Empey. An Ulster Unionist 'dream ticket'? Nightmare on Downing Street? Or a daft idea waiting (if ever put to the test) to fall apart under the weight of its inherent contradictions?

Sir Reg may feel some impatience at finding the idea once more in the public domain. Only recently, after all, did he confirm his view that David Trimble would and should lead the UUP into next year's Assembly elections. No, he had not been party to discussions about replacing Mr Trimble, nor had he authorised others to act on his behalf. Fellow party officers or Assembly members engaged in such talk should, he advised, 'desist'.

Clear enough, as far as it goes. However, Sir Reg did not quite close the door on the possibility that, in some future circumstance, he and Mr Donaldson might provide the nucleus of a new unionist leadership. Asked if the dream ticket scenario was credible, he replied that, because of his answers in respect of Mr Trimble's position, this was not an issue.

In fairness, we are not necessarily entitled to make too much of this. Sir Reg may have declined to speak on the record, and confined himself to very limited replies to the questions subsequently submitted, because he had no wish to give the story legs.

Be that as it may, he left it with legs enough — certainly for those pro-agreement Assembly members who believe that, between them, Sir Reg and Mr Donaldson probably represent the UUP's best alternative to electoral disaster next May. And, of course, it is the fact that it is pro-agreement unionists who have been sponsoring this plan which spells real potential danger for Mr Trimble.

For some time it has seemed clear that Mr Donaldson and his allies cannot muster the necessary numbers to oust the First Minister. They appear determined to have another tilt in September and may yet prove that wrong. Their high point until now was the Rev Martin Smyth's audacious bid for the leadership, on just two days' notice, and his staggering forty-six per cent share of the vote. Since then Mr Trimble's majority on the Ulster Unionist Council has marginally increased, twice.

The dissidents believe they will get Mr Trimble in the end, if only after their party's defeat at the hands of the DUP. However, that must be an unappealing prospect for Mr Donaldson, who might find himself leading a UUP rump but playing second-fiddle in a changed unionist landscape increasingly dominated by Dr Paisley's deputy, Mr Peter Robinson.

So the Lagan Valley MP will hardly have discouraged those pro-agreement unionists when they sought to persuade him that he and Sir Reg offered the best chance of reuniting the UUP and staving off the prospect of a Robinson ascendancy — not to mention their own best hope of keeping their Stormont seats.

Such personal calculations are hardly surprising. Indeed he would be a poor and ultimately doomed politician who did not remain properly focused on the imperatives of securing re-election. It's perfectly plain what might be in it for the plotters. What is less clear is why they might imagine Mr Donaldson and Sir Reg a better bet than Mr Trimble to preserve them and the entire devolution project.

For is there not a glaring inherent contradiction in the concept of coalition between Sir Reg, the man who actually negotiated the Strand One part of the Good Friday settlement, and Mr Donaldson who, had he had his way, would by now have collapsed the entire edifice?

Ah, comes the soothing reply, but Jeffrey is too cute for that. He knows that would finally split the party and ensure the DUP's dominance. And why would he want to do that anyway, they retort, when even the DUP does not really want to wreck the Assembly?

So the dream-ticket theory runs on. A party grown weary of warfare seizes the opportunity to unite behind a new leadership team, which in turn uses the traditional 'honeymoon' period to confront the DUP with its own alleged hypocrisies and inconsistencies over the agreement. The pitch for electoral survival would obviously necessitate lots of tough talk about holding paramilitaries to account and preserving the integrity of the democratic process. And after — with the DUP challenge successfully repelled? With Sinn Féin still entitled to a place in government? Well, says one dreamer, 'Jeffrey can explain that he didn't start with a clean slate and that there were always going to be limits to what he could do to improve on the situation he inherited from Trimble.'

This is not convincing. For starters, it suggests an approach to politics which might incline the unionist electorate to kick the lot of them out with contempt. As they would surely be contemptuous, having endured the trauma of Trimble's removal only to discover that Donaldson, Empey or who-ever had claimed the top job while changing little else. It is also almost certainly based on a complete misunderstanding of Mr Donaldson.

He rejected the Belfast Agreement because it did not guarantee IRA decommissioning — a position he certainly has considered vindicated by every tortured UUP twist and turn on the issue in the intervening years. Unlike Mr Trimble, he was serious in recent weeks in seeking Sinn Féin's exclusion because of Colombia and Castlereagh. If he became leader before the Assembly election, he would have to frame a policy to match the DUP's pledge to force a renegotiation of the agreement. And, above all, Mr Donaldson knows that he cannot (any more, by the way, than can the DUP) promise to remove Sinn Féin from office while somehow maintaining the structure of devolved government.

Unionists may well decide to finish with Mr Trimble — in the autumn, or next May. But they should not delude themselves that in doing so they would be choosing a better way to save Stormont. The alternative to devolution with Sinn Féin is Direct Rule.

TUESDAY, 19 AUGUST 2002

We Watched as Hope Slowly Faded in the Face of Unspeakable Evil

Kathy Sheridan

One of the hardest truths we've learned from the disappearance of Holly Wells and Jessica Chapman is that, short of locking our children in the attic, we are helpless in the face of random evil.

Looking back, the achievement — or the mis-fortune — of the Cambridgeshire police was to keep hope alive for so long. They squared up to the statistics, which show that children abducted in this way are usually dead within forty-eight hours, and determined that this time, their little force would confound them.

They transmitted it to the families. It was written in the strong, intelligent face of Kevin Wells, father of Holly, as he sat alert and composed at press conferences, holding his wife's hand, handling multi-part questions in the orderly, meticulous way of a man in possession of every scintilla of information and still in control, still capable of rational thought.

A father clasps his son's hand outside St Andrew's Church, Soham, Cambridgeshire, 18 August, after a special church service to give prayers for missing schoolgirls Holly Wells and Jessica Chapman. Photograph: Toby Melville.

If he had reason to hope, then why wouldn't we? The images of two shiny-faced, bright-eyed little girls, captured on camera ninety minutes before their disappearance, barely suppressing the giggles and the glee in their matching Manchester United kits, would come to haunt us as their parents endured a stomach-turning, two-week crucifixion.

Library photograph of Holly Wells (left) and her best friend, Jessica Chapman, pictured in their Manchester United shirts shortly before they disappeared. Nearly 2,000 people gathered at Ely Cathedral in Cambridgeshire on 30 August to celebrate the girls' lives. Holly and Jessica, both from Soham, Cambridgeshire, vanished on 4 August. Their bodies were found near a track in Wangford, Suffolk, on 17 August. Photograph: PA.

With it, came a willing suspension of belief. Who could bring themselves to snuff out the lives of two innocents? Who would want to? And against that, came the constant struggle to bury that insistent part of the mind, the part that threatens to engulf us with images of such horror and depravity that it can only drive decent people to thoughts of murderous vengeance and despair.

Courtesy of the twenty-four-hour television news channels, we accompanied the Wells and the Chapman families on a small part of their journey to Golgotha.

With their voracious hunger for news and instant reporting, for better or worse, these channels brought to us every rumour, every stray word, every talkative villager, every 'breakthrough', most of it unfiltered or unleavened by time or reflection. It seemed that this calamity had befallen good neighbours just a few miles down the road in a place alive with gossip and speculation.

So when they returned to interview the woman who had reported an unlikely sighting of the girls on the motorway the morning after their disappearance, we saw her certainty fade before our eyes.

When they told us that Huntley and Carr had been called in for questioning on Friday afternoon, we were able, just like the people of Soham, to dissect the nondescript pair who had been talking for the cameras only a day before.

And when soon after we heard that Holly's mother, Nicola, had come out shopping in the village, looking cheerful, we put the gloss on it that we wanted: she had clearly been told something that had come out of the questioning and it must be good.

From these small omens, for a few hours on Friday, it was possible to believe that the two little girls were coming home, a bit tearful maybe but miraculously unscathed, leaving the name of Soham to stand forever as a beacon of hope, defiance and redemption.

Instead, it will rank in the same chilling roll-call as a Dunblane or a Hungerford, a name resonant of horrors that surpass human understanding.

After Soham, school caretakers and classroom assistants will never be above suspicion and like Dunblane, children will feel threatened in a place which should be a monument to security.

After Soham, can the red shirt of Manchester United ever evoke anything other than two lovely, smiling faces? Represent anything other than an image of innocence crucified? Soham this weekend was a place where the mutual need of locals and media suddenly became redundant and its forbearance showed signs of snapping. A place where the grieving process must take its course and anger and recrimination will have its turn.

Cambridgeshire police will be among the prime targets. Time will tell whether different tactics might have yielded other results or at least a swifter conclusion.

But the announcement finally that they were dealing with a murder case was surely devastating for those who led by flying the flag of hope. Though clearly vital for police morale, was it sensible to sustain it at such a pitch? Only the parents of Holly and Jessica can tell us that.

But we do know, or can guess at, some other truths. That for all the talk of a different policing system, of Internet supervision, of sex offender registers, of more vigilant parenting, it is probable that none could have helped Holly and Jessica. As events unfold, we will probably find that their terrible fate had nothing to do with the Internet, nothing to do with the hundreds of known sex offenders who live within reach of Soham, nothing that the best-organised police force on earth or most brilliant psychiatrist could have predicted. Paedophiles may invest vast amounts of time in 'grooming' their prey. Or may pounce in seconds.

The fact is that having taken all the preventative steps open to us, short of locking our children in the attic, we are helpless in the face of random evil. That is the hardest truth of all.

But as we stare into the darkest heart of humanity in these coming days, we should also remind ourselves of another truth: that of all the terrible violations perpetrated against children every day, by far the least likely are abuse or abduction by a stranger. Like the people of Soham, we must learn first, to look to our own.

TUESDAY, 26 AUGUST 2002

Rough Guide to One Man's Lonely Planet

LockerRoom: Tom Humphries

Keano — The Index That Shocked a Generation:

Austria: 178, annexation plan 180-81.

Bambi: early relationship with 27-29, eats raw 119, relatives, sued by 126-32.

Beckham: David, affection for 100, request to play central midfield 100, visiting hours 100.

Charlton: Jack, fishing, RK discovers that JC knows nothing of 111-14, fraud 113-14, Irish, not even 113, war against 113-17.

De Rossa: Proinsias 238.

Dervan: Cathal, early relationship with 39-40, eats raw 40, finds greasy 41, relatives, thanked by 147.

Evans: Ian 'Taff', Welsh, not even 120.

Fawkes, Guy: funding for 56-7, plays testimonial for 60.

Ferguson: Alex, first apparition 47-49, first miracle 58-60, God, mistaken for 165, 166.

Frequent Flyer Miles better than World Cup: 213, gets bonus 214, gets gold card 215.

God: Cork, by grace of 3, 7, 10, dispute with 139-142, settlement with 144.

Haaland: Alf Inge, Christmas card from 77, joke, practical (with) 99-101, misunderstanding 101-105, prison, because of 106-110.

Hasselbaink: Jimmy Floyd, dairy products 142, dietary patterns 139-42, pizza ordering technique of 143, wonders what JFH is eating right now 143, 178, 218.

Kahn: Aga, RK's charitable donations to 192.

The controversial new book by Roy Keane and Eamon Dunphy which went on sale at Easons Bookshop, O'Connell Street, Dublin. Photograph: Bryan O'Brien.

Kahn: Chaka, grand girl 195, romantic notions 195, tribe of Keane-Kahns? 195.

Kahn: Genghis, influence of 193.

Kahn: Oliver, performance versus Ireland 194.

Kennedy: JF, Monroe, dispute over 67-68.

Kennedy: Michael, burning bush incident 244, infallibility of 223, inflammability of 244.

Libel laws: 238, fallibility of 239, innocent victims of 240.

Locomotiv Moscow: 236-37.

Manchester United: career 23-26,

walks with 8, 10, 24, 97, 120.

Mass: occasions missed 193.

McCarthy: Mick, assessment of as b★★★ocks 109, as c★★t 110, as w★★★er 111, first touch 112-113.

Moon: cow jumps over 220, howls at 201, Keith, drinking with 23-24.

Mouse: Mickey, analysis of performance within FAI 234-5, criticism of dress sense 236-7.

Oswald: Lee Harvey, uses as patsy 67-68.

Presley: Elvis, arraignment and trial 245-6, as room-mate 241-2, friendship with 243, RK's You're-Not-Singing-Anymore taunt 245, wedding, best man 244, writes 'Are You Lonesome Tonight' for RK 245.

Quinn: Niall, assessment of 191-2, hell, prospects in 240.

Robinson: Mary, liberal agenda killing football 201-03.

Rolexes: mass smashing of 236.

Saipan: barbecue location 239, bumpiness 240-46, flight schedules from 247-249.

Sandwiches: cheese 213-216.

Satan: Steve captains Ireland 230-35, RK rejects deeds of 241-42.

Simpson: Bart, comparison with Dervan, Cathal 132.

Simpson: Homer, comparison with McCarthy, Mick 132.

Simpson: Marge, comparison with Evans, Ian 132.

Spring: Dick, b★★★ocks, 135.

Stone: Oliver, key errors in movie JFK 70.

Taliban: captain of 195-196, flirts with 194, goes home from 197, takes revenge on 198, 'waited long enough' 198.

Theresa: Mother, mistaken for 193, pace similar to 194.

Triggs: assessment of 19-27, dislike of cats, shared 28, first touch, (see Mick McCarthy above)

World Cup: assessment of as televisual experience 290, compared to frequent flyer miles 213.

World, News of: breaks heart 57, 89, 123; gets it wrong 45, 89, 90, 178, 203; invades privacy 67, 89, 103, 145, 245; sale of serialisation rights to 289-90.

SATURDAY, 28 AUGUST 2002

Leading Labour Into Government was the One Prize that Eluded an Ambitious, Driven Quinn

Mark Brennock

A flamboyant European social democrat who used power well and took pleasure in it, Ruairí Quinn did not fulfil his ambition as Labour leader. Throughout his thirty-eight-year career in the Labour Party, Ruairí Quinn's attitude to power has been unambiguous: politicians need to be in power, he has said regularly, adding that he personally enjoys power.

But since his election as Labour Party leader in 1997, many close to him have speculated that his ambition may have been modified. Sure, he would have loved to enter government after June's general election, but this would not be enough. After all, his predecessor, Mr Dick Spring, had enjoyed a tremendous period of power and influence, and had ended bitter divisions in Labour. But he had also left the party, electorally, in as bad a condition as he had found it.

Mr Quinn wanted to leave behind a stronger party than he had inherited. But he has neither led them to power, nor left them electorally stronger — apart from the effect of the merger with Democratic Left.

His critics argue that his failure to join an alternative government platform with Fine Gael was a miscalculation. Deprived of the chance to change the Government, many people voted to change the Opposition, they maintain. Labour's measured election message failed to attract the significant number of anti-Government voters, who instead supported the Green Party, Sinn Féin and Independents.

Mr Quinn's supporters say they had no alternative. Ruling out coalition with Fianna Fáil, thus binding themselves to a deeply unpopular Fine Gael, would have damaged them further, they argue. Their electoral strategy, they say, was forced on them by circumstances. In addition, it was approved overwhelmingly at a Labour Party conference before the election.

Mr Quinn tried to put a positive gloss on Labour's election result yesterday, but coming back with the same number of seats he entered the campaign with was probably his greatest political disappointment.

He spent five bruising years as an Opposition leader with little to show for it. Yesterday, he said frankly that he might not have the energy to give the job the same level of commitment for the next six years. He would stay in politics and had no plans to do anything else, he said.

Ruairí Quinn has been a Labour Party member for thirty-eight years, but did not come to the party through the traditional trade union route. There has always been some muttering among Labour's members about Mr Quinn's attachment to power and his willingness to deal with, what for many Labour people was the traditional enemy, Fianna Fáil.

His liking of good wine, fine cigars, contemporary Irish art and other 'bourgeois' trappings were commented upon as marking him out from the traditional Labour Party image.

Much of this was unfair. He is a genuine democratic socialist or social democrat (the preferred epithet within the party changes with fashion) and could never see himself in any other party. His natural ideological home is among the left of centre social democratic parties of western Europe who have held or shared power in their respective states for many years since the Second World War.

When he said, on the day of his election as party leader, that it was the achievement of 'a lifetime's political ambition … a dream come true', he meant it.

His political consciousness was formed during student protests in UCD in the late 1960s. He has always had a penchant for the flamboyant gesture and image: the light-coloured suit in the Dáil chamber's sea of grey, navy and black; the loud tie; the campaign car blasting Manfred Mann's 'The Mighty Quinn' at election time; the red roses.

He comes from a Ranelagh-born, Sandymount-bred family of achievers. One brother, Lochlann, is a successful businessman and chairman of AIB. Another, Conor, is managing director of the QMP advertising agency. Another brother, Declan, is professor of medicine at the University of Saskatchewan, Canada, while another, Colm, is a doctor. His cousin, Feargal, is a senator and owner of Superquinn.

He was educated at Blackrock College and UCD, where he quickly became involved in the political activism that swept European campuses in the 1960s, but he was regarded as a moderate by many of his fellow activists.

His activism spread outside UCD into the housing action committees that were active at the time, and he campaigned for the opening of Merrion Square to the public.

'It seemed to everyone that he would end up in politics,' says one fellow student activist from that time.

On his return from post-graduate study in Athens, he began working as an architect and, at the same time, began building up the depleted Labour organisation in Dublin South East and his own position within it. The depletion was due to the fact that many in Dr Noel Browne's 1969 organisation had been expelled from the party or had resigned after the party's bitter coalition conference.

When the selection convention for the 1973 general election took place, Dr Browne stood down and Mr Quinn took the nomination. In the subsequent general election, he was just thirty-nine votes short of a Dáil seat, despite a collapse in Labour's vote from twenty-four per cent to eleven per cent.

He held the nomination, despite opposition from a lively left within the constituency which eventually dissipated. Mr Quinn's election to Dublin Corporation in 1974, and nomination to the Seanad in 1976, gave him the base from which he finally won the seat in 1977 by 250 votes.

He lost the seat briefly in 1981 and scraped back on the eleventh count in February 1982. He has held it comfortably at every election since, although he had only a narrow margin over Fine Gael's Frances Fitzgerald in June.

In November 1982, the new Tánaiste and Labour leader, Mr Dick Spring, picked Mr Quinn to be his junior minister in the Department of the Environment. As an architect, Mr Quinn had written considerably on the social problems of urban growth in Ireland and the area suited his interests.

However, when Frank Cluskey resigned from cabinet in late 1983 and Mr Spring decided to

move to another department, it was to Labour, and not Environment that Mr Quinn was appointed as a minister.

In coalition with Fianna Fáil from 1992, he was the Labour TD given the most senior economic brief, Enterprise and Employment. But this turned out to be only a warm-up for his appointment as minister for finance in the rainbow government.

It was during the crisis that led to the collapse of the coalition with Fianna Fáil and the formation of the rainbow government that Mr Quinn uttered his most quoted political phrase. Walking into a meeting with then Taoiseach Mr Albert Reynolds, he said: 'We have come for a head, yours or Harry's. It does not appear we are getting Harry's.'

However, Mr Quinn was seen as much less hostile to continuing in government with Fianna Fáil than were many of his colleagues.

Labour's achievement during Mr Quinn's time in Finance was to show that it could handle the government's most senior ministry. With Mr Quinn, this came as no surprise: his pragmatism and commitment to being in government ensured there was no major loosening of the purse strings and no run on the pound.

As chairman of the European Council of Economic Ministers, during Ireland's EU presidency, he steered through crucial agreements to lay the foundations for the single currency.

He said yesterday that when Mr Spring became party leader, he thought his chance of the top job was gone.

However, it came again in 1997 when Mr Quinn defeated Mr Brendan Howlin, now his deputy leader. He had a good first year, steering through the merger with Democratic Left and

Ruairí Quinn, TD at Leinster House announcing that he is stepping down as leader of the Labour Party.
Photograph: Dara MacDonaill.

winning by-elections in Limerick East and Dublin North.

He adopted a very different style from his predecessor. His kitchen cabinet was dominated by deputies such as Mr Howlin, Mr Derek McDowell and Mr Emmet Stagg, rather than the outside advisers who were much resented during Mr Spring's time.

But with Sinn Féin moving closer to mainstream politics and the Green Party attracting more support, he struggled to establish Labour as a clear voice for change.

During the biggest economic boom in Irish history, as Mr Quinn said yesterday: 'We seem to have failed to convince people that you cannot have your cake and eat it. You cannot have such low tax rates and still have the public services we require.'

Letters to the Editor August 2002

Dr Empey's Retirement

Sir, — Might the obvious inconsistency of Dr Walton Empey's valedictory claim (Irish Times, *29 July*) to aspire to better Anglican relations with Catholics while yet again taking one last impertinent swipe at an internal memorandum of the Catholic Church addressed to her members only by authority of the Pope himself, namely Dominus Iesus, be acknowledged? — Yours, etc., Rev Fr David O'Hanlon, CC, Parochial House, Kentstown, Navan, Co Meath. 1 August 2002

Sir, — I never cease to be amazed at the outpourings in the press (and in other media) of Fr David O'Hanlon (1 August).

His latest attack on a leading member of the Church of Ireland — our fellow Christians — on the occasion of the retirement of Archbishop Walton Empey makes me feel ashamed to be a Roman Catholic.

Fr O'Hanlon's arrogance — as displayed both in the question he poses and in the intemperate wording of the question — is all the more to be deplored at a time when the Hierarchy of the Catholic Church in Ireland is featuring prominently in the media for reasons relating to rather unChristian policies/practices (to put it mildly).

His talk of an 'impertinent swipe' on the part of Dr Empey beggars belief when account is taken of his own outpourings in the press and his performances on TV.

Perhaps Fr O'Hanlon could do all Christians in this country a big favour by taking early retirement or a long career break. — Yours, etc., Tony Forde, Shenick Avenue, Skerries, Co Dublin. 3 August 2002

Sir, — Fr David O'Hanlon has added his pinch of silly seasoning to the thymes that are in it.

His tetchy strictures on the gentle aspirations toward unity expressed, on retiring, by Archbishop Walton Empey (1 August) have a more than passing resonance to the deplorable sneer made some time back by his own ecclesiastical superior regarding Dr Empey's theological expertise.

When both David O'Hanlon and his cardinal shall come to retire, I hope they may be held in the kind of love and regard which Walton Empey enjoys and which he has merited by his shining Christian ministry over the years.

Dr Empey's pained disappointment at the reiteration of sterile and self-righteous exclusivity featured in that 'internal memorandum for Catholics, Dominus Iesus' — and cited by David O'Hanlon — is echoed by the few who may have read it, and regarded with indifference by the many who haven't, but deem such views to be little more than hoary canards wheeled out by time-warped and fossilised obscurantists of the Roman Curia.

After all, Jesus wasn't a Roman Catholic, but he did instigate a great reformation in his day. Is not another such renewal urgently overdue? — Yours, etc., David Grant, Mount Pleasant, Waterford. 7 August 2002

Dunboyne School Dispute

Sir, — What seems to be lacking in the Dunboyne school dispute is an appreciation of the nature of religious education. It is a subject in its own right and has nothing whatever to do with the preparation of children for first Holy Communion and Confirmation.

The Roman Catholic Church has been very quiet in this controversy and it is not hard to guess the reason. For if Holy Communion and Confirmation preparation took place outside the school curriculum (as it should), then the numbers being presented for these sacraments are likely to be significantly reduced. The Church seems happy that, instead, almost everyone should be prepared for nothing more than rites of puberty by teachers who may never darken the church doors themselves. — Yours, etc., Robert MacCarthy, Dean of St Patrick's, The Deanery, Upper Kevin Street, Dublin 8. 10 August 2002

Sir, — As a committed and enthusiastic ecumenist, I was thoroughly dismayed at the content and tone of Dean McCarthy's letter in The Irish Times (10 August) and subsequent interview on 'Morning Ireland'.

To imply that the differences between the Anglican and Catholic Churches are merely trivial and scarcely worth discussing does a serious disservice to the cause of ecumenism. The nature of the Eucharist, the role of Mary, the Papacy, the Catholic Church's teachings on sexual morality, are all matters of serious difference and cannot be minimised. The suggestion that the Catholic Church is interested only in numbers is insulting and does Dean McCarthy little credit. A recent correspondent to your columns has described his intervention as 'a low in ecumenism' — and many would agree.

One of the most helpful comments on ecumenism ever heard came from a wise and committed Christian woman, the Rev Ruth Paterson, at an ecumenical conference in Dublin some years ago: The key element in ecumenism, she said, is respect for your own tradition. She is absolutely right and I wish more people in

positions of influence (like, for instance, the present Dean of St. Patrick's Cathedral) would take cognisance of the truth of what she said. — Yours, etc., Louis Power, Killiney, Co Dublin 20 August 2002.

Dublin Traffic Changes

Sir, — Could you confirm that the new road signs will be recycled to point to the Millennium Clock? — Yours, etc., Laurence Paveau, Lucan, Co Dublin. 29 August 2002.

THURSDAY, 5 SEPTEMBER 2002

FF Research to Dictate What Voters Will be Told

Mark Brennock

The Government parties will be selling a different pro-Nice Treaty message than last year. Then their narrowly focused and largely technical campaign was outmanoeuvred by a broad alliance of anti-Nice campaigners who raised broader concerns about the direction of Europe.

This time, the Government parties will put forward a broader argument: that EU membership has been good for the Irish economy over almost three decades, and that a Yes vote is needed to keep Ireland at the heart of the Union. Ministers have been told to emphasise the economy at every opportunity.

They also hope to neutralise the argument that the treaty could compromise Irish neutrality. At the EU summit in Seville in June, the Government and EU leaders issued separate declarations affirming Irish neutrality. The Government will emphasise this strongly.

While the campaign against Nice will be strong, the Dáil has a substantial Yes majority. Fianna Fáil, Fine Gael, Labour and the PDs will all be campaigning for a Yes vote. They will face vigorous opposition from the Green Party, Sinn Féin,

Part of a group from VHI Health Care Finance Department on a team building day at The Orchard Conference Centre, Tinahely, Co Wicklow. Photograph: David Sleator.

the Socialist Party and a number of Independents.

Fianna Fáil has reassembled the team that managed its general election campaign earlier this year. Mr P.J. Mara is director of elections again while general secretary Mr Martin Mackin, former Taoiseach's adviser Mr Peter McDonagh and the party's press office staff will form the nucleus of the campaign.

Just as then they have conducted substantial market research to find out what the public wants to hear. And so the party will emphasise the economic benefits that have accrued during EU membership because the research suggests this will strike a chord among voters. The economy will be better served through full EU membership rather than a 'semi-detached' status that could result from a second No vote, it will say.

Fianna Fáil has also appointed each deputy as a director of elections in his/her Dáil constituency or part of it. The party will produce posters and leaflets, but finances may limit the amount of material it can pay for.

Fine Gael begins a series of 17 regional meetings around the State in Navan tomorrow night. Party front-bench members and guest speakers such as former EU Commissioner Mr Peter Sutherland and current Commissioner Mr David Byrne will address the meetings seeking a Yes vote. Later in the campaign, Fine Gael will produce leaflets and posters. A party spokeswoman said yesterday it would not decide on what pro-Nice argument to concentrate on until it received feedback on the public's concerns through the public meetings.

Labour and the Progressive Democrats will also mount poster and leaflet campaigns seeking a Yes vote. According to a Labour spokesman, the party will emphasise the desire to show solidarity with the applicant states. The PDs, like Fianna Fáil, will push economic arguments and warn of possible economic damage should Ireland vote No again. The party will set up a Vote Yes marquee at the National Ploughing Championships later this month.

All of the Dáil-based opponents said they will steer clear of anyone seeking to put the race issue into the public debate. The Green Party has appointed Dublin Mid West TD Mr Paul Gogarty as director of its campaign. The party will campaign under the slogan 'For a Democratic Europe', arguing that the EU's decision-making processes are

undemocratic, and the decision to hold a second referendum on the same issue is also undemocratic.

'We will be steering clear of those with xenophobic tendencies, and arguing that we are pro-enlargement and pro-Europe,' said Mr Gogarty. 'Our argument is not against Europe, but the direction Europe is now taking.'

Sinn Féin will highlight its desire for an independent Irish foreign policy and will also campaign heavily on the proposition that holding a second

Liam O'Grady shows off his work on his first day at school in Scoil Chroí Naofa, Athenry, Co. Galway. Photograph: Joe O'Shaughnessy.

referendum is undemocratic. A spokesman said the party will produce a newsletter on the topic for distribution around the country, a poster campaign and a series of press conferences. The party's president and other senior figures from Northern Ireland will also get involved. Sinn Féin expects to mount a significant door-to-door canvas in the constituencies where it has TDs and a number of others.

Mr Joe Higgins of the Socialist Party will campaign for a No vote, with his party canvassing door to door in a number of areas.

Mr Finian McGrath of Independent Health Alliance (Dublin North Central) and Mr Seamus Healy, Independent (Tipperary South), said they will work vigorously against the treaty, producing leaflets and campaigning door to door. 'I am concerned about the reduced power for Ireland, the threat to our ability to conduct an independent foreign policy and the ability of the Rapid Reaction Force to carry out offensive military operations four thousand kilometres outside the EU,' said Mr McGrath.

Mr Tony Gregory, Independent (Dublin Central), will not mount a constituency campaign, but will speak against the treaty in the Dáil and at a number of public meetings. Mr Niall Blaney, Independent (Donegal North East), has not formally adopted a position, but said he called for a No vote last time and has heard nothing to change his mind.

Of the thirteen Independents, five are on the Yes side, four on the No side with three saying they have not made up their minds. One, Mr Paudge Connolly (Cavan-Monaghan) could not be contacted for comment yesterday.

Dr Liam Twomey (Wexford) said he is inclined to vote Yes. 'But I am as confused as the next person as to what the result will be for Ireland in the years to come.' He said he was concerned that the public would use the opportunity to make an anti-Government protest vote.

Dr Jerry Cowley (Mayo) is also a Yes voter, but feels the Government may have undermined its campaign through the recent health cuts. He said the democratic deficit — where there is no prior Oireachtas scrutiny of EU directives — must be addressed properly. Ms Marian Harkin (Sligo Leitrim) said she will be canvassing for a Yes vote, although some of her supporters will be seeking a No vote. Ms Mildred Fox (Wicklow) and Mr Michael Lowry (Tipperary South) will also be calling for a Yes vote.

Three Independents put themselves in the 'don't know' category. According to Mr Paddy McHugh (Galway East): 'There are good arguments on both sides and what I decide in the end will be based on what I think will be best for the country.' Similarly Mr James Breen (Clare) and Mr Jackie Healy-Rae (Kerry South) said they have not yet made up their minds, but will do so after the Dáil debate this week and next.

SATURDAY, 7 SEPTEMBER 2002

The View of Hell

Conor O'Clery

When I think of September 11th, I recall the man at the window. He was on the ninety-second or ninety-third floor of the North Tower, eighteen stories below the Windows on the World Restaurant. There was black smoke pouring from a line of narrow, church-like windows beside and above him. He stood on the narrow ledge, his body hanging out above Vesey Street 300 metres below. He waved a white cloth.

It looked like his shirt. He was in his thirties, I would say, and a little overweight. I spotted him first about 8.50 a.m., about four minutes after American Airlines Boeing 767 smashed into the tower just above him at 470 miles an hour laden with 10,000 gallons of fuel.

The plane had flown past my apartment just 300 metres north of the World Trade Centre. I don't remember hearing it, though it came low over central Manhattan. When the explosion occurred I thought it was a bomb. I saw a gaping hole in the side of the tower high above with flames and smoke pouring out.

I made several quick telephone calls, to my newsdesk, to my colleague Paddy Smyth in Washington, DC and my wife, Zhanna, in her office uptown. I also called RTÉ. It was 2 p.m. in Ireland.

As I was waiting to go on air there was a news flash about an aircraft hitting the World Trade Centre. Only then did I realise what it was. I focused again on the man with the white cloth. As I watched him through binoculars still waving futilely, United Airlines flight 175 came roaring over the Hudson and slammed into the South Tower behind and below him.

I knew immediately then that this was an act of war. It hit between the seventy-eighth and eighty-fourth floors, creating a huge orange and black fire-ball. Flaming jet fuel rained down on Broadway.

By now about two dozen fire engines had come wailing down West Side highway and parked outside the World Trade Centre, filling the wide roadway. Hundreds of firemen ran into the buildings laden down with gear. I decided to go to the scene. As I passed through the lobby of my building, a woman there was in hysterics; her husband worked in the stricken trade centre (he survived).

I went to the corner of Vesey Street and West Side Highway. People ran past me in panic towards Battery Park. Others stood in absolute shock, hands over open mouths, craning upwards. I recall a security man pushing me back. Bodies were falling on to Vesey Street and on to the plaza between the towers. They fell with arms extended, taking about ten seconds to reach the ground.

I thought I had better get back to my office. Apartment buildings were being evacuated all around, and I was afraid that I would not be allowed back. I also had a guest for whom I was responsible: twenty-one-year-old Dublin student Aoife Keane, who was witnessing from the

window scenes of unimaginable terror. I just made it back minutes before all tenants were ordered to leave. Somehow we were overlooked.

Jim Dwyer called from the *New York Times* in a panic about his daughter Maura at Stuyvesant High School next to my building. I was able to establish that all the children were evacuated safely. As I watched from the window, a helicopter buzzed low over the North Tower. I remember thinking in frustration — why doesn't it take people off the roof or lower a rope to the windows? Only later did I learn that the doors to the roof were locked and that the helicopter pilots could not approach because of the heat.

At around 10 a.m., I saw office workers gathered in Battery Park suddenly turn and run as fast as they could. The South Tower had started to fall. The top seemed to tilt over towards the river and then crush the whole building beneath it. It collapsed onto fire-engines and firemen who were just arriving. I was by now completely numb, working on my reflexes.

As the dust cleared, I scanned the windows of the North Tower for the man who had been waving. Incredibly, he was still there, holding desperately on to a pillar between two windows as smoke poured out past him. He most likely worked for Carr Futures, the finance company on the ninety-second floor which lost sixty-eight staff there that morning, or perhaps the Marsh & McLennan insurance company which had offices on several floors above.

I will never know. Nobody survived in the North Tower above the ninety-first floor. As I watched, two bodies fell past him from the higher floors, then two more, and I saw the building was shuddering violently.

Much has been written about people jumping. I believe that many were clinging desperately to life but were simply unable to hold on. Intense smoke and heat gave people little choice. They could not breathe and crowded around windows smashed open with computers and chairs. It was later estimated that 200 people fell to their death, most from the North Tower. None were ever classified as 'jumpers', i.e. people who deliberately commit suicide.

The North Tower was now in its death throes. The end came seconds later, at 10.28 a.m. The man suddenly went down as if on a fast elevator as the building slipped away beneath him. He disappeared as the 110-storey tower imploded floor by floor, spewing out particles of debris and irradiated flesh. A mass of yellow-brown dust obliterated every-thing. Rescue workers fled from its advance towards the river. Some jumped in and were pulled on board ferry boats. The cloud approached our apartment. We could almost reach out and touch it. Then it retreated, ever so slowly, pushed back by a breeze from the Hudson.

It left a scene like that from a nuclear winter. A thick layer of grey dust covered the whole area, coating the streets and parks. A line of cars at Vesey and West Side Highway were on fire, ignited by firey debris.

More cars were burning on Greenwich Street. The massive walkway from the Winter Gardens lay crushed on the highway. Beyond it, the Marriott Hotel was on fire. Thousands of scraps of paper floated in the air. Some firemen stood absolutely

A police officer kneels in prayer in the centre of the 'Circle of Honor' at Ground Zero on 11 September 2002, during the reading of the names at a commemoration ceremony to mark the first anniversary of the event. Photograph: Ruth Fremson/Reuters.

stunned at a distance, coated from head to foot in dust. The telephone lines were disrupted when the towers collapsed, and I could not call anyone in New York after that. Incredibly, the long-distance service still worked. I was able to call my family, keep up contact with my office in Dublin, send digital photographs and do more radio interviews throughout the afternoon.

The firemen vainly tried to fight a blaze at No 7 World Trade Centre, a forty-seven-storey building housing the Secret Service. At 5.20 p.m., we watched it, too, collapse, falling straight down on to Greenwich Street. On its own, such an event would have made world headlines. Its collapse cut off electricity to our building. It was time to leave. We made our way down forty-one flights of concrete emergency stairs.

For days afterwards, my muscles ached. I kept thinking, what must it have been like for those fleeing down the stairwells in the World Trade Centre? Now hardly a day goes by that I don't feel a spasm of guilt at the inadequacy and helplessness we all experienced as onlookers that morning. This week, with its memorial services and replays of the horrific footage, will be an especially distressing time for those touched by the catastrophe. Many find it very difficult, even now, to look at images of the burning towers, as they bring back a flood of personal memories and threaten to release powerful suppressed emotions. I'll be glad when it's over.

SATURDAY, 7 SEPTEMBER 2002

Poverty in Developing Regions Gets a Hearing

Frank McDonald

South Africa's president, Mr Thabo Mbeki, summed it all up when he spoke to the press after the final plenary session of the World Summit on Sustainable Development in Johannesburg this week. 'The critical issue is what happens after this,' he said. And after ten days of intensive horse-trading at the Sandton Convention Centre, that remains an open question.

For some, such as the World Development Movement, what went on there amounted to a 'zero sum game' in which there were no real winners. For others, the outcome was little better than feeble, even gutless. Yet even after all the compromises had been made to keep everyone on board, delegates who didn't get a lot of what they wanted still hailed it as a success.

'Some people go from summit to summit, others from abyss to abyss,' observed Mr Hugo Chavez, the president of Venezuela. And if the world is facing the abyss, the US must be regarded as the principal culprit.

Instead of taking a progressive stance in advancing the sustainable development agenda, it dug in its heels at every turn on all of the crunch issues.

The fact that President Bush was too busy preparing for his assault on President Saddam Hussein to bother coming to Johannesburg was seen by many as a major snub to the rest of the world. That his Secretary of State, Mr Colin Powell, didn't turn up until the last day only compounded this US contempt, and it was little wonder that he was roasted when he finally came to the podium.

Few could credit Mr Powell's assertion that 'President Bush and the American people have an enduring commitment to sustainable development,' when the US had already reneged on the Kyoto Protocol — the only international instrument to deal with the adverse effects of climate change — and sought to have all references to it omitted from the Johannesburg Plan of Action.

Yet despite US recalcitrance on the world's most serious environmental threat, some of its closest allies at the summit — Canada, Australia and Japan — declared that they were moving towards ratifying Kyoto. The announcement by

Russia that it, too, will sign up means that the protocol will now come into force early next year, to become the only concrete result from the Rio Summit in 1992.

What will Johannesburg produce? For a start, as President Mbeki noted, it has succeeded in projecting sustainable development on to the world stage. While Rio emphasised environmental protection, there is now a more balanced view that encompasses social and economic development and, in particular, the amelioration of grinding poverty in the poorest developing nations.

Thus, this summit can be seen as a significant contribution to 'the evolution of global discussion', as Mr Mbeki put it. The UN Secretary General, Mr Kofi Annan, also saw the outcome in a positive light — he would, wouldn't he? — provided that the momentum was maintained to implement the targets and timetables agreed after so much haggling between the 187 participating countries.

Specific targets are few however. The most important is the commitment to extend basic sanitation at least to half the people without access to it by 2015. That means millions of taps and toilets, which should be good news for the plumbing industry — if there was any indication of where all the money was going to come from. Optimists say the funding required will be found from somewhere.

The US, whose $10 billion development aid budget represents just over 0.1 per cent of its GNP, opposed the sanitation target. Its delegation at the summit only went along with it in return for a major concession from the EU and 'like-minded countries', notably Norway and Brazil, to drop a specific target for boosting the share of renewables in the global energy mix.

Not only that. The EU even had to concede to the inclusion of 'clean' fossil fuel technologies in the final text on energy. This was a shameful climb-down, but one that had to be made — however reluctantly — in the interest of brokering a deal. As a result, greenhouse gas–belching coal, oil

and gas-fired power stations can still be supplied to developing countries on 'concessional terms'.

But Europe, which has made more progress than anywhere else in promoting wind power — whatever about Ireland's dismal record so far — stole the moral high ground by declaring that it would go ahead anyway with firm targets for renewables. And its fifteen member-states were joined in this upstaging of the US and OPEC by numerous others, including many of the countries lining up to join the EU.

Globalisation, which wasn't even mentioned in any of the first Earth Summit's documents a decade ago, was another of the dominant issues in Johannesburg — specifically, corporate power and the World Trade Organisation's agenda. But environment and development lobbyists won at least a partial victory in persuading delegates to delete a clause that would have given WTO rules primacy over environmental protection.

Further discussions on this emotive issue are to take place at the next WTO ministerial meeting in Mexico next year. And even this week, the WTO's new director-general, Dr Supachai Panitchpakdi, was able to say with confidence that Johannesburg had kept its current Doha trade round on track — including the need to ensure that tariff barriers are not replaced by non-tariff barriers such as environmental 'restrictions'.

His predecessor, Mr Renato Ruggeiro, made no bones about the WTO's agenda. 'We are writing a constitution for the world,' he said quite openly on one occasion. Indeed, the extent to which it managed to get its trade agenda through the Johannesburg summit is reflected by the fact that there are around 200 references to the WTO or its rules in the final text, according to a word count by Friends of the Earth. 'Doha is what this summit was all about,' according to Dennis Brutus (77), emeritus professor of African literature at the University of Pittsburgh. Once regarded by South Africa's apartheid regime as being among its twenty most dangerous opponents, he is now actively involved in the anti-globalisation movement; he was in Seattle in November 1999 when the WTO's ministerial meeting came under siege.

Later this month, after an extensive speaking tour in the US, Prof Brutus will be among those who will head for Washington DC to carry on the struggle at a three-day meeting of the World Bank. The next stage in the campaign will to develop an 'alternative people's agenda' at the World Social Forum in Porto Allegre, Brazil, in February. Then it will be on to the WTO in Cancun, Mexico, the following November.

The WTO's Doha round of trade talks is already under way in Geneva, and it will be instructive to see how such issues as environmental protection, agricultural subsidies and corporate accountability will be dealt with there. Certainly, environment and development groups at the Johannesburg summit have no confidence that the WTO will embrace an agenda based on their interpretation of sustainable development.

Despite the fall-out from the Enron and Woldcom 'accounting' scandals, the US entered a caveat to the text covering corporate accountability, by insisting that it was limited to existing rather than future agreements. This does not inspire much hope for new, binding international rules for big business. 'Voluntary partnerships' involving the corporate sector, governments and civil society are no substitute.

Friends of the Earth cite the Congo Basin Initiative as an example of what can go wrong.

Harvey M. Soning, left, Chairman and Chief Executive James Andrew, international property consultants representing Red Sea Hotels Ltd with Amos Pickel, Chief Executive Red Sea, at the Gresham Hotel Group Plc's extraordinary General Meeting. Photograph: Brenda Fitzsimons.

Though ostensibly intended to benefit forest protection in this ecologically important region, it has 'put more money into flawed programmes that have not reduced illegal logging, empowered local communities or enabled sustainable forest management'. The only real winners are the timber barons.

Irish NGOs at the Johannesburg summit complained that its Plan of Implementation 'represents the lowest common denominator'. It contained only limited references to human rights, made no serious commitments on aid or debt alleviation for developing countries, set no targets or timetables for renewable energy or debt and left reform of EU and US agricultural subsidies 'entirely to the WTO'.

The final paragraph of the thirty-two-point political declaration adopted by world leaders before they flew home solemnly pledged — 'from the African continent, the Cradle of Humankind', in Mr Mbeki's phrase — 'to the peoples of the world, and the generations that will surely inherit this Earth, that we are determined to ensure that our collective hope for sustainable development is realised'.

Two days earlier, in a fiery speech, President Jacques Chirac of France had posed this awkward question: 'Can mankind, who is at the forefront of evolution, become the enemy of life itself?' Referring to the multitude of problems facing the world, he even suggested that 'the house is burning' and reminded his colleagues, particularly those in the rich north, that none of them could say that they did not know.

Incidentally, the organisational cost of the summit was put at $50 million — not counting all the air fares, hotel bills and lavish meals. Altogether, it was attended by 45,000 people and consumed enough energy to boil a billion kettles. And all the carbon dioxide — or hot air — it generated would have met the energy needs of half-a-million Africans for a full year.

Attempt to Unite Iraqi Opposition Leaves Americans Bewildered

Chris Stephen

The scene came straight from James Bond. In the rolling grounds of a discreet hotel in deepest Surrey, dark-suited American security men patrolled in pairs, stopping to have conversations with their watches.

In the hotel itself, more thick-necked security people, all of them with funny things in their ears, were watched by curious chamber maids in pretty white aprons. Among them mingled mysterious Arabs, also in sharp suits but more portly, muttering to each other as they wandered the corridors.

Improbable as it sounds, this hotel was the site of the US's grandly-named Future of Iraq project, a desperate attempt to get the Iraqi opposition to agree on a new government to replace that of Saddam Hussein.

More than twenty-five opposition groups were flown in from exile around the world for the two-day meeting. On Wednesday I was the only journalist present, having been tipped off by a friendly Iraqi, but I was not welcome.

'What are you doing here?' asked a US diplomat summoned by hotel staff. 'It's a closed meeting. I can't let you in. You'll have to go.' His anxiety was understandable, because behind the firmly closed doors of the hotel's main conference room, US plans to set up a new democratic Iraq were turning to dust.

This is bad news for the White House, which needs to demonstrate that removing Saddam will usher in democracy, rather than civil war.

Though nobody here will say so publicly, most expect Iraq to suffer a Yugoslavia-style melt-down if Saddam Hussein's dictatorship is removed.

Consider the parallels: Iraq, like Yugoslavia, is an artificial creation by the West: They were even created at the same time — out of the ruins of the first World War.

Like Yugoslavia, Iraq is in effect a clumsy welding operation, throwing together three ethnic groups — Kurds, Shias and Sunnis — with a long history of mutual antagonism. Coups and dictatorships are the norm and democratic government unknown.

Complicating things still further is the bewildering array of splinter groups scrambling for a slice of the post-Saddam cake: fundamentalists vie with liberals, communists oppose monarchists, tribal chieftains squabble among themselves and nobody trusts the growing band of defectors from Saddam's own regime.

'They hate each other more than they hate Saddam Hussein,' observed Abdul Bari Atwani, editor of the influential Arabic newspaper *Al Quds*.

But the real problem is with the Big Three ethnic groups: Once the US army completes its 'regime change', the Kurds in the north and the Shias in the south plan to tear out great chunks of territory for themselves at the expense of the Sunnis in the centre.

The Kurds are best placed for this, with 40,000 troops waiting in the north and one objective — the oil rich city of Kirkuk. Ten years ago, Kurds were ethnically cleansed, and replaced by Arabs, by Saddam Hussein.

Now the Kurds want it back and plan to reverse the cleansing process. 'Don't worry, there won't be any violence,' joked one observer. 'You think the Arabs of Kirkuk are going to wait around for the Kurdish army to arrive?' The Kurds, however, have their own factionalism to sort out first: They are split evenly between the Kurdish Democratic Party, under Massoud Barzani, and the Patriotic Union of Kurdistan, controlled by Jalal Talabani.

Ten years ago I interviewed Barzani in Barzan, the bombed-out ruins of his village in northern Iraq. 'I'm used to it,' he said. 'My village was bombed fifteen times in the past century, once by the British.' Complicating their relationship is the fact that Talibani deserted the KDP in the 1970s, and animosity between the two groups is strong. What is likely to bring them together, however, is the prospect of the huge riches of the Kirkuk oil fields.

Down south, the Shias have a 3,000-strong army based just over the border in Iran under the command of the Supreme Council for the Islamic Revolution.

The council's leader, Ayatollah Mohammad Baqir al-Hakim, pointedly refused to show up at the Surrey talks, instead giving interviews in Tehran voicing opposition to the planned US attack.

Trying to hold it together is the umbrella group Iraqi National Congress, which fears that the US may simply give up on democracy and install a new dictator to replace Saddam.

'The Iraqi people do not want something like US intelligence operations in Latin America, which replaced regimes and left power in the hands of dictators,' said congress leader Ahmad Chalabi.

Chalabi s the nearest thing the Iraqi opposition has to a figurehead, enjoying the support of several Sunni parties and the big Kurdish power brokers.

But his calls for unity went unheeded. 'We cannot agree a government in advance, I do not think so,' said one participant. 'Please do not mention my name.' The problem with Iraq, as with Afghanistan, is that the forces pulling the country apart are stronger then those holding it together — or rather, they will be if Saddam Hussein's iron grip is broken.

The Americans may not want to believe this, but the British know better.

British officials preferred to sit on the hotel veranda drinking tea rather than get involved in the haggling taking place within. The man from the Foreign and Commonwealth Office insisted British officials were there strictly as 'observers'. Translation: when it all falls apart, blame the Americans, not us.

By the end of two days of exhausting talks, the Iraqis seemed happy enough, trooping out for the trip back to the airport still arguing and looking forward to a whirl around the Duty Free before returning to their points of exile.

The Americans looked shattered, their officials wearing faces like crumpled paper bags, bewildered by the failure of the world's most powerful nation to force Iraq's opposition to speak with one voice.

For them the task now is to return to Washington empty-handed, to explain to the White House that, as with Afghanistan last year, invading Iraq will be the easy part.

SATURDAY, 7 SEPTEMBER 2002

The Year of Political Confusion Continues in Full Swing

Dick Walsh

This ought to have been a week in which the promises and problems of the next three or four years in politics began to take shape. We have a Government; the full outline of the Opposition will soon be visible.

We should have a clear idea of the social, economic, Northern and European issues likely to occupy the Dáil and the Government by the time Labour finds a direction and leader at the end of next month.

But this week has been far from a brisk start to a busy new season.

Indeed, it fits all too neatly into a year of political confusion during which the only thing to compare with the mound of questions raised by its critics at the Government's door was the Government's determination to ignore them.

Why, for instance, did Fianna Fáil, senior partners in the old coalition, go out of their way to

deny that they stood a chance of winning an overall majority in the new Dáil?

And why did Fianna Fáil's once and future partners — or guardians in government — the Progressive Democrats, continue to claim that an overall majority for FF would be the worst of all outcomes for the electorate?

Even when poll after poll, some in the regular series commissioned by newspapers and broadcasters, others of doubtful provenance and questionable quality, a few plainly fictional, showed Fianna Fáil well ahead?

An overall majority was clearly in the party's sights.

Indeed, FF might well have formed a government with a little help from its friends, two or three nominally Independent backbenchers who had helped prop up the previous government and would be perfectly happy to do the same again.

As it happened the help wasn't needed: no sooner had the results been studied than it was obvious the Progressive Democrats were ready, willing and able to serve unreconstructed Fianna Fáil.

More to the point, the member of the PDs who had most vociferously denounced FF, Michael McDowell, was ready to move, lock, stock and barrel, from the Attorney General's office into the Department of Justice.

Never mind the contradictions: Niccolo Machiavelli, who matched the Medicis in Florence, survived in style the murkier waters of Dublin South East.

But the most confusing week of a confusing year neither began nor ended with the reconciliation of FF and the PDs, a political odd couple if ever there was one; the Coalition reached an extraordinary agreement as to how some other potentially disastrous affairs might be handled.

They decided to reopen the Dáil early so that TDs could get down to business without delay.

A final gesture, you might have thought, in view of public criticism of the Dáil's predilection

Niall and Keadie Reilly from Newbridge, Co. Kildare enjoying the weather at the Old Mill, Naas. Photograph: Brenda Fitzsimons.

for taking off at the slightest excuse, leaving unanswered — and unasked — questions in every corner.

An early resumption would be especially valuable on this occasion as so many TDs were newcomers from the Green Party, Sinn Féin or the biggest assortment of Independents to have been elected for a long time.

They could do with the help of old hands who'd show them the ropes.

Worries about the State's finances, taxation and public services, which were evident but not debated during the campaign, had intensified with the resumption of the FF-PD partnership during the campaign.

The confusion had grown because Bertie Ahern and Charlie McCreevy stubbornly refused to explain or even discuss the crises their policies provoked. Ahern oozed reassurance. McCreevy cackled on about miracles.

And when the campaign was over and the new Coalition — well, the old coalition with a lick of paint and a new retainer or two — returned to office, there were some other curiosities which might have been explained.

There were cutbacks where none had been expected, promised or threatened. Ahern snapped at journalists' use of the word 'cutbacks' and, when it came to complaints about reductions in overseas development aid, he and his colleagues argued about definitions and targets.

The Dáil had resumed early to pass legislation allowing us to have a second referendum on the Treaty of Nice.

Its rejection in the first referendum had been deeply embarrassing all round.

Enda Kenny and Ruairí Quinn continued to call for a Yes vote, not in support of the Government but in spite of it. It's a reasonable approach, not only to Nice but to the European project as a whole.

A point made, I believe, whenever we are reminded of the risk of finding ourselves at the mercy of George W. Bush and his gaggle of corporatist crooks and fundamentalists. Here, unfortunately, FF's broken election promises and a clumsy start to the Coalition's campaign have become a focus of resistance.

Even some of the Government's old friends are turning against it, which causes Ahern and colleagues to react in uncharacteristic style.

This was clear from a discussion on Tuesday's edition of Liveline, the RTÉ radio program presented by Joe Duffy.

It featured Micheál Martin and the *Sunday World*'s crime correspondent, Paul Williams, who had last week attacked Ahern.

Williams was angered by the state of the health services. He listed examples as well as the causes and consequences of failure. Some had doubted, in the aftermath of the election, that such feelings were abroad: now, here, on Radio One, Williams's anger blazed and a majority of listeners appeared to agree with him. And when someone said that his might have been an opposition view he made a more telling point: he said he'd voted for Fianna Fáil. Several listeners said they had also.

It was the kind of thing that party leaders hate to hear; especially if, like Ahern, they'd been at that moment advocating sustainable development in far off Johannesburg: 'It matters for many many millions who are poor and starving,' he said.

'It matters for our children and future generations. Let us not fail in this historic task.'

His Government had just cut €40 million from its budget for overseas development aid. But that's the kind of year it is.

Kilkenny Perfection

Tom Humphries, at Croke Park

Kilkenny 2-20 Clare 0-19

For the great teams, excellence supplies its own narrative. There are no stepping stones from contention to achievement, no guff about having to lose one to win one. There's just the game and the pursuit of perfection.

Kilkenny brushed Clare aside yesterday in an All-Ireland final that was about introversion and obsession. As DJ Carey said afterwards, they had nothing against Clare, virtually no history with them. This was about a journey within the game. This was about Kilkenny being as good as they can be.

Last summer, in the popular imagination at least, Kilkenny threatened perfection as they cut through Leinster. They came to Croke Park for an All-Ireland semi-final with Galway and were widely advertised as possessing a full-forward line that was the eighth wonder of the world. They lost.

The time since then hasn't been spent sticking pins through maroon-coloured voodoo dolls.

It's been a movement towards the type of performance which Kilkenny gave yesterday. Two goals and twenty points scored. Three wides over the seventy minutes. Sublime contributions from all parts of the pitch. McGarry. Kavanagh. Barry. Shefflin. Carey. All wondrous. Just about everyone else outstanding.

And when Kilkenny began introducing their subs, two of them, McEvoy and Carter, hit wonder points just for fun.

Few teams have done what Kilkenny have this year in winning both league and championship. They have maintained a standard that is impressive even within the context of their own history and in the latter stages of the All-Ireland series they have handed in two performances which were sublime.

Could they be as good yesterday as they were against Tipperary some weeks ago, we wondered?

They answered emphatically.

For Clare, the achievement was in keeping the crowd from seeping out of the ground. They played with the heat and the passion which is their modern hallmark, but the winning of twenty-seven All-Ireland titles means that hurling craft is congenital in Kilkenny and acquired in Clare. That's a lot to overcome. Their pride was their defiance.

'We were beaten by seven points today,' said Cyril Lyons, their manager. 'I don't know if we were seven points the lesser team, but it doesn't matter now anyway. They were always ahead by five or six and when the score is that way you can try things and they come off.'

They come off because excellence makes its own rules too. The world must bend to accommodate its prodigies. Nobody who heard that DJ Carey intended coming back to the black and amber of Kilkenny when the spadework of the provincial championships had been done could have demurred.

If he had left it until yesterday to step from the stands and declare himself available again there could have been no objections. What would be the point of building a cathedral like Croke Park if DJ Carey were not to soar within it.

The joy of the game and the thrill of yesterday was seeing DJ's genius unfold again under the command of his will. DJ came back to the game eight weeks ago. He won his fourth All-Ireland yesterday and one suspects that the two games he played all year will be enough to secure him a ninth All Star. He brushes it all away. Even his goal, another chunky contribution to the cause he

Clare's David Hoey and Kilkenny's Martin Comerford in action during the All Ireland Hurling Final in Croke Park. Photograph: Alan Betson.

has served, was played down until it assumed the significance of a man removing lint from his pocket.

'Ah, I took the chance and put the hurl up and flicked it in the net. Just one of those things.'

And his resurrection? His journey back from being hurling's most talked about retiree to the Croke Park pastures?

'It's been worthwhile. You dream when you are a youngster of this. It's occasions like this that matter. I didn't do as much this year as the rest of the lads, but today is fantastic. We knew that Clare would come at us in the second half.

'They got points. And we hoped we'd tack on a point or two when they did. They came back to within three points and then Henry got a great point and we got it back to six.'

His mind wanders off into the mechanics of the game he loves. Shefflin. He wishes he had ten years left playing with Shefflin. Charlie Carter, his old confederate, how Charlie can still illuminate Croke Park when he walks on stage.

DJ was at the Leinster Final this summer and he had that edginess within himself, that little insistence that he was gone before he was ready to go.

'I felt disappointed that my year was gone. Watching in the stand that day I was very passionate. I've never been a spectator. I knew then. At this stage I have the heart to go on some more . . . it's all about the legs next year, though.'

He went out and trained and lifted weights on his own. He trained when the panel he had rejoined were still resting. And he found the sessions had changed. Every session was like an All-Ireland. Brian Cody had marked out a pitch the precise size as Croke Park. Training on that every night makes lead of a man's legs.

Fortunately, Kilkenny's hunger for excellence matched his own. When their paths intersected a September afternoon like this was inevitable. The team he rejoined was making its own journey. They were convincing champions this summer and will start next season as favourites to repeat.

In the Kilkenny dressing-room, with the Liam McCarthy Cup lying on his kitbag, Andy Comerford stands on the bench and speaks to the players he has captained all year. This is the soul of the GAA we are prying on, those moments when an ordinary man expands his horizons and seizes the respect of others. He speaks passionately.

'You can all hold your heads high lads. Thirty men got us here and every one of them was needed. I'll say one thing, lads, respect yourselves and respect your families. Celebrate for sure, but Kilkenny were always men that were humble.

'Always remember that you're Kilkenny hurlers. Whatever way you celebrate, do it with dignity and do it with pride. Be proud of what you achieved. Respect the jersey. Always remember that you are Kilkenny hurlers.'

He stands down with the roar of applause coming towards him. Kilkenny hurlers. All-Ireland champions.

The jersey. The dignity. The pride. That's the story of the season. That's the narrative of one team's excellence.

TUESDAY, 10 SEPTEMBER 2002

Harvesting a Rich Crop of New Ideas

Olivia Kelly

Farmers have had a terrible couple of years. But instead of abandoning their land, many are finding new ways of making it pay — from flooding fields to create a lake for fishing to growing worms for compost.

Things weren't going too well down on the Robinson family farm. Margins had got very tight, dry stock — sheep and cattle, weren't making the prices they used to and thirty-five acres had become too small a holding to make any real money.

Tom Robinson's only son Dave had studied agriculture in college, but had decided he didn't want to be a farmer and went off to work in insurance instead and Tom no longer felt it was worth keeping on the farm on his own.

So one day, Tom and Dave decided to flood the farm. It may sound drastic but, Dave Robinson says, it was the best decision they ever made.

'We had to do something, the land was just not paying its way,' he says. 'So we took two flat ordinary grazing fields of seven-and-a-half and eight-and-a-half acres each, dug them out and flooded them.'

The flooded fields were then stocked with rainbow trout and coarse fish; carp, perch and bream. The Robinsons planted 3,500 trees, erected walk-ways, built a log cabin lodge, stocked it with fishing tackle and in 1998 Rathbeggan Lakes Angling Centre was born.

'I had the idea in my head for about seven or eight years. I had gone away from farming completely and year by year it looked like an even lousier option,' Dave Robinson says. 'Dad was not earning a living from the farm, but we didn't want to sell, so instead we went into partnership together.'

As a rural leisure facility, Rathbeggan Lakes is ideally situated: little more than a thrity-minute drive from Dublin, near the village of Dunshaughlin, Co Meath. It offers fly and coarse fishing to groups and individuals, with full instruction if required. The enterprise supports five full-time staff and three part-time. The lakes take up between fifteen and sixteen acres of the Robinsons' farm land. The remainder of the thirty-five-acre holding is given over to grazing sheep and breeding show ponies.

Now in its fourth year, the angling centre has a well-established feel, but says Robinson, getting it off the ground, or into the ground, wasn't all plain sailing.

'We had great difficulty raising the loan, because it was such a new project. So in 1995/96 I did a Teagasc alternative enterprise course and a County Enterprise Board start your own business course. I developed a business plan and it made it easier to secure a loan.'

He was also able to avail of some start-up grants, including a EU agri-tourism grant and a Leader grant through the National Rural Development plan.

'This was something I'd had in my head for a long time and I knew in my heart and soul it was what I wanted. It was a brilliant challenge and it keeps two families and three full-time staff. It's more work than farming, but it's also more enjoyable.'

The Robinsons' enterprise, though innovative, typifies a trend in farming. The fat of the land no longer offers the rich rewards it once did and the man with the fine big milk quota and the glint in his eye has lost something of his sheen. Farmers have had it particularly tough this year. Record rains made it difficult to cut hay, with the result that more money will have to go on supplementary feeds this winter. Yields of soft fruits and apples are expected to be down this autumn and blight is an ever-present threat. Add to this the recent animal health crises of BSE and foot-and-mouth, and life on the land starts to look pretty grim.

Some farmers have given up, taking off-farm jobs, but others, determined to stay, have developed new ways to make money from their biggest asset: the land.

'It's in the national interest that farmers stay on the land but it's increasingly difficult, particularly on smaller holdings, to get a full income from farming,' says Dr Larry Kennedy, development manager with Teagasc.

'Farm incomes have come under pressure in recent years as farming hasn't reached the income-earning potential of other industries. Expectations of the quality of life people should have are also growing, so farmers are seeking ways to supplement the household income,' he adds.

Alternative farm enterprises and farm diversification are nothing new. For years, farmers have sold home-made jams and cheeses or offered bed-and-breakfast in the farmhouse. However, falling farm-income margins have pushed more

Emer Kelly (8), from Rochfordbridge, Co Westmeath, showing a Friesian Holstein calf at the Powers Gold Label National Livestock Show at the Charleville Estate in Tullamore, Co Offaly. Photograph: Frank Miller

farmers to get in on the act and created a need for more formal development of the alternative farm enterprise system.

'There's always been an entrepreneurial culture of farmyard enterprise and there will always be people out there looking for opportunities, but greater numbers of people need assistance in developing the right opportunities for them,' Kennedy says.

Teagasc has long offered advice and assistance in setting up alternative businesses, but since last November, it has been working a new rural viability programme geared to help farm families to explore the opportunities for generating new income.

'The idea of the programme is to get farm families to take a look at their present situations and identify what options might be there for them to improve their quality of life. It's just getting going now but we're hoping that people will consider a wide range of options.'

Teagasc offers farmers a large number of alternative enterprise ideas. They may choose to take on new animals such as deer or goats; build on their existing resources, with butter or ice-cream production; get into floristry, with tulip bulb, cut foliage or Christmas tree production; or take the rural tourism route.

'What we want is for people not to be blinkered in their approach. Farmers need to look at what's going on in their areas, make sure the product is right for them, that there's a market for it and that they can raise the right capital to match any grants there might be. We would also encourage them to look at their own skills and resources and come up with fresh ideas,' says Kennedy.

One farmer who certainly embraced the challenge of developing a fresh idea is Jimmy Austin from Summerhill, Co Meath. Not only is Austin's alternative enterprise innovative, but it appeals to the ecologically minded and has many organic possibilities. Austin is a worm farmer, or to give him his proper title, a vermiculturalist.

'I got into worms about twelve years ago. I saw the effect they had on rotting farmyard manure and considered the option of the live bait market, but after further research I came across the idea of blending compost using worm casting,' he says.

Austin spent a number of years developing worm beds and harvesting castings (worm manure) as a hobby on his beef and dairy farm. Five years ago he began to take a greater interest in vermiculture and for the last three years he has been in business with another local farmer, Michael Newman, as Irish Earthworm Technology Ltd.

Worms can be fed pretty much any type of organic waste, including paper, kitchen waste and farm manure. On Austin's farm, approximately three million blue-nosed worms (a particularly good composting worm) work in 100 foot by ten foot beds, surrounded by an electric fence for herding. For every 100 tons of waste, the worms produce sixty tons of castings, which can then be used to develop an organic compost.

'It has been discovered that the compost they produce has properties which mimic a plant growth hormone,' Austin says. 'They are remarkable creatures. They take on a waste product and turn it into something positive.'

The Irish market has been slow to realise the potential of vermiculture, Austin says, however, he hopes its value as a recycling tool will begin to gain recognition.

'It would be wrong to says it's a lucrative business, it seems that it's just not fancy enough. It's a limited interest for me at the moment but if milk prices keep falling, who knows?'

WEDNESDAY, 11 SEPTEMBER 2002

The End of US Benign Isolation in a World that Has Been Changed Forever

Jonathan Eyal

Prudence, commonsense or even just a casual glance at various crisis locations would suggest that the world has not changed fundamentally since September 11th last year.

The Palestinian-Israeli conflict remains as intractable as ever. The Middle East as a whole is still a powder keg. The Taliban regime has been dismantled, but the future of Afghanistan remains uncertain. Disease and economic decay still afflict Africa, and Latin America's economic and political institutions are shakier today than they were a year ago.

Even the 'war on terrorism' remains for the moment a highly-qualified success: the main organisers of the atrocities against the US have been deprived of permanent bases and training camps, but they have escaped capture and are assumed to be planning further attacks.

Yet appearances are deceiving for, in one crucial respect, the world today is different: the US, the sole remaining superpower, has changed its priorities, overturning most of the assumptions which underpinned global strategic arrangements.

For many decades ordinary Americans believed in their territorial invincibility, a myth which US strategists called 'benign isolation'. Apart from Soviet nuclear missiles — now quietly rusting away — few other nations on Earth could hit at continental US and fewer still had any cause to do so.

Wars happened in other countries, and US governments sometimes had to decide whether to become involved or not. The choice, however, was always Washington's, and usually on its own terms.

This American myth died in the rubble of the Twin Towers in New York a year ago today: the threat of sudden death at the hands of enemies is now part of the American psyche. And the fact that destruction can come suddenly, perpetrated by people difficult to identify and seemingly impervious to reason, is now accepted as fact by every ordinary American citizen.

Europeans are still struggling to understand the sheer enormity of this psychological transformation across the Atlantic. Living in close proximity in relatively small countries, the Europeans have long grown accustomed to such risks.

Europe's preoccupation since the end of the second World War has therefore been to limit these dangers, rather than eliminate them altogether. This was accomplished by reducing the importance of the nation-state, while increasing the role of international or regional co-operation institutions.

The outcome is a continent which instinctively believes that military force is the last option to be used when all other diplomatic and economic measures have failed. But the US response to its current vulnerability has been precisely the opposite.

None of this was obvious immediately after September 11th. The atrocities were so horrendous that Europe's first response was to swing behind the US. And Washington initially surprised the Europeans by biding its time, building up a coalition of forces for its war in Afghanistan.

Yet the cracks across the Atlantic soon reappeared and they have widened ever since. The US administration has elaborated a host of new policies, with the explicit purpose of using military force as a first, rather than last, option.

The growth in US military expenditure is staggering: the Pentagon's current budget is equal to the combined spending of all the next fifteen top military nations put together; the US accounts for half of the entire world's defence expenditure. And, crucially, the US is responsible for no less than seventy per cent of all the world's military research and development.

It is at best useless and at worst counterproductive for the Europeans to dismiss these moves as just the misguided policies of an unruly Texan sheriff, eager to shoot from the hip. For the divide is much more profound.

The Europeans instinctively wish to manage risk; the US still strives to eliminate its vulnerabilities altogether.

The Europeans believe that their nation-states have failed to solve their problems; the US asserts that the nation-state is the starting point for any solution.

The Europeans underestimated the effectiveness of military power; the US probably overestimates what sheer military force can achieve.

For relatively small European countries international institutions are a necessity; for the world's only superpower, such institutions are a luxury, to be used when necessary and discarded when inconvenient. The current debate over Iraq is merely a manifestation of this deeper divide, and it is unlikely to disappear for decades to come.

Beyond Europe, the strategic situation of almost any country around the world has changed during the last year. Having been merely a 'partner', Russia is now an active ally of the US. President Vladimir Putin's response has finally dispelled the last lingering doubts which Washington had about this successor to the communist Soviet Union.

The scope of this alliance is now being expanded to the management of oil prices around the world, and joint action against weapons of mass destruction. There is no doubt that Russia has been a significant winner during the last year. And, conversely, there is little doubt that China has been a strategic loser.

Pakistan, China's old ally, is now a trusted partner of the US. American troops are in Central Asia as well as the Pacific, virtually encircling China from all directions. Furthermore, a host of

The Greenpeace vessel the **Rainbow Warrior** *leaving Dublin port and making its way into the Irish Sea on a misty morning to intercept the ships bringing nuclear waste to Sellafield. Photograph: Bryan O'Brien.*

other Asian countries — India, Singapore, Malaysia, Thailand, Indonesia, the Philippines — have either rekindled or established military links with Washington.

In short, an old superpower has been embraced, while China, a budding future major power, has been temporarily eclipsed. Meanwhile, Europe's own common foreign and security policy efforts have simply been ignored: the only major security event later this year will be NATO enlargement to the countries of eastern Europe, a project managed and mandated by the US.

And, behind the scenes, more subtle changes remain just as important. Support for Israel in the US is now widespread, not only among various ethnic lobbies which were traditionally grouped around the Democratic Party, but is particularly strong with the Christian fundamentalist right-

wing organisations, which have a hold over the Republicans.

And disdain for Saudi Arabia, the country which has claimed to be a chief US ally while exporting a boorish, narrow-minded interpretation of Islam around the world, is now common in Washington.

This does not mean that the US cannot implement a coherent policy in the Middle East. But it does imply that President Bush's options in dealing with the Palestinian-Israeli conflict remain severely circumscribed.

And, in the long term, it must mean that the US would look for other regional key allies, beyond the desert monarchy of Saudi Arabia. One of the unspoken assumptions behind the determination to overthrow Saddam Hussein in Iraq is precisely the search for new Arab regimes which could be more democratic and pro-Western, but not dependent on Islamic fundamentalism for their legitimacy at the same time.

Whether this US strategy works or not, Saudi Arabia's importance for Washington seems destined to decline.

In essence, therefore, the kind of profound strategic changes which would have usually taken decades to become obvious have now happened in less than a year. A Japanese admiral, who was

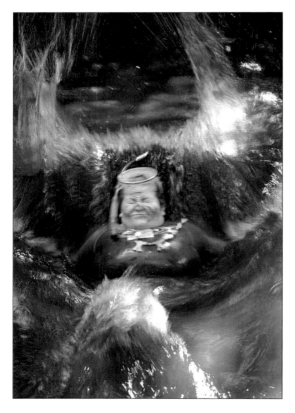

Tralee school teacher Julie Galvin makes quite a splash as she enters a bog near her home town of Listowel while training for the World Bog Snorkelling Championships which take place in Wales at the weekend. This is Julie's second attempt at the world title which involves bog snorkelling through 120m of bog water in the fastest possible time. Photograph: Don MacMonagle.

responsible for the attack on Pearl Harbour in 1941, later remarked ruefully that he had awakened a giant. If he can indulge in any thinking while hiding from the Americans, Osama Bin Laden should come to the same conclusion.

MONDAY, 23 SEPTEMBER 2002

Armagh's Divine Deliverance

Tom Humphries, at Croke Park

Armagh 1-12 Kerry 0-14

Armagh wake up this morning blinking against the glare of a new era. It's their time. It's their world. The rest of us just live in it.

They came to Croke Park this weekend timidly fancied in some quarters, dismissed in most others. By half time they had squandered the benefits of a good wind and a cheap penalty. We wondered were they lingering in the dressing-room so long because they were looking for a pulse. Nothing but the same old story, we said. Pity the oul Dubs aren't here, we said. Then Armagh came out and told us that everything we knew about football was wrong.

This was the All-Ireland that proved that the world ain't flat, even if teams drop off the end of it sometimes. This proved that what goes around comes around again. Armagh have been waiting for Kerry, waiting patiently. They got roughed up in a final in 1953 and got pickpocketed in a semi-final in 1990. Yesterday they gave Kerry a four-point lead at half time, gave them the wind, gave them every chance. And they won. They out-played and they out-thought Kerry.

It's not flat. It isn't. You can miss a penalty in an All-Ireland final against Kerry and still win. You can hold a great Kerry forward line to a point from play in the second half of an All-Ireland final. You can hold them scoreless entirely for the final

THE IRISH TIMES BOOK OF THE YEAR

fifteen minutes. These are things we never knew before yesterday.

They say the first time is the best time and if Armagh go on to win a hatful of All-Ireland titles none will be better than this. It was one of the great finals. The football ran pure for long stretches and even when it didn't the play was thoughtful and crisp. More than any other side in recent memory, Armagh's win was built on cerebration. Everybody in football works hard, everybody in football has talent, few teams could have thought their way out of the corner they were in at about ten past four yesterday. It took conviction and it took something more visceral, a wild hunger born out of defeat and bad times. At half time Joe Kernan, who lost a famous final here twenty-five years ago, fished into his kit-bag and took out the bauble he'd been given for being on the losing side that day. He fired it against the wall of the dressing-room and told his team that it wasn't worth two balls of glue. They sat up.

Armagh had the players when it was white-knuckle time. Oisín McConville missed a penalty, but stepped up and hit a tough forty-five which was just as invigorating. Tony McEntee came in from the bench like a transfusion of life. The full-forward line scored three points each from play. And they had Kieran McGeeney.

The defining moment perhaps came twelve minutes from the end and involved the two pedigree players on the pitch. Seamus Moynihan swept out of the Kerry goalmouth and whipped a ball from under the nose of Ronan Clarke. He had a quick look up and played a fifty-yard hoof downfield. It fell straight into Kieran McGeeney's hands and almost in the same movement he planted it back to the vicinity it had come from, only this time straight to the paws of Clarke. Clarke levelled the scores for the first time since the fifteenth minute.

All through the remarkable second half of yesterday's final the growing influence of McGeeney seemed likely to be the deciding factor between the two sides. Benny Tierney, the Armagh goalkeeper, grew up a little ahead of McGeeney in Mullabawn,

but all these years later he's still amazed by the neighbour's child.

'Kieran McGeeney doesn't talk,' said Tierney, 'he does. He said at half time that he wasn't producing. That he could talk the talk but he wasn't walking the walk. It started with him. He trains harder, he drives more miles. He's just a leader. We follow him.'

McGeeney himself said over and over again that he hadn't the words to describe yesterday. He said it from the Hogan Stand as he grasped the great gleaming canister in his hand. He said it again in the tunnel outside the dressing-rooms as the media swamped him and he said it quietly in his own dressing-room, leaning thoughtfully with his back to the wall. His own renaissance had prompted that of the team around him. There is no better mark of leadership or influence. He conceded at least that a renaissance was needed at half time.

'Kerry moved the ball so quick I knew they were going to move it around me, they weren't going to kick it down my throat. It had to go into their corner forwards. I could have cried about it and said they're not kicking the ball to me, but that usually doesn't happen in Gaelic football. I had to go out and win it myself. I wasn't going to point the finger at other people when I wasn't doing it myself. You have to bury your woes and come out and change.'

Again the curious mix of thoughtfulness and feral hunger. McGeeney found a way into the match. Early in the second half he went and claimed two balls he had little right to and pumped huge deliveries down the main causeway to the Kerry goal.

Thirteen years he's been on this road to fulfilment. None of them easy. Each of them making him the player he was yesterday.

'I've never come close to quitting. After Galway last year I felt like it. Days like today don't feel good unless you have days like that. Paul McGrane, myself and Benny; you sacrifice your life. I know people say it's a choice, but after a while it stops being a choice. You have to do it. It's something in your blood. You set out to do it. Ten or eleven years ago in the Botanic Inn in Belfast I remember saying that and I was just a year or two on the Armagh team. The people I was talking to just laughed at me. They said I wouldn't win an Ulster. Wee things like that stick in your head.'

Yesterday and the shrill of the final whistle was what he lived for. He inverts the dressing-room cliche. There is an I in 'team', he says. You have to get yourself right before you can present yourself to the team. More than almost anyone in football, McGeeney has had himself right for years now. This was a journey for a team and a county, but at

the heart of it was one man's quest for personal fulfilment. Culture and circumstance and good luck meant that football was the vehicle he chose for the journey.

'To be honest, I'm not trying to belittle Ulster, but I never dreamed of winning an Ulster medal. It's like beating your neighbours, but it doesn't make you the best. Today we proved we are the number one team in Ireland. It's more about proving it to yourself. The only way to do that is on a football pitch.'

It goes around and all the particles gather themselves and come around again and again. When McGeeney was walking behind the Artane

The Armagh team celebrate their victory over Kerry in the All-Ireland Football Championship at Croke Park. Photograph: Matt Kavanagh.

Boys Band yesterday, he did something he doesn't usually do, he looked up into the stands at the fields of swaying orange and his gaze fell upon the face of an old friend and mentor. Charlie Grant. When McGeeney first started kicking a football in the flatlands of Mullabawn it was Charlie Grant who had charge of the team.

'He introduced me to football. He had a great love for it. He used to say, go out and play Kieran. He never tried to mould us at under-ten and under-twelve. Amazing how the full circles come. It's men like him and Joe McNulty, Justin and Enda's father who took me at minor, men like Peter McDonald and Pilar Caffrey in Na Fianna, all the people who shape you. It all comes out there today. Other players. Neil Smyth and John Rafferty and Kieran McGurk, fellas who show you wee things along the way. It all comes out on days like today when you throw every single thing in. A wee piece of all those people was playing today in every one of us.'

Kieran McGeeney started by saying that he wished he had the words to describe the day. He had. On a day when he lacked nothing he had the words, too.

Letters to the Editor September 2002

US War Plans Against Iraq

A chara, — I am disturbed by the lack of support within Europe — with the honourable exception of Tony Blair — for the possible war against Iraq.

People seem to oppose war with Iraq on two grounds: that it would be outside the auspices of the United Nations and that it would be another manifestation of American unilateral action. Neither reason is sufficient.

Saddam Hussein must be considered the gravest threat to international security as long as he remains in power. Since his bloody rise to power Saddam has shown he is willing to massacre. He has disregarded international borders and laws, invading Iran and Kuwait, as well as launching unprovoked missile attacks on Israel. The real possibility that a man who would rather let his people die from a lack of medicine than surrender his ambitions to develop nuclear weapons should be allowed to continue his rule, when regime change is eminently possible, is sickening. Yet this seems to be the attitude of the European governments.

Rather than pursue the failed policy of weapons inspection, we in the EU must develop a common military and foreign policy with regard to any invasion of Iraq. If Europe stands idly by and lets the US act alone, or manages to scupper American plans, Europe will have again failed collectively as it did in 1938 at the Munich peace talks.

A democratic, secular Iraq is within the grasp of the world but because of hysterical noises from the cowards that populate the governments of Europe, it may slip away. A federal Iraq with equal rights for all its citizens would provide a beacon of hope for the oppressed majorities in the Middle East.

Rather than suffer without hope under regimes such as that of Saudi Arabia or Egypt, Arab peoples would see a vibrant, healthy and wealthy alternative in the traditional Arab heartland of Iraq.

A change of regime would also be good for Europe; it would stem the tide of immigrants from Iraq as well as providing the West with a large supply of cheap oil free from the greedy hands of OPEC. This would surely fuel a global economic recovery that would be good for all the world's citizens. — *Is mise,* John J. Carroll, Ratoath, Co Meath. 7 September 2002.

Sir, — I wish to respond to John J. Carroll's myopic letter of 7 September. Firstly, the main reason people oppose such a war is that it would gravely threaten the stability of the Middle East as a whole, and thus have frightening consequences for the entire world. The same holds true, of course, if Iraq has or is developing weapons of mass destruction. Yet until this is proven, war cannot be justified.

Saddam Hussein is certainly guilty of disregarding international borders and laws, yet should action be taken without such evidence, the US will be guilty of the same (and not for the first time).

Secondly, it is sadly true that Saddam let his people die due to a lack of medical aid rather than allow unhindered weapons inspection. Yet this bleak fact does not cleanse the rest of the world of their deaths. Rather than impose sanctions on such aid, would it not have been wiser to adopt a boycott of Iraqi oil, the profits from which have undoubtedly allowed Saddam to finance his weapons development? Alas, yet again oil proved a more valuable commodity than human life.

Thirdly, the idea of a 'democratic, secular Iraq' is naïve at best. Entire political systems cannot be simply imported. They are often as closely interwoven with the history of a country as a language or a religion. Mr Carroll suggests that the people of Saudi Arabia would view a democratic Iraq as a 'beacon of hope'. They might, but not as long as their good friend the US continues to find a willing political and economic ally in the Saudi ruling family.

Finally, the idea of a global boom benefiting all the world's citizens, were the West to acquire Iraq's oil supply, is patently ridiculous. Such benefits can come only when the wealthier nations step off the necks of the poorer and allow them to climb out of the economic black holes in which they are mired.

Saddam Hussein is indeed a despicable man who has massacred his own people. Yet he is also a shrewd political animal, having excelled in his role as the most malign influence in the region for years. Once more he is proving successful in this role, helping to polarise the US 'war on terror' into an attack on the Arab world, and create schisms in the international community.

I would like to see an end to him, yet I would also like to see an end to the infuriating hypocrisy of US foreign policy. Perhaps a trade-off could be arranged: Saddam goes if Ariel Sharon steps down to be replaced by someone less barbaric and more worthy of leading the Israeli people and what they stand for? I won't hold my breath. — Yours, etc., Shane O'Hara, Fivemilebourne, Co Sligo. 10 September 2002.

Debate on the Nice Treaty

Sir, — The Irish people voted No to the Nice Treaty in June 2001. Immediately after the result became known, the Government rejected our democratic decision and assured European bureaucrats that the same treaty would be put before us again in order to obtain the 'correct' result.

This unprecedented abuse of the democratic process, if allowed to succeed, will have serious consequences for Irish and European democracy in the future. While the many issues in the Nice Treaty are of great importance, they all pale into insignificance in the face of this threat to democracy.

When considering how they will vote in the next referendum, Irish citizens should first and foremost consider the following question: 'Is it acceptable that politicians should have the power to act in an undemocratic manner if they feel that the people have made an incorrect decision?'

All who vote Yes in the next Nice referendum will, in effect, be accepting this dangerous situation. All who vote No will be making it crystal clear to the Irish Government and European bureaucrats that they will not be bullied into giving up their democratic rights. — Yours, etc., Anthony Sheridan, Carraig Eoin, Cobh, Co Cork. 11 September 2002.

Demise of the Bertie Bowl

Sir, — Is it merely a coincidence that the demise of the 'Bertie Bowl' was announced on the eve of the first anniversary of the September 11th attacks? On almost any other day, the cancellation of such a project would have been certain to dominate the headlines. Another case of using September 11th to bury bad news? — Yours etc., Martin Loughnan, Skerries, Co Dublin. 12 September 2002.

Sir, — Now that Bertie has accepted financial reality, is it not time for Charlie McCreevy to revisit the massive fiscal overhang of the SSIA scheme on the public finances? — Yours, etc., David McDermott, Coolrua Drive, Dublin 9. 12 September 2002.

Index